Take You to

North America

带你到北美学习

管理会计

to Learn
Managerial Accounting

杜玮 著

西北工业大学出版社
西安

图书在版编目（CIP）数据

带你到北美学习管理会计/杜玮著. —西安：西北工业
大学出版社，2018.10
ISBN 978 - 7 - 5612 - 6053 - 1

Ⅰ. ①带… Ⅱ. ①杜… Ⅲ. ①管理会计 Ⅳ. ①F234.3

中国版本图书馆 CIP 数据核字（2018）第 139495 号

DAI NI DAO BEIMEI XUEXI GUANLI KUAIJI
带你到北美学习管理会计

策划编辑：李　萌
责任编辑：李文乾

出版发行	西北工业大学出版社
通信地址	西安市友谊西路 127 号　　邮编：710072
电　　话	(029) 88493844　88491757
网　　址	www.nwpup.com
印　刷　者	陕西金德佳印务有限公司
开　　本	787 mm×1 092 mm　　1/16
印　　张	30.5
字　　数	515 千字
版　　次	2018 年 10 月第 1 版　　2018 年 10 月第 1 次印刷
定　　价	145.00 元

前　言

为减轻在美国和加拿大攻读商科学位的中国留学生的学业压力，更快、更好地融入北美大学教育体系，笔者于 2016 年 8 月出版了《带你到北美学习财务会计》，基于该书出版后的各方反馈，笔者于 2017 年 1 月萌生出写作《带你到北美学习管理会计》的想法，并历时 20 个月完成。相较于前书，本书语言更为简练，例题和案例更为丰富，配图和说明也更为具体、清晰和翔实。

《带你到北美学习管理会计》是为欲赴美国和加拿大攻读会计学、金融学、经济学、管理类、市场类学士学位，工商管理、金融学、会计学硕士学位和其他准备在美国和加拿大学习管理会计课程的留学生量身打造的。本书可作为留学预科课程的教辅用书，亦可作为留学生在海外求学时的辅导书、参考书或工具书使用。

本书分五个主题讲解管理会计：

（1）管理会计的主要内容。为有效运用管理会计信息，管理会计师和企业管理者需要了解一些基本的管理会计术语。第 1、2 章介绍管理会计学基本知识与常见术语。

（2）产品成本计算。企业为获取利润，产品价格必须高于产品成本。那么，就需要知道如何确定产品成本和产品价格。第 3、4 章介绍如何计算产品成本。一旦获知产品成本，企业管理层便可规划、监督、控制及决策企业运营。

（3）企业决策。为实现盈亏平衡，企业需要获知产品产量。在计算盈亏平衡点之前，还必须了解企业的成本习性。第 5、6 章介绍成本习性知识、如何确定盈亏平衡点、如何运用成本习性知识进行决策。第 10 章讨论企业如何制定短期决策。第 11 章阐述企业如何制定资本投资决策。

（4）企业规划。预算是呈现企业规划的主要工具。企业管理者利用预算阐明企业规划，评估企业目标的实现情况。第 7 章讲解总预算及其辅助性预算的相关知识，如销售预算、生产预算和经营费用预算等。

（5）评估与控制。企业管理层通过差异分析可以更好地控制企业运营。第8章介绍企业管理层如何通过差异分析，调整企业运营。第9章讨论如何通过其他方法和工具，评估企业的业务部门是否实现企业目标。

本书共分11章，涉及221道真题和456个专业名词。每章由内容讲解、例题综述和专业名词汇编三部分组成。

（1）内容讲解。对每章知识点进行完整且细致的讲解。针对每个知识点，均配有北美大学管理会计课程所使用的真实案例，并对案例进行深度剖析。这样，留学生可以在短时间内充分理解和掌握所学知识。

（2）例题综述。所选题目均来自北美大学管理会计课程的作业及考试真题，每道例题均提供深入的题目分析、逻辑清晰且详尽的解题过程及准确的答案。这不仅有助于巩固每章所学知识、了解出题意图、熟悉题型，更有助于留学生进行有效的自学与复习。

（3）专业名词汇编。精心总结每章出现的学术名词，并配有中文权威注解，这有利于提高留学生对管理会计专业名词的理解与记忆。

本书给留学生提供的不仅是管理会计的知识讲解和题目剖析，更是一套行之有效的学习方法，不仅帮助留学生在管理会计课程考试中取得高分，更帮助他们提升在海外求学时的自学能力。

预祝大家在海外学业有成，早日实现自我抱负、体现人生价值。

杜 玮

2018 年 7 月 10 日

于北京百万庄

目 录

第 1 章

管理会计概述

An Introduction to
Managerial Accounting

带你到北美学习
管理会计
Take You to
North America
to Learn
Managerial Accounting

1.1　管理会计定义
The Managerial Accounting Definition

《带你到北美学习财务会计》已经介绍了，财务会计（financial accounting）可以为外部使用者（external user）提供制定投资与借贷决策所需的信息，这些信息通常以财务报表（financial statement）的形式呈现。财务报表包括收益表（income statement）、股东权益变化表（statement of changes in equity）、资产负债表（statement of financial position）和现金流量表（statement of cash flows）。外部使用者一般包括投资人（investor）、债权人（creditor）、税务机关（taxing authority）、监管机构（regulatory agency）和工会（labor union）等。

与财务会计不同，管理会计（managerial accounting）可以为内部使用者（internal user）提供高效运营企业所需的财务信息。内部使用者一般包括首席执行官（chief executive officer）、市场营销主管（marketing executive）、人力资源经理（human resource manager）、生产主管（production supervisor）和财务总监（finance director）等。

1.2　管理会计与财务会计之间的区别
The Differences between Managerial Accounting and Financial Accounting

管理会计信息在许多方面不同于财务会计信息，"说明1-1"总结了两者之间的不同。

说明 1-1：对比管理会计与财务会计		
Issue	Managerial Accounting	Financial Accounting
1. Who are the primary users of the accounting information?	内部使用者一般包括首席执行官、市场营销主管、人力资源经理、生产主管和财务总监等	外部使用者一般包括投资人、债权人、税务机关、监管机构和工会等
2. What is the purpose of the accounting information?	帮助管理者筹划、监督和控制企业运营，制定企业相关决策	帮助外部使用者制定投资与借贷决策
3. What are the primary accounting products?	提供对企业管理者有价值和有益的内部会计报告	收益表、股东权益变化表、资产负债表和现金流量表

Issue	Managerial Accounting	Financial Accounting
4. What must be included in the accounting reports, and how must they be formatted?	企业管理层决定管理会计报告的内容与形式。当管理会计报告带来的益处超过编写报告产生的成本时，企业管理层编写管理会计报告	财务会计报告标准包括《国际财务报告准则》(International Financial Reporting Standards, IFRS)、《美国通用会计准则》(Generally Accepted Accounting Principles, US GAAP) 和《非上市企业会计准则》(Accounting Standards for Private Enterprises, ASPE)
5. How often are the accounting reports prepared	根据企业管理层的不同需求，有些管理会计报告需要每日编写一次，而有些管理会计报告则在需要时方才编写	每年和每季度
6. What are the underlying basises of the accounting information?	虽然有些管理会计信息与企业历史交易有关，但管理会计更注重企业未来，提供更多关于企业决策方面的信息。管理会计既呈现企业内部交易信息，又揭示企业外部交易信息	财务会计信息与企业外部历史交易有关
7. What accounting information characteristics are emphasized?	管理会计信息必须是相关的 (relevant)	财务会计信息必须是可靠的 (reliable)、客观的 (objective)
8. Does anyone verify the accounting information?	企业无需对管理会计进行独立审计 (independent audit)，但企业内部审计工作可以对管理会计报告的编写流程进行审查	独立注册会计师 (certified public accountant) 对上市公司的年度财务报表进行审计，并针对所公布财务信息的公正性提出自己的意见
9. What business unit is the accounting report about?	关于企业的具体业务部门、地区分支机构，如产品部门、市场部门和人力资源部门等	关于整个企业
10. Is the accounting information required by a government agency?	政府部门不要求企业公布管理会计报告	政府部门要求上市企业公布经审计的年度财务报表 (annual audited financial statement)

　　财务会计系统可以向企业投资人 (investor) 与债权人 (creditor) 提供制定投资与借贷决策所需的财务报表。财务报表客观地总结并呈现了企业过去一年发生的外部交易。从 2011 年 1 月 1 日起，加拿大要求，上市企业在编写财务报表时必须使用《国际财务报告准则》，而非上市企业可以选择《国际财务报告准则》或《非上市企业会计准则》。美国企业在提供财务信息时，要求使用《美国通用会计准则》。国际会计准则委员会 (International Accounting Standards Board, IASB) 负责制定《国际财务报告准则》。当前，超过 125 个国家允许使用《国际财务报告准则》。美国财务

带你到北美学习
管理会计
Take You to
North America
to Learn
Managerial Accounting

会计标准委员会（Financial Accounting Standards Board，FASB）负责制定《美国通用会计准则》。《国际财务报告准则》与《美国通用会计准则》之间没有明显差异，且国际会计准则委员会与美国财务会计标准委员会正在紧密合作，以求减小两种会计准则之间存在的差异。

虽然财务报表可以向企业投资人或债权人提供有价值的财务信息，却不能为企业管理者提供其所需要的财务信息，而管理会计系统为企业管理者提供了在规划、监督、控制和决策等方面所需的会计信息。为获取有效的会计信息、制定更好的决策，企业可以定制适合自己的管理会计系统，因此不同企业拥有不同的管理会计系统。在定制系统时，企业必须权衡开发与运营系统产生的成本以及系统带来的益处。

相较于财务报表，管理会计报告更关注企业未来的发展，能够为企业决策提供更多的信息。为更好地制定企业决策，管理者可能更需要企业业务部门或地区分支机构的信息，而非企业整体信息。例如，餐饮企业需要单个菜品和每个分店的收入与成本数据，因为单个菜品的销售额与利润信息可以协助管理层决定哪些菜品可以成为招牌菜，也可以提醒企业管理者，销售欠佳的菜品是否存在菜品口感不佳、不符合当地居民饮食习惯等问题。与财务报表不同，管理会计报告在需要时便可编写或修改，而非每年或每季度编写一次。此外，因为管理会计可以为内部使用者提供企业运营所需的财务信息，所以《国际财务报告准则》《非上市企业会计准则》《美国通用会计准则》以及独立审计均不适用于管理会计。

1.3 企业管理者的主要职责
The Primary Responsibilities of Managers

管理会计协助企业管理者履行四项主要职责，即规划（planning）、监督（directing）、控制（controlling）和决策（decision making）。图 1-1 所示为上述四项主要职责之间的相互关系。

（1）规划指为企业设定目标，决定如何实现这些目标。例如，一家餐饮企业的目标是选用高质量的食材和配料以建立良好的企业品牌与客户口碑。为实现这一目标，企业应与食材质量可靠的原料供应商建立长期合作关系，以保证原料质量。此外，管理会计可以将企业计划进行量化（quantitative expression），这种量化被称为预算（budget）。

（2）监督指对企业日常运营进行监管。通过产品成本报告、产品销售信息及其他管理会计报告，管理层可以对企业日常运营进行监督与管理。例如，餐饮企业可以通过菜品销售数据知道，哪些菜品可以为企业带来更大的销售额，从而调整菜单和市场策略。

（3）控制指根据企业规则评估企业的实际运营结果。企业通过绩效报告（performance report）对比实际运营情况与预算，从而对企业规划与监督提出反馈意见（feedback），必要时也可以采取矫正措施（corrective action）。例如，当实际销售额低于预算销售额或实际成本高于预算成本时，企业可以适当修正计划，调整运营。

（4）决策。在规划、监督和控制企业运营的同时，企业管理层也在制定决策。比如餐饮企业必须针对新餐厅的选址、每道菜品的价位、主菜选用的菜品等问题做出决策。管理会计可以协助企业管理层收集、汇总、分析每项决策需要的相关数据。

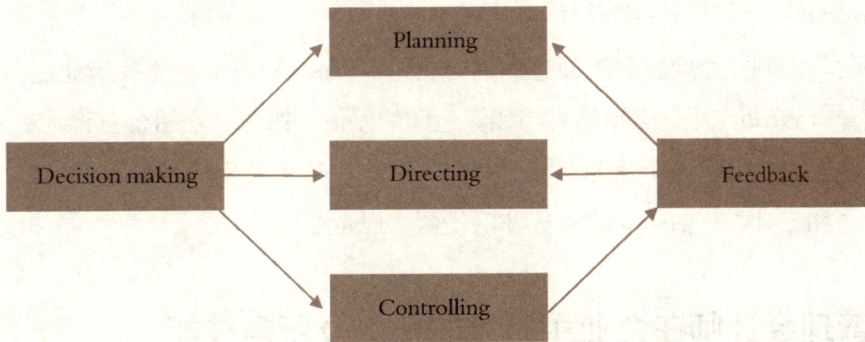

图 1-1　企业管理者的四项主要职责

1.4　企业管理者运用管理会计信息履行职责
Managers Fulfill Their Responsibilities Using Managerial Accounting Information

本书分五个主题讲解管理会计如何协助企业管理者履行职责：①管理会计的主要内容；②产品成本计算（product costing）；③企业决策（decision making）；④企业规划（planning）；⑤评估与控制（evaluating and controlling）。

（1）管理会计的主要内容。为有效运用管理会计信息，管理会计师和企业管理者需

带你到北美学习
管理会计
Take You to
North America
to Learn
Managerial Accounting

要了解一些基本的管理会计术语。第 1 章和第 2 章介绍管理会计学的基本知识与常见术语。

（2）产品成本计算。企业为获取利润，产品价格必须高于产品成本。那么如何确定产品成本和产品价格？第 3 章和第 4 章介绍如何计算产品成本。一旦获知产品成本，企业管理层便可规划、监督、控制及决策企业运营。

（3）企业决策。为实现盈亏平衡（breakeven），企业需要获知产品产量。在计算盈亏平衡点（breakeven point）之前，必须了解企业的成本习性（cost behaviour）。第 5 章和第 6 章介绍成本习性知识、如何确定盈亏平衡点、如何运用成本习性知识进行决策。第 10 章讨论如何制定短期决策。第 11 章阐述如何制定资本投资决策。

（4）企业规划。预算（budget）是呈现企业规划的主要工具。企业管理者运用预算，阐明企业规划，评估企业目标的实现。第 7 章讲解总预算（master budget）及其辅助性预算（supporting budget），如销售预算（sales budget）、生产预算（production budget）和经营费用预算（operating expenses budget）等。

（5）评估与控制。企业管理层通过差异分析（variance analysis）监控企业运营情况。差异（variance）是实际结果与预算之间的差值。第 8 章介绍企业管理层如何通过差异分析，获知企业运营需要调整的环节。第 9 章分析企业管理层通过其他方法和工具，评估企业的业务部门是否实现企业目标。

1.5 管理会计师在企业中扮演的角色及所需技能
The Roles Played and the Skills Required of Management Accountants in a Corporation

接下来，介绍管理会计师如何融入企业组织管理架构及他们所需的技能。

1.5.1 企业组织架构
The Organizational Structure of Corporations

股东（shareholder）本身很难直接管理大型企业，因此需要选举董事会（board of directors）监管企业。由于董事会按期会面，所以需要聘请首席执行官（chief executive officer）对企业进行日常管理。首席执行官需要聘请企业部门主管，这其中包括首席运营官（chief operating officer）和首席财务官（chief financial officer）。首席运营官负责企业运营，如产品的研发、生产和配送。首席财务官负责企业财务业务，直接听取财务长（treasurer）和会计长（controller）的汇报。财务长负责筹集、管理和投资企业资金，维护企业与投资者的良好关系；会计长负责企业财务会计、管理会计和税务申报（tax reporting）。

纽约证券交易所（New York Stock Exchange）规定，上市企业不仅需要外部审计，也需要内部审计。内部审计可以确保企业内部控制（internal control）和风险管理政策（risk management policy）的正确落实与执行。为使管理层不得干扰企业的内部审计工作，内部审计部门直接向审计委员会汇报。作为董事会的附属委员会（subcommittee），审计委员会（audit committee）审查企业内部审计工作、独立审计师（会计师事务所）提供的经审计的年度财务报表（annual audited financial statement）。由于审计委员会仅按期会面，而非每日会面，不能对内部审计工作进行日常管理，所以内部审计工作也向高级主管（首席财务官和首席执行官）进行汇报。

多伦多证券交易所（Toronto Stock Exchange）要求，上市公司董事会成员必须具有上市公司管理及行业从业经验，而且至少两名董事会成员独立于公司事务。

图1-2所示为企业组织架构，其中绿色部分代表企业雇员，非绿色部分代表非企业雇员。管理会计师在企业组织架构中扮演什么角色？管理会计师一般具有企业管理职位所需的金融、会计和管理知识，战略思维（strategic thinking），决策（decision making）和沟通能力，因此管理会计师在跨职能团队中更具优势。跨职能团队（cross-functional team）一般由负责企业价值链各环节的员工组成，这些环节包括研发、设计、生产或采购、市场营销、配送和客户服务。因为团队成员来自于价值链

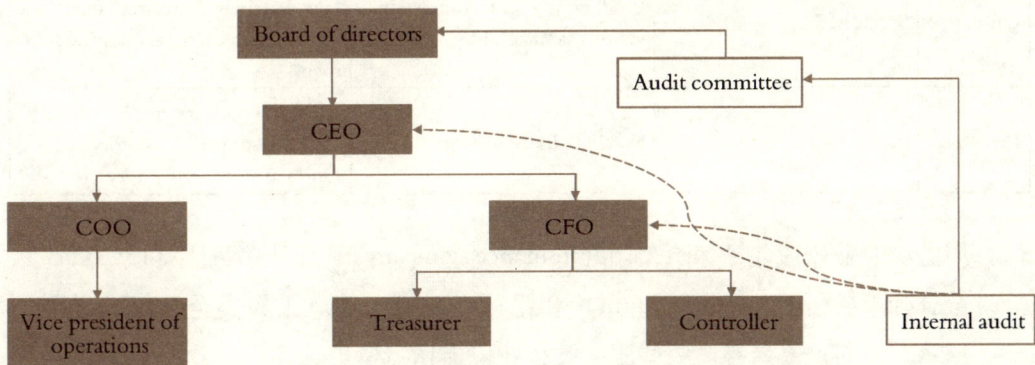

图 1 - 2　企业组织架构

带你到北美学习
管理会计
Take You to
North America
to Learn
Managerial Accounting

的不同环节，所以跨职能团队可以从不同角度思考企业决策、处理企业问题。在工作配合默契的前提下，跨职能团队的工作往往特别有效率。管理会计师一般在跨职能团队中起到领导作用。

1.5.2 管理会计师所需技能
The Skills Required of Management Accountants

管理会计师需要具备以下六种技能：①财务会计和管理会计知识；②解决问题（problem-solving）和决策能力；③企业运营与管理知识；④团队领导力和团队协作力；⑤遵守道德标准（ethical standard）和专业化（professionalism）；⑥口头和书面表达能力（oral and written communication skills）。

1.6 企业种类与价值链
The Types of Companies and the Value Chain

企业可以分为如下三类：①服务类企业（service company）；②商业类企业（merchandising company）；③制造类企业（manufacturing company）（见说明1-2）。

说明 1-2：服务类、商业类和制造类企业			
	Service Companies	Merchandising Companies	Manufacturing Companies
Examples	Insurance companies Law offices Accounting firms Banks	Retailers Wholesalers eBay. com Amazon. com	Audil Bombardier Boeing Canada Goose
Outputs	Services	Products bought from suppliers or manufacturers	New products manufactured when raw materials converted into new products by workers and equipment.
Inventory	None	Merchandise inventory	Raw materials inventory Work in process inventory Finished goods inventory

（1）服务类企业一般包括保险公司（insurance company）、律师事务所（law office）、会计师事务所（accounting firm）和银行（bank）等。服务类企业仅提供无形服务，没有产品库存。一些服务类企业仅保留日常办公用品，这些日常办公用品库存仅用于企业内部运营，而非出售营利。

（2）商业类企业一般转售供应商提供的实体商品。商业类企业出售实体商品，因此备有商品库存。商业类企业一般包括批发商（wholesaler）和零售商（retailer）。批发商从制造商（manufacturer）手中采购大批商品，出售给零售商；零售商则从批发商手中采购商品，出售给消费者。

（3）制造类企业使用原材料、设备和其他生产资源，将原材料加工为制成品。制造类企业一般向零售商或批发商销售产品，但也有许多制造类企业直接向客户出售产品。制造类企业的库存一般分为三类：①原材料库存；②在制品库存；③制成品库存。原材料指在生产过程中使用的基本材料、零部件。在制品（work in process）指在生产过程中尚未完工的产品。制成品（finished good）指完工但尚未出售的产品。

许多人认为，制造类企业仅生产、制造产品。其实不然，制造类企业也有许多其他业务，如研发、设计、市场营销、配送和客户服务，这些业务同样增加企业产品与服务价值，因此研发（research and development）、设计（design）、生产（production）、市场营销（marketing）、配送（distribution）和客户服务（customer service）共同组成了制造类企业价值链。价值链各个环节均产生成本。为制定既有市场竞争力又可盈利的产品价格，企业必须考虑与价值链有关的所有成本，而非仅考虑生产环节产生的成本。

（1）研发指研发新产品，改善现有产品、产品生产加工流程，诸如为减少汽车对环境的污染，汽车制造企业研发新技术，以求减少汽车尾气排放，降低能耗和噪声。一些企业也将研制减少环境污染的新技术作为企业社会责任的一部分。

（2）设计指企业产品、服务、生产加工流程的详细设计。在设计新产品时，企业需要考虑新产品带来的相关服务，如产品的运行与维护、技术支持以及客户服务。

（3）生产指企业运用生产资源制造产品或提供服务。价值链生产环节产生的成本包括直接材料成本（direct materials cost）、直接人工成本（direct labour cost）和制造费用（manufacturing overhead）。

（4）市场营销指企业宣传、推广产品与服务。市场营销的主要目的是使消费者产生对企业产品和服务的需求与兴趣。

（5）配送指企业向客户出售与配送产品并提供相关服务。每个行业都有各自的销售与配送机制，如飞机制造商通过投标（bidding）出售飞机，互联网公司通过互

带你到北美学习
管理会计
Take You to
North America
to Learn
Managerial Accounting

联网出售商品。

（6）客户服务指企业为客户提供的客户服务。

图1-3所示为制造类企业价值链环节的先后顺序。然而现实中，在研发新产品、设计产品新功能的同时，跨职能团队还需要考虑生产、市场营销、产品配送以及产品的客户服务等，所以在现实商业环境中，企业一般要同时考虑价值链的六大环节。

| Research and development | Design | Production | Marketing | Distribution | Customer service |

图1-3　制造类企业价值链

图1-4所示为商业类企业价值链。商业类企业一般转售供应商提供的实体商品。与制造类企业价值链略有差异，商业类企业价值链包括研发、设计、采购、市场营销、配送和客户服务。

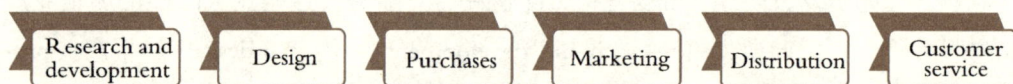

| Research and development | Design | Purchases | Marketing | Distribution | Customer service |

图1-4　商业类企业价值链

企业管理者应控制价值链的整体成本，而非具体环节产生的成本。比如一家企业在研发与设计产品上投入资金，以求提升产品质量。因为产品质量的提升可以降低产品客户服务成本；换言之，降低的产品客户服务成本可以抵销产品研发与设计上的巨大投入，如果降低的产品客户服务成本大于产品研发与设计上的资金投入，那么企业价值链的整体成本将降低。

1.7　企业管理者提升产品质量

Managers Improve the Quality of Products

劣质原材料、有缺陷的生产加工流程会导致企业生产不景气，甚至停产。对于经营成功的企业，持续生产高质量的产品是非常必要和极具挑战的。为客户提供优质的产品与服务，许多企业实施全面质量管理（total quality management）；换言之，企业应检查价值链各个环节，以求提升产品质量，减少产品损耗与缺陷，降低无附加值活动。大部分企业发现，如果在价值链前端（研发和设计）加大投入，就可以节省价值链末端（生产、市场营销、配送和客户服务）产生的成本，如在研发、设计产品与生产流程上加大投入，可以缩短生产时间，降低检验、返工、保修产品的成本。

1.7.1 质量成本
Quality Costs

作为全面质量管理的一部分，企业需要编写质量成本报告（report of quality costs）。质量成本报告分类显示了与质量有关的成本。质量成本分为四类：①预防成本（prevention cost）；②鉴定成本（appraisal cost）；③内部损失成本（internal failure cost）；④外部损失成本（external failure cost），这四类质量成本构成了质量成本报告的主体框架。"说明1-3"提供了四类质量成本的常见例子。

说明 1-3：质量成本	
Prevention Costs	**Appraisal Costs**
Training employees	Inspecting raw materials
Evaluating potential suppliers	Inspecting equipment
Using good-quality raw materials	Inspecting finished goods
Periodic maintenance	Inspecting manufacturing processes
Redesigning manufacturing processes	Testing products
Improving equipment	
Internal Failure Costs	**External Failure Costs**
Production losses caused by downtime	Lost profits from lost customers
Reworking poor-quality products	Warranty costs
Discarding products with quality problems	Recall costs
Disposing discarded products	Sales returns and allowances due to poor-quality products

（1）预防成本指为避免生产劣质产品而产生的成本。劣质产品一般是生产流程中的不稳定因素、复杂的产品设计造成的。因此，简化产品设计和生产流程可以降低生产问题、劣质产品的出现概率与风险。为统一生产流程，减少生产流程中的不稳定因素，企业尽可能使用自动化生产流程。对于非自动化生产流程，企业可以通过员工培训，减少生产流程中的不稳定因素。

（2）鉴定成本指检测劣质产品而产生的成本。

（3）内部损失成本指企业在交货前，不合格产品带来的损失与成本，诸如重新提供

带你到北美学习
管理会计
Take You to
North America
to Learn
Managerial Accounting

服务，重新鉴定、返工、加工产品，报废产品等。最糟糕的一种情况就是一件不合格产品已不能返修而只能报废，出现这种情况时，内部损失成本包括制造不合格产品的成本和清理不合格产品产生的成本。

（4）外部损失成本指企业在交货后，不合格产品带来的损失，诸如召回、保修产品，产品质量问题引发的销售退货与折价（sales return and allowance）。此外，外部损失成本还包括不合格产品造成客户流失而引发的企业未来亏损。比如出于对油门踏板安全隐患的考虑，某知名汽车生产商分别于 2009 年、2010 年召回 400 万辆和 230 万辆汽车，随着修理和替换不合格油门踏板产生的巨额费用，企业在公众中建立的良好声誉也会因召回事件严重受损，这将极大损害企业形象和未来销售业绩。

预防成本一般出现在价值链的研发和设计环节，鉴定成本和内部损失成本则出现在价值链的生产环节，价值链的客户服务环节通常产生外部损失成本。预防成本和鉴定成本是为确保产品符合最初设计而产生的成本，因此它们也被称为符合性成本（conformance cost），而内部损失成本和外部损失成本是在制造商生产不合格产品之后产生的成本，因此这些成本也被称为非符合性成本（non-conformance cost）。

1.7.2 质量成本报告
Report of Quality Costs

质量成本报告为企业管理层呈现了四类质量成本。通过"案例 1-1"，学习如何编写质量成本报告。

案例 1-1

The CEO of Meals Corporation is concerned about the amount of resources currently spent on customer warranty claims. Since the claims are so high, she would like to evaluate what costs should be incurred to ensure the quality of products. The following information was collected from the various departments within the company:

Warranty claims	$210,000
Costs of the defective products found at inspection points	47,000
Training factory employees	13,000

Recall of Batch 59374	87,500
Inspecting products when halfway through production processes	27,500
Costs of disposing rejected products	6,000
Preventive maintenance on factory equipment	3,500
Production losses due to machine breakdowns	7,500
Inspecting raw materials	2,500

Required:

Prepare a report of quality costs in good form (listing the costs by category and determining the percentage of the total costs of quality incurred in each cost category).

讲解: Training factory employees, Preventive maintenance on factory equipment 属于预防成本; Inspecting raw materials, Inspecting products when halfway through production processes 属于鉴定成本; Costs of the defective products found at inspection points, Costs of disposing rejected products, Production losses due to machine breakdowns 属于内部损失成本; Warranty claims, Recall of batch 59374 属于外部损失成本。

在将质量成本分为预防成本、鉴定成本、内部损失成本和外部损失成本之后，Meals Corporation 可以分别计算预防成本总额、鉴定成本总额、内部损失成本总额和外部损失成本总额，如预防成本总额为 $16 500，外部损失成本总额为 $297 500。

在获知预防成本总额、鉴定成本总额、内部损失成本总额和外部损失成本总额之后，Meals Corporation 可以计算质量成本总额、每类质量成本占质量成本总额的百分比，如预防成本占质量成本总额的4.08% ($16 500 ÷ $404 500 ≈ 4.08%)，外部损失成本占质量成本总额的73.55% ($297 500 ÷ $404 500 ≈ 73.55%)。

说明 1 - 4：质量成本报告

	Costs Incurred	Total Costs of Quality	Percentage of Total Costs of Quality
Prevention costs:			
Training factory employees	$13,000		
Preventive maintenance on factory equipment	3,500		
Total prevention costs		$16,500	4.08%
Appraisal costs:			
Inspecting raw materials	2,500		

带你到北美学习
管理会计
Take You to
North America
to Learn
Managerial Accounting

	Costs Incurred	Total Costs of Quality	Percentage of Total Costs of Quality
Inspecting products when halfway through production processes	27,500		
Total appraisal costs		30,000	7.42%
Internal failure costs:			
Costs of the defective products found at inspection points	47,000		
Costs of disposing rejected products	6,000		
Production losses due to machine breakdowns	7,500		
Total internal failure costs		60,500	14.96%
External failure costs:			
Warranty claims	210,000		
Recall of Batch 59374	87,500		
Total external failure costs		297,500	73.55%
Total costs of quality		$404,500	100.00%

　　质量成本报告表明，Meals Corporation 在符合性成本部分（预防成本和鉴定成本）投入较小，仅占质量成本总额的 11.50%（4.08% + 7.42% = 11.50%），而非符合性成本（内部损失成本和外部损失成本）却占质量成本总额的 88.51%（14.96% + 73.55% = 88.51%）。企业减少内部损失与外部损失成本的最好方法是加大对预防和鉴定环节的投入（见说明1-4）。

　　如何通过加大对预防和鉴定环节的投入，降低内部损失与外部损失成本？在分析质量成本报告之后，Meals Corporation 正在考虑是否对预防和鉴定环节加大投入，以求提升产品质量，降低内部损失与外部损失成本。Meals Corporation 希望在检查原材料、审查供应商、维护设备和重新设计生产流程等方面进行以下投入。

Inspecting raw materials	$30,000
Reengineering production processes to improve product quality	100,000
Supplier screening and certification	20,000
Preventive maintenance on factory equipment	10,000
Total costs	$160,000

　　虽然不能完全消除内部损失和外部损失成本，但通过在检查原材料、审查供应商、维护设备和重新设计生产流程等方面进行投入与改进，Meals Corporation 可以

降低以下内部损失成本和外部损失成本。

Reduction in lost profits from lost sales due to impaired reputation	$110,000
Fewer sales returns	20,000
Reduction in rework costs	30,000
Reduction in warranty costs	30,000
Total costs	$190,000

Meals Corporation 在预防和鉴定环节新增投入 $160 000，节省非符合性成本 $190 000，产生净效益（net benefit） $30 000。

根据成本效益分析（cost-benefit analysis），Meals Corporation 新增预防成本 $130 000、鉴定成本 $30 000，节省内部损失成本 $30 000、外部损失成本 $160 000，降低质量成本总额 $30 000（ $30 000 + $160 000 − $130 000 − $30 000 = $30 000）。通过加大对符合性成本的投入，Meals Corporation 可以节省更多的非符合性成本，进而降低整体质量成本（见说明 1-5）。

说明 1-5: 成本效益分析	Additional (Costs) and Cost Savings	Total New (Costs) or Cost Savings
Prevention costs:		
Reengineering production processes to improve product quality	($100,000)	
Supplier screening and certification	(20,000)	
Preventive maintenance on factory equipment	(10,000)	
Total additional prevention costs		($130,000)
Appraisal costs:		
Inspecting raw materials	(30,000)	
Total additional appraisal costs		(30,000)
Internal failure costs:		
Reduction in rework costs	30,000	
Total internal failure cost savings		30,000
External failure costs:		
Reduction in lost profits from lost sales due to impaired reputation	110,000	
Fewer sales returns	20,000	

带你到北美学习
管理会计
Take You to
North America
to Learn
Managerial Accounting

	Additional (Costs) and Cost Savings	Total New (Costs) or Cost Savings
Reduction in warranty costs	30,000	
Total external failure cost savings		160,000
Total savings (costs)		$ 30,000

例题综述
Summary of Examples

例题 1 - 1

What is the value chain? What are the six elements of the value chain?

讲解： 许多人认为，制造类企业仅仅生产制造产品。其实不然，制造类企业也有许多其他业务，如研发、设计、市场营销、配送和客户服务，这些业务同样增加企业产品或服务价值，因此研发、设计、生产、市场营销、配送和客户服务组成了制造类企业价值链。

商业类企业一般转售供应商提供的实体商品。与制造类企业价值链略有差异，商业类企业价值链包括研发、设计、采购、市场营销、配送和客户服务。

答案： The value chain is the activities that add value to a company's products or services. The value chain of a company consists of research and development, design, production or purchases, marketing, distribution, and customer service.

例题 1 - 2

Overseeing a company's day-to-day operations is considered controlling. True or False?

讲解： 监督（directing）指对企业日常运营进行监管。通过产品成本报告、产品销售信息及其他管理会计报告，管理层对企业日常运营进行监督与管理。

答案： False

例题 1 - 3

When the management of a corporation uses feedback to take corrective actions on the budgets, which of the following management responsibilities are being fulfilled?

A. Controlling and decision-making

B. Planning and controlling

C. Planning and decision-making

D. Directing and planning

讲解： 控制（controlling）指根据企业规划，评估企业的实际运营结果。通过绩效报告（performance report），对比企业实际运营情况与预算，进而对企业规划与监督

带你到北美学习
管理会计
Take You to
North America
to Learn
Managerial Accounting

提出反馈意见（feedback），必要时也可以采取矫正措施（corrective action）。例如，实际销售额低于预算销售额，实际成本高于预算成本，企业可以适当修正计划，调整运营。在规划、监督和控制企业运营的同时，企业管理层也在制定决策。

答案： A

例题 1－4

Planning involves which of the following activities?

A. Overseeing a company's day-to-day operations

B. Directing a company's operations

C. Setting goals and objectives for a company

D. Evaluating the actual results of operations

讲解： 规划（planning）指为企业设定目标，并决定如何实现这些目标。

答案： C

例题 1－5

Research and development, design, production, marketing, distribution, and customer service are all elements of _____.

A. the planning and controlling cycle

B. the value chain

C. total quality management

D. the cost of goods manufactured and sold schedule

讲解： 制造类企业价值链包括研发（research and development）、设计（design）、生产（production）、市场营销（marketing）、配送（distribution）和客户服务（customer service）。

答案： B

例题 1－6

Managerial accounting focuses on _____.

A. internal reporting

B. external reporting

C. auditing

D. historic transactions

讲解： 管理会计（managerial accounting）可以为内部使用者（internal user）提供高效运营企业所需的财务信息。

答案： A

例题 1 - 7

The person most likely using only financial accounting information would be the
_____.

A. plant manager

B. marketing executive

C. human resource manager

D. investor

讲解： 财务会计（financial accounting）可以为外部使用者（external user）提供制定投资与借贷决策所需的信息，这些信息通常以财务报表（financial statement）的形式呈现。外部使用者一般包括投资人（investor）、债权人（creditor）、税务机关（taxing authority）、监管机构（regulatory agency）和工会（labor union）等。

与财务会计不同，管理会计（managerial accounting）可以为内部使用者（internal user）提供高效运营企业所需的财务信息。内部使用者一般包括首席执行官（chief executive officer）、市场营销主管（marketing executive）、人力资源经理（human resource manager）、生产主管（production supervisor）和财务总监（finance director）等。

答案： D

例题 1 - 8

Which of the following would report to the audit committee, a subcommittee of the board of directors?

A. The treasurer and controller

B. The CFO and the independent auditor (CPA firm)

C. The CFO and CEO

带你到北美学习
管理会计
Take You to
North America
to Learn
Managerial Accounting

D. The internal audit department and the independent auditor（CPA firm）

讲解： 内部审计可以确保企业内部控制（internal control）和风险管理政策（risk management policy）的正确落实与执行。为使管理层不干扰企业的内部审计工作，内部审计部门向审计委员会直接汇报。作为董事会的附属委员会（subcommittee），审计委员会（audit committee）审查企业内部审计工作、独立审计师（会计师事务所）提供的经审计的年度财务报表（annual audited financial statement）。由于审计委员会仅按期会面，而非每日会面，不能对内部审计工作进行日常管理，所以内部审计工作也向高级主管（首席财务官和首席执行官）进行汇报。

答案： D

例题 1 - 9

Who is primarily responsible for raising capital and investing funds?

A. The controller

B. The treasurer

C. The CEO

D. The CFO

讲解： 首席财务官（chief financial officer）负责企业财务业务，直接听取财务长（treasurer）和会计长（controller）的汇报。财务长负责筹集、管理和投资企业资金，维护与企业投资者的良好关系；会计长负责企业财务会计、管理会计和税务申报（tax reporting）。

答案： B

例题 1 - 10

The primary goal of managerial accounting is to provide information to _____.

A. investors and creditors

B. regulatory agency

C. internal users

D. taxing authority

讲解： 同"例题1-7"。

答案： C

例题 1 - 11

Which type(s) of companies prepare financial statements?

A. Service company

B. Merchandising company

C. Manufacturing company

D. All of the above

讲解： 企业需要财务报表（financial statement）提供财务信息。财务报表包括收益表（income statement）、股东权益变化表（statement of changes in equity）、资产负债表（statement of financial position）和现金流量表（statement of cash flows）。

答案： D

例题 1 - 12

Before these raw materials are used to manufacture its autos, an auto manufacturer classifies steel, glass, and plastic as _____.

A. raw materials inventory

B. work in process inventory

C. finished goods inventory

D. merchandise inventory

讲解： 制造类企业的库存一般分为三类：①原材料库存；②在制品库存；③制成品库存。原材料指在生产过程中使用的基本材料、零部件。在制品指在生产过程中尚未完工的产品。制成品指完工但尚未出售的产品。

答案： A

例题 1 - 13

An income tax preparation service firm is what type of company?

A. Manufacturer

B. Service company

C. Retailer

D. Wholesaler

讲解： 服务类企业（service company）一般包括保险公司（insurance company）、律

带你到北美学习
管理会计
Take You to
North America
to Learn
Managerial Accounting

师事务所（law office）、会计师事务所（accounting firm）和银行（bank）等。服务类企业仅提供无形服务，没有产品库存。

答案： B

例题 1 - 14

Briefly discuss the differences between financial accounting and managerial accounting.

讲解： 见"说明1-1"。

答案： Managerial accounting information differs from financial accounting information in many aspects. A company's financial accounting information system is geared toward creating annual and quarterly consolidated financial statements that will be used by potential investors and creditors to make investment and lending decisions. The financial statements objectively show and summarize the transactions that occurred between a company and its external parties during the previous fiscal year. As of January 1, 2011, publicly accountable corporations must use International Financial Reporting Standards in Canada, while private corporations in Canada can voluntarily select an option: International Financial Reporting Standards (IFRS) or Accounting Standards for Private Enterprises (ASPE).

In contrast to financial accounting information system, a company's managerial accounting information system is designed to present its management with the enough accounting information the management needs to plan, direct, control, and make decisions. Most managerial accounting reports focus on the future and shows the relevant information that helps management to make better business decisions. Because of the primary goal of managerial accounting is to provide information to internal users, ASPE or IFRS guidelines are not required for managerial accounting. Each company can tailor its own managerial accounting information system, so different companies have different managerial accounting systems. When designing a managerial accounting information system, the management must consider how the system will affect employees' behaviours.

例题 1 - 15

For each of the following users of accounting information, specify whether the user would primarily use financial accounting information, managerial accounting information, or both?

a．Potential investor

b．Taxing authority

c．Plant's manager

d．Accounting department

e．Human resource manager

f．Regulatory agency

g．Current shareholder

h．New York Stock Exchange analyst

i．News reporter

j．New Brunswick Securities Commission employee

k．External independent auditor（public accounting firm）

l．Controller

m．Board of directors

n．Internal auditing department

讲解： 财务会计（financial accounting）可以为外部使用者（external user）提供制定投资与借贷决策所需的信息，这些信息通常以财务报表（financial statement）的形式呈现。外部使用者一般包括投资人（investor）、债权人（creditor）、税务机关（taxing authority）、监管机构（regulatory agency）和工会（labor union）等。

与财务会计不同，管理会计（managerial accounting）可以为内部使用者（internal user）提供高效运营企业所需的财务信息。内部使用者一般包括首席执行官（chief executive officer）、市场营销主管（marketing executive）、人力资源经理（human resource manager）、生产主管（production supervisor）和财务总监（finance director）等。

董事会（board of directors）、首席执行官（chief executive officer）、首席财务官、会计长（controller）和内部审计部门既需要企业财务会计信息，又需要企业管理会计信息。

答案：

a．Financial accounting information

b．Financial accounting information

c．Managerial accounting information

带你到北美学习

管理会计

Take You to
North America
to Learn
Managerial Accounting

d．Financial accounting information

e．Managerial accounting information

f．Financial accounting information

g．Financial accounting information

h．Financial accounting information

i．Financial accounting information

j．Financial accounting information

k．Financial accounting information

l．Both

m．Both

n．Both

例题 1－16

Classify each of the following five items as either a prevention cost, an appraisal cost, an internal failure cost, or an external failure cost for an electronic manufacturer.

	Classification
a．Salaries of staffs who are designing components to withstand electrical overloads	
b．Costs of electronic products returned by customers	
c．Costs of repairing defective electronic components after discovery by a manufacturer's inspectors	
d．Costs incurred by a manufacturer's customer representatives travelling to customer sites to repair defective products	
e．Costs of inspecting components in production processes	

讲解： 质量成本分为四类：①预防成本（prevention cost）；②鉴定成本（appraisal cost）；③内部损失成本（internal failure cost）；④外部损失成本（external failure cost）。预防成本指为避免生产劣质产品而产生的成本。鉴定成本指检测劣质产品而产生的成本。内部损失成本指企业在交货前，不合格产品带来的损失与成本。外部损失成本指企业在交货后，不合格产品带来的损失。

答案：

	Classification
a. Salaries of staffs who are designing components to withstand electrical overloads	Prevention cost
b. Costs of electronic products returned by customers	External failure cost
c. Costs of repairing defective electronic components after discovery by a manufacturer's inspectors	Internal failure cost
d. Costs incurred by a manufacturer's customer representatives travelling to customer sites to repair defective products	External failure cost
e. Costs of inspecting components in production processes	Appraisal cost

例题 1 – 17

The following information was collected from the various departments of a manufacturer：

Litigation on product liability claims	$ 350,000
Warranty returns	240,000
Production losses due to machine breakdowns	90,000
Training employees	20,000
Repairing defective products	20,000
Inspecting final products	10,000
Inspecting raw materials	10,000

Required：

Prepare a report of quality costs in good form (listing the costs by category and determining the percentage of the total costs of quality incurred in each cost category).

讲解： 同 "例题 1-16"。Training employees 属于预防成本；Inspecting raw materials，Inspecting final products 属于鉴定成本；Repairing defective products，Production losses due to machine breakdowns 属于内部损失成本；Warranty returns，Litigation on product liability claims 属于外部损失成本。

在将质量成本分为预防成本、鉴定成本、内部损失成本和外部损失成本之后，企业可以分别计算预防成本总额、鉴定成本总额、内部损失成本总额和外部损失成本总额。

在获知预防成本总额、鉴定成本总额、内部损失成本总额和外部损失成本总额之后，企业可以计算质量成本总额和每类质量成本占质量成本总额的百分比。

带你到北美学习
管理会计
Take You to
North America
to Learn
Managerial Accounting

答案：

	Costs Incurred	Total Costs of Quality	Percentage of Total Costs of Quality
Prevention costs：			
Training employees	$ 20,000		
Total prevention costs		$ 20,000	2.70%
Appraisal costs：			
Inspecting raw materials	10,000		
Inspecting final products	10,000		
Total appraisal costs		20,000	2.70%
Internal failure costs：			
Repairing defective products	20,000		
Production losses due to machine breakdowns	90,000		
Total internal failure costs		110,000	14.86%
External failure costs：			
Warranty returns	240,000		
Litigation on product liability claims	350,000		
Total external failure costs		590,000	79.73%
Total costs of quality		$ 740,000	100.00%

例题 1 - 18

The following information was collected from the various departments within a manufacturing company：

Warranty claims	$ 475,000
Costs of recalling batches	130,000
Costs of the defective products found at inspection points	75,000
Inspecting work in process	50,000
Training factory employees	25,000
Production losses due to machine breakdowns	18,000
Costs of disposing the defective products found at inspection points	13,000
Preventive maintenance on factory equipment	8,000
Inspecting raw materials	5,000

Required:

1. Prepare a report of quality costs in good form (listing the costs by category and determining the percentage of the total costs of quality incurred in each cost category).

2. Do any additional subjective costs or qualitative issues that need to be addressed here?

3. What can be learned from the report of quality costs?

1. Prepare a report of quality costs in good form (listing the costs by category and determining the percentage of the total costs of quality incurred in each cost category).

讲解: 同"例题1-16"。Training factory employees, Preventive maintenance on factory equipment属于预防成本; Inspecting raw materials, Inspecting work in process 属于鉴定成本; Production losses due to machine breakdowns, Costs of the defective products found at inspection points, Costs of disposing the defective products found at inspection points 属于内部损失成本; Warranty claims, Costs of recalling batches 属于外部损失成本。

答案:

	Costs Incurred	Total Costs of Quality	Percentage of Total Costs of Quality
Prevention costs:			
Training factory employees	$ 25,000		
Preventive maintenance on factory equipment	8,000		
Total prevention costs		$ 33,000	4.13%
Appraisal costs:			
Inspecting work in process	50,000		
Inspecting raw materials	5,000		
Total appraisal costs		55,000	6.88%
Internal failure costs:			
Production losses due to machine breakdowns	18,000		
Costs of the defective products found at inspection points	75,000		
Costs of disposing the defective products found at inspection points	13,000		
Total internal failure costs		106,000	13.27%

	Costs Incurred	Total Costs of Quality	Percentage of Total Costs of Quality
External failure costs:			
Warranty claims	475,000		
Costs of recalling batches	130,000		
Total external failure costs		605,000	75.72%
Total costs of quality		$799,000	100.00%

2. Do any additional subjective costs or qualitative issues that need to be addressed here?

答案： A manufacturer has warranty claims and has had the recall of batches. Along with incurring substantial costs for repairing the warranty claims or replacing the recalled products, the manufacturer may suffer from the reputation for poor-quality products. If so, they are probably losing profits from losing potential clients and their sales. Unsatisfied clients will be reluctant to purchase from the manufacturer again in the future. Even worse, unsatisfied clients tend to tell their neighbours, friends and family members about their any poor experience with products and not to buy from the manufacturer. As a result, the manufacturer's reputation for poor quality can increase at an exponential rate. To capture the extent of this problem, external failure costs should involve an estimate of how much sales and profit the manufacturer is losing due to the reputation of poor-quality products. However, the report of quality costs does not include the estimate of the lost sales and profits arising from poor-quality products.

3. What can be learned from the report of quality costs?

答案： The report of quality costs shows that very little is being spent on the prevention and appraisal areas, which is probably why the internal and external failure costs are so high. It appears that the company is only inspecting raw materials and work in process, and not again at the end of the production process. Perhaps that is the reason why their external failure costs are so high. The management can now begin to focus on how they might be able to prevent future internal and external failure costs from occurring. The management should use this information and develop quality programs in the areas of prevention and appraisal, which can reduce future failure costs.

带你到北美学习
管理会计
Take You to
North America
to Learn
Managerial Accounting

例题 1 - 19

Classify each of a cellphone manufacturer's costs as one of the six elements in the value chain.

a. Depreciation on the manufacturer's plant

b. Costs of a customer support center website

c. Transportation costs to deliver cellphones to retailers

d. Depreciation on research labs

e. Costs of a prime-time TV advertisement featuring a new logo

f. Salaries of scientists at the manufacturer's laboratories that are developing new cellular technologies

g. Salaries of engineers who are redesigning a new interactive screen

h. Depreciation on delivery vehicles

i. Plant managers' salaries

讲解： 制造类企业价值链包括研发、设计、生产、市场营销、配送和客户服务。研发（research and development）指研发新产品，提升现有产品、产品生产加工流程。设计（design）指企业产品、服务、生产加工流程的详细设计。生产（production）指企业运用生产资源，制造产品或提供服务。价值链生产环节产生的成本包括直接材料成本（direct materials cost）、直接人工成本（direct labour cost）、制造费用（manufacturing overhead）。市场营销（marketing）指企业宣传、推广产品与服务。配送（distribution）指企业向客户提供服务，出售与配送产品。客户服务（customer service）指企业为客户提供的客户服务。

根据上述定义，Depreciation on research labs, Salaries of scientists at the manufacturer's laboratories that are developing new cellular technologies 属于研发环节；Salaries of engineers who are redesigning a new interactive screen 属于设计环节；Depreciation on the manufacturer's plant, Plant managers' salaries 属于生产环节；Costs of a prime-time TV advertisement featuring a new logo 属于市场营销环节；Transportation costs to deliver cellphones to retailers, Depreciation on delivery vehicles 属于配送环节；Costs of a customer support center website 属于客户服务环节。

答案：

a. Production

带你到北美学习
管理会计
Take You to
North America
to Learn
Managerial Accounting

b. Customer service

c. Distribution

d. Research and development

e. Marketing

f. Research and development

g. Design

h. Distribution

i. Production

例题 1 - 20

A cola manuafacturer produces a cherry-lime cola and incurs the following costs:

a. Plant utilities

b. Payments for new recipes

c. Salt

d. Freight-in on materials

e. Cherry syrup

f. Lime flavoring

g. Plant janitors' wages

h. Depreciation on plant and equipment

i. Bottles

j. Sales commissions

k. Depreciation on delivery trucks

l. Rearranging plant layouts

m. Wages of workers who mix syrup

n. Replacing products with expired dates upon customer complaints

o. Customer hotline

p. Production costs of "cent-off" store coupons for customers

q. Delivery truck drivers' wages

Required:

Use the following format to classify each of the above costs as one of the six elements in the value chain.

Research and development	
Design	
Production	
Marketing	
Distribution	
Customer service	

讲解： 同"例题1-19"。Payments for new recipes 属于研发环节；Rearranging plant layouts 属于设计环节；Plant utilities，Depreciation on plant and equipment，Salt，Cherry syrup，Lime flavoring，Bottles，Plant janitors' wages，Wages of workers who mix syrup，Freight-in on materials 属于生产环节；Production costs of "cent-off" store coupons for customers，Sales commissions 属于市场营销环节；Delivery truck drivers' wages，Depreciation on delivery trucks 属于配送环节；Replacing products with expired dates upon customer complaints，Customer hotline 属于客户服务环节。

答案：

Research and development	Payments for new recipess
Design	Rearranging plant layouts
Production	Plant utilities, Depreciation on plant and equipment, Salt, Cherry syrup, Lime flavoring, Bottles, Plant janitors' wages, Wages of workers who mix syrup, Freight-in on materials
Marketing	Production costs of "cent-off" store coupons for customers, Sales commissions
Distribution	Delivery truck drivers' wages, Depreciation on delivery trucks
Customer service	Replacing products with expired dates upon customer complaints, Customer hotline

带你到北美学习
管理会计
Take You to
North America
to Learn
Managerial Accounting

专业名词汇编
Glossary of Accounting Terms

在制品	work in process	保修	warranty
财务报表	financial statement	财务会计	financial accounting
财务长	treasurer	财务总监	finance director
差异分析	variance analysis	产品成本计算	product costing
成本	cost	成本习性	cost behaviour
成本效益分析	cost-benefit analysis	规划	planning
道德标准	ethical standard	定价	pricing
董事会	board of directors	独立审计	independent audit
多伦多证券交易所	Toronto Stock Exchange	非符合性成本	non-conformance cost
风险管理政策	risk management policy	服务类企业	service company
符合性成本	conformance cost	附属委员会	subcommittee
工会	labor union	供应商	supplier
股东	shareholder	管理会计	managerial accounting
会计长	controller	监督	directing
监管机构	regulatory agency	鉴定成本	appraisal cost
矫正措施	corrective action	进货运费	freight-in cost
进口税	import duty	决策	decision making
客户服务	customer service	控制	controlling
库存	inventory	跨职能团队	cross-functional team
利润	profit	量化	quantitative expression
零售商	retailer	内部控制	internal control
内部使用者	internal user	内部损失成本	internal failure cost
纽约证券交易所	New York Stock Exchange	配送	distribution
批发商	wholesaler	全面质量管理	total quality management
人力资源经理	human resource manager	商业类企业	merchandising company
设计	design	审计委员会	audit committee
生产	production	生产主管	production supervisor
市场营销	marketing	收入	revenue
收益表	income statement	首席财务官	chief financial officer
首席运营官	chief operating officer	首席执行官	chief executive officer

税务机关	taxing authority	税务申报	tax reporting
投标	bidding	投资人	investor
外包	outsourcing	外部使用者	external user
外部损失成本	external failure cost	解决问题	problem-solving
无形服务	intangible service	现金流量表	statement of cash flows
销售退货与折价	sales return and allowance	市场营销主管	marketing executive
研发	research and development	绩效报告	performance report
盈亏平衡	breakeven	盈亏平衡点	breakeven point
预防成本	prevention cost	预算	budget
原材料	raw materials	债权人	creditor
战略思维	strategic thinking	直接材料成本	direct materials cost
直接人工成本	direct labour cost	制成品	finished good
制造费用	manufacturing overhead	制造类企业	manufacturing company
制造商	manufacturer	质量成本	quality cost
质量成本报告	report of quality costs	注册会计师	certified public accountant
资产负债表	statement of financial position	总预算	master budget
非上市企业会计准则	Accounting Standards for Private Enterprises, ASPE		
股东权益变化表	statement of changes in equity		
国际财务报告准则	International Financial Reporting Standards, IFRS		
经审计的年度财务报表	annual audited financial statement		
美国通用会计准则	Generally Accepted Accounting Principles, US GAAP		
国际会计准则委员会	International Accounting Standards Board, IASB		
美国财务会计标准委员会	Financial Accounting Standards Board, FASB		

第 2 章

管理会计的主要内容

The Main Contents of
Managerial Accounting

带你到北美学习
管理会计
Take You to
North America
to Learn
Managerial Accounting

2.1 成本对象、直接成本与间接成本
Cost Objects, Direct Costs, and Indirect Costs

　　成本对象（cost object）指在计算成本时，企业管理者归属和分配成本所需的载体。成本对象可以是一件产品、一件模具、一个部门、一个厂房或一个地区分支机构。根据成本对象，成本可以分为直接成本和间接成本。直接成本（direct cost）指与成本对象有关，并基于成本对象容易确定的成本；简言之，根据成本对象，企业可以直接确定的成本被视为直接成本。间接成本（indirect cost）指与成本对象有关，但基于成本对象不易确定的成本；简言之，根据成本对象，企业不能直接确定的成本被视为间接成本（见图2-1）。

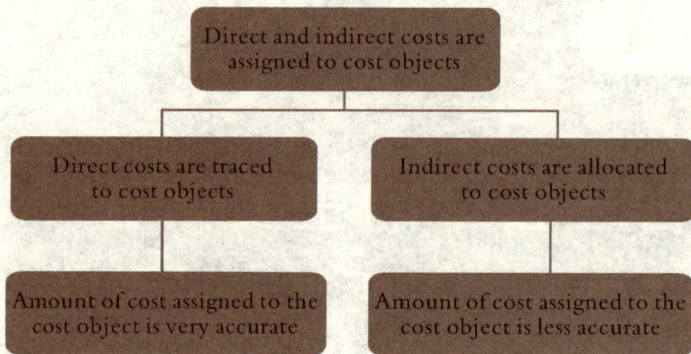

图 2 - 1　直接成本与间接成本之间的区别

　　成本究竟属于直接成本还是间接成本取决于成本对象；换言之，同样的成本对于某类成本对象可能属于直接成本，而对于另一类成本对象可能属于间接成本。例如某知名汽车生产商需要获知生产一辆汽车的成本。作为汽车主要零部件之一，座椅成本可以很容易被直接确定，因此座椅成本是汽车成本中的直接成本；而在生产汽车时，工厂产生的水电费用、折旧费用、不动产税费用不能直接计入汽车成本，因此这些费用是汽车成本中的间接成本。如果这家汽车生产商想要获知运营一家工厂所需的成本，那么工厂的水电费用、折旧费用、不动产税费用就是工厂成本中的直接成本。请注意：本书中的案例与例题均将产品作为成本对象。

　　在计算成本对象的成本时，必须考虑与成本对象有关的直接成本与间接成本。继续使用上述例子说明生产一辆汽车的总成本。作为汽车的主要零部件，汽车座椅成本、方向盘成本、发动机成本可以被直接确定，并计入一辆汽车的成本，这将为企业提供非常精准的成本数据；而在生产汽车时，工厂产生的水电费用、折旧费用、

不动产税费用不能直接计入汽车成本，因此这些费用必须被分摊至所生产的每辆汽车。第 3 章将详细讲解关于成本分摊（cost allocation）的知识。

2.2 两种不同的成本界定：企业内部决策与对外公布财务报告
The Two Different Definitions of Costs：Internal Decision Making and External Reporting

企业一般使用两种不同的成本界定方式：①企业内部决策使用的总成本；②对外公布财务报告使用的产品成本。

2.2.1 企业内部决策使用的总成本
Total Costs for Internal Decision Making

总成本（total cost）指企业在价值链中所用资源的成本之和。企业总成本一般由两部分组成：①产品成本（product cost）；②期间成本（period cost）。一件产品的总成本就是该产品在研发、设计、生产、市场营销、配送和客户服务等环节产生的成本总和。企业通过预估该产品的成本来确定产品的售价，通过比较每种产品的销售额、价格、成本，来了解哪些产品可以获取更大的利润。

2.2.2 对外公布财务报告使用的产品成本
Product Costs for External Reporting

财务会计报告准则不允许企业使用总成本计算企业库存账目余额和售出商品成本账目余额。对外公布财务报告时，企业必须使用产品成本。产品成本指企业在价值链生产环节或采购环节产生的成本。在出售产品之前，产品成本被视为企业资产，计入库存账目。在出售产品之后，所售产品成本从企业库存账目移出，计入售出商品成本账目（cost of goods sold）。

我们知道，企业在价值链生产环节或采购环节产生的成本被视为产品成本，而在价值链其他五个环节（研发、设计、市场营销、配送和客户服务）产生的成本则被视为期间成本，期间成本也称为经营费用（operating expense）或销售、常规与行政费用（selling, general, and administrative expense）。

带你到北美学习
管理会计
Take You to
North America
to Learn
Managerial Accounting

2.3 制造类企业的产品成本
The Product Costs of Manufacturing Companies

制造类企业的产品成本是指在价值链生产环节产生的成本。在生产产品时，制造商一般承担三类制造成本（manufacturing cost）：①直接材料成本（direct materials cost）；②直接人工成本（direct labour cost）；③制造费用（manufacturing overhead）（见图2-2）。

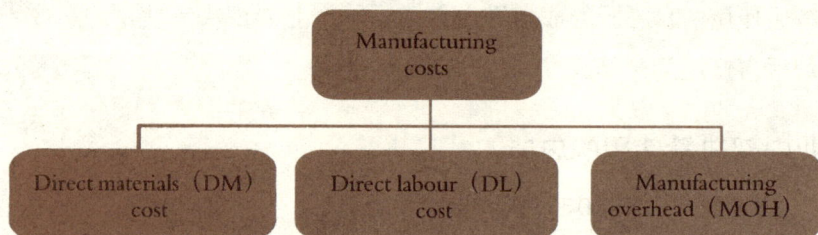

图 2 - 2　制造成本分类

2.3.1 直接材料成本
Direct Materials Cost

制造商一般将原材料（raw materials）加工为制成品（finished goods）。原材料指在生产过程中使用的基本材料、零部件。原材料包括直接材料（direct materials）和间接材料（indirect materials）。直接材料指在生产过程中使用的主要原材料。因为直接材料是制成品的实体，所以直接材料与制成品有直接关联，且易于确定制成品的直接材料成本，如烘烤面包所用的面粉、瓶装饮料所用的瓶子、汽车生产中所用的座椅和发动机等。

2.3.2 直接人工成本
Direct Labour Cost

在生产过程中，直接参与将原材料加工为制成品的员工被视为直接人工，如汽车生产中的机器操作员和技术员、饮料生产中的装瓶工、面包店的烘焙师等。

2.3.3 制造费用

Manufacturing Overhead

制造费用指直接材料成本和直接人工成本以外的制造成本；换言之，制造费用包含了所有间接制造成本（indirect manufacturing cost），一般由三部分组成：①间接材料成本（indirect materials cost）；②间接人工成本（indirect labour cost）；③其他间接制造成本（other indirect manufacturing cost）。制造费用英文也称为"factory overhead"（见图2-3）。

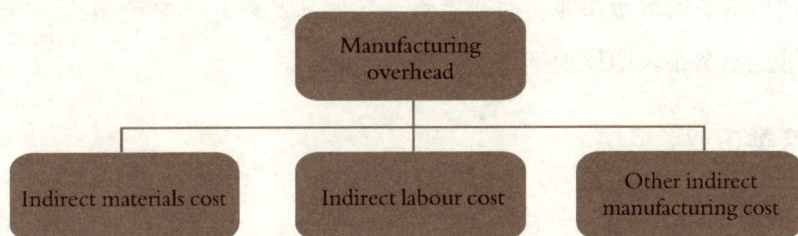

图 2 - 3　制造费用分类

（1）间接材料指不易确定的制成品原材料。间接材料具有如下两个特点：①间接材料不是制成品的实体；②间接材料与制成品无直接关联且不易确定，如工厂机器的清洁剂、润滑油，使用的电焊条、砂轮、燃料等。

（2）间接人工指不直接参与将原材料加工为制成品的工厂员工，如工厂升降机操作员、保安、保洁工人等。

（3）其他间接制造成本指间接材料成本和间接人工成本以外的间接制造成本，如厂房与设备的保险费用、折旧费用、维护费用和水电费用等。

2.3.4 主要成本与加工成本

Prime Costs and Conversion Costs

主要成本（prime cost）指产品的直接材料成本与直接人工成本之和。加工成本（conversion cost）指产品的直接人工成本与制造费用之和，这些成本主要是将直接材料加工为制成品产生的成本（见图2-4和图2-5）。

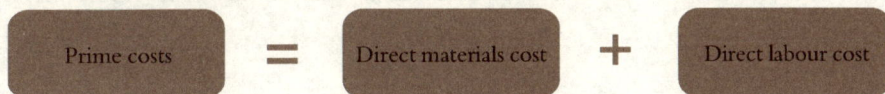

图 2 - 4　主要成本计算公式

带你到北美学习
管理会计
Take You to
North America
to Learn
Managerial Accounting

$$\boxed{\text{Conversion costs}} \quad = \quad \boxed{\text{Direct labour cost}} \quad + \quad \boxed{\text{Manufacaturing overhead}}$$

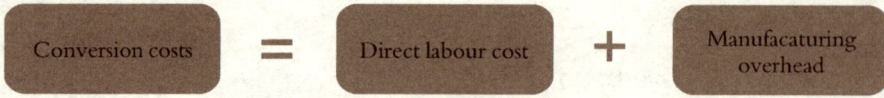

图 2 - 5　加工成本计算公式

2.4　财务报表中的产品成本与期间成本

The Product Costs and Period Costs Presented in the Financial Statements

企业可以分为服务类企业、商业类企业和制造类企业。接下来，学习如何在三类不同企业的财务报表中体现产品成本和期间成本。

2.4.1 服务类企业

Service Companies

服务类企业仅提供无形服务，没有库存产品，因此没有售出商品成本账目和库存账目（inventory）。如"说明2-1"所示，服务类企业收益表没有售出商品成本（cost of goods sold）。如"说明2-2"所示，服务类企业资产负债表没有库存账目。

说明 2 - 1: 服务类企业收益表		
Service Company Income Statement For the year ended by December 31，2017		
Service revenue		$ 16,000
Operating expenses		
Salaries expense	$ 3,000	
Office rent expense	1,500	
Depreciation expense	800	
Marketing expense	1,000	
Utilities expense	300	
Total operating expenses		(6,600)
Operating income		$ 9,400

说明 2-2：服务类企业资产负债表短期资产部分	
Service Company Balance Sheet（Partial） At December 31，2017	
Cash	$ 4,000
Accounts receivable	1,000
Prepaid expenses	1,000
Office supplies	2,000
Total current assets	$ 8,000

《带你到北美学习财务会计》介绍了收益表体现的最终结果，即净收益（net income）或净亏损（net loss），而非经营收益（operating income）。由于企业管理者更关心企业运营创造的收益或产生的亏损，所以本书一般使用经营收益作为收益表的最终结果，而非净收益或净亏损。

2.4.2 商业类企业

Merchandising Companies

商业类企业一般转售供应商提供的实体商品，因此存在商品库存。与服务类企业相比，商业类企业资产负债表有商品库存账目。因为商业类企业依靠转售供应商提供的商品赚取收入，所以在赚取销售额的同时，此类企业也产生售出商品成本，且售出商品成本是商业类企业的主要费用。

"说明 2-3"中的绿色部分说明了如何计算商业类企业的售出商品成本。商品库存账目期初余额加上购买商品成本（cost of goods purchased）等于可供销售商品成本（cost of goods available for sale），可供销售商品成本减去商品库存账目期末余额等于售出商品成本（cost of goods sold）（见图 2-6）。商品成本包括获得产品和使产品可以出售而产生的所有必要支出，这些必要支出包括所购商品价格、进货运费（freight-in cost）和进口税（import duty）等。

说明 2-3：商业类企业收益表		
Merchandising Company Income Statement For the year ended by December 31，2017		
Sales revenue		$ 180,000

带你到北美学习
管理会计
Take You to
North America
to Learn
Managerial Accounting

Cost of goods sold:			
Beginning merchandise inventory		$10,000	
Cost of goods purchased		110,000	
Cost of goods available for sale		120,000	
Ending merchandise inventory		(20,000)	(100,000)
Gross profit			80,000
Operating expenses			
Salaries expense		20,000	
Office supplies expense		10,000	(30,000)
Operating income			$50,000

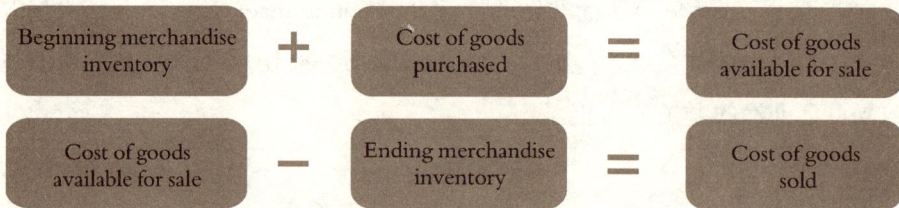

图2-6 商业类企业售出商品成本计算公式

如"说明2-4"中绿色部分所示，商业类企业资产负债表短期资产部分含有商品库存账目。

说明2-4：商业类企业资产负债表短期资产部分	
Merchandising Company Balance Sheet（Partial） At December 31，2017	
Cash	$12,000
Accounts receivable	8,000
Inventory（见说明2-3）	20,000
Prepaid expenses	10,000
Office supplies	2,000
Total current assets	$52,000

2.4.3 制造类企业

Manufacturing Companies

制造类企业使用原材料、设备和其他生产资源，将原材料加工成制成品。制造类企业一般向零售商或批发商销售产品，但也有许多制造类企业直接向客户出售产品。制造类企业的库存一般分为三类：①原材料库存；②在制品库存；③制成品库存。原材料指在生产过程中使用的基本材料、零部件。在制品（work in process）指在生产过程中尚未完工的产品。制成品（finished good）指完工但尚未出售的产品。与商业类企业仅有商品库存账目不同，制造类企业资产负债表短期资产部分有原材料库存账目、在制品库存账目和制成品库存账目，如"说明 2-7"中的绿色部分所示。

"说明 2-5"中的绿色部分为制造类企业的售出商品成本的计算过程。制成品库存账目期初余额加上制成商品成本（cost of goods manufactured）等于可供销售商品成本（cost of goods available for sale），可供销售商品成本减去制成品库存账目期末余额等于售出商品成本（cost of goods sold）（见图 2-7）。

说明 2-5：制造类企业收益表		
Manufacturing Company Income Statement For the year ended by December 31, 2017		
Sales revenue		$ 280,000
Cost of goods sold:		
Beginning finished goods inventory	$ 60,000	
Cost of goods manufactured	240,000	
Cost of goods available for sale	300,000	
Ending finished goods inventory	(100,000)	(200,000)
Gross profit		80,000
Operating expenses		
Delivery expense	30,000	
Office supplies expense	10,000	(40,000)
Operating income		$ 40,000

图 2-7　制造类企业售出商品成本计算公式

商业类企业在计算售出商品成本时，使用购买商品成本数据；而制造类企业在

带你到北美学习
管理会计
Take You to
North America
to Learn
Managerial Accounting

计算售出商品成本时，使用制成商品成本数据。什么是制成商品成本？制成商品成本指在给定财务周期所用直接材料、直接人工和制造费用制成产品的成本；换言之，制成商品成本就是制造商为获得新产品而产生的成本。

制成商品成本表明，制造工厂在给定财务周期产生的成本。在加工产品之前，制造商采购直接材料，将直接材料计入原材料库存（raw materials inventory）。在开始加工后，生产所用直接材料将从原材料库存移入在制品库存（work in process inventory）。在加工过程中，制造商需要支付直接人工成本、制造费用，这些直接人工成本和制造费用计入在制品库存。在制成产品之后，产品将从在制品库存移入制成品库存（finished goods inventory）。在给定财务周期，从在制品库存账目移入制成品库存账目的产品成本被视为制成商品成本（cost of goods manufactured）。在制成品出售之后，所售制成品成本将计入售出商品成本账目（见图 2-8）。

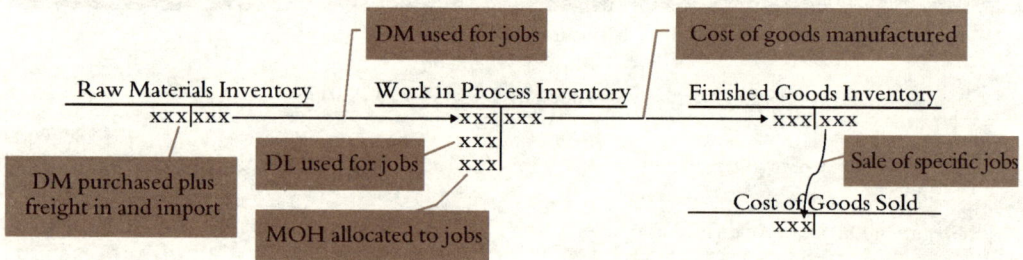

图 2-8　制造工厂内的成本流转

"说明 2-6"为制成商品成本的计算过程。

说明 2-6：计算制成商品成本			
Manufacturing Company Schedule of Cost of Goods Manufactured For the year ended by December 31，2017			
Beginning work in process inventory			$ 20,000
Direct materials used：			
Beginning direct materials inventory	$ 60,000		
Purchases of direct materials	120,000		
Direct materials available for use	180,000		
Ending direct materials inventory	(80,000)	$ 100,000	
Direct labour		80,000	
Manufacturing overhead			
Indirect materials	10,000		

Indirect labour	30,000		
Depreciation on plant and equipment	20,000		
Plant utilities, insurances, and property taxes	<u>40,000</u>	<u>100,000</u>	
Total manufacturing costs incurred during year			<u>280,000</u>
Total manufacturing costs to account for			300,000
Ending work in process inventory			(60,000)
Cost of goods manufactured			<u>$ 240,000</u>

讲解：

1. 制成商品成本指在给定财务周期所用直接材料、直接人工和制造费用制成产品的成本，因此首先计算所用直接材料成本。直接材料库存账目期初余额（$60 000）加上购买直接材料成本（$120 000）等于可供使用直接材料成本（$180 000），可供使用直接材料成本（$180 000）减去直接材料库存账目期末余额（$80 000）等于所用直接材料成本（$100 000）。其次，制造商承担的直接人工成本为 $80 000。最后，计算制造费用（manufacturing overhead）。制造费用指直接材料成本和直接人工成本以外的制造成本；换言之，制造费用包含了所有间接制造成本（indirect manufacturing cost），一般由三部分组成：①间接材料成本（indirect materials cost）；②间接人工成本（indirect labour cost）；③其他间接制造成本（other indirect manufacturing cost）。根据制造费用定义，Indirect materials，Indirect labour，Depreciation on plant and equipment，Plant utilities，insurances and property taxes 属于制造费用，因此制造费用总额为 $100 000（$10 000 + $30 000 + $20 000 + $40 000 = $100 000）。
2. 2017 年，制造商所用直接材料成本为 $100 000，直接人工成本为 $80 000，制造费用为 $100 000，共计 $280 000。制造商产生的直接材料成本、直接人工成本和制造费用之和代表了 2017 年度的年内承担制造成本总额（total manufacturing cost incurred during the year）。
3. 制成商品成本计算表表明，2017 年年初的在制品库存账目余额为 $20 000，即截至 2016 年 12 月 31 日，企业拥有价值为 $20 000 的未完工产品，这些产品需要在 2017 年继续完成。在制品库存账目年初余额（$20 000）加上年内承担制造成本总额（$280 000）等于需核算制造成本总额（total manufacturing cost to account for）（$300 000）。
4. 需核算制造成本总额（$300 000）减去在制品库存账目年末余额（$60 000）等于制成商品成本（$240 000）。在制品库存账目年末余额为 $60 000，即截至 2017 年 12 月 31 日，制造商仍有价值为 $60 000 的未完工产品，这些产品需要在 2018 年继续完成。

如"说明 2-7"中的绿色部分所示，制造类企业资产负债表短期资产部分含有原材料库存账目、在制品库存账目和制成品库存账目。

说明 2-7：制造类企业资产负债表短期资产部分

Manufacturing Company Balance Sheet (Partial) At December 31, 2017		
Cash		$ 25,000
Accounts receivable		35,000
Inventories：		
Raw materials inventory（见说明 2-6）	$ 80,000	

带你到北美学习
管理会计
Take You to
North America
to Learn
Managerial Accounting

Work in process inventory（见说明 2-6）	60,000	
Finished goods inventory（见说明 2-5）	100,000	
Total inventories		240,000
Prepaid expenses		6,000
Office supplies		10,000
Total current assets		$316,000

例题综述
Summary of Examples

例题 2 - 1

Inventorial product costs for a manufactured product include _____.

A. marketing, research and development costs

B. prime costs

C. conversion costs

D. the costs of direct materials, direct labour and manufacturing overhead

讲解： 产品成本（product cost）指企业在价值链生产环节或采购环节产生的成本。制造类企业的产品成本指在价值链生产环节产生的成本。在加工产品时，制造商一般承担三类制造成本（manufacturing cost）：①直接材料成本（direct materials cost）；②直接人工成本（direct labour cost）；③制造费用（manufacturing overhead）。

答案： D

例题 2 - 2

A typical manufacturing overhead would be _____.

A. direct materials

B. period costs

C. direct labour

D. depreciation on factory equipment

讲解： 制造费用指直接材料成本和直接人工成本以外的制造成本；换言之，制造费用包含了所有间接制造成本（indirect manufacturing cost），一般由三部分组成：①间接材料成本（indirect materials cost）；②间接人工成本（indirect labour cost）；③其他间接制造成本（other indirect manufacturing cost）。

答案： D

例题 2 - 3

What is meant by the term, product cost? How does it differ from period cost?

讲解： 企业总成本一般由两部分组成：①产品成本（product cost）；②期间成本

47

带你到北美学习
管理会计
Take You to
North America
to Learn
Managerial Accounting

（period cost）。

《财务会计报告准则》不允许企业使用总成本计算企业库存账目余额和售出商品成本账目余额。对外公布财务报告时，企业必须使用产品成本。产品成本（product cost）指企业在价值链生产环节或采购环节产生的成本。在出售产品之前，产品成本被视为企业资产，计入库存账目。在出售产品之后，所售产品成本从企业库存账目移出，计入售出商品成本账目（cost of goods sold）。在价值链其他五个环节（研发、设计、市场营销、配送和客户服务）产生的成本则被视为期间成本（period cost），期间成本也被称为经营费用（operating expense）或销售、常规与行政费用（selling, general, and administrative expense）。

制造类企业的产品成本是指在价值链生产环节产生的成本。在加工产品时，制造商一般承担三类制造成本（manufacturing cost）：①直接材料成本（direct materials cost）；②直接人工成本（direct labour cost）；③制造费用（manufacturing overhead）。

答案： Product costs include only the costs incurred during the production or purchases stage of the value chain. Product costs are treated as an asset (inventory) until the product is sold. When the product is sold, these costs are removed from inventory and expensed as cost of goods sold. Manufacturers' product costs include only those costs incurred during the production element of the value chain. Manufacturers incur three types of manufacturing costs when making a product: direct materials, direct labour, and manufacturing overhead.

Since product costs include only costs incurred during the production or purchases stage of the value chain, all costs incurred in the other stages of the value chain must be expensed in the period in which they are incurred. Therefore, we refer to research and development, design, marketing, distribution, and customer service costs as period costs. Period costs are often called operating expenses or selling, general, and administrative expenses on the income statement.

例题 2 - 4

Classify the following items as direct or indirect costs with respect to a local store of DVDs Corporation (the store is the cost object).

a. Store utilities and depreciation

b. Salaries of the corporation's top executives

c．Costs of DVDs

d．Costs of the corporate advertising

e．Wages of the store employees

f．Costs of operating the corporate human resource department

g．Costs of popcorn and candy sold at the store

讲解： 成本对象（cost object）指在计算成本时，企业管理者归属和分配成本所需的载体；成本对象可以是一件产品、一件模具、一个部门、一个厂房或一个地区分支机构。根据成本对象，成本可以分为直接成本和间接成本。直接成本（direct cost）指与成本对象有关，并基于成本对象容易确定的成本；简言之，根据成本对象，企业可以直接确定的成本被视为直接成本。间接成本（indirect cost）指与成本对象有关，但基于成本对象不易确定的成本；简言之，根据成本对象，企业不能直接确定的成本被视为间接成本。成本究竟属于直接成本还是间接成本取决于成本对象；换言之，同样的成本对于某类成本对象可能属于直接成本，而对于另一类成本对象可能属于间接成本。

答案：

a．Direct cost

b．Indirect cost

c．Direct cost

d．Indirect cost

e．Direct cost

f．Indirect cost

g．Direct cost

例题 2 - 5

Wood Ltd. is a manufacturer of stud lumber, veneer, and wood chips. Classify each of the manufacturer's costs as either a product cost or a period cost.

a．Depreciation on a veneer plant

b．Purchases of lumber to be cut into boards

c．Life insurances on the corporate staffs

d．Salaries of scientists studying ways to speed forest growth

带你到北美学习
管理会计
Take You to
North America
to Learn
Managerial Accounting

e. Costs of new softwares to track inventory during production

f. Costs of electricity at one of the company's paper mills

g. Salaries of the corporation's top executives

h. Costs of chemical applied to lumber to inhibit mould from developing

i. Costs of TV advertisements promoting environmental awareness

讲解： 同 "例题 2-3"。

答案：

a. Product cost

b. Product cost

c. Period cost

d. Period cost

e. Product cost

f. Product cost

g. Period cost

h. Product cost

i. Period cost

例题 2 - 6

Classify each of the following costs as a period cost or a product cost. If you classify the cost as a product cost, further classify it as direct materials (DM), direct labour (DL), or manufacturing overhead (MOH).

Description	Is it a Period or Product Cost?	If it is a Product Cost, is it DL, DM or MOH
a. Depreciation on automated production equipment		
b. Telephone bills relating to customer service centre		
c. Wages and benefits paid to assembly line workers in manufacturing plants		
d. Repairs and maintenance on plant equipment		
e. Lease payments for administrative headquarters		
f. Salaries paid to product quality inspectors in manufacturing plants		

Description	Is it a Period or Product Cost?	If it is a Product Cost, is it DL, DM or MOH
g. Property insurances – 40% of buildings are used for offices and the remainder are used for plants		
h. Standard packaging materials used to package individual units of finished goods for sale		
i. Lubricants used in running machines in manufacturing plants		
j. Depreciation on trucks used to collect raw materials from local suppliers		
k. Property taxes on manufacturing plants		
l. Television advertisements for corporate products		
m. Gasoline used to operate trucks that used to deliver finished goods to retailers		
n. CEO's annual bonus		
o. Plastic bottles in which products are packaged		
p. Depreciation on human resource department's computers		
q. Wages and salaries paid to machine operators in manufacturing plants		
r. Research and development on improving manufacturing processes		

讲解： 企业总成本一般由两部分组成：①产品成本（product cost）；②期间成本（period cost）。产品成本指企业在价值链生产环节或采购环节产生的成本。在出售产品之前，产品成本被视为企业资产，计入库存账目。在出售产品之后，所售产品成本从企业库存账目移出，计入售出商品成本账目（cost of goods sold）。在价值链其他五个环节（研发、设计、市场营销、配送和客户服务）产生的成本则被视为期间成本。

制造类企业的产品成本是指在价值链生产环节产生的成本。在加工产品时，制造商一般承担三类制造成本（manufacturing cost）：①直接材料成本（direct materials cost）；②直接人工成本（direct labour cost）；③制造费用（manufacturing overhead）。

直接材料指在生产过程中使用的主要原材料。因为直接材料是制成品的实体，所以直接材料与制成品有直接关联，且易于确定制成品的直接材料成本。

在生产过程中，直接参与将原材料加工为制成品的员工被视为直接人工。

制造费用指直接材料成本和直接人工成本以外的制造成本；换言之，制造费用

带你到北美学习
管理会计
Take You to
North America
to Learn
Managerial Accounting

包含了所有间接制造成本（indirect manufacturing cost），一般由三部分组成：①间接材料成本（indirect materials cost）；②间接人工成本（indirect labour cost）；③其他间接制造成本（other indirect manufacturing cost）。

答案：

Description	Is it a Period or Product Cost?	If it is a Product Cost, is it DL, DM or MOH
a . Depreciation on automated production equipment	Product	MOH
b . Telephone bills relating to customer service centre	Period	
c . Wages and benefits paid to assembly line workers in manufacturing plants	Product	DL
d . Repairs and maintenance on plant equipment	Product	MOH
e . Lease payments for administrative headquarters	Period	
f . Salaries paid to product quality inspectors in manufacturing plants	Product	MOH
g . Property insurances – 40% of buildings are used for offices and the remainder are used for plants	Period（40%） Product（60%）	– MOH
h . Standard packaging materials used to package individual units of finished goods for sale	Product	DM
i . Lubricants used in running machines in manufacturing plants	Product	MOH
j . Depreciation on trucks used to collect raw materials from local suppliers	Product	MOH
k . Property taxes on manufacturing plants	Product	MOH
l . Television advertisements for corporate products	Period	
m. Gasoline used to operate trucks that used to deliver finished goods to retailers	Period	
n . CEO's annual bonus	Period	
o . Plastic bottles in which products are packaged	Product	DM
p . Depreciation on human resource department's computers	Period	
q . Wages and salaries paid to machine operators in manufacturing plants	Product	DL
r . Research and development on improving manufacturing processes	Period	

例题 2 - 7

The following amounts were taken from the general ledger of a manufacturer：

Direct materials inventory, beginning	$ 50,000
Direct materials inventory, ending	56,000
Work in process inventory, beginning	100,000
Work in process inventory, ending	70,000
Finished goods inventory, beginning	36,000
Finished goods inventory, ending	50,000
Purchases of direct materials	30,000
Indirect labour	30,000
Direct labour	164,000
Depreciation expense on plant	26,000
Repairs and maintenance expenses on plant	8,000
Insurance expense on plant	18,000
General and administrative expenses	25,000
Marketing expense	40,000

Required：

Prepare a schedule of cost of goods manufactured and a schedule of cost of goods sold for the manufacturer for the year ended by December 31, 2017.

讲解： 制成商品成本指在给定财务周期所用直接材料、直接人工和制造费用制成产品的成本，因此首先计算所用直接材料成本。直接材料库存账目期初余额（ $ 50 000）加上购买直接材料成本（ $ 30 000）等于可供使用直接材料成本（ $ 80 000），可供使用直接材料成本（ $ 80 000）减去直接材料库存账目期末余额（ $ 56 000）等于所用直接材料成本（ $ 24 000）。其次，制造商承担的直接人工成本为 $ 164 000。最后，计算制造费用。制造费用指直接材料成本和直接人工成本以外的制造成本；换言之，制造费用包含了所有间接制造成本，一般由三部分组成：①间接材料成本；②间接人工成本；③其他间接制造成本。根据制造费用定义和题目信息，Indirect labour，Depreciation expense on plant，Repairs and maintenance expenses on plant，Insurance expense on plant 属于制造费用，因此制造费用总额为 $ 82 000（ $ 30 000 + $ 26 000 + $ 8 000 + $ 18 000 = $ 82 000）。

制造商所用直接材料成本为 $ 24 000，直接人工成本为 $ 164 000，制造费用为

带你到北美学习
管理会计
Take You to
North America
to Learn
Managerial Accounting

$82 000，因此年内承担制造成本总额为 $270 000（$24 000 + $164 000 + $82 000 = $270 000）。

在制品库存账目期初余额（$100 000）加上年内承担制造成本总额（$270 000）等于需核算制造成本总额（$370 000），需核算制造成本总额（$370 000）减去在制品库存账目期末余额（$70 000）等于制成商品成本（$300 000）。

制成品库存账目期初余额（$36 000）加上制成商品成本（$300 000）等于可供销售商品成本（$336 000），可供销售商品成本（$336 000）减去制成品库存账目期末余额（$50 000）等于售出商品成本（$286 000）。

答案：

The Manufacturing Company Schedule of Cost of Goods Manufactured For the year ended by December 31, 2017			
Beginning work in process inventory			$100,000
Direct materials used:			
Beginning direct materials inventory	$50,000		
Purchases of direct materials	30,000		
Direct materials available for use	80,000		
Ending direct materials inventory	(56,000)	$24,000	
Direct labour		164,000	
Manufacturing overhead			
Indirect labour	30,000		
Depreciation expense on plant	26,000		
Repairs and maintenance expenses on plant	8,000		
Insurance expense on plant	18,000	82,000	
Total manufacturing costs incurred during year			270,000
Total manufacturing costs to account for			370,000
Ending work in process inventory			(70,000)
Cost of goods manufactured			$300,000

The Manufacturing Company Schedule of Cost of Goods Sold For the year ended by December 31, 2017	
Beginning finished goods inventory	$ 36,000
Cost of goods manufactured	300,000
Cost of goods available for sale	336,000
Ending finished goods inventory	(50,000)
Cost of goods sold	$ 286,000

例题 2 - 8

Using the information in the table below, fill in the missing items.

Direct materials inventory, beginning	$ 15,000
Purchases of direct materials	
Direct materials inventory, ending	10,000
Direct materials used	95,000
Direct labour	150,000
Manufacturing overhead	
Manufacturing costs to account for	340,000
Work in process inventory, beginning	30,000
Work in process inventory, ending	
Cost of goods manufactured	315,000
Finished goods inventory, beginning	
Finished goods inventory, ending	50,000
Cost of goods sold	390,000
Prime costs	
Conversion costs	

讲解： 首先，计算购买直接材料成本。直接材料账目期初余额加上购买直接材料成本，减去直接材料账目期末余额，等于所用直接材料成本。直接材料账目期初余额为 $ 15 000，直接材料账目期末余额为 $ 10 000，所用直接材料成本为 $ 95 000，因此购买价值为 $ 90 000 的直接材料（$ 95 000 + $ 10 000 - $ 15 000 = $ 90 000）。

带你到北美学习
管理会计
Take You to
North America
to Learn
Managerial Accounting

Direct materials inventory, beginning	$ 15,000
Purchases of direct materials	X
Direct materials inventory, ending	(10,000)
Direct materials used	$ 95,000

其次，计算制造费用、在制品库存账目期末余额、制成品库存账目期初余额。

在制品库存账目期初余额加上年内承担制造成本总额等于需核算制造成本总额。在制品库存账目期初余额为 $30 000，需核算制造成本总额为 $340 000，因此年内承担制造成本总额为 $310 000（$340 000 – $30 000 = $310 000）。

需核算制造成本总额减去在制品库存账目期末余额等于制成商品成本。需核算制造成本总额为 $340 000，制成商品成本为 $315 000，所以在制品库存账目期末余额为 $25 000（$340 000 – $315 000 = $25 000）。

年内承担制造成本总额指年内产生的直接材料成本、直接人工成本和制造费用之和。年内承担制造成本总额为 $310 000，所用直接材料成本为 $95 000，直接人工成本为 $150 000，因此制造费用为 $65 000（$310 000 – $95 000 – $150 000 = $65 000）。

制成品库存账目期初余额加上制成商品成本等于可供销售商品成本，可供销售商品成本减去制成品库存账目期末余额等于售出商品成本。售出商品成本为 $390 000，制成品库存账目期末余额为 $50 000，因此可供销售商品成本为 $440 000；可供销售商品成本为 $440 000，制成商品成本为 $315 000，所以制成品库存账目期初余额为 $125 000。

Finished goods inventory, beginning	$ X
Cost of goods manufactured	315,000
Cost of goods available for sale	440,000
Finished goods inventory, ending	(50,000)
Cost of goods sold	$ 390,000

最后，计算主要成本和加工成本。主要成本指产品的直接材料成本与直接人工成本之和。加工成本指产品的直接人工成本与制造费用之和。所用直接材料成本为 $95 000，直接人工成本为 $150 000，所以主要成本为 $245 000；直接人工成本为 $150 000，制造费用为 $65 000，因此加工成本为 $215 000。

答案：

Direct materials inventory, beginning	$ 15,000
Purchases of direct materials	90,000
Direct materials inventory, ending	10,000
Direct materials used	95,000
Direct labour	150,000
Manufacturing overhead	65,000
Manufacturing costs to account for	340,000
Work in process inventory, beginning	30,000
Work in process inventory, ending	25,000
Cost of goods manufactured	315,000
Finished goods inventory, beginning	125,000
Finished goods inventory, ending	50,000
Cost of goods sold	390,000
Prime costs	245,000
Conversion costs	215,000

例题 2 - 9

A small manufacturer has presented the following items about the last year's operations：

Sales revenue	$ 83,600
Sales salaries	2,500
Travelling and entertainment expenses	1,400
Administrative expense	2,600
Advertising expense	1,500
Direct materials inventory, beginning	2,100
Direct materials inventory, ending	3,200
Work in process inventory, beginning	1,600
Work in process inventory, ending	1,200
Finished goods inventory, beginning	65,400
Finished goods inventory, ending	59,500
Freight-in on direct materials	650

带你到北美学习
管理会计
Take You to
North America
to Learn
Managerial Accounting

General liability insurance expense	240
Indirect labour	13,800
Indirect materials used	1,500
Insurance expense on factory	1,300
Purchases of direct materials	14,000
Property taxes on factory	600
Property taxes on office buildings	300
Repairs and maintenance on factory	900
Depreciation expense on factory	3,300
Depreciation expense on office buildings	1,100
Direct labour	27,500

Required:

1. Prepare a schedule of cost of goods manufactured in good form for the year ended by December 31, 2016.

2. Prepare an income statement in good form for the year ended by December 31, 2016, including a schedule of cost of goods sold in good form.

1. Prepare a schedule of cost of goods manufactured in good form for the year ended by December 31, 2016.

讲解： 制成商品成本指在给定财务周期所用直接材料、直接人工和制造费用制成产品的成本，因此首先计算所用直接材料成本。直接材料账目期初余额（＄2 100）加上购买直接材料成本（＄14 000）和直接材料进货费用（＄650）等于可供使用直接材料成本（＄16 750），可供使用直接材料成本（＄16 750）减去直接材料账目期末余额（＄3 200）等于所用直接材料成本（＄13 550）。其次，制造商承担的直接人工成本为＄27 500。最后，计算制造费用。制造费用指直接材料成本和直接人工成本以外的制造成本；换言之，制造费用包含了所有间接制造成本，一般由三部分组成：①间接材料成本；②间接人工成本；③其他间接制造成本。根据制造费用定义和题目信息，Indirect materials used，Indirect labour，Insurance expense on factory，Property taxes on factory，Repairs and maintenance on factory，Depreciation expense on factory 属于制造费用，所以制造费用总额为＄21 400（＄1 500 + ＄13 800 + ＄1 300 + ＄600 + ＄900 + ＄3 300 = ＄21 400）。

制造商所用直接材料成本为 $13 550，直接人工成本为 $27 500，制造费用为 $21 400，因此年内承担制造成本总额为 $62 450（$13 550 + $27 500 + $21 400 = $62 450）。

在制品库存账目期初余额（$1 600）加上年内承担制造成本总额（$62 450）等于需核算制造成本总额（$64 050），需核算制造成本总额（$64 050）减去在制品库存账目期末余额（$1 200）等于制成商品成本（$62 850）。

答案：

Small Manufacturer Schedule of Cost of Goods Manufactured For the year ended by December 31, 2016			
Beginning work in process inventory			$1,600
Direct materials used：			
Beginning direct materials inventory	$2,100		
Purchases of direct materials	14,000		
Freight-in on direct materials	650		
Direct materials available for use	16,750		
Ending direct materials inventory	(3,200)	$13,550	
Direct labour		27,500	
Manufacturing overhead			
Indirect materials used	1,500		
Indirect labour	13,800		
Insurance expense on factory	1,300		
Property taxes on factory	600		
Repairs and maintenance on factory	900		
Depreciation expense on factory	3,300	21,400	
Total manufacturing costs incurred during year			62,450
Total manufacturing costs to account for			64,050
Ending work in process inventory			(1,200)
Cost of goods manufactured			$62,850

2. **Prepare an income statement in good form for the year ended by December 31, 2016, including a schedule of cost of goods sold in good form.**

讲解： 制成品库存账目期初余额加上制成商品成本等于可供销售商品成本，可供销

带你到北美学习
管理会计
Take You to
North America
to Learn
Managerial Accounting

售商品成本减去制成品库存账目期末余额等于售出商品成本。制成品库存账目期初余额为 $65 400，制成商品成本为 $62 850，因此可供销售商品成本为 $128 250；可供销售商品成本为 $128 250，制成品库存账目期末余额为 $59 500，所以售出商品成本为 $68 750。

销售额（$83 600）减去售出商品成本（$68 750）等于毛利润（$14 850）。

价值链其他五个环节（研发、设计、市场营销、配送和客户服务）产生的成本被视为期间成本（period cost）。根据期间成本定义和题目信息，Administrative expense，Advertising expense，Depreciation expense on office buildings，General liability insurance expense，Property taxes on office buildings，Sales salaries，Travelling and entertainment expenses 属于经营费用，所以经营费用总额为 $9 640（$2 600 + $1 500 + $1 100 + $240 + $300 + $2 500 + $1 400 = $9 640）。

毛利润（$14 850）减去经营费用总额（$9 640）等于经营收益（$5 210）。

答案：

Small Manufacturer Income Statement For the year ended by December 31, 2016		
Sales revenue		$83,600
Cost of goods sold:		
Beginning finished goods inventory	$65,400	
Cost of goods manufactured	62,850	
Cost of goods available for sale	128,250	
Ending finished goods inventory	(59,500)	(68,750)
Gross profit		14,850
Operating expenses		
Administrative expense	2,600	
Advertising expense	1,500	
Depreciation expense on office buildings	1,100	
General liability insurance expense	240	
Property taxes on office buildings	300	
Sales salaries	2,500	
Travelling and entertainment expenses	1,400	(9,640)
Operating income		$5,210

例题 2 - 10

ABC Company used $71,000 of direct materials and incurred $37,000 of direct labour during 2009. Indirect labour amounted to $2,700 while indirect materials used totaled $1,600. Other operating costs pertaining to the plant included utilities of $3,100, maintenance of $4,500, supplies of $1,800, depreciation of $7,900, and property taxes of $2,600. There was no beginning or ending finished goods inventory, but work in process inventory began the year (January 1, 2009) with a $5,500 balance, and ended the year (December 31, 2009) with a $7,500 balance.

Required:

Prepare a schedule of cost of goods manufactured for ABC Company for the year ended by December 31, 2009.

讲解: 制成商品成本指在给定财务周期所用直接材料、直接人工和制造费用制成产品的成本。所用直接材料成本为 $71 000,直接人工成本为 $37 000。制造费用指直接材料成本和直接人工成本以外的制造成本;换言之,制造费用包含了所有间接制造成本,一般由三部分组成:①间接材料成本;②间接人工成本;③其他间接制造成本。根据制造费用定义和题目信息,Indirect materials used, Indirect labour, Plant utilities, Plant maintenance, Plant supplies, Depreciation on plant, Property taxes on plant 属于制造费用,因此制造费用总额为 $24 200($1 600 + $2 700 + $3 100 + $4 500 + $1 800 + $7 900 + $2 600 = $24 200)。

制造商所用直接材料成本为 $71 000,直接人工成本为 $37 000,制造费用为 $24 200,因此年内承担制造成本总额为 $132 200($71 000 + $37 000 + $24 200 = $132 200)。

在制品库存账目期初余额($5 500)加上年内承担制造成本总额($132 200)等于需核算制造成本总额($137 700),需核算制造成本总额($137 700)减去在制品库存账目期末余额($7 500)等于制成商品成本($130 200)。

答案:

ABC Company Schedule of Cost of Goods Manufactured For the year ended by December 31, 2009		
Beginning work in process inventory		$5,500
Direct material used	$71,000	

带你到北美学习
管理会计
Take You to
North America
to Learn
Managerial Accounting

Direct labour		37,000	
Manufacturing overhead			
Indirect materials	$1,600		
Indirect labour	2,700		
Depreciation on plant	7,900		
Plant utilities	3,100		
Plant supplies	1,800		
Property taxes on plant	2,600		
Plant maintenance	4,500	24,200	
Total manufacturing costs incurred during year			132,200
Total manufacturing costs to account for			137,700
Ending work in process inventory			(7,500)
Costs of goods manufactured			$130,200

例题 2 - 11

Certain item descriptions and amounts are missing from the monthly schedule of cost of goods manufactured and the monthly income statement of DEF Manufacturing below. Fill in the missing items.

DEF Manufacturing Schedule of Cost of Goods Manufactured For the month ended by December 31, 2009			
Beginning _____			$21,000
Direct _____:			
Beginning direct materials inventory	$X		
Purchases of direct materials	51,000		
_____	78,000		
Ending direct materials inventory	(23,000)	$X	
Direct _____		X	
Manufacturing overhead		40,000	
Total _____ costs _____			166,000
Total _____ costs _____			X
Ending _____			(25,000)
_____			$X

DEF Manufacturing Income Statement For the year ended by December 31, 2009		
Sales revenue		$ X
Cost of goods sold:		
Beginning _____	$ 115,000	
_____	X	
Cost of goods _____	X	
Ending _____	(X)	(209,000)
Gross profit		254,000
_____ Expenses		
Marketing expense	99,000	
Administrative expense	X	(154,000)
_____ Income		$ X

答案:

DEF Manufacturing Schedule of Cost of Goods Manufactured For the month ended by December 31, 2009		
Beginning work in process inventory		$ 21,000
Direct materials used:		
Beginning direct materials inventory	$ 27,000	
Purchases of direct materials	51,000	
Direct materials available for use	78,000	
Ending direct materials inventory	(23,000) $ 55,000	
Direct labour	71,000	
Manufacturing overhead	40,000	
Total manufacturing costs incurred during year		166,000
Total manufacturing costs to account for		187,000
Ending work in process inventory		(25,000)
Cost of goods manufactured		$ 162,000

带你到北美学习
管理会计
Take You to
North America
to Learn
Managerial Accounting

DEF Manufacturing The Income Statement For the year ended by December 31, 2009		
Sales revenue		$463,000
Cost of goods sold:		
Beginning finished goods inventory	$115,000	
Cost of goods manufactured	162,000	
Cost of goods available for sale	277,000	
Ending finished goods inventory	(68,000)	(209,000)
Gross profit		254,000
Operating expenses		
Marketing expense	99,000	
Administrative expense	55,000	(154,000)
Operating income		$100,000

例题 2 - 12

XYZ Inc. experienced a plant fire on December 31, 2013. Most of the company's accounting records were destroyed, but the following information was remained:

Beginning inventories on December 1, 2013 were as follows:

Direct materials	$64,000
Work in process	68,000
Prime costs: 70% of total manufacturing costs Manufacturing overhead: 40% of conversion costs	

Actual operating data for the year ended by December 31, 2013 were as follows:

Cost of goods manufactured	$1,540,000
Purchases of direct materials	440,000
Direct labour	720,000

Required:

Using the above information, prepare a schedule of cost of goods manufactured in good form for the month ended by December 31, 2013.

讲解: 加工成本指产品的直接人工成本与制造费用之和。根据题目信息,制造费用占加工成本的40%,直接人工成本为 $720 000,因此制造费用为 $480 000。

主要成本指产品的直接材料成本与直接人工成本之和。根据题目信息，主要成本占制造成本总额的 70%，直接人工成本为 $720 000，制造费用为 $480 000，因此所用直接材料成本为 $400 000。

直接材料账目期初余额为 $64 000，购买直接材料成本为 $440 000，所用直接材料成本为 $400 000，因此直接材料账目期末余额为 $104 000。

Direct materials inventory, beginning	$64,000
Purchases of direct materials	440,000
Direct materials inventory, ending	(X)
Direct materials used	$400,000

制造商所用直接材料成本为 $400 000，直接人工成本为 $720 000，制造费用为 $480 000，因此年内承担制造成本总额为 $1 600 000（$400 000 + $720 000 + $480 000 = $1 600 000）。在制品库存账目期初余额（$68 000）加上年内承担制造成本总额（$1 600 000）等于需核算制造成本总额（$1 668 000），需核算制造成本总额（$1 668 000）减去制成商品成本（$1 540 000）等于在制品库存账目期末余额（$128 000）。

答案：

XYZ Inc. Schedule of Cost of Goods Manufactured For the month ended by December 31, 2013			
Beginning work in process inventory			$68,000
Direct materials used:			
Beginning direct materials inventory	$64,000		
Purchases of direct materials	440,000		
Direct materials available for use	504,000		
Ending direct materials inventory	(104,000)	$400,000	
Direct labour		720,000	
Manufacturing overhead		480,000	
Total manufacturing costs incurred during year			1,600,000
Total manufacturing costs to account for			1,668,000
Ending work in process inventory			(128,000)
Cost of goods manufactured			$1,540,000

带你到北美学习
管理会计
Take You to
North America
to Learn
Managerial Accounting

专业名词汇编
Glossary of Accounting Terms

中文	英文	中文	英文
在制品	work in process	不动产税费用	property tax expense
产品成本	product cost	成本	cost
成本对象	cost object	成本分摊	cost allocation
服务类企业	service company	购买商品成本	cost of goods purchased
加工成本	conversion cost	间接材料	indirect materials
间接材料成本	indirect materials cost	间接成本	indirect cost
间接人工	indirect labour	间接人工成本	indirect labour cost
间接制造成本	indirect manufacturing cost	进货运费	freight-in cost
进口税	import duty	净亏损	net loss
净收益	net income	毛利润	gross profit
期间成本	period cost	商业类企业	merchandising company
收益表	income statement	售出商品成本	cost of goods sold
售价	selling price	水电费用	utility expense
销售额	sales revenue	原材料	raw materials
经营费用	operating expense	经营收益	operating income
折旧费用	depreciation expense	直接材料	direct materials
直接材料成本	direct materials cost	直接成本	direct cost
直接人工	direct labour	直接人工成本	direct labour cost
制成品	finished good	制成商品成本	cost of goods manufactured
制造成本	manufacturing cost	制造费用	manufacturing overhead
制造类企业	manufacturing company	主要成本	prime cost
总成本	total cost		
可供销售商品成本	cost of goods available for sale		
年内承担制造成本总额	total manufacturing cost incurred during the year		
其他间接制造成本	other indirect manufacturing cost		
销售、常规与行政费用	selling, general, and administrative expense		
需核算制造成本总额	total manufacturing cost to account for		

分批成本计算法

Job Costing

带你到北美学习
管理会计
Take You to
North America
to Learn
Managerial Accounting

3.1 确定产品的制造成本
Determining the Cost of Manufacturing a Product

为确定产品的制造成本，大部分制造商使用如下两种成本计算法：①分步成本计算法（process costing）；②分批成本计算法（job costing）。虽然两种产品成本计算法的使用条件和计算方法不同，但它们有同样的目的，即确定产品的制造成本（见说明 3-1）。

说明 3-1：对比分批成本计算法与分步成本计算法		
	Job Costing	Process Costing
Cost Object	Job	Process
Outputs	Unique, custom-ordered products or small batches of different products	Large number of identical units
How to Average?	Costs are averaged over the small number of units in a job (often one unit in a job).	Costs are averaged over the large number of identical products that pass through a series of uniform production steps or processes.

3.1.1 分步成本计算法
Process Costing

通过一系列统一的生产流程，制造商可以大量生产完全相同的产品，如面粉、水泥、石油、食品、饮料、卫生纸、纸张等，这类制造商使用分步成本计算法。理论上，这样生产的单件产品是完全相同的，因此单件产品的制造成本也应相同。在给定财务周期，分步成本计算法对制造商生产的同一种产品平均分摊制造成本，因此单件产品承担相同的产品成本，比如为生产 100 万个汉堡，一家食品企业在购买和使用原材料上花费了 200 万美元，因此单个汉堡的原材料成本为 2 美元。第 4 章将详细讲解分步成本计算法的知识。

3.1.2 分批成本计算法
Job Costing

与制造大量完全相同的产品不同，另一类制造商生产独特、客户定制、小批量商品，如飞机、别墅、高端定制珠宝、高档定制汽车等，这类企业使用分批成本计算法。一件独特商品、一小批定制商品被视为一张订单，因此分批成本计算法也被称为订单成本计算法（job - order costing）。不但制造商可以使用分批成本计算法，专业性服务提供商，如律师事务所、会计师事务所、顾问公司、市场公关公司等，也可以使用分批成本计算法，确定所提供定制服务的成本。

不同订单对直接材料、直接人工和制造费用的使用程度不同，因此每张订单产生不同的生产成本。由于每张订单的生产成本不同，所以制造商不能平均分摊生产成本。那么，如何确定一张订单的成本？接下来，我们将详细学习。

3.2 确定一张订单的成本
Determining a Job's Costs

生产独特、客户定制、小批量商品的制造商使用分批成本计算法。在讲解分批成本计算法之前，我们先复习一下，制造商生产实体产品（physical product）和生产产品带来的成本如何在工厂内流转。

在加工产品之前，制造商采购直接材料，并将直接材料计入原材料库存（raw materials inventory）。在开始加工之后，生产所用直接材料将从原材料库存移入在制品库存（work in process inventory）。在加工过程中，制造商需要支付直接人工成本、制造费用，这些直接人工成本和制造费用计入在制品库存。在产品制成后，产品将从在制品库存移入制成品库存（finished goods inventory）。在给定财务周期，从在制品库存账目移入制成品库存账目的产品成本被视为制成商品成本（cost of goods manufactured）。在制成品出售后，所售制成品成本将计入售出商品成本账目（见 P44 图 2-8）。

订单成本记录（job cost record）详细记录了制造商完成订单所产生的直接材料成本、直接人工成本以及分摊至订单的制造费用。因为一张订单成本记录仅记录与这张订单有关的三类制造成本：①直接材料成本；②直接人工成本；③制造费用，所以每张订单都有自己的订单成本记录。订单成本记录既可使用电子版形式，也可使用复印件形式（见说明 3-2）。

带你到北美学习
管理会计
Take You to
North America
to Learn
Managerial Accounting

Job Cost Record

Job Number：

Customer：

Job Description：

Date Started：

Date Completed：

Manufacturing Cost Information	Cost Summary
Direct Materials	
Direct Labour	
Manufacturing Overhead	
Total Job Costs	
Number of Units	
Costs per Unit	

Shipping Information			
Date	Quantity Shipped	Units Remaining	Cost Balance

对于尚未完工的订单，订单成本记录出现在资产负债表的在制品库存账目。在订单完成后，这些产品将从在制品库存账目移至制成品库存账目，因此对于已完工的订单，订单成本记录出现在资产负债表的制成品库存账目。从"说明 3-2"中的绿色区域可以发现，出售制成品的具体数量及日期、制成品剩余数量、制成品账目余额均出现在订单成本记录中。

接下来，通过"案例 3-1"，学习计算一张订单的直接材料成本、直接人工成本以及分摊的制造费用。

案例 3 - 1

Glass Corporation makes custom glass tiles. The management estimates total manufacturing overhead for the coming year to be ＄280,000 and has chosen direct labour (DL) hour as the allocation base. Furthermore, it estimates that 20,000 direct labour hours will be used in the coming year.

During May, the corporation started and finished Job 915. Job 915 has included 1,000 custom glass tiles. The corporation's records show the following direct materials for Job 915：

Clear white tile	3,000 units at ＄3 per unit
Specialty colour	8 quarts at ＄5 per quart
Mirror glass	6 quarts at ＄10 per quart

The corporation's labour time records show the following employees worked on Job 915：

Sarah Goodson	20 DL hours at ＄25 per DL hour
Micah McWhorter	10 DL hours at ＄15 per DL hour

Required：

Compute the total amounts of direct materials, direct labour, and manufacturing overhead that should be shown on the job cost record of Job 915.

讲解： 在分批成本计算系统中，订单成本记录 (job cost record) 扮演了重要角色。我们现在看一下，Glass Corporation 如何在订单成本记录中累计制造成本 (manufacturing cost)。

(1) 确定 915 号订单的直接材料成本。根据生产计划 (production schedule)，制造商将在 5 月份开始加工 915 号订单且当月完成。在生产 915 号订单之前，生产工人 (Sarah Goodson 和 Micah McWhorter) 必须列出所需直接材料：Clear white tile, Specialty colour, Mirror glass, 并填写领料单 (materials requisition form)（见说明 3-3）。领料单显示从库房中领取原材料的种类、数量、成本信息。领料单既可使用电子版形式，也可使用复印件形式。只要库房收到领料单，生产工人便可领取所需原材料。库房拥有各种原材料的记录。根据每种原材料记录 (raw materials record) 显示的成本信息，所领取原材料的单位成本 (unit cost) 和总成本 (total cost) 被转账至领料单，因此一旦领取原材料，原材料记录将随之更新（见说明 3-4、说明 3-5、说明 3-6）。

带你到北美学习
管理会计
Take You to
North America
to Learn
Managerial Accounting

说明 3 - 3：领料单

Materials Requisition Form

Date：May 2nd   **Form Number**：1234

Job Number：915

Date	Description	Quantity	Unit Cost	Amount
05/02	Clear white tile	3,000 units	$ 3	$ 9,000
05/02	Specialty colour	8 quarts	$ 5	40
05/02	Mirror glass	6 quarts	$ 10	60
			Total	$ 9,100

说明 3 - 4：Clear White Tile 的原材料记录

Raw Materials Record

Description：Clear White Tile   **Minimum Balance**：5,000 units

Date	Received			Used				Balance		
	Units	Cost	Total	Job No.	Units	Cost	Total	Units	Cost	Total
05/01	5,000	$ 3	$ 15,000					10,000	$ 3	$ 30,000
05/02				915	3,000	$ 3	$ 9,000	7,000	$ 3	$ 21,000

说明 3 - 5：Specialty Colour 的原材料记录

Raw Materials Record

Description：Specialty Colour   **Minimum Balance**：50 quarts

Date	Received			Used				Balance		
	Quarts	Cost	Total	Job No.	Quarts	Cost	Total	Quarts	Cost	Total
05/01	10	$ 5	$ 50					60	$ 5	$ 300
05/02				915	8	$ 5	$ 40	52	$ 5	$ 260

说明 3 - 6：Mirror Glass 的原材料记录

Raw Materials Record

Description：Mirror Glass   **Minimum Balance**：30 quarts

	Received			Used				Balance		
Date	Quarts	Cost	Total	Job No.	Quarts	Cost	Total	Quarts	Cost	Total
05/01	20	$ 10	$ 200					40	$ 10	$ 400
05/02				915	6	$ 10	$ 60	34	$ 10	$ 340

如 "说明 3-7" 中的绿色部分所示，915 号订单成本记录显示了这张订单产生的直接材料成本。

说明 3 - 7：915 号订单产生的直接材料成本转账至订单成本记录

Job Cost Record

Job Number：915

Customer：Unknown

Job Description：Custom Glass Tile

Date Started：May 1st

Date Completed：May 31st

Manufacturing Cost Information	Cost Summary
Direct Materials： 　　Clear white tile： 3,000 units at $ 3 per unit 　　Specialty colour： 8 quarts at $ 5 per quart 　　Mirror glass： 6 quarts at $ 10 per quart	$ 9,100
Direct Labour	
Manufacturing Overhead	
Total Job Costs	
Number of Units	
Costs per Unit	

（2）确定 915 号订单的直接人工成本。根据直接人工工资率和订单所用直接人工工时，计算出 915 号订单的直接人工成本。Sarah Goodson 为 915 号订单工作 20 小时，每小时工资为 $ 25，Micah McWhorter 为 915 号订单工作 10 小时，每小时工资为 $ 15，因此 915 号订单的直接人工成本为 $ 650。如 "说明 3-10" 的

带你到北美学习
管理会计
Take You to
North America
to Learn
Managerial Accounting

绿色部分所示，915 号订单成本记录显示这张订单产生的直接人工成本
（$650）。此外，Sarah Goodson 和 Micah McWhorter 还需填写工作时间记录
（labour time record）（见说明3-8 和说明3-9）。工作时间记录显示一名工人每
天为完成各种订单付出的时间。

说明 3 - 8：Sarah Goodson 的工作时间记录

Labour Time Record

Employee：Sarah Goodson   **Month**：05/01 – 05/31

Hourly Wage Rate：$25   **Record Number**：23

Date	Job Number	Start Time	End Time	Hours	Cost
05/03	901	8：00	10：00	2	$50
05/03	915	10：00	12：00	2	$50
05/03	915	13：00	17：00	4	$100
05/05	915	8：00	12：00	4	$100
05/05	915	13：00	17：00	4	$100
05/07	915	8：00	12：00	4	$100
05/07	915	13：00	15：00	2	$50
Etc.					

说明 3 - 9：Micah McWhorter 的工作时间记录

Labour Time Record

Employee：Micah McWhorte   **Month**：05/01 – 05/31

Hourly Wage Rate：$15   **Record Number**：45

Date	Job Number	Start Time	End Time	Hours	Cost
05/05	901	8：00	12：00	4	$60
05/07	912	8：00	12：00	4	$60
05/07	912	13：00	17：00	4	$60
05/09	912	8：00	12：00	4	$60
05/09	915	13：00	17：00	4	$60
05/11	915	8：00	12：00	4	$60
05/11	915	13：00	15：00	2	$30
Etc.					

说明 3 - 10：915 号订单产生的直接人工成本转账至订单成本记录

Job Cost Record

Job Number：915

Customer：Unknown

Job Description：Custom Glass Tile

Date Started：May 1st

Date Completed：May 31st

Manufacturing Cost Information			Cost Summary
Direct Materials：			$9,100
Clear white tile：	3,000 units at $3 per unit		
Specialty colour：	8 quarts at $5 per quart		
Mirror glass：	6 quarts at $10 per quart		
Direct Labour：			$650
Sarah Goodson：	20 DL hours at $25 per DL hour		
Micah McWhorter：	10 DL hours at $15 per DL hour		
Manufacturing Overhead			
Total Job Costs			
Number of Units			
Costs per Unit			

那么，Glass Corporation 为两位工人承担的员工福利费用（employee benefit expense），如员工报酬计划（employee compensation plan）、雇主发起的健康与养老金计划（employer-sponsored health and pension plan）、就业保险金的雇主份额等，是否属于直接人工成本？其实不然，许多企业将这些额外薪资费用归为制造费用，而非直接人工成本。

(3) 我们已经确定了 915 号订单的直接材料成本和直接人工成本。与此同时，为完成 915 号订单和其他订单，Glass Corporation 也产生了许多不易直接确定的制造成本，这些制造成本被称为间接制造成本或制造费用，一般包括间接材料成本、间接人工成本以及厂房和设备的保险与折旧费用、维护费用和水电费用等。财务会计报告准则规定，制造商产生的制造费用必须属于产品成本（product cost），而非期间成本（period cost）。由于制造费用的自身性质，我们不能直接确定订单的制造费用，所以不得不将制造费用分摊至订单。由于每张订单使用的资源不同，因此不能平均分摊制造费用。那么，如何将制造费用分摊至订单？这里，介绍大部分制造商使用的传统制造费用分摊法。传统制造费用分

带你到北美学习
管理会计
Take You to
North America
to Learn
Managerial Accounting

摊法一般需要如下四步：①预估未来一年的制造费用总额（total manufacturing overhead）；②选择分摊基础（allocation base），预估未来一年的分摊基础总额；③使用从"第1步"和"第2步"获知的信息，计算预定制造费用分摊率；④将制造费用分摊至订单。请注意：前三步在财务年度开始之前完成。

第1步：预估未来一年的制造费用总额。

根据"案例3-1"信息，Glass Corporation 预估未来一年的制造费用总额为 $280 000。

第2步：选择分摊基础，预估未来一年的分摊基础总额。

根据"案例3-1"信息，分摊基础为直接人工工时（direct labour hour），未来一年的直接人工工时为 20 000 小时。

分摊基础也称为成本动因（cost driver）；顾名思义，成本动因指的是成本（制造费用）产生的主要因素（primary factor）。过去，大部分制造商将直接人工工时或直接人工成本作为制造费用的分摊基础（成本动因）；如今，更多制造商使用机器生产加工产品，而非人工，且机器运转会产生水电费用、维护费用和折旧费用，这些费用属于制造费用，因此机器运转时长（machine hour）也逐渐成为制造费用的分摊基础（成本动因）。

第3步：使用从 "第1步" 和 "第2步" 获知的信息， 计算预定制造费用分摊率。

预定制造费用分摊率（predetermined manufacturing overhead rate）等于预估制造费用总额（estimated total manufacturing overhead）除以预估分摊基础总额（estimated total amount of allocation base）（见说明3-11）。

说明 3 - 11：计算预定制造费用分摊率

$$\text{Predetermined manufacturing overhead rate} = \frac{\text{Estimated total manufacturing overhead}}{\text{Estimated total amount of allocation base}}$$

未来一年的预估制造费用总额为 $280 000，直接人工工时（分摊基础）为 20 000小时，因此预定制造费用分摊率为 $14 per DL hour（$280 000 ÷ 20 000 = $14）。为什么使用预定制造费用分摊率，而非实际制造费用分摊率（actual manufacturing overhead rate）？因为实际制造费用分摊率需要实际数据，而制造商到年底才可获知实际数据，所以为及时获知完工订单的成本信息，以制定产品售价和其他决策，制造商不得不使用预定制造费用分摊率，并牺牲一些成本信息的精确性。

第 4 步：将制造费用分摊至订单。

一张订单的分摊制造费用（manufacutring overhead allocated to a job）等于预定制造费用分摊率（predetermined manufacutring overhead rate）乘以该订单所用分摊基础的实际数额（actual amount of allocation base used by the job）（见说明 3-12）。

> **说明 3-12：计算一张订单的分摊制造费用**
>
> Manufacutring overhead allocated to a job =
> Predetermined manufacutring overhead rate × Actual amount of allocation base used by the job

根据"案例 3-1"信息，为完成 915 号订单，Sarah Goodson 和 Micah McWhorter 分别工作 20 小时和 10 小时，因此 915 号订单的直接人工工时为 30 小时。从"第 3 步"计算出预定制造费用分摊率为 $14 per DL hour。预定制造费用分摊率（$14 per DL hour）乘以 915 号订单所用分摊基础实际数额（30 DL hours）等于 915 号订单的分摊制造费用（$420）。如"说明 3-13"中的绿色部分所示，915 号订单成本记录显示分摊至该订单的制造费用为 $420。

> **说明 3-13：915 号订单的分摊制造费用转账至订单成本记录**

Job Cost Record

Job Number：915

Customer：Unknown

Job Description：Custom Glass Tile

Date Started：May 1st

Date Completed：May 31st

Manufacturing Cost Information			Cost Summary
Direct Materials：			$9,100
Clear white tile：	3,000 units at $3 per unit		
Specialty colour：	8 quarts at $5 per quart		
Mirror glass：	6 quarts at $10 per quart		
Direct Labour：			$650
Sarah Goodson：	20 DL hours at $25 per DL hour		
Micah McWhorter：	10 DL hours at $15 per DL hour		
Manufacturing Overhead：			$420
$14 per DL hour × 30 DL hours = $420			
Total Job Costs			$10,170
Number of Units			÷ 1,000 units
Costs per Unit			$10.17

带你到北美学习
管理会计
Take You to
North America
to Learn
Managerial Accounting

在"3.5 改善成本分摊系统"部分，将学习其他两种制造费用分摊法：①通过部门制造费用分摊率（departmental manufacturing overhead rate）将制造费用分摊至订单；②通过作业活动成本法（activity-based costing）将制造费用分摊至订单。

3.3 处理多分摊或少分摊的制造费用
Dealing with Overallocated or Underallocated Manufacturing Overhead

通过填写领料单和记录工作时间，制造商可以直接确定订单的直接材料成本和直接人工成本；然而，由于制造费用的自身性质，制造商不能直接确定订单的制造费用，而是通过预定制造费用分摊率将制造费用分摊至订单。

我们知道，因为实际制造费用分摊率需要实际数据，而制造商到年底才可获知实际数据，所以为及时获知完工订单的成本信息，以制定产品售价和其他决策，制造商不得不使用预定制造费用分摊率，并牺牲一些成本信息的精确性，这将产生一个新问题：制造商在年底知晓的企业本年度为完成订单所产生的实际制造费用（actual manufacturing overhead）不同于分摊制造费用。这样，会出现两种情况：如果实际制造费用大于分摊制造费用，制造费用少分摊，订单成本估值过低；如果实际制造费用小于分摊制造费用，制造费用多分摊，订单成本估值过高（见图3-1）。

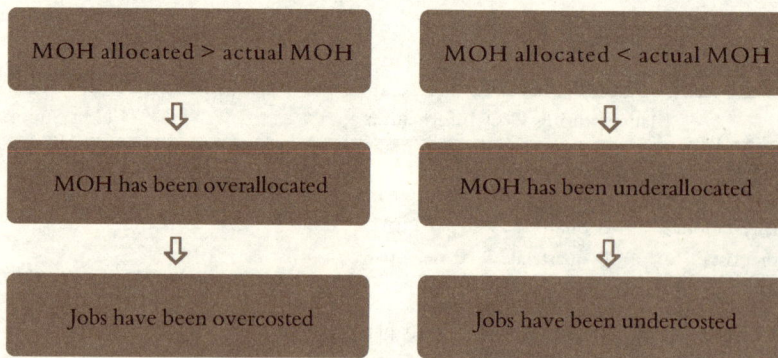

MOH allocated > actual MOH	MOH allocated < actual MOH
⇩	⇩
MOH has been overallocated	MOH has been underallocated
⇩	⇩
Jobs have been overcosted	Jobs have been undercosted

图 3-1　对比分摊制造费用与实际制造费用

案例 3-2

At the beginning of the year, Freeman prepared the following budgeted information:

Machine hours	75,000 hours
Manufacturing overhead (MOH)	$600,000
Direct labour	$1,500,000

At the end of the year, the company had incurred the following actual results:

Machine hours	55,000 hours
Direct labour	$1,210,000
Depreciation on plant and equipment	$480,000
Property taxes on plant	$20,000
Salespersons' salaries	$25,000
Delivery drivers' wages	$15,000
Plant janitors' wages	$10,000

Freeman always allocates manufacturing overhead to individual jobs based on machine hour.

Required:

1. How much manufacturing overhead was allocated to the jobs during the year?

2. How much manufacturing overhead was incurred during the year?

3. Was manufacturing overhead underallocated or overallocated at the end of the year? By how much?

4. Were the jobs overcosted or undercosted? By how much?

讲解: 未来一年的预估制造费用总额为 $600 000, 分摊基础为机器运转时长 (machine hour), 未来一年的机器运转时长为 75 000 小时, 因此预定制造费用分摊率为 $8 per machine hour。为生产和加工订单, 全年实际机器运转时长为 55 000 小时, 因此分摊制造费用为 $440 000 ($8 × 55 000 = $440 000)。

制造费用包括所有间接制造成本, 一般由三部分组成: ①间接材料成本; ②间接人工成本; ③其他间接制造成本。根据制造费用定义和"案例 3-2"信息, Depreciation on plant and equipment, Property taxes on plant, Plant janitors' wages 属于制造费用, 因此实际制造费用总额为 $510 000 ($480 000 + $20 000 + $10 000 = $510 000)。分摊制造费用 ($440 000) 小于实际制造费用 ($510 000), 说明少分摊制造费用 $70 000, 低估订单成本 $70 000; 换言之, 相比于订单成本记录显示的制造费用 ($440 000), Freeman 还应向订单多分摊制造费用 $70 000。

那么, 如何处理少分摊制造费用的问题? 如果少 (多) 分摊制造费用的金额是

带你到北美学习
管理会计
Take You to
North America
to Learn
Managerial Accounting

无关紧要的，且大部分库存商品在给定财务周期已售出，制造商可以通过调整售出商品成本账目（cost of goods sold），解决少（多）分摊制造费用的问题。

制造费用少分摊，订单成本估值过低，将使制造商的售出商品成本过低，制造商应上调售出商品成本，上调金额为少分摊的制造费用。制造费用多分摊，订单成本估值过高，将使制造商的售出商品成本过高，制造商应下调售出商品成本，下调金额为多分摊的制造费用（见图 3-2）。对于"案例 3-2"，制造费用少分摊 $70 000，造成低估订单成本 $70 000，因此需要上调售出商品成本 $70 000。

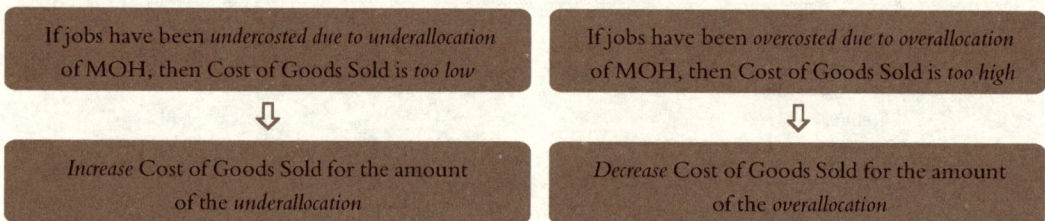

If jobs have been *undercosted due to underallocation* of MOH, then Cost of Goods Sold is *too low*	If jobs have been *overcosted due to overallocation* of MOH, then Cost of Goods Sold is *too high*
⇩	⇩
Increase Cost of Goods Sold for the amount of the *underallocation*	*Decrease* Cost of Goods Sold for the amount of the *overallocation*

图 3-2 调整售出商品成本账目

如果少（多）分摊制造费用的金额巨大，且大部分库存商品在给定财务周期尚未售出，制造商根据给定财务周期生产或加工订单的情况，按在制品库存（work in process inventory）、制成品库存（finished goods inventory）、售出商品成本（cost of goods sold）之间的比例，分配少（多）分摊的制造费用。

在继续使用"少分摊制造费用 $70 000，造成低估订单成本 $70 000"的前提下，我们增加一些新数据，比如："在给定财务周期，30% 的订单为在制品，20% 的订单为制成品，50% 的订单已出售"。那么，分配至在制品库存账目的制造费用为 $21 000（$70 000×30% = $21 000），分配至制成品库存账目的制造费用为 $14 000（$70 000×20% = $14 000），分配至售出商品成本账目的制造费用为 $35 000（$70 000×50% = $35 000）。

3.4 使用日记账分录结算制造费用账目
Using a Journal Entry to Close Manufacturing Overhead

我们知道，如果实际制造费用大于分摊制造费用，制造费用少分摊，制造费用账目产生借方余额（debit balance）；如果实际制造费用小于分摊制造费用，制造费用多分摊，制造费用账目产生贷方余额（credit balance）。制造费用账目是一种临时性账目（temporary account），不在财务报表中出现。在财务周期结束之际，制造商必须结算制造费用账目，那么如何结算制造费用账目？

根据"案例 3 - 2"信息，分摊制造费用（＄440 000）小于实际制造费用
（＄510 000），说明少分摊制造费用 ＄70 000，低估订单成本 ＄70 000；换言之，相
比于订单成本记录出现的制造费用（＄440 000），Freeman 还应向订单多分摊制造
费用 ＄70 000。实际制造费用（＄510 000）记录在制造费用账目的借方，而分摊制
造费用（＄440 000）则记录在制造费用账目的贷方，因此制造费用账目呈现借方余额
＄70 000。制造费用账目借方余额为给定财务周期少分摊的制造费用（见图 3-3）。

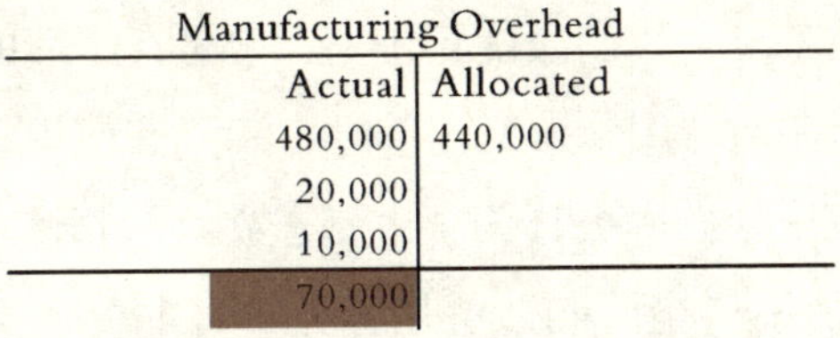

Manufacturing Overhead	
Actual	Allocated
480,000	440,000
20,000	
10,000	
70,000	

图 3 - 3　制造费用账目

我们知道，制造商可以通过调整售出商品成本账目（cost of goods sold），解决
少（多）分摊制造费用的问题。如果制造费用少分摊，订单成本估值过低，将使制
造商的售出商品成本过低，制造商应上调售出商品成本，上调金额为少分摊的制造
费用。为结算少分摊的制造费用账目，售出商品成本账目增长 ＄70 000，制造费用
账目减小 ＄70 000。日记账分录借方和贷方分别记录售出商品成本账目（cost of
goods sold）和制造费用账目（manufacturing overhead）。

Cost of goods sold	70,000	
Manufacturing overhead		70,000
(To close the manufacturing overhead account)		

过账上述日记账分录信息之后，制造费用账目减少 ＄70 000，余额为 ＄0；售出
商品成本账目余额增长 ＄70 000，少分摊的制造费用（＄70 000）得到调整（见图
3-4）。

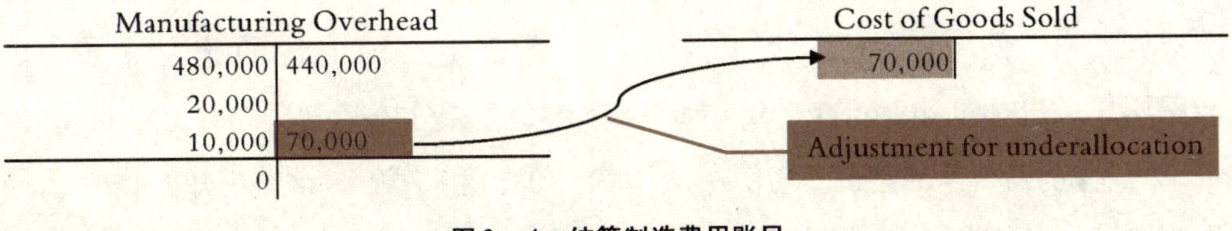

Manufacturing Overhead		Cost of Goods Sold
480,000	440,000	70,000
20,000		
10,000	70,000	Adjustment for underallocation
0		

图 3 - 4　结算制造费用账目

相反，如果制造费用多分摊，订单成本估值过高，将使制造商的售出商品成本
过高，制造商应下调售出商品成本，下调金额为多分摊的制造费用。为结算多分摊

带你到北美学习
管理会计
Take You to
North America
to Learn
Managerial Accounting

的制造费用账目，售出商品成本账目减少，制造费用账目增长，日记账分录借方和贷方分别记录制造费用账目（manufacturing overhead）和售出商品成本账目（cost of goods sold）。

3.5　改善成本分摊系统
Refining the Cost Allocation System

在分析一张订单成本时，我们假设，无论订单是在工厂的一个部门加工，还是在几个部门加工，在将制造费用分摊至订单时，制造商使用统一的预定制造费用分摊率，这种预定制造费用分摊率被称为全厂制造费用分摊率（plantwide manufacturing overhead rate），而使用"全厂制造费用分摊率"的分摊系统则被称为全厂成本分摊系统（plantwide cost allocation system）。使用该系统经常造成一些订单成本估值过高，而另一些订单成本估值过低，从而造成成本扭曲（cost distortion）现象，那么如何降低这种成本扭曲现象出现的可能性？制造商可以将使用的"全厂制造费用分摊率"改为使用"部门制造费用分摊率"或"作业活动成本法"分摊制造费用，进而改善成本分摊系统，降低成本扭曲现象出现的可能性，提高订单成本信息的精确性。

3.5.1　部门成本分摊系统
Departmental Cost Allocation System

若出现以下两种情况：①工厂不同部门承担不同种类、金额的制造费用；②不同订单、产品对于工厂部门的依赖程度不同。制造商更应通过部门制造费用分摊率（departmental manufacturing overhead rate）分摊制造费用，这种使用"部门制造费用分摊率"的分摊系统被称为部门成本分摊系统（departmental cost allocation system）。

我们知道，使用全厂制造费用分摊率，一般需要如下四步：①预估未来一年的制造费用总额（total manufacturing overhead）；②选择分摊基础（allocation base），预估未来一年的分摊基础总额；③使用从"第1步"和"第2步"获知的信息，计算预定制造费用分摊率；④将制造费用分摊至订单。使用部门制造费用分摊率，同样需要上述四步。接下来，通过"案例3-3"，讲解部门制造费用分摊率的使用。

案例 3 – 3

GG Corporation manufactures wooden furniture and uses a job costing system at its Nova Scotia factory. The factory has two departments (Cutting and Assembly) used in the production of tables and chairs. The job costing system has two categories of direct costs (direct materials and direct labour (DL)) and two manufacturing overhead. Manufacturing overhead is allocated using machine hour in the Cutting Department and using direct labour hour in the Assembly Department. The annual budgeted amounts for 2014 are as follows:

	Cutting Department	Assembly Department
Manufacturing overhead	$1,200,000	$1,732,500
Direct labour costs	$1,080,000	$4,800,000
Direct labour hours	30,000 hours	315,000 hours
Machine hours	200,000 hours	33,000 hours

Job 431 was begun in September 2014 but was not completed until October. On September 30, the balance of the work in process account for Job 431 was $8,500. In order to finish Job 431, the following resources were consumed during October:

	Cutting Department	Assembly Department
Direct materials used	$16,800	$3,600
Direct labour costs	$720	$1,500
Direct labour hours	70 hours	350 hours
Machine hours	280 hours	50 hours

Required:

1. What is the predetermined manufacturing overhead rate for Cutting Department?

2. What is the predetermined manufacturing overhead rate for Assembly Department?

3. How much manufacturing overhead was allocated to Job 431?

讲解:

第 1 步:预估每个部门未来一年的制造费用总额。

根据"案例 3-3"信息,GG Corporation 预估,Cutting Department 未来一年的制造费用总额为 $1 200 000,Assembly Department 未来一年的制造费用总额为 $1 732 500。请注意:预估的部门制造费用总额也被视为部门制造费用成本库(cost pool)。

带你到北美学习
管理会计
Take You to
North America
to Learn
Managerial Accounting

第 2 步：为每个部门选择分摊基础，预估每个部门未来一年的分摊基础总额。

Cutting Department 的分摊基础为机器运转时长（machine hour），未来一年的机器运转时长为 200 000 小时；Assembly Department 的分摊基础为直接人工工时（direct labour hour），未来一年的直接人工工时为 315 000 小时。请注意：不同部门拥有不同的分摊基础，分摊基础也称为成本动因（cost driver）。

第 3 步：使用从 "第 1 步" 和 "第 2 步" 获知的信息，计算部门制造费用分摊率。

部门制造费用分摊率（departmental manufacturing overhead rate）等于预估部门制造费用总额（estimated total departmental manufacturing overhead）除以预估部门分摊基础总额（estimated total amount of departmental allocation base）（见说明 3-14）。

说明 3-14：计算部门制造费用分摊率

$$\text{Predetermined manufacturing overhead rate} = \frac{\text{Estimated total departmental manufacturing overhead}}{\text{Estimated total amount of departmental allocation base}}$$

GG Corporation 预估，Cutting Department 未来一年的制造费用总额为 \$1 200 000，分摊基础为机器运转时长（machine hour），未来一年的机器运转时长为 200 000 小时，因此 Cutting Department 的部门制造费用分摊率为 \$6 per machine hour。Assembly Department 未来一年的制造费用总额为 \$1 732 500，分摊基础为直接人工工时（direct labour hour），未来一年的直接人工工时为 315 000 小时，所以 Assembly Department 的部门制造费用分摊率为 \$5. 50 per DL hour。

第 4 步：将部门的制造费用分摊至部门加工的订单。

一张订单的分摊制造费用（manufacturing overhead allocated to a job）等于部门制造费用分摊率（departmental manufacturing overhead rate）乘以该订单所用部门分摊基础的实际数额（actual amount of departmental allocation base used by the job）（见说明 3-15）。

说明 3-15：计算一张订单的分摊制造费用

Manufacturing overhead allocated to a job =
　Departmental manufacturing overhead rate × Actual amount of departmental allocation base used by the job

根据 "案例 3-3" 信息，为完成 431 号订单，Cutting Department 的机器运转时长为 280 小时，Assembly Department 的直接人工工时为 350 小时。从 "第 3 步" 计

算可知，Cutting Department 的部门制造费用分摊率为 $ 6 per machine hour，Assembly Department 的部门制造费用分摊率为 $ 5.50 per DL hour，因此 431 号订单的分摊制造费用为 $ 3 605 （ $ 6 × 280 + $ 5.50 × 350 = $ 3 605）。

3.5.2 作业活动成本法
Activity-Based Costing

如果制造商想要一个更加精确的成本分摊系统，以求降低成本扭曲现象出现的可能性，它们可以使用作业活动成本法（activity-based costing）。作业活动成本法聚焦于产品加工作业活动，而非加工产品的部门或工厂，因此加工作业活动是作业活动成本法的主要成本对象（cost object）。使用作业活动成本法，一般基于以下两种情况：①不同的加工作业活动；②产品或订单对于加工作业活动的依赖程度不同。因此，作业活动成本法造成成本扭曲的可能性最低。

与全厂成本分摊系统、部门成本分摊系统相似，作业活动成本分摊系统也运用相同的分摊步骤，将制造费用分摊至订单。全厂成本分摊系统使用全厂制造费用分摊率，部门成本分摊系统使用部门制造费用分摊率，而作业活动成本法则使用作业活动成本分摊率。接下来，通过"案例 3-4"，讲解作业活动成本法的使用。

案例 3-4

As a family-run small manufacturer, Berg Inc. adopts an activity-based costing system. The following manufacturing activities, indirect manufacturing costs, and usages of cost drivers have been estimated for the year:

Activity	Cost Pool	Estimated Amount of Cost Driver
Machine set-ups	$ 150,000	3,000 set-ups
Machining	1,000,000	5,000 machine hours
Controlling quality	337,500	4,500 tests

During May, Evan and Sajiah Berg manufactured Job 624. Evan worked 10 hours on the job, while Sajiah worked five hours on the job. Evan's wage rate is $ 25 per hour, while Sajiah is paid $ 30 per hour because of her additional experience level. The direct materials requisitioned for Job 624 totaled $ 1,050. The following additional information was col-

带你到北美学习
管理会计
Take You to
North America
to Learn
Managerial Accounting

lected on Job 624: the job required one machine set-up, five machine hours, and two quality-control tests.

Required:

1. Compute the cost allocation rate for each activity.

2. How much manufacturing overhead was allocated to Job 624?

讲解:

第1步: 鉴别主要加工作业活动, 预估每种作业活动未来一年的制造费用总额。

根据"案例3-4"信息, Berg 的主要加工作业活动包括 Machine set-ups, Machining 和 Controlling quality。Berg 预估, Machine set-ups 未来一年的制造费用总额为 $150 000, Machining 未来一年的制造费用总额为 $1 000 000, Controlling quality 未来一年的制造费用总额为 $337 500。请注意: 每种作业活动的制造费用也被视为这种作业活动的成本库 (cost pool)。

第2步: 为每种作业活动选择分摊基础, 预估每种作业活动未来一年的分摊基础总额。

Machine set-ups 的分摊基础为装置数量 (set-up), 未来一年使用 3 000 架装置; Machining 的分摊基础为机器运转时长 (machine hour), 未来一年的机器运转时长为 5 000 小时; Controlling quality 的分摊基础为测试数量 (test), 未来一年进行 4 500 次测试。请注意: 不同作业活动拥有不同的分摊基础。

第3步: 使用从 "第1步" 和 "第2步" 获知的信息, 计算作业活动成本分摊率。

作业活动成本分摊率 (activity cost allocation rate) 等于预估作业活动制造费用总额 (estimated total activity manufacturing overhead) 除以预估作业活动分摊基础总额 (estimated total amount of activity allocation base) (见说明3-16)。

说明 3-16: 计算作业活动成本分摊率

$$\text{Activity cost allocation rate} = \frac{\text{Estimated total activity manufacturing overhead}}{\text{Estimated total amount of activity allocation base}}$$

Berg 预估, Machine set-ups 未来一年的制造费用总额为 $150 000, 分摊基础为装置数量 (set-up), 未来一年使用 3 000 架装置, 因此 Machine set-ups 的作业活动成本分摊率为 $50 per set-up。Machining 未来一年的制造费用总额为 $1 000 000,

分摊基础为机器运转时长（machine hour），未来一年的机器运转时长为 5 000 小时，所以 Machining 的作业活动成本分摊率为 $ 200 per machine hour。Controlling quality 未来一年的制造费用总额为 $ 337 500，分摊基础为测试数量（test），未来一年进行 4 500 次测试，因此 Controlling quality 的作业活动成本分摊率为 $ 75 per test。

第 4 步：将每种作业活动的制造费用分摊至作业活动加工的订单。

一张订单的分摊制造费用（manufacturing overhead allocated to a job）等于作业活动成本分摊率（activity cost allocation rate）乘以该订单所用作业活动分摊基础的实际数额（actual amount of activity allocation base used by the job）（见说明 3-17）。

说明 3 - 17：计算一张订单的分摊制造费用

Manufacturing overhead allocated to a job =
Activity cost allocation rate × Actual amount of activity allocation base used by the job

为完成 624 号订单，Berg 使用 1 架装置，运转机器 5 小时，进行 2 次测试。从"第 3 步"计算可知，Machine set-ups 的作业活动成本分摊率为 $ 50 per set-up，Machining 的作业活动成本分摊率为 $ 200 per machine hour，Controlling quality 的作业活动成本分摊率为 $ 75 per test，因此 624 号订单的分摊制造费用为 $ 1 200（$ 50 × 1 + $ 200 × 5 + $ 75 × 2 = $ 1 200）。

3.5.3 对比三种成本分摊系统
Contrasting the Three Cost Allocation Systems

我们总结一下，三种成本分摊系统的异同点（见说明 3-18）。全厂成本分摊系统（plantwide cost allocation system）、部门成本分摊系统（departmental cost allocation system）、作业活动成本法（activity-based costing）具有相同的分摊步骤，但三种成本分摊系统使用不同的分摊率，因此对于同一张订单，三种成本分摊系统给出了不同的答案。在三种不同成本分摊系统中，哪个分摊系统可以提供最精确的成本信息？

在三种成本分摊系统中，作业活动成本法考虑：①每种产品、订单使用的特定资源或生产作业活动；②每种产品、订单对特定资源或生产作业活动的依赖程度。因此，作业活动成本法被视为最精确的成本分摊系统。

请牢记：成本扭曲是订单的分摊制造费用（间接成本）所致，而非订单的直接材料成本或直接人工成本所致；换言之，订单的直接材料成本或直接人工成本不能引起成本扭曲。

带你到北美学习
管理会计
Take You to
North America
to Learn
Managerial Accounting

说明 3 - 18：对比三种成本分摊系统			
	全厂成本分摊系统	部门成本分摊系统	作业成本法分摊系统
第1步	预估未来一年的制造费用总额	预估每个部门未来一年的制造费用总额	鉴别主要加工作业活动，预估每种作业活动未来一年的制造费用总额
第2步	选择分摊基础，预估未来一年的分摊基础总额	为每个部门选择分摊基础，预估每个部门未来一年的分摊基础总额	为每种作业活动选择分摊基础，预估每种作业活动未来一年的分摊基础总额
第3步	计算全厂制造费用分摊率	计算部门制造费用分摊率	计算作业活动成本分摊率
第4步	一张订单的分摊制造费用＝全厂制造费用分摊率×该订单所用分摊基础的实际数额	一张订单的分摊制造费用＝部门制造费用分摊率×该订单所用部门分摊基础的实际数额	一张订单的分摊制造费用＝作业活动成本分摊率×该订单所用作业活动分摊基础的实际数额

3.5.4 成本层级

Cost Hierarchy

制造商可能面对成百上千、不同的生产作业活动。为运用作业活动成本法，制造商必须归类不同的生产作业活动，以建立作业活动成本库（cost pool），这种分类系统被称为成本层级（cost hierarchy）。成本层级可以帮助制造商了解每种作业活动成本库的性质和成本动因（cost driver）。成本层级将作业活动分为：①单位水准作业活动（unit-level activity）；②批量水准作业活动（batch-level activity）；③产品水准作业活动（product-level activity）；④设备水准作业活动（facility-level activity）（见图3-5）。

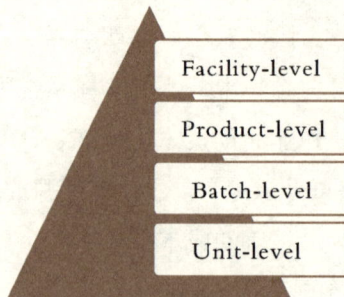

图 3 - 5　成本层级

（1）单位水准作业活动。为生产或加工单件产品而引起的作业活动被称为单位水准作业活动，如检测、包装每件产品。检测和包装每件产品产生的成本属于单位水准作业活动成本库。

（2）批量水准作业活动。无论一批产品的具体数量是 1 件、10 件、100 件，还是 1 000件，为生产或加工一批产品而引起的作业活动被称为批量水准作业活动。为满足生产运营需求，制造商安装机器；一旦机器安装完成，机器可以完成数量为 1 件、10 件或 100 件产品的批量生产。安装机器产生的成本属于批量水准作业活动成本库。

（3）产品水准作业活动。无论生产多少件产品，还是多少批产品，为生产或加工一种产品而引起的作业活动被称为产品水准作业活动，如研发、设计和市场营销新产品。研发、设计和市场营销新产品产生的成本属于产品水准作业活动成本库。

（4）设备水准作业活动。无论生产多少件、多少批，还是多少种产品，工厂内设备的作业活动被称为设备水准作业活动，如设备保养。设备的折旧、保险、财产税和维护费用均属于设备水准作业活动成本库。

3.6 分批成本计算系统中的日记账分录

The Journal Entries Required in a Job Costing System

在确定订单成本之后，如何将这些成本信息输入会计系统？换言之，如何使用日记账分录记录加工订单过程中的成本流转？接下来，通过"案例 3-5"详细学习。

在讲解"案例 3-5"之前，先复习一下日记账分录的借贷记账定则。

（1）资产账目（asset account）增长通过借方（debit）记录，资产账目减小通过贷方（credit）记录。资产账目通常呈现借方余额（debit balance）。

（2）负债账目（liability account）增长通过贷方记录，负债账目减小通过借方记录。负债账目通常呈现贷方余额（credit balance）。

（3）股东权益账目（shareholders' equity account）增长通过贷方记录，股东权益账目减小通过借方记录。股东权益账目通常呈现贷方余额。

（4）收入账目（revenue account）增长通过贷方记录，收入账目减小通过借方记录。收入账目通常呈现贷方余额。

（5）费用账目（expense account）增长通过借方记录，费用账目减小通过贷方记录。

带你到北美学习
管理会计
Take You to
North America
to Learn
Managerial Accounting

　　费用账目通常呈现借方余额。

（6）股息账目（dividend account）增长通过借方记录，股息账目减小通过贷方记录。股息账目通常呈现借方余额。

案例 3 - 5

In May, Micro Speakers had the following transactions：

a．Purchased raw materials on account，$ 14,750.

b．Used raw materials in production：direct materials，$ 7,000，indirect materials，$ 3,000.

c．Incurred manufacturing labour costs，$ 15,000，70% of which was direct labour and the remainder was indirect labour.

d．Recorded manufacturing overhead：depreciation on plant，$ 13,000，prepaid plant insurances expired，$ 1,700，plant property taxes，$ 4,200.

e．Allocated manufacturing overhead to jobs，200% of direct labour costs.

f．Costs of jobs completed during the month，$ 33,000.

g．Sold all jobs completed during the month for $ 52,000 on credit.

Required：

Record the above transactions of May in Micro Speakers' general journal.

a．Purchased raw materials on account，$ 14,750.

讲解：Micro Speakers 赊账购买价值为 $ 14 750 的原材料,因此原材料库存账目和应付账款账目增长 $ 14 750。日记账分录借方和贷方分别记录原材料库存账目（raw materials inventory）和应付账款账目（accounts payable）。

a	Raw materials inventory	14,750	
	Accounts payable		14,750
	(To record the purchase of raw materials on account)		

b．Used raw materials in production：direct materials，$ 7,000，indirect materials，$ 3,000.

讲解：　在生产过程中，Micro Speakers 使用了价值为 $ 7 000 的直接材料。所用直接材料将从原材料库存移入在制品库存，因此在制品库存账目增长 $ 7 000，原材料库存账目减少 $ 7 000。日记账分录借方和贷方分别记录在制品库存账目（work in process inventory）和原材料库存账目（raw materials inventory）。

b	Work in process inventory	7,000	
	Raw materials inventory		7,000
	（To record the use of direct materials on jobs）		

制造费用包含所有间接制造成本（indirect manufacturing cost），一般由三部分组成：①间接材料成本；②间接人工成本；③其他间接制造成本。Micro Speakers 在生产过程中使用价值为 $3 000 的间接材料，因此制造费用账目增长 $3 000，原材料库存账目减少 $3 000。日记账分录借方和贷方分别记录制造费用账目（manufacturing overhead）和原材料库存账目（raw materials inventory）（见图 3-6）。

b	Manufacturing overhead	3,000	
	Raw materials inventory		3,000
	（To record the use of indirect materials on jobs）		

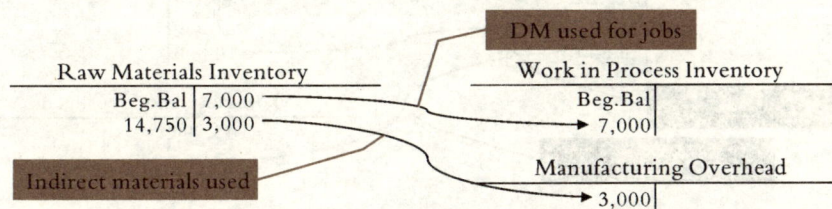

图 3 - 6　记录生产中产生的直接材料成本和间接材料成本

c. Incurred manufacturing labour costs, $15,000, 70% of which was direct labour and the remainder was indirect labour.

讲解： 在生产过程中，Micro Speakers 产生了直接人工成本 $10 500（$15 000 × 70% = $10 500）。在加工订单过程中，制造商不但需要使用直接材料，还需要承担直接人工成本；这些直接人工成本将计入在制品库存账目，因此在制品库存账目增长 $10 500，应付工资账目增长 $10 500。日记账分录借方和贷方分别记录在制品库存账目（work in process inventory）和应付工资账目（wages payable）。

带你到北美学习
管理会计
Take You to
North America
to Learn
Managerial Accounting

c	Work in process inventory	10,500	
	Wages payable		10,500
	(To record the use of direct labour on jobs)		

制造费用包含所有间接制造成本（indirect manufacturing cost），一般由三部分组成：①间接材料成本；②间接人工成本；③其他间接制造成本。Micro Speakers 在生产过程中产生间接人工成本 $4 500（$15 000 × 30% = $4 500），因此制造费用账目增长 $4 500，应付工资账目增长 $4 500。日记账分录借方和贷方分别记录制造费用账目（manufacturing overhead）和应付工资账目（wages payable）（见图3-7）。

c	Manufacturing overhead	4,500	
	Wages payable		4,500
	(To record the use of indirect labour on jobs)		

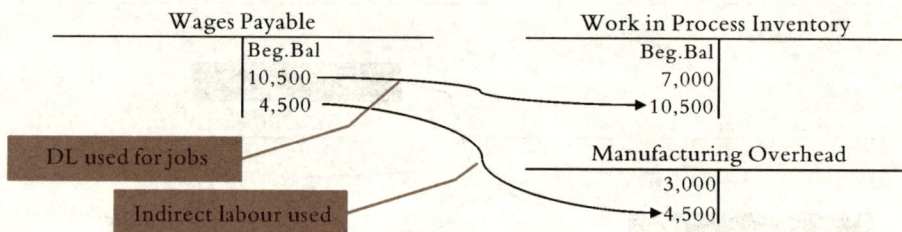

图 3 - 7　记录生产中产生的直接人工成本和间接人工成本

d. Recorded manufacturing overhead: depreciation on plant, $13,000, prepaid plant insurances expired, $1,700, plant property taxes, $4,200.

讲解： 在生产过程中，Micro Speakers 还产生了其他间接制造成本，如 Depreciation on plant，Plant insurances，Plant property taxes。在将制造费用分摊至订单之前，这些其他间接制造成本计入制造费用账目，因此制造费用账目增长 $18 900（$13 000 + $1 700 + $4 200 = $18 900）。日记账分录借方记录制造费用账目（manufacturing overhead），贷方分别记录工厂累计折旧账目（accumulated depreciation – plant）、工厂预付保险账目（prepaid insurances – plant）、工厂应付财产税（property taxes payable – plant）（见图3-8）。

d	Manufacturing overhead	18,900	
	Accumulated depreciation – plant		13,000
	Prepaid insurances – plant		1,700

	Property taxes payable – plant		4,200
	(To record other indirect manufacturing costs incurred)		

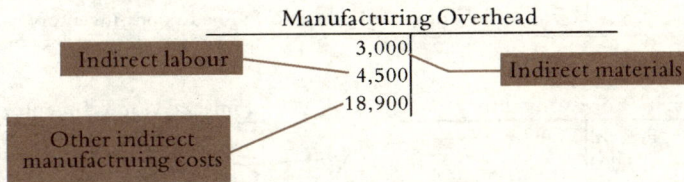

Manufacturing Overhead

Indirect labour   3,000   Indirect materials
4,500
18,900

Other indirect
manufactruing costs

图 3 – 8　记录生产中产生的其他间接制造成本

e. Allocated manufacturing overhead to jobs, 200% of direct labour costs.

讲解： 分摊基础为直接人工成本（direct labour cost）。在生产过程中，Micro Speakers 产生直接人工成本 $10 500，预定制造费用分摊率为 200%，因此分摊至订单的制造费用为 $21 000（$10 500 × 200% = $21 000）。在加工过程中，制造商不但使用直接材料，还需要承担直接人工成本，并将制造费用分摊至订单；这些分摊制造费用计入在制品库存，因此在制品库存账目增长 $21 000，制造费用账目减少 $21 000。日记账分录借方和贷方分别记录在制品库存账目（work in process inventory）和制造费用账目（manufacturing overhead）（见图3-9）。

e	Work in process inventory	21,000	
	Manufacturing overhead		21,000
	(To allocate manufacturing overhead to specific jobs)		

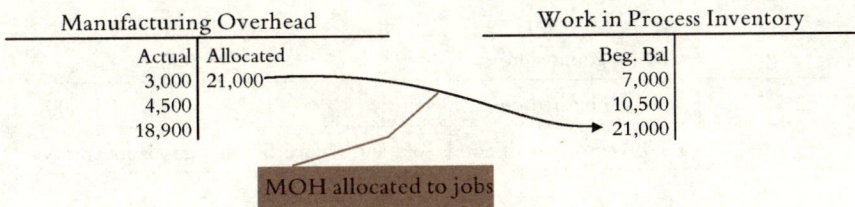

Manufacturing Overhead   Work in Process Inventory

Actual	Allocated		Beg. Bal	
3,000	21,000		7,000	
4,500			10,500	
18,900			21,000	

MOH allocated to jobs

图 3 – 9　记录制造费用分摊至订单

f. Cost of jobs completed during the month, $33,000.

讲解： 本月，Micro Speakers 完成了价值为 $33 000 的订单。一旦完工，订单将从在制品库存移入制成品库存，因此在制品库存账目减少 $33 000，制成品库存账目增长 $33 000。日记账分录借方和贷方分别记录制成品库存账目（finished goods in-

带你到北美学习
管理会计
Take You to
North America
to Learn
Managerial Accounting

ventory）和在制品库存账目（work in process inventory）（见图3-10）。

f	Finished goods inventory	33,000	
	Work in process inventory		33,000
	（To move the completed jobs into finished goods inventory）		

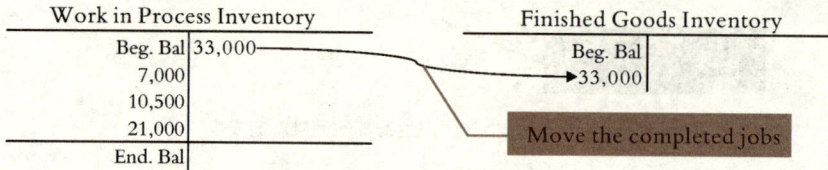

Work in Process Inventory
Beg. Bal 33,000
7,000
10,500
21,000
End. Bal

Finished Goods Inventory
Beg. Bal
33,000

Move the completed jobs

图3－10　记录订单完成

g. Sold all jobs completed during the month for $52,000 on credit.

讲解： Micro Speakers 向客户赊销定制产品，赚取销售额 $52 000，因此应收账款账目增长 $52 000，销售额账目增长 $52 000。日记账分录借方和贷方分别记录应收账款账目（accounts receivable）和销售额账目（sales revenue）。

g	Accounts receivable	52,000	
	Sales revenue		52,000
	（To record the sale of specific jobs on credit）		

在订单出售后，所售订单成本（$33 000）计入售出商品成本账目，因此售出商品成本账目增长 $33 000，制成品库存账目减少 $33 000。日记账分录借方和贷方分别记录售出商品成本账目（cost of goods sold）和制成品库存账目（finished goods inventory）（见图3-11）。

g	Cost of goods sold	33,000	
	Finished goods inventory		33,000
	（To record cost of goods sold and reduce finished goods inventory）		

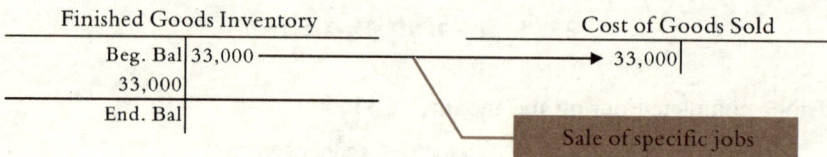

Finished Goods Inventory
Beg. Bal 33,000
33,000
End. Bal

Cost of Goods Sold
33,000

Sale of specific jobs

图3－11　记录订单出售

3.7 使用订单成本记录制定商业决策
Using a Job Cost Record to Make Business Decisions

企业管理者可以使用订单、产品成本信息，在以下六个方面制定商业决策：①降低未来订单、产品成本；②评估、对比每种产品的盈利能力（profitability）；③处理来自于同行业竞争者的价格压力；④对于大批量采购，给予销售折扣；⑤竞购定制订单；⑥编写财务报表。

通过"案例 3-6"，学习如何为订单制定销售价格。制造商一般使用成本加成定价法（cost-plus pricing）制定产品销售价格。成本加成价格（cost-plus price）等于产品成本（cost）加上成本加成（markup on cost）（见图 3-12）。

| Cost-plus price | = | Cost | + | Markup on cost |

图 3-12 成本加成定价法计算公式

案例 3-6

WGCC is a distributor and processor of different blends of coffee. The company buys coffee beans from around the world and roasts, blends, and packages them for resale. Some blends of coffee are very popular and sold in large sales volumes, while some newer blends have very low sales volumes. WGCC prices its coffee at a full product cost (including allocated manufacturing overhead) plus a markup of 30 percent.

Data for the 2011 budget include manufacturing overhead of \$3,000,000, which has been allocated based on direct labour cost. The budgeted direct labour costs for 2011 total \$600,000.

The expected prime costs for one-kilogram bags of two of the company's products are as follows:

	Kona	Malaysian
Direct materials	\$3.20	\$4.20
Direct labour	0.30	0.30

Required:

1. Determine the company's predetermined manufacturing overhead rate using direct labour

带你到北美学习
管理会计
Take You to
North America
to Learn
Managerial Accounting

cost as the cost driver.

2. Determine the full product costs and selling prices of one kilogram of Kona coffee and one kilogram of Malaysian coffee.

讲解： 生产 1 千克 Kona 咖啡，WGCC 产生直接材料成本 $3.20、直接人工成本 $0.30；生产 1 千克 Malaysian 咖啡，WGCC 产生直接材料成本 $4.20、直接人工成本 $0.30。未来一年的制造费用总额为 $3 000 000，分摊基础为直接人工成本（direct labour cost），未来一年的直接人工成本为 $600 000，因此制造费用分摊率为 500%。生产 1 千克 Kona 咖啡，企业承担直接人工成本 $0.30，所以 1 千克 Kona 咖啡的分摊制造费用为 $1.50（500% × $0.30 = $1.50）；生产 1 千克 Malaysian 咖啡，企业承担直接人工成本 $0.30，因此 1 千克 Malaysian 咖啡的分摊制造费用为 $1.50（500% × $0.30 = $1.50）。通过每种咖啡的直接材料成本、直接人工成本和分摊制造费用，计算出 1 千克 Kona 咖啡和 1 千克 Malaysian 咖啡的成本分别为 $5 和 $6。

	Kona	Malaysian
Direct materials	$3.20	$4.20
Direct labor	0.30	0.30
Manufacturing overhead	1.50	1.50
Unit costs	$5.00	$6.00

根据题目信息，1 千克咖啡的成本加上 30% 的成本加成（markup on cost），计算出 1 千克咖啡的售价；换言之，1 千克 Kona 咖啡的成本为 $5，30% 的成本加成为 $1.50（$5×30% = $1.50），因此 1 千克 Kona 咖啡的售价为 $6.50（$5 + $1.50 = $6.50）；1 千克 Malaysian 咖啡的成本为 $6，30% 的成本加成为 $1.80（$6×30% = $1.80），因此 1 千克 Malaysian 咖啡的售价为 $7.80（$6 + $1.80 = $7.80）。

	Kona	Malaysian
Unit costs	$5.00	$6.00
Markup (30%)	1.50	1.80
Selling price	$6.50	$7.80

■ 例题综述
Summary of Examples

例题 3 - 1

An equal amount of manufacturing overhead should be allocated to each job. True or False?

讲解： 不同订单对直接材料、直接人工和制造费用的使用有不同程度的变化，因此每张订单产生不同的生产成本。由于每张订单的生产成本不同，所以制造商不能平均分摊生产成本。

答案： False

例题 3 - 2

Product - level activities and costs are incurred for a particular product, regardless of the number of units or batches of the product produced. True or False?

讲解： 无论生产多少件产品，还是多少批产品，为生产或加工一种产品而引起的作业活动被称为产品水准作业活动，如研发、设计和市场营销新产品。研发、设计和市场营销新产品而产生的成本属于产品水准作业活动成本库。

答案： True

例题 3 - 3

The allocation base selected for each activity should be the cost driver of the activity cost pool. True or False?

讲解： 分摊基础也称为成本动因（cost driver）；顾名思义，成本动因指的是成本（制造费用）产生的主要因素（primary factor）。

答案： True

例题 3 - 4

Companies use a process costing system when their products or services vary in terms of raw materials needed, time required and the complexity of production processes. True or False?

讲解： 通过一系列统一的生产流程，制造商可以大量生产完全相同的产品，如面粉、水泥、石油、食品、饮料、卫生纸、纸张等，这类制造商使用分步成本计算法

带你到北美学习
管理会计
Take You to
North America
to Learn
Managerial Accounting

（process costing）。理论上，这样生产的单件产品是完全相同的，因此单件产品的制造成本也应相同。

答案： False

例题 3 - 5

The use of which of the following costing systems is most likely to minimize cost distortion?

A. Plantwide cost allocation system

B. Departmental cost allocation system

C. Activity-based costing system

D. All of the above

讲解： 如果制造商想要一个更加精确的成本分摊系统，以求降低成本扭曲现象出现的可能性，它们可以使用作业活动成本法（activity-based costing）。作业活动成本法聚焦于产品加工作业活动，而非加工产品的部门或工厂，因此加工作业活动是作业活动成本法的主要成本对象（cost object）。使用作业活动成本法，一般基于以下两种情况：①不同的加工作业活动；②产品或订单对于加工作业活动的依赖程度不同。因此，作业活动成本法造成成本扭曲的可能性最低。

答案： C

例题 3 - 6

Which of the following describes how the activity cost allocation rate is computed in an activity-based costing system?

A. The estimated total activity cost pool is divided by the estimated total amount of activity allocation base.

B. The estimated total amount of activity allocation base is divided by the estimated total activity cost pool.

C. The estimated total amount of activity allocation base is multiplied by the estimated total activity cost pool.

D. You take the estimated total amount of activity allocation base and subtract the estimated total activity cost pool.

讲解： 作业活动成本分摊率（activity cost allocation rate）等于预估作业活动制造费

用总额（estimated total activity manufacturing overhead）除以预估作业活动分摊基础总额（estimated total amount of activity allocation base）。

答案： A

例题 3-7

Assigning manufacturing overhead and other indirect costs is called _____.

A. cost allocation

B. cost driver

C. materials requisition

D. predetermined manufacturing overhead rate

讲解： 成本分摊（cost allocation）是指运用成本分摊系统，将制造费用分摊至订单或产品。

答案： A

例题 3-8

What products are a job costing system appropriate for? Also, what products are a process costing system appropriate for?

讲解： 通过一系列统一的生产流程，制造商可以大量生产完全相同的产品，如面粉、水泥、石油、食品、饮料、卫生纸、纸张等，这类制造商使用分步成本计算法（process costing）。理论上，这样生产的单件产品是完全相同的，因此单件产品的制造成本也应相同。在给定财务周期，分步成本计算法对制造商生产的同一种产品，平均分摊制造成本，因此单件产品承担相同的产品成本。

与通过统一生产流程，制造大量完全相同的产品不同，另一类制造商生产独特、客户定制、小批量商品，如飞机、别墅、高端定制珠宝、高档定制汽车等，这类企业使用分批成本计算法（job costing）。一件独特商品、一小批定制商品被视为一张订单，因此分批成本计算法也被称为订单成本计算法（job-order costing）。不但制造商可以使用分批成本计算法，专业性服务提供商，如律师事务所、会计师事务所、顾问公司、市场公关公司等，也可以使用分批成本计算法，确定所提供定制服务的成本。不同订单对直接材料、直接人工和制造费用的使用程度不同，因此每张订单产生不同的生产成本。

带你到北美学习
管理会计
Take You to
North America
to Learn
Managerial Accounting

答案： Job costing is appropriate for the production of unique products that vary in their needs for raw materials or labour, however, process costing is appropriate for the large volume of same or similar products.

例题 3 - 9

Therrien Pools manufactures swimming pool equipment. Therrien estimates total manufacturing costs to be \$1,200,000 next year. Therrien also estimates it will use 50,000 direct labour (DL) hours and incur \$1,000,000 of direct labour costs next year. In addition, its machines are expected to be run for 40,000 hours next year.

Required：

Compute the predetermined manufacturing overhead rate for next year under the following independent situations.

1. Assume that Therrien uses direct labour hour as its manufacturing overhead allocation base.

2. Assume that Therrien uses direct labour cost as its manufacturing overhead allocation base.

3. Assume that Therrien uses machine hour as its manufacturing overhead allocation base.

1. Assume that Therrien uses direct labour hour as its manufacturing overhead allocation base.

讲解： 未来一年的制造费用总额为 \$1 200 000，分摊基础为直接人工工时，未来一年的直接人工工时为 50 000 小时，因此预定制造费用分摊率为 \$24 per DL hour。

答案： Using direct labour hour as the manufacturing overhead allocation base, the predetermined manufacturing overhead rate for next year is \$24 per DL hour.

2. Assume that Therrien uses direct labour cost as its manufacturing overhead allocation base.

讲解： 未来一年的制造费用总额为 \$1 200 000，分摊基础为直接人工工时，未来一年的直接人工成本为 \$1 000 000，因此预定制造费用分摊率为120%。

答案： If the manufacturing overhead allocation base is direct labour cost, the predetermined manufacturing overhead rate for next year is 120%.

3. Assume that Therrien uses machine hour as its manufacturing overhead allocation base.

讲解： 未来一年的制造费用总额为 $1 200 000，分摊基础为机器运转时长，未来一年的机器运转时长为 40 000 小时，因此预定制造费用分摊率为 $30 per machine hour。

答案： Using machine hour as the manufacturing overhead allocation base, the predetermined manufacturing overhead rate for next year is $30 per machine hour.

例题 3 - 10

At the beginning of January, the following account balances were selected from the general ledger of Model Industries:

Work in process inventory	$0
Direct materials inventory	29,500
Finished goods inventory	51,200

Additional data:

a. Actual manufacturing overhead for January was $78,200.

b. Actual direct labour (DL) costs for January were $72,000, actual direct labour hours for January were 3,600 hours.

c. The predetermined manufacturing overhead rate is based on direct labour hour. The budget for the year called for $325,000 of direct labour costs and $410,400 of manufacturing overhead. Estimated direct labour hours for the year were expected to be 15,200 hours.

d. The only job unfinished on January 31 was Job 619, for which direct labour costs were $18,000 (900 direct labour hours) and direct materials were $15,700.

e. Direct materials used in production during January totaled $125,000.

f. Direct materials inventory balance on January 31 was $32,000.

g. Finished goods inventory balance on January 31 was $42,300.

Required：

1. Determine the predetermined manufacturing overhead rate.

带你到北美学习
管理会计
Take You to
North America
to Learn
Managerial Accounting

2. Determine the amount of direct materials purchased during January.

3. Determine the work in process inventory balance on January 31.

4. Determine the cost of goods manufactured for January.

5. Determine the cost of goods sold for January.

6. Determine whether manufacturing overhead is overallocated or underallocated and by what amount at January 31.

1. Determine the predetermined manufacturing overhead rate.

讲解： 未来一年的制造费用总额为 $410 400，分摊基础为直接人工工时，未来一年的直接人工工时为 15 200 小时，因此预定制造费用分摊率为 $27 per DL hour。

答案： The predetermined manufacturing overhead rate is $27 per DL hour.

2. Determine the amount of direct materials purchased during January.

讲解： 直接材料账目期初余额为 $29 500，直接材料账目期末余额为 $32 000，所用直接材料成本为 $125 000，因此购入价值为 $127 500 的直接材料（$32 000 + $125 000 − $29 500 = $127 500）。

答案： The amount of direct materials purchased during January is $127,500.

3. Determine the work in process inventory balance on January 31.

讲解： 1 月 31 日，Logan Industries 仅剩 619 号订单尚未完工，因此在制品账目余额仅有这张订单的成本。619 号订单的直接材料成本为 $15 700，直接人工成本为 $18 000，分摊制造费用为 $24 300（$27 × 900 = $24 300），因此总成本为 $58 000（$15 700 + $18 000 + $24 300 = $58 000）。1 月 31 日的在制品账目余额为 $58 000。

答案： The work in process inventory balance on January 31 is $58,000.

4. Determine the cost of goods manufactured for January.

讲解： 为完成订单，Logan Industries 在 1 月份使用直接材料 $125 000，支付直接人工 $72 000，分摊制造费用 $97 200（$27 × 3 600 = $97 200），因此在制品库存账目增长 $294 200（$125 000 + $72 000 + $97 200 = $294 200）。1 月份，在制品

库存账目月初余额为 $0，在制品库存账目增长 $294 200，在制品库存账目月末余额为 $58 000，因此从在制品库存账目转至制成品库存账目的产品成本为 $236 200（$0 + $294 200 − $58 000 = $236 200），制成商品成本为 $236 200。

	Work in Process Inventory	
DM used for jobs	Beg. Bal	0
DL used for jobs		125,000	X → Cost of goods manufactured
		72,000
MOH allocated to jobs		97,200
	End. Bal	58,000

答案： The cost of goods manufactured for January is $236,200.

5. Determine the cost of goods sold for January.

讲解： 在产品制成后，产品将从在制品库存移入制成品库存。在给定财务周期，从在制品库存账目移入制成品库存账目的产品成本被视为制成商品成本。Logan Industries 的制成商品成本为 $236 200，因此制成品库存账目增长 $236 200。1 月份，制成品库存账目月初余额为 $51 200，制成品库存账目增长 $236 200，制成品库存账目月末余额为 $42 300，因此售出商品成本为 $245 100（$51 200 + $236 200 − $42 300 = $245 100）。

	Finished Goods Inventory	
Cost of goods manufactured	Beg. Bal	51,200
		236,200	X → Cost of goods sold
	End. Bal	42,300

答案： The cost of goods sold for January is $245,100.

6. Determine whether manufacturing overhead is overallocated or underallocated and by what amount at January 31.

讲解： 如果实际制造费用大于分摊制造费用，制造费用少分摊，订单成本估值过低；如果实际制造费用小于分摊制造费用，制造费用多分摊，订单成本估值过高。订单的实际制造费用为 $78 200，分摊制造费用为 $97 200（$27 × 3 600 = $97 200），实际制造费用（$78 200）小于分摊制造费用（$97 200），因此多分摊制造费用 $19 000。

答案： The manufacturing overhead is overallocated by 19,000.

带你到北美学习
管理会计
Take You to
North America
to Learn
Managerial Accounting

例题 3 - 11

Deerfoot Corporation produces (manufactures) and sells hockey equipment. The corporation allocates manufacturing overhead to each job based on machine hours used and has provided the following selected items from its budget for the upcoming year, 2014:

Direct labour (DL) hours	5,000 hours
Machine hours	8,000 hours
Direct labour (5,000 hours × $21 per DL hour)	$105,000
Plant utilities	$12,000
Depreciation on salespersons' cars	$22,000
Indirect materials	$80,000
Direct materials	$80,000
Depreciation on delivery trucks	$14,000
Depreciation on factory equipment	$20,000
Indirect labour	$40,000

Required:

1. Determine Deerfoot Corporation's predetermined manufacturing overhead rate.

2. Job 3 required $1,200 in direct materials, 55 direct labour hours and 25 machine hours. Compute the costs of Job 3.

3. Given your answer to Part 2. above, show the appropriate journal entry to record the completion of Job 3.

4. In order to determine the selling price for the goods that Deerfoot Corporation manufactures, the corporation applies a markup of 70%. What price will Deerfoot charge for Job 3? Show the journal entries related to the sale of Job 3 on account.

1. Determine Deerfoot Corporation's predetermined manufacturing overhead rate.

讲解： 未来一年的制造费用总额为 $152 000 ($12 000 + $80 000 + $20 000 + $40 000 = $152 000)，分摊基础为机器运转时长，未来一年的机器运转时长为 8 000小时，因此预定制造费用分摊率为 $19 per machine hour。

答案： Deerfoot Corporation's predetermined manufacturing overhead rate is $19 per machine hour.

2. Job 3 required ＄1,200 in direct materials, 55 direct labour hours and 25 machine hours. Compute the costs of Job 3.

讲解： 为完成 3 号订单，产生直接材料成本 ＄1 200、直接人工成本 ＄1 155（＄21 × 55 = ＄1 155），运转机器 25 小时，预定制造费用分摊率为 ＄19 per machine hour，因此 3 号订单的分摊制造费用为 ＄475（19 × 25 = ＄475）、成本为 ＄2 830。

Direct materials	＄1,200
Direct labour	1,155
Manufacturing overhead	475
Total costs	＄2,830

答案： The costs of Job 3 are ＄2,830.

3. Given your answer to Part 2. above, show the appropriate journal entry to record the completion of Job 3.

讲解： 在 3 号订单完成后，订单将从在制品库存移入制成品库存，因此在制品库存账目减少 ＄2 830，制成品库存账目增长 ＄2 830。日记账分录借方和贷方分别记录制成品库存账目（finished goods inventory）和在制品库存账目（work in process inventory）。

答案：

| Finished goods inventory | 2,830 | |
| Work in process inventory | | 2,830 |

4. In order to determine the selling price for the goods that Deerfoot Corporation manufactures, the corporation applies a markup of 70%. What price will Deerfoot charge for Job 3? Show the journal entries related to the sale of Job 3 on account.

讲解一： 根据题目信息，订单售价等于订单成本加上 70% 的成本加成（markup on cost）；换言之，订单成本为 ＄2 830，70% 的成本加成为 ＄1 981（＄2 830 × 70% = ＄1 981），因此订单售价为 ＄4 811（＄2 830 + ＄1 981 = ＄4 811）。

Deerfoot Corporation 向客户赊销定制产品，赚取销售额 ＄4 811，因此应收账款账目增长 ＄4 811，销售额账目增长 ＄4 811。日记账分录借方和贷方分别记录应收账款账目（accounts receivable）和销售额账目（sales revenue）。

带你到北美学习
管理会计
Take You to
North America
to Learn
Managerial Accounting

答案一：

Accounts receivable	4,811	
Sales revenue		4,811

讲解二： 在订单出售后，所售订单成本计入售出商品成本账目，因此售出商品成本账目增长 $2 830，制成品库存账目减少 $2 830。日记账分录借方和贷方分别记录售出商品成本账目（cost of goods sold）和制成品库存账目（finished goods inventory）。

答案二：

Cost of goods sold	2,830	
Finished goods inventory		2,830

例题 3 - 12

September production generated the following activities in Digital's work in process inventory：

Production was completed in September, but is not recorded yet. September production consisted of Job B-78 and G-65 with total costs of $41,000 and $37,000 respectively.

Required：

1. Compute the work in process inventory balance at September 30.

2. Prepare the journal entry for the production completed in September.

3. Prepare the journal entry to record the sale (on credit) of Job G-65 for $45,000.

4. What is the gross profit of Job G-65? What other costs must this gross profit cover?

1. Compute the work in process inventory balance at September 30.

讲解： 为完成订单，Digital 在 9 月份产生直接材料成本 $29 000，承担直接人工成本 $32 000，分摊制造费用 $12 000，因此在制品库存账目增长 $73 000（$29 000 + $32 000 + $12 000 = $73 000）。9 月份，Digital 完成 B-78 和 G-65 订单，这 2 张订

单成本分别为 $ 41 000 和 $ 37 000，因此在制品库存账目减少 $ 78 000（$ 41 000 + $ 37 000 = $ 78 000）。9 月份，在制品库存账目月初余额为 $ 16 000，在制品库存账目增长 $ 73 000，在制品库存账目减少 $ 78 000，因此在制品库存账目月末余额为 $ 11 000（$ 16 000 + $ 73 000 − $ 78 000 = $ 11 000）。

答案： The work in process inventory balance at September 30 is $ 11,000.

2. Prepare the journal entry for the production completed in September.

讲解： 9 月份，Digital 完成 B-78 和 G-65 订单，这 2 张订单将从在制品库存移入制成品库存，因此在制品库存账目减少 $ 78 000（$ 41 000 + $ 37 000 = $ 78 000），制成品库存账目增长 $ 78 000。日记账分录借方和贷方分别记录制成品库存账目（finished goods inventory）和在制品库存账目（work in process inventory）。

答案：

Finished goods inventory	78,000	
Work in process inventory		78,000

3. Prepare the journal entry to record the sale（on credit）of Job G-65 for $ 45,000.

讲解一： Digital 向客户赊销定制产品（Job G-65），赚取销售额 $ 45 000，因此应收账款账目增长 $ 45 000，销售额账目增长 $ 45 000。日记账分录借方和贷方分别记录应收账款账目（accounts receivable）和销售额账目（sales revenue）。

答案一：

Accounts receivable	45,000	
Sales revenue		45,000

讲解二： 在订单出售后，所售订单成本计入售出商品成本账目，因此售出商品成本账目增长 $ 37 000，制成品库存账目减少 $ 37 000。日记账分录借方和贷方分别记录售出商品成本账目（cost of goods sold）和制成品库存账目（finished goods inventory）。

带你到北美学习
管理会计
Take You to
North America
to Learn
Managerial Accounting

答案二：

Cost of goods sold	37,000	
Finished goods inventory		37,000

4. What is the gross profit of Job G-65? What other costs must this gross profit cover?

讲解： 订单销售额（$45 000）减去订单成本（$37 000）等于订单利润（$8 000）。

答案： The gross profit of Job G-65 is $8,000. The gross profit must cover operating expenses, including all non-manufacturing costs: research and development, design, marketing, distribution, and customer service, and other costs such as interest expense and income taxes.

例题 3 - 13

Rhapsody Corporation manufactures several different products and uses an activity-based costing system. The information from the activity-based costing system for the year for all products is as follows:

Activity	Cost Pool	Allocation Base	Estimated Usage of Allocation Base
Assembly	$120,000	Machine hours	12,000 hours
Processing	80,750	Orders	4,750 orders
Inspecting	22,888	Inspection hours	1,760 hours

The annual production and sales of sizzlers, one of the corporation's products, are 1,000 units. The data related to the production and sales of sizzlers in the most recent year are as follows:

Annual machine hours	750 hours
Annual number of orders	180 orders
Annual inspection hours	350 hours
Direct materials per unit	$125
Direct labour per unit	$67

Required:

1. Calculate the activity cost pool rate for each of the three activities listed.

2. Calculate the average costs of one sizzler.

1. Calculate the activity cost pool rate for each of the three activities listed.

讲解： Rhapsody Corporation 的主要加工作业活动包括 Assembly，Processing 和 Inspecting。

Assembly 未来一年的制造费用总额为 $120 000，分摊基础为机器运转时长，未来一年的机器运转时长为 12 000 小时，作业活动成本分摊率为 $10 per machine hour。

Processing 未来一年的制造费用总额为 $80 750，分摊基础为订单数量，未来一年处理 4 750 张订单，作业活动成本分摊率为 $17 per order。

Inspecting 未来一年的制造费用总额为 $22 888，分摊基础为检测时长，未来一年的检测时长为 1 760 小时，作业活动成本分摊率为 $13 per inspection hour。

答案：

Activity	Cost Pool	Estimated Usage of Allocation Base	Cost Allocation Rate
Assembly	$120,000	12,000 machine hours	$10 per machine hour
Processing	80,750	4,750 orders	$17 per order
Inspecting	22,888	1,760 inspection hours	$13 per inspection hour

2. Calculate the average costs of one sizzler.

讲解： 为生产 1 000 件 sizzler，企业运转机器 750 小时，产生 180 张订单，检测时长为 350 小时。Assembly 的作业活动成本分摊率为 $10 per machine hour，Processing 的作业活动成本分摊率为 $17 per order，Inspecting 的作业活动成本分摊率为 $13 per inspection hour，因此 1 000 件 sizzler 的分摊制造费用为 $15 110（$10 × 750 + $17 × 180 + $13 × 350 = $15 110），1 件 sizzler 的分摊制造费用为 $15.11。单件 sizzler 的直接材料成本为 $125，直接人工成本为 $67，分摊制造费用为 $15.11，因此 1 件sizzler的总成本为 $207.11。

Direct materials	$125.00
Direct labour	67.00
Manufacturing overhead	15.11
Total costs	$207.11

答案： The average costs of one sizzler are $207.11.

带你到北美学习
管理会计
Take You to
North America
to Learn
Managerial Accounting

例题 3 - 14

Tires Corporation uses an activity-based costing system to account for its wheel manufacturing processes. The corporation managers have identified four manufacturing activities that incur manufacturing overhead. The budgeted activity costs for the upcoming year and their allocation bases are as follows:

Activity	Cost Pool	Allocation Base	Estimated Amount of Cost Driver
Materials handling	$6,000	Number of parts	3,000 parts
Machine set-ups	8,500	Number of set-ups	34 set-ups
Inserting parts	36,000	Number of parts	3,000 parts
Finishing	98,000	Direct labour (DL) hours	2,800 DL hours

Required:

1. Compute the cost allocation rate for each activity.

2. Assume Job 504 used 250 parts, required 2 set-ups, and consumed 168 direct labour hours. Compute the manufacturing overhead that should be allocated to the job.

1. Compute the cost allocation rate for each activity.

讲解: Tires Corporation 的主要加工作业活动包括 Materials handling, Machine set-ups, Inserting parts 和 Finishing。

Materials handling 未来一年的制造费用总额为 $6 000,分摊基础为零部件数量,未来一年使用 3 000 件零部件,因此作业活动成本分摊率为 $2 per part。

Machine set-ups 未来一年的制造费用总额为 $8 500,分摊基础为装置数量,未来一年使用 34 架装置,所以作业活动成本分摊率为 $250 per set-up。

Inserting parts 未来一年的制造费用总额为 $36 000,分摊基础为零部件数量,未来一年使用 3 000 件零部件,因此作业活动成本分摊率为 $12 per part。

Finishing 未来一年的制造费用总额为 $98 000,分摊基础为直接人工工时,未来一年的直接人工工时为 2 800 小时,因此作业活动成本分摊率为 $35 per DL hour。

答案:

Activity	Cost Pool	Allocation Base	Cost Allocation Rate
Materials handling	$6,000	3,000 parts	$2 per part

Machine set‑ups	8,500	34 set‑ups	$250 per set‑up
Inserting parts	36,000	3,000 parts	$12 per part
Finishing	98,000	2,800 DL hours	$35 per DL hour

2. Assume Job 504 used 250 parts, required 2 set‑ups, and consumed 168 direct hours. Compute the manufacturing overhead that should be allocated to the job.

讲解: 为完成 504 号订单，Tires Corporation 使用 250 件零部件、2 架装置，付出直接人工 168 小时。Materials handling 的作业活动成本分摊率为 $2 per part，Machine set‑ups 的作业活动成本分摊率为 $250 per set‑up，Inserting parts 的作业活动成本分摊率为 $12 per part，Finishing 的作业活动成本分摊率为 $35 per DL hour，因此 504 号订单的分摊制造费用为 $9 880（$2×250 + $250×2 + $12×250 + $35×168 = $9 880）。

答案: The manufacturing overhead that should be allocated to Job 504 is $9,880.

例题 3 - 15

Winkle and Zale is a small law firm operating in Atlantic Canada. The firm uses a job-order costing system to accumulate the costs chargeable to each client (job). The firm is organized into two departments: Research & Documents Department and Litigation Department.

Job costs are made up of three items: materials and supplies used, direct lawyer costs incurred, and an allocated amount of manufacturing overhead. In the Research & Documents Department, manufacturing overhead is allocated based on research hour. In the Litigation Department, manufacturing overhead is allocated based on direct lawyer cost.

At the beginning of the year, the firm's accountant came up with the following estimates for the year:

	Research & Documents Department	Litigation Department
Research hours	20,000 hours	
Direct lawyer hours	9,000 hours	16,000 hours
Materials and supplies	$18,000	$5,000
Direct lawyer costs	$430,000	$800,000
Manufacturing overhead	$700,000	$320,000

带你到北美学习
管理会计
Take You to
North America
to Learn
Managerial Accounting

The following actual costs and time were recorded on Job 2014-56：

	Research & Documents Department	Litigation Department
Research hours	18 hours	
Direct lawyer hours	9 hours	42 hours
Materials and supplies	$ 50	$ 30
Direct lawyer costs	$ 410	$ 2,100

Required：

1. Calculate the predetermined manufacturing overhead rate used by Research & Documents Department during the year.

2. Calculate the predetermined manufacturing overhead rate used by Litigation Department during the year.

3. Using the rates you calculated in Part 1. and Part 2. above, compute the total manufacturing overhead applied to Job 2014-56.

1. Calculate the predetermined manufacturing overhead rate used by Research & Documents Department during the year.

讲解： Research & Documents Department 未来一年的制造费用总额为 $ 700 000，分摊基础为研究时长，未来一年的研究时长为 20 000 小时，因此预定制造费用分摊率为 $ 35 per research hour。

答案： The predetermined manufacturing overhead rate used by Research & Documents Department during the year is $ 35 per research hour.

2. Calculate the predetermined manufacturing overhead rate used by Litigation Department during the year.

讲解： Litigation Department 未来一年的制造费用总额为 $ 320 000，分摊基础为直接律师费，未来一年的直接律师费为 $ 800 000，因此预定制造费用分摊率为 40% 。

答案： The predetermined manufacturing overhead rate used by Litigation Department during the year is 40% .

3. Using the rates you calculated in Part 1. and Part 2. above, compute the total manu-

facturing overhead applied to Job 2014-56.

讲解： 为完成 2014-56 号订单，Research & Documents Department 研究了 18 小时，支付直接律师费 $2 100 。Research & Documents Department 的制造费用分摊率为 $35 per research hour，Litigation Department 的制造费用分摊率为 40% ，因此 2014-56 号订单的分摊制造费用为 $1 470 （ $35 × 18 + $2 100 × 40% = $1 470）。

答案： The total manufacturing overhead applied to Job 2014-56 is $1,470.

例题 3 - 16

Suit Up produces uniforms. The company allocates manufacturing overhead based on machine hour. Suit Up reports the following cost data for the past year:

	Budgeted	Actual
Direct labour hours	7,000 hours	6,200 hours
Machine hours	6,920 hours	6,400 hours
Depreciation on salespersons' autos	$22,000	$22,000
Indirect materials	$50,000	$52,000
Depreciation on delivery trucks	$14,000	$12,000
Depreciation on plant and equipment	$65,000	$67,000
Indirect labour	$40,000	$43,000
Customer service hotline	$19,000	$21,000
Plant utilities	$18,000	$20,000
Direct labour	$70,000	$85,000

Required：

1. Calculate the predetermined manufacturing overhead rate.

2. Calculate the allocated manufacturing overhead for the past year.

3. Calculate the underallocated or overallocated manufacturing overhead. How will this underallocated or overallocated manufacturing overhead be disposed of?

4. How can managers use accounting information to help control manufacturing overhead?

1. Calculate the predetermined manufacturing overhead rate.

讲解： 未来一年的制造费用总额为 $173 000 （ $50 000 + $40 000 + $65 000 + $18 000 = $173 000），分摊基础为机器运转时长，未来一年的机器运转时长为

带你到北美学习
管理会计
Take You to
North America
to Learn
Managerial Accounting

6 920 小时，因此预定制造费用分摊率为 $25 per machine hour。

答案： The predetermined manufacturing overhead rate is $25 per machine hour.

2. Calculate the allocated manufacturing overhead for the past year.

讲解： 过去一年，机器实际运转时长为 6 400 小时，预定制造费用分摊率为 $25 per machine hour，因此分摊制造费用为 $160 000。

答案： The allocated manufacturing overhead for the past year is $160,000.

3. Calculate the underallocated or overallocated manufacturing overhead. How will this underallocated or overallocated manufacturing overhead be disposed of?

讲解： 如果实际制造费用大于分摊制造费用，制造费用少分摊，订单成本估值过低，因此制造商的售出商品成本过低，制造商应上调售出商品成本，上调金额为少分摊的制造费用。如果实际制造费用小于分摊制造费用，制造费用多分摊，订单成本估值过高，所以制造商的售出商品成本过高，制造商应下调售出商品成本，下调金额为多分摊的制造费用。

实际制造费用为 $182 000（ $52 000 + $67 000 + $43 000 + $20 000 = $182 000），分摊制造费用为 $160 000。分摊制造费用（ $160 000）小于实际制造费用（ $182 000），说明少分摊制造费用 $22 000，低估订单成本 $22 000，因此制造商的售出商品成本过低，Suit Up 应上调售出商品成本 $22 000。为结算少分摊的制造费用账目，售出商品成本账目增长 $22 000，制造费用账目减小 $22 000。日记账分录借方和贷方分别记录售出商品成本账目（cost of goods sold）和制造费用账目（manufacturing overhead）。

答案： The Suit Up's manufacturing overhead is underallocated by $22,000, therefore Suit Up will increase the cost of goods sold by $22,000 to dispose of the underallocated manufacturing overhead.

Cost of goods sold	22,000	
Manufacturing overhead		22,000

4. How can managers use accounting information to help control manufacturing overhead?

答案: Managers compare the actual manufacturing overhead with the budgeted data. Managers investigate the large differences between actual and budgeted amounts to identify the reasons why actual costs differ from budgeted costs.

例题 3 - 17

Happy Cleaning is a small family-owned business, serving customers within a 40-kilometre radius. The company has always charged a flat fee of $0.25 per square metre of carpet cleaned. The company is questioning whether or not it is making money by charging that rate, especially when some jobs are very far away in distance, requiring considerable travel time. The owner's son has just completed a course in managerial accounting and he began investigating whether an activity-based costing system might be better. The following activity cost pools and measures were developed:

Activity	Cost Pool	Allocation Base	Estimated Amount of Allocation Base
Cleaning carpets	$137,000	Square metres cleaned	1,000,000 square metres
Travelling to/from jobs	45,000	Kilometres driven	50,000 kilometres
Jobs supporting	58,500	Number of jobs	1,800 jobs
Total	$240,500		

Required:

1. Calculate the cost allocation rate for each activity.

2. The company recently completed a 600-square meter carpet cleaning job, which was a 52-kilometer round-trip journey from the company's office. Compute the costs of the job.

3. Assuming the company charged the standard $0.25 per squar meter of carpet cleaned, prepare a condensed income statement to show whether or not the company made a profit or loss.

1. Calculate the cost allocation rate for each activity.

讲解: Happy Valley Carpet Cleaning 的主要加工作业活动包括 Cleaning carpets, Travelling 和 Jobs supporting。

Cleaning carpets 未来一年的制造费用总额为 $137 000, 分摊基础为平方米, 未

带你到北美学习
管理会计
Take You to
North America
to Learn
Managerial Accounting

来一年清洗 1 000 000 平方米，因此作业活动成本分摊率为 $ 0. 137 per square meter。

Travelling 未来一年的制造费用总额为 $ 45 000，分摊基础为千米（kilometer），未来一年的行程为 50 000 千米，所以作业活动成本分摊率为 $ 0. 90 per kilometer。

Jobs supporting 未来一年的制造费用总额为 $ 58 500，分摊基础为订单数量，未来一年完成 1 800 张订单，因此作业活动成本分摊率为 $ 32. 50 per job。

答案： The activity cost allocation rate for cleaning carpets is $ 0. 137 per square meter. The activity cost allocation rate for travelling is $ 0. 90 per kilometer. The activity cost allocation rate for jobs supporting is $ 32. 50 per job.

2. The company recently completed a 600 - square meter carpet cleaning job, which was a 52 - kilometer round - trip journey from the company's office. Compute the costs of the job.

讲解： 为完成一张清洁订单，Happy Valley Carpet Cleaning 往返 52 千米，清洁地毯 600 平方米。Cleaning carpets 的作业活动成本分摊率为 $ 0. 137 per square meter，Travelling 的作业活动成本分摊率为 $ 0. 90 per kilometer，Jobs supporting 的作业活动成本分摊率为 $ 32. 50 per job，因此这张订单的分摊成本为 $ 161. 50（ $ 0. 137 × 600 + $ 0. 90 × 52 + $ 32. 50 × 1 = $ 161. 50）。

答案： Using the activity - based costing, the costs of the job are $ 161. 50.

3. Assuming the company charged the standard $ 0. 25 per squar meter of carpet cleaned, prepare a condensed income statement to show whether or not the company made a profit or loss.

讲解： Happy Valley Carpet Cleaning 清洁地毯 600 平方米，赚取销售额 $ 150（ $ 0. 25 × 600 = $ 150）。Cleaning carpets 产生费用 $ 82. 20（ $ 0. 137 × 600 = $ 82. 20），Travelling 产生费用 $ 46. 80（ $ 0. 90 × 52 = $ 46. 80），Jobs supporting 产生费用 $ 32. 50（ $ 32. 50 × 1 = $ 32. 50），因此费用总额为 $ 161. 50（ $ 82. 20 + $ 46. 80 + $ 32. 50 = $ 161. 50）。销售额为 $ 150，费用总额为 $ 161. 50，造成损失 $ 11. 50（ $ 150 − $ 161. 50 = − $ 11. 50）。

答案：

Sales revenue		$ 150. 00
Expenses		
Cleaning carpets	$ 82. 20	
Travelling	46. 80	
Jobs supporting	32. 50	
Total expenses		(161. 50)
Net loss		($ 11. 50)

例题 3 - 18

The following information pertains to Glass Corporation for the year just ended is provided below：

Budgeted direct labour (DL) (79,500 DL hours × $ 16. 90 per DL hour)	$ 1,343,550
Actual direct labour (84,500 DL hours × $ 18. 40 per DL hour)	1,554,800
Budgeted manufacturing overhead	1,128,900
Budgeted selling and administrative expenses	480,000
Actual manufacturing overhead：	
Depreciation	276,000
Property taxes	25,500
Indirect labour	86,500
Supervisors' salaries	245,000
Utilities	63,500
Insurances	34,500
Rental of space	345,000
Indirect materials used	83,500

Required：

1. Calculate the firm's predetermined manufacturing overhead rate based on direct labour hour.

2. Calculate the overapplied or underapplied manufacturing overhead for the year.

3. Explain how to record the overapplied or underapplied manufacturing overhead.

带你到北美学习
管理会计
Take You to
North America
to Learn
Managerial Accounting

1. Calculate the firm's predetermined manufacturing overhead rate based on direct labour hour.

讲解： 未来一年的制造费用总额为 $ 1 128 900，分摊基础为直接人工工时，未来一年的直接人工工时为 79 500 小时，因此预定制造费用分摊率为 $ 14.20 per DL hour。

答案： Based on direct labour hour, the firm's predetermined manufacturing overhead rate is $ 14.20 per DL hour.

2. Calculate the overapplied or underapplied manufacturing overhead for the year.

讲解： 制造费用一般由三部分组成：①间接材料成本；②间接人工成本；③其他间接制造成本。根据制造费用定义，计算出实际制造费用总额为 $ 1 159 500。直接人工的实际工时为 84 500 小时，预定制造费用分摊率为 $ 14.20 per DL hour，因此分摊制造费用为 $ 1 199 900 ($ 14.20 × 84 500 = $ 1 199 900)。

Indirect materials used	$ 83,500
Depreciation	276,000
Property taxes	25,500
Indirect labour	86,500
Supervisors' salaries	245,000
Utilities	63,500
Insurances	34,500
Rental of space	345,000
Total actual manufacturing overhead	$ 1,159,500

分摊制造费用 ($ 1 199 900) 大于实际制造费用 ($ 1 159 500)，说明多分摊制造费用 $ 40 400，高估订单成本 $ 40 400，因此制造商的售出商品成本过高，Glass Corporation 应下调售出商品成本 $ 40 400。

答案： The manufacturing overhead of Glass Corporation is overallocated by $ 40,400.

3. Explain how to record the overapplied or underapplied manufacturing overhead.

讲解： 实际制造费用为 $ 1 159 500，分摊制造费用为 $ 1 199 900。分摊制造费用 ($ 1 199 900) 大于实际制造费用 ($ 1 159 500)，说明多分摊制造费用 $ 40 400，高估订单成本 $ 40 400，因此制造商的售出商品成本过高，Glass Corporation 应下调售出商品成本 $ 40 400。售出商品成本账目降低 $ 40 400，制造费用账目增长

$40 400，日记账分录借方和贷方分别记录制造费用账目（manufacturing overhead）和售出商品成本账目（cost of goods sold）。

答案：Glass Corporation will decrease the cost of goods sold by $40,400 to dispose of the overallocated manufacturing overhead.

Manufacturing overhead	40,400	
Cost of goods sold		40,400

例题 3 - 19

GG Corporation manufactures two wooden chairs: Model A and Model B. Model B is a higher quality and requires two direct labour hours per unit to manufacture compared to one-half hour for Model A.

Indirect costs are currently allocated to products based on direct labour hour. GG Corporation estimates that total manufacturing overhead will be $375,000 this year to produce 20,000 Model A chairs and 8,000 Model B chairs.

Unit costs for direct materials and direct labour are as follows:

	Model A	Model B
Direct labour	$8	$32
Direct materials	12	18

Indirect costs are as follows:

Activity	Cost Pool	Expected Activity		
		Model A	Model B	Total
Machine set-ups	$150,000	600 set-ups	1,000 set-ups	1,600 set-ups
Materials handling	28,000	380 events	320 events	700 events
Machining	165,000	6,500 machine hours	4,500 machine hours	11,000 machine hours
Maintenance requests	32,000	1,000 requests	600 requests	1,600 requests
Total	$375,000			

Required:

1. Determine the unit costs of Model A and Model B using the traditional costing system with direct labour hour as the allocation base.

2. Determine the unit costs of the two products using an activity-based costing system.

带你到北美学习
管理会计
Take You to
North America
to Learn
Managerial Accounting

1. Determine the unit costs of Model A and Model B using the traditional costing system with direct labour hour as the allocation base.

讲解： 预估间接成本总额为 $375 000，分摊基础为直接人工工时，未来一年的直接人工工时为 26 000 小时（2 × 8 000 + 0.50 × 20 000 = 26 000），因此预定间接成本分摊率为 $14.42 per DL hour。制造 1 件 Model B 需要 2 小时，而制造 1 件 Model A 需要 0.50 小时，因此 1 件 Model B 的分摊间接成本为 $28.84（$14.42 × 2 = $28.84），1 件 Model A 的分摊间接成本为 $7.21（$14.42 × 0.50 = $7.21）。

生产 1 件 Model A，产生直接材料成本 $12，付出直接人工成本 $8，分摊间接成本 $7.21，因此 1 件 Model A 的成本为 $27.21。生产 1 件 Model B，产生直接材料成本 $18，付出直接人工成本 $32，分摊间接成本 $28.84，因此 1 件 Model B 的成本为 $78.84。

答案：

	Model A	Model B
Direct materials	$12.00	$18.00
Direct labour	8.00	32.00
Indirect costs	7.21	28.84
Total costs	$27.21	$78.84

2. Determine the unit costs of the two products using an activity-based costing system.

讲解： GG Corporation 的主要加工作业活动包括 Machine set-ups，Materials handling，Machining 和 Maintenance requests。根据题目信息和作业活动成本分摊率公式，计算出如下作业活动成本分摊率。

Activity	Cost Pool	Allocation Base	Cost Allocation Rate
Machine set-ups	$150,000	1,600 set-ups	$93.75 per set-up
Materials handling	28,000	700 events	$40 per event
Machining	165,000	11,000 machine hours	$15 per machine hour
Maintenance requests	32,000	1,600 requests	$20 per request

根据每种作业活动成本分摊率和作业活动的分摊基础实际数额，计算出 1 件 Model A 和 1 件 Model B 的分摊间接成本。

Model A			
Activity	Cost Allocation Rate	Used Allocation Base	Allocated Indirect Cost
Machine set-ups	$93.75 per set-up	600 set-ups	$56,250
Materials handling	$40 per event	380 events	15,200
Machining	$15 per machine hour	6,500 machine hours	97,500
Maintenance requests	$20 per request	1,000 requests	20,000
		Total costs	$188,950
		Number of units	÷ 20,000 units
		Unit costs	$9.45

Model B			
Activity	Cost Allocation Rate	Used Allocation Base	Allocated Indirect Cost
Machine set-ups	$93.75 per set-up	1,000 set-ups	$93,750
Materials handling	40 per event	320 events	12,800
Machining	15 per machine hour	4,500 machine hours	67,500
Maintenance requests	20 per request	600 requests	12,000
		Total costs	$186,050
		Number of units	÷ 8,000 units
		Unit costs	$23.26

生产 1 件 Model A, 产生直接材料成本 $12, 付出直接人工成本 $8, 分摊间接成本 $9.45, 因此 1 件 Model A 的成本为 $29.45。生产 1 件 Model B, 产生直接材料成本 $18, 付出直接人工成本 $32, 分摊间接成本 23.26, 因此 1 件 Model B 的成本为 $73.26。

答案:

	Model A	Model B
Direct materials	$12.00	$18.00
Direct labour	8.00	32.00
Indirect costs	9.45	23.26
Total costs	$29.45	$73.26

例题 3 - 20

Chester Corporation manufactures two products: table and chair. The annual production

带你到北美学习
管理会计
Take You to
North America
to Learn
Managerial Accounting

and sales of tables are 2,000 units, while 8,000 chairs are produced and sold. The company has traditionally used direct labour (DL) hour to allocate its manufacturing overhead (MOH) to products. Tables require one direct labour hour per unit, while chairs require one-half direct labour hour per unit. The estimated total manufacturing overhead for the period is $235,000. The company is looking at the possibility of changing from a plant-wide manufacturing overhead rate to an activity-based costing system. If the company uses an activity-based costing system, it will have the following three activity cost pools:

Activity	Cost Pool	Expected Activity		
		Table	Chair	Total
Machine set-ups	$12,000	200 batches	400 batches	600 batches
Machining	136,000	900 machine hours	800 machine hours	1,700 machine hours
Finishing	87,000	2,000 DL hours	4,000 DL hours	6,000 DL hours
Total	$235,000			

Required:

1. Calculate the manufacturing overhead per unit for one chair and for one table (separately) using the traditional cost allocation system.

2. Determine the activity cost allocation rate for each of the three activities listed.

3. Job 14 is an order to manufacture 20 tables and 80 chairs for a restaurant. The 20 tables require only one batch set-up, 10 machine hours, and given direct labour hours. Also, the 80 chairs will require only one batch set-up, 20 machine hours, and given direct labour hours. Calculate the total manufacturing overhead for Job 14 using the activity-based costing system.

1. Calculate the manufacturing overhead per unit for one chair and for one table (separately) using the traditional cost allocation system.

讲解： 未来一年的制造费用总额为 $235 000，分摊基础为直接人工工时，未来一年的直接人工工时为 6 000 小时 （2 000 × 1 + 8 000 × 0.50 = 6 000），因此预定制造费用分摊率为 $39.17 per DL hour。

生产 1 张桌子，直接人工需要工作 1 小时，因此 1 张桌子的分摊制造费用为 $39.17；而生产 1 把椅子，直接人工需要工作 0.50 小时，所以 1 把椅子的分摊制

造费用约为 $ 19.59 （ $ 39.17 \times 0.50 = $ 19.585 \approx $ 19.59）。

答案： Using the traditional cost allocation system, the manufacturing overhead is $ 19.59 for one chair and $ 39.17 for one table.

2. Determine the activity cost allocation rate for each of the three activities listed.

讲解： Chester Corporation 的主要加工作业活动为 Machine set-ups，Machining 和 Finishing。根据题目信息和作业活动成本分摊率公式，计算出作业活动成本分摊率。

答案：

Activity	Cost Pool	Allocation Base	Cost Allocation Rate
Machine set-ups	$ 12,000	600 batches	$ 20 per batch
Machining	136,000	1,700 machine hours	$ 80 per machine hour
Finishing	87,000	6,000 DL hours	$ 14.50 per DL hour

3. Job 14 is an order to manufacture 20 tables and 80 chairs for a restaurant. The 20 tables require only one batch set-up, 10 machine hours, and given direct labour hours. Also, the 80 chairs will require only one batch set-up, 20 machine hours, and given direct labour hours. Calculate the total manufacturing overhead for Job 14 using the activity-based costing system.

讲解： 根据每种作业活动的成本分摊率和分摊基础实际数额，计算出 14 号订单的分摊制造费用。20 张桌子的分摊制造费用为 $ 1 110，80 把椅子的分摊制造费用为 $ 2 200，因此 14 号订单的分摊制造费用为 $ 3 310。

20 Tables			
Activity	Cost Allocation Rate	Used Allocation Base	Allocated MOH
Machine set-ups	$ 20 per batch	1 batch	$ 20
Machining	$ 80 per machine hour	10 machine hours	800
Finishing	$ 14.50 per DL hour	20 DL hours[①]	290
① 20 tables ×1 DL hour per table = 20 DL hours		Total MOH	$1,110

80 Chairs			
Activity	Cost Allocation Rate	Used Allocation Base	Allocated MOH
Machine set-ups	$ 20 per batch	1 batch	$ 20

带你到北美学习
管理会计
Take You to
North America
to Learn
Managerial Accounting

Machining	$ 80 per machine hour	20 machine hours	1,600
Finishing	$ 14. 50 per DL hour	40 DL hours[②]	580
② 80 chairs ×0. 50 DL hour per chair = 40 DL hours		Total MOH	$ 2,200

答案： Using the activity-based costing system, the total manufacturing overhead for Job 14 is $ 3,310.

例题 3 - 21

Farm Products Ltd. manufactures organic-based and poultry-based food products. The estimated plantwide manufacturing overhead for the year is $ 265,200. Direct labour costs are expected to be $ 162,500 and machine hours are expected to be 2,400 hours for the year. In order to allocate manufacturing overhead to jobs, the business uses a predetermined manufacturing overhead rate based on machine hour. At year-end, the business had incurred the following costs:

Direct labour	$ 210,000
Plant property taxes	$ 32,000
Production supervisors' salaries	$ 60,000
Delivery drivers' wages	$ 19,000
Depreciation on plant equipment	$ 174,500
Salespersons' salaries	$ 28,500
Plant janitorial supplies	$ 3,500
Machine hours	2,200 hours

Required:

1. Calculate the amount of manufacturing overhead allocated to jobs at Farm Products Ltd. during the year.

2. Was manufacturing overhead underallocated or overallocated to the year's jobs? By how much?

3. Assuming the difference is considered immaterial, show the journal entry to correct the underallocated or overallocated manufacturing overhead.

1. **Calculate the amount of manufacturing overhead allocated to jobs at Farm Products**

Ltd. during the year.

讲解： 未来一年的制造费用总额为 \$265 200，分摊基础为机器运转时长，未来一年的机器运转时长为 2 400 小时，因此预定制造费用分摊率为 \$110. 50 per machine hour。机器的实际运转时长为 2 200 小时，所以分摊制造费用为 \$243 100（\$110. 50 × 2 200 = \$243 100）。

答案： The amount of manufacturing overhead allocated to jobs at Farm Products Ltd. during the year is \$243,100.

2. Was manufacturing overhead underallocated or overallocated to the year's jobs? By how much?

讲解： 制造费用一般由三部分组成：①间接材料成本；②间接人工成本；③其他间接制造成本。根据制造费用定义，计算出实际制造费用总额为 \$270 000。

Plant property taxes	\$32,000
Production supervisors' salaries	60,000
Depreciation on plant equipment	174,500
Plant janitorial supplies	3,500
Total actual manufacturing overhead	\$270,000

实际制造费用为 \$270 000，分摊制造费用为 \$243 100，分摊制造费用（\$243 100）小于实际制造费用（\$270 000），因此少分摊制造费用 \$26 900。

答案： The manufacturing overhead underallocated to the year's jobs is \$26,900.

3. Assuming the difference is considered immaterial, show the journal entry to correct the underallocated or overallocated manufacturing overhead.

讲解： 分摊制造费用（\$243 100）小于实际制造费用（\$270 000），说明少分摊制造费用 \$26 900，低估订单成本 \$26 900，因此制造商的售出商品成本过低，Farm Products Ltd. 应上调售出商品成本 \$26 900。售出商品成本账目增长 \$26 900，制造费用账目减小 \$26 900，日记账分录借方和贷方分别记录售出商品成本账目（cost of goods sold）和制造费用账目（manufacturing overhead）。

带你到北美学习
管理会计
Take You to
North America
to Learn
Managerial Accounting

答案:

Cost of goods sold	26,900
Manufacturing overhead	26,900

例题 3 – 22

Owens Inc. manufactures only two products, Medium TV and Large TV. To generate adequate profit and cover its expenses throughout the value chain, Owens prices its TVs at 300% of manufacturing costs. The company is concerned because the Large model is facing a severe pricing competition, whereas the Medium model is a low-price leader in the market. The CEO questions whether the cost information created by the accounting system is correct and wants to reanalyze the past year's product costs using an activity-based costing system.

The information about the past year's products is as follows:

Medium TV	
Direct materials	$660,000
Direct labour	$216,000
Production volume	3,000 units
Large TV	
Direct materials	$1,240,000
Direct labour	$384,000
Production volume	4,000 units

Currently, the company applies manufacturing overhead (MOH) on the basis of direct labour (DL) hour. The company incurred $800,000 of manufacturing overhead this year and 25,000 direct labour hours (9,000 direct labour hours making Medium TVs and 16,000 direct labour hours making Large TVs). The activity-based costing system identified three primary production activities that generate manufacturing overhead:

Materials handling activity ($150,000) driven by orders handled
Machine processing activity ($560,000) driven by machine hours
Packaging activity ($90,000) driven by packaging hours

The company's only two products required the following activity levels during the year:

	Orders Handled	Machine Hours	Packaging Hours
Medium TV	300 orders	20,000 hours	4,000 hours
Large TV	200 orders	20,000 hours	6,000 hours

Required:

1. Use the company's current costing system to find the total costs of producing all Medium TVs and the total costs of producing all Large TVs. Compute the average costs of making each unit of each model. Round your answers to the nearest cent.

2. Use the activity-based costing system to find the total costs of producing all Medium TVs and the total costs of producing all Large TVs. Compute the average costs of making each unit of each model. Round your answers to the nearest cent.

3. How much the cost distortion was occurring between Owens' two products? Calculate the cost distortion in total and on a per-unit basis. Could the cost distortion explain the CEO's confusion about the pricing competition? Explain.

1. Use the company's current costing system to find the total costs of producing all Medium TVs and the total costs of producing all Large TVs. Compute the average costs of making each unit of each model. Round your answers to the nearest cent.

讲解: 未来一年的制造费用总额为 $800 000,分摊基础为直接人工工时,未来一年的直接人工工时为 25 000 小时,因此预定制造费用分摊率为 $32 per DL hour。

为生产 3 000 台 Medium TV,产生直接材料成本 $660 000,承担直接人工成本 $216 000,付出 9 000 小时的直接人工工时,分摊制造费用 $288 000($32 × 9 000 = $288 000),因此 3 000 台 Medium TV 的成本为 $1 164 000,每台 Medium TV 的成本为 $388。

为生产 4 000 台 Large TV,产生直接材料成本 $1 240 000,承担直接人工成本 $384 000,付出 16 000 小时的直接人工工时,分摊制造费用 $512 000($32 × 16 000 = $512 000),因此 4 000 台 Large TV 的成本为 $2 136 000,每台 Large TV 的成本为 $534。

Medium TV	
Direct materials	$ 660,000
Direct labour	216,000

带你到北美学习
管理会计
Take You to
North America
to Learn
Managerial Accounting

Manufacturing overhead	288,000
Total costs	$1,164,000
Production volume	÷ 3,000 units
Unit costs	$388

Large TV	
Direct materials	$1,240,000
Direct labour	384,000
Manufacturing overhead	512,000
Total costs	$2,136,000
Production volume	÷ 4,000 units
Unit costs	$534

答案： The average costs of making each unit of Medium TV are ＄388, the average costs of making each unit of Large TV are ＄534.

2. Use the activity-based costing system to find the total costs of producing all Medium TVs and the total costs of producing all Large TVs. Compute the average costs of making each unit of each model. Round your answers to the nearest cent.

讲解： Owens Inc. 的主要加工作业活动包括 Materials handling，Machine processing 和 Packaging。根据题目信息和作业活动成本分摊率公式，计算出如下作业活动成本分摊率。

Activity	Cost Pool	Estimated Amount of Allocation Base	Cost Allocation Rate
Materials handling	$150,000	500 orders	$300 per order
Machine processing	560,000	40,000 machine hours	$14 per machine hour
Packaging	90,000	10,000 packaging hours	$9 per packaging hour

　　根据每种作业活动的成本分摊率和分摊基础实际数额，计算出 Medium TV 和 Large TV 的分摊制造费用。

Medium TV			
Activity	Cost Allocation Rate	Used Allocation Base	Allocated MOH
Materials handling	$300 per order	300 orders	$90,000

Machine processing	$ 14 per machine hour	20,000 machine hours	280,000
Packaging	$ 9 per packaging hour	4,000 packaging hours	36,000
		Total MOH	$ 406,000

Large TV			
Activity	Cost Allocation Rate	Used Allocation Base	Allocated MOH
Materials handling	$ 300 per order	200 orders	$ 60,000
Machine processing	$ 14 per machine hour	20,000 machine hours	280,000
Packaging	$ 9 per packaging hour	6,000 packaging hours	54,000
		Total MOH	$ 394,000

为生产 3 000 台 Medium TV，产生直接材料成本 $ 660 000，承担直接人工成本 $ 216 000，分摊制造费用 $ 406 000，因此 3 000 台 Medium TV 的成本为 $ 1 282 000，每台 Medium TV 的成本为 $ 427. 33。

为生产 4 000 台 Large TV，产生直接材料成本 $ 1 240 000，承担直接人工成本 $ 384 000，分摊制造费用 394 000，因此 4 000 台 Large TV 的成本为 $ 2 018 000，每台 Large TV 的成本为 $ 504. 50。

Medium TV	
Direct materials	$ 660,000
Direct labour	216,000
Manufacturing overhead	406,000
Total costs	$ 1,282,000
Production volume	÷ 3,000 units
Unit costs	$ 427. 33

Large TV	
Direct materials	$ 1,240,000
Direct labours	384,000
Manufacturing overhead	394,000
Total costs	$ 2,018,000
Production volume	÷ 4,000 units
Unit costs	$ 504. 50

答案： The average costs of making each unit of Medium TV are $ 427. 33, the average costs of making each unit of Large TV are $ 504. 50.

带你到北美学习
管理会计
Take You to
North America
to Learn
Managerial Accounting

3. How much the costs distortion was occurring between Owens' two products? Calculate the cost distortion in total and on a per-unit basis. Could the cost distortion explain the CEO's confusion about the pricing competition? Explain.

答案： The Medium TVs had been undercosted and the Large TVs had been overcosted. Since Owens Inc. sets its sales price at 300% of manufacturing costs, the resulting sales price should have been about $117.99 higher for the Medium TVs ($39.33 × 300%) and about $88.50 lower for the Large TVs ($29.50 × 300%). This helps to explain why Owens Inc. is the low-cost leader for Medium TVs but faces competitive pressures on Large TVs.

	Medium TV	Large TV
Costs per unit using the current system	$388	$534
Costs per unit using the activity-based costing system	427.33	504.50
Overcosting / (Undercosting)	($39.33)	$29.50
Number of units	× 3,000	× 4,000
Total cost distortion	($117,990①)	$118,000①

① The $10 difference between the total amount overcosted and undercosted is due to the fact that unit answers were rounded to the nearest cent.

例题 3 - 23

Bakerston Company is a manufacturing firm that uses a job-order costing system. The company's inventory balances were as follows at the beginning and end of the year:

	Beginning Balance	Ending Balance
Raw materials inventory	$14,000	$22,000
Work in process inventory	27,000	9,000
Finished goods inventory	62,000	77,000

The company applies manufacturing overhead (MOH) to jobs using the predetermined manufacturing overhead rate based on machine hour. At the beginning of the year, the company estimated that it would work 33,000 machine hours and incur $231,000 in manufacturing overhead. The following transactions were recorded for the year:

a. Raw materials were purchased, $315,000.

b. $307,000 in raw materials were used in production: $281,000 direct materials

(DM), $26,000 indirect materials.

c. The following employee costs were incurred:

- · Direct labour (DM), $377,000;
- · Indirect labour, $96,000;
- · Sales administrative, $172,000.

d. Advertising, $147,000.

e. Factory utilities, $10,000.

f. Amortization for the year was $127,000 of which $120,000 was related to factory operations and $7,000 was related to selling and administrative activities.

g. Manufacturing overhead was applied to jobs.

- · The actual level of activity for the year was 34,000 machine hours.

h. Sales for the year totaled $1,253,000.

Required:

1. Calculate the cost of goods manufactured.

2. Was the manufacturing overhead underapplied or overapplied? By how much?

3. Prepare an income statement in good form for the year.

1. Calculate the cost of goods manufactured.

讲解: 未来一年的制造费用总额为 $231 000,分摊基础为机器运转时长,未来一年的机器运转时长为 33 000 小时,因此预定制造费用分摊率为 $7 per machine hour。机器的实际运转时长为 34 000 小时,所以分摊制造费用为 $238 000。

为加工订单,Bakerston Company 产生直接材料成本 $281 000,付出直接人工成本 $377 000,分摊制造费用 $238 000,因此在制品库存账目增长 $896 000。在制品库存账目月初余额为 $27 000,在制品库存账目增长 $896 000,在制品库存账目月末余额为 $9 000,因此从在制品库存账目移入制成品库存账目的产品成本为 $914 000($27 000 + $896 000 – $9 000 = $914 000),制成商品成本为 $914 000。

DM used for jobs		Work in Process Inventory		
	Beg. Bal	27,000		
DL used for jobs		281,000	X	Cost of goods manufactured
		377,000		
		238,000		
MOH allocated to jobs	End. Bal	9,000		

带你到北美学习
管理会计
Take You to
North America
to Learn
Managerial Accounting

答案： The cost of goods manufactured is $914,000.

2. Was the manufacturing overhead underapplied or overapplied? By how much?

讲解： 实际制造费用为 $252 000（$26 000 + $96 000 + $10 000 + $120 000 = $252 000），分摊制造费用为 $238 000。分摊制造费用（$238 000）小于实际制造费用（$252 000），因此少分摊制造费用 $14 000。

答案： The manufacturing overhead was underapplied by $14,000.

3. Prepare an income statement in good form for the year.

讲解： 分摊制造费用（$238 000）小于实际制造费用（$252 000），少分摊制造费用 $14 000，低估订单成本 $14 000，因此制造商的售出商品成本过低，Bakerston Company 应上调售出商品成本 $14 000。

答案：

Bakerston Company Income Statement		
Sales revenue		$1,253,000
Cost of goods sold:		
Beginning finished goods inventory	$62,000	
Cost of goods manufactured	914,000	
Adjusting for underallocated MOH	14,000	
Cost of goods available for sale	990,000	
Ending finished goods inventory	(77,000)	(913,000)
Gross profit		340,000
Operating expenses		
Advertising expense	147,000	
Amortization expense	7,000	
Sales administrative expense	172,000	(326,000)
Operating income		$14,000

专业名词汇编
Glossary of Accounting Terms

产品水准作业活动	product-level activity	成本层级	cost hierarchy
成本动因	cost driver	成本分摊系统	cost allocation system
成本加成	markup on cost	成本加成定价法	cost-plus pricing
成本加成价格	cost-plus price	成本库	cost pool
成本扭曲	cost distortion	贷方	credit
贷方余额	credit balance	单位成本	unit cost
单位水准作业活动	unit-level activity	订单成本计算法	job-order costing
订单成本记录	job cost record	费用账目	expense account
分步成本计算法	process costing	分批成本计算法	job costing
分摊基础	allocation base	负债账目	liability account
股东权益账目	shareholders' equity account	股息账目	dividend account
机器运转时长	machine hour	计时工资率	hourly wage rate
间接材料	indirect materials	间接人工	indirect labour
间接制造成本	indirect manufacturing cost	借方	debit
借方余额	debit balance	累计折旧	accumulated depreciation
临时性账目	temporary account	领料单	materials requisition form
批量水准作业活动	batch-level activity	设备水准作业活动	facility-level activity
生产计划	production schedule	实体产品	physical product
收入账目	revenue account	售出商品成本	cost of goods sold
售价	selling price	销售额	sales revenue
盈利能力	profitability	应付财产税	property tax payable
应付工资	wage payable	应付账款	account payable
应收账款	account receivable	预付保险	prepaid insurance
员工报酬计划	employee compensation plan	原材料记录	raw materials record
原材料库存	raw materials inventory	在制品库存	work in process inventory
直接材料	direct materials	直接人工工时	direct labour hour
直接人工	direct labour	直接人工成本	direct labour cost
制成品库存	finished goods inventory	制成商品成本	cost of goods manufactured
制造成本	manufacturing cost	制造费用	manufacturing overhead
制造费用总额	total manufacturing overhead	主要因素	primary factor

带你到北美学习
管理会计
Take You to
North America
to Learn
Managerial Accounting

资产账目	asset account	总成本	total cost
部门成本分摊系统	departmental cost allocation system		
部门制造费用分摊率	departmental manufacturing overhead rate		
少分摊的制造费用	underallocated manufacturing overhead		
多分摊的制造费用	overallocated manufacturing overhead		
雇主发起的健康与养老金计划	employer-sponsored health and pension plan		
全厂成本分摊系统	plantwide cost allocation system		
全厂制造费用分摊率	plantwide manufacturing overhead rate		
实际制造费用	actual manufacturing overhead		
实际制造费用分摊率	actual manufacturing overhead rate		
预定制造费用分摊率	predetermined manufacturing overhead rate		
预估分摊基础总额	estimated total amount of allocation base		
预估部门分摊基础总额	estimated total amount of departmental allocation base		
预估部门制造费用总额	estimated total departmental manufacturing overhead		
预估作业活动分摊基础总额	estimated total amount of activity allocation base		
预估作业活动制造费用总额	estimated total activity manufacturing overhead		
预估制造费用总额	estimated total manufacturing overhead		
员工福利费用	employee benefit expense		
作业活动成本法	activity-based costing		
作业活动成本分摊率	activity cost allocation rate		

分步成本计算法

Process Costing

带你到北美学习
管理会计
Take You to
North America
to Learn
Managerial Accounting

4.1 对比分步成本计算法与分批成本计算法
Contrasting Process Costing and Job Costing

第 3 章简单介绍了分步成本计算法与分批成本计算法。生产独特、客户定制、小批量商品的企业使用分批成本计算法（job costing）。一件独特商品、一小批定制商品被视为一张订单，因此分批成本计算法也被称为订单成本计算法（job - order costing）。不但制造商可以使用分批成本计算法，专业性服务提供商，如律师事务所、会计师事务所、顾问公司、市场公关公司等，也可以使用分批成本计算法，以此确定所提供定制服务的成本。不同订单对直接材料、直接人工和制造费用的使用程度不同，因此每张订单产生的生产成本不同。由于每张订单的生产成本不同，所以制造商不能平均分摊生产成本。

通过一系列统一的生产流程，生产大量完全相同产品的企业使用分步成本计算法（process costing）。理论上，这样生产的单件产品是完全相同的，因此单件产品的制造成本也应相同。在给定财务周期，分步成本计算法对制造商生产的同一种产品平均分摊制造成本，因此单件产品承担相同的产品成本。通过图 4 - 1 和图 4 - 2，对比两种成本计算法之间实体产品与成本流转的不同。

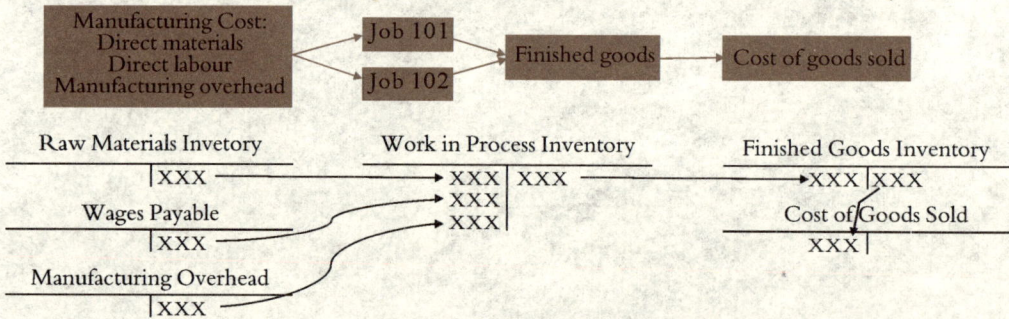

图 4 - 1　分批成本计算法的成本流转

如图 4-2 所示，依据每步生产流程产生的制造成本，直接材料成本、直接人工成本和制造费用计入各自生产流程的在制品库存账目，因此不同生产流程产生不同的直接材料成本、直接人工成本和制造费用；在完成裁剪流程之后，在制品从裁剪流程转入包装流程，因此在制品将从裁剪流程的在制品库存账目转出，并转入包装流程的在制品库存账目；在完成生产流程最后一步（包装流程）之后，在制品将从包装流程的在制品库存账目转至制成品账目；在制成品出售后，所售制成品成本计入售出商品成本账目。

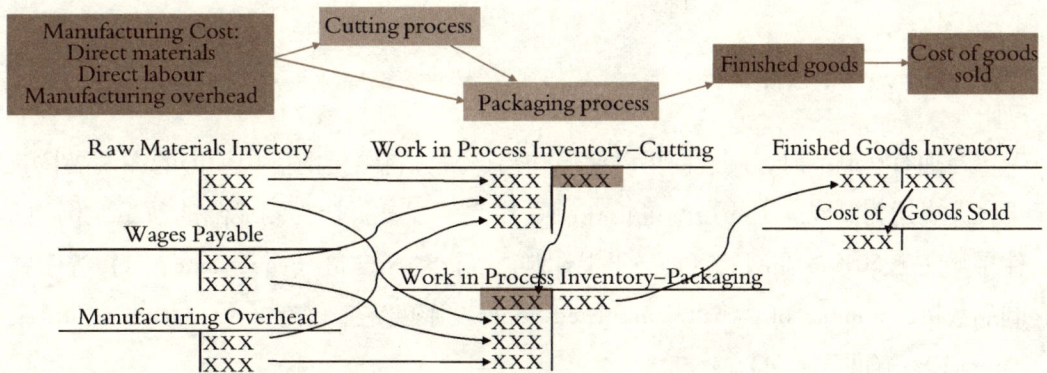

图 4 - 2　分步成本计算法的成本流转

4.2　分步成本计算法的主要内容

The Main Contents of Process Costing

在讲解分步成本计算法之前，首先需要了解该方法的四个基本要素：①直接材料成本与加工成本；②约当产量（equivalent unit）；③库存流转假设；④生产成本报告（production cost report）。

4.2.1　直接材料与加工成本

Direct Materials and Conversion Costs

在加工产品时，制造商一般承担三类制造成本（manufacturing cost）：①直接材料成本；②直接人工成本；③制造费用。因为大部分制造商使用自动化生产流程实现大规模生产，所以直接人工成本仅占制造成本的一小部分。鉴于此，使用自动化生产流程的制造商一般将直接人工成本和制造费用归为加工成本，三类制造成本缩减为两类，即直接材料成本和加工成本。将直接人工成本和制造费用归为加工成本，也简化了分步成本计算法。

加工成本（conversion cost）指产品的直接人工成本与制造费用之和，这些成本是将直接材料加工为制成品产生的成本（见图 4-3）。

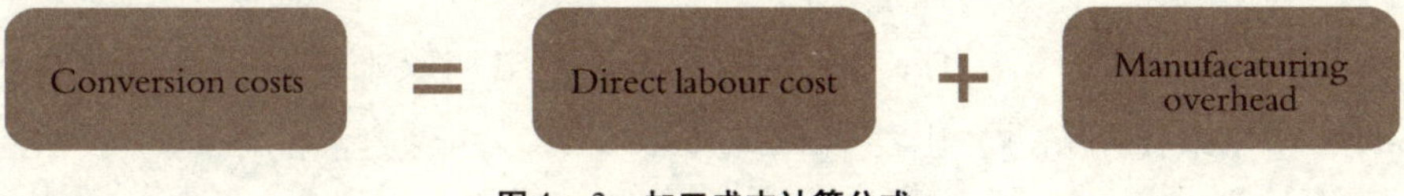

图 4 - 3　加工成本计算公式

带你到北美学习
管理会计
Take You to
North America
to Learn
Managerial Accounting

4.2.2 约当产量

Equivalent Units

当拥有在制品时，制造商可以使用约当产量，将给定财务周期内的在制品按完工程度表述为制成品。约当产量指在制品按完工程度折合为制成品的数量，例如 2 件平均完工 50% 的在制品，相当于 1 件制成品。约当产量（equivalent unit）等于在制品数量（number of partially completed goods）乘以完工程度（percentage of process completed）（见图 4-4）。

图 4-4　约当产量计算公式

案例 4-1

For the current period, Jones started 15,000 units and completed 10,000 units, the remaining 5,000 units were only 30% of the way through the production process. How many equivalent units of production did Jones have for the period?

A. 10,000

B. 11,500

C. 13,500

D. 15,000

讲解：　当前财务周期，Jones 加工 15 000 件商品，完工 10 000 件，尚未完工 5 000 件。10 000 件制成品，100% 完成，相当于 10 000 件制成品；5 000 件在制品，平均完工 30%，相当于 1 500 件制成品，因此约当产量为 11 500 件制成品。

4.2.3 库存流转假设

The Assumptions of Inventory Flow

在使用分步成本计算法时，制造商既可以运用加权平均法（weighted average method），也可以使用先进先出法（FIFO method）。两种方法的不同在于如何处理给定财务周期的期初库存商品。先进先出法要求区别对待给定财务周期的期初库存产品与开始加工的产品，而加权平均法对给定财务周期的期初库存产品与开始加工

第4章
分步成本计算法
Process Costing

的产品不作区别。

由于加权平均法和先进先出法计算结果之间的差异微乎其微，且加权平均法更简单，因此大部分制造商偏向于使用加权平均法。本章将重点讲解加权平均法。

4.2.4 生产成本报告
Production Cost Report

制造商一般将分步成本计算法涉及的计算过程、数据以报表形式呈现，这张报表被称为生产成本报告。对于制造商，每个生产部门要按月编写生产成本报告。

4.3 加权平均法
Weighted Average Method

使用加权平均法编写生产成本报告需要如下四步：①分析产品流转；②计算各种直接材料与加工成本的约当产量（equivalent unit）；③计算单件产品成本；④将成本计入完工产品、在制品期末库存（ending work in process inventory）。通过"案例4-2"，掌握加权平均法的应用。

案例 4 - 2

Drimo Tile produces ceramic tiles using two sequential production departments：Forming Department and Finishing Department. During May, the following information was created for Drimo Tile's first production process department，Forming Department：

Forming Department For the month ended by May 31	
Information about units：	
Work in process, May 1（100% complete as to direct materials, 10% complete as to conversion costs）	2,000
Started in production in May	18,000
Completed and transferred to Finishing Department in May	16,000
Work in process, May 31（25% complete as to direct materials, 55% complete as to conversion costs）	4,000

带你到北美学习
管理会计
Take You to
North America
to Learn
Managerial Accounting

Information about costs:	
Work in process, May 1 ($800 of direct materials and $4,000 of conversion costs)	$4,800
Direct materials used in May	6,000
Direct labour incurred in May	2,400
Manufacturing overhead allocated in May	30,000
Conversion costs incurred in May	32,400

During May, Drimo Tile reported the following information about Finishing Department:

Finishing Department For the month ended by May 31	
Information about units:	
Work in process, May 1 (20% complete as to direct materials, 70% complete as to conversion costs)	4,000
Transferred in from Forming Department in May	16,000
Completed and transferred out to finished goods inventory in May	15,000
Work in process, May 31 (36% complete as to direct materials, 80% complete as to conversion costs)	5,000
Information about costs:	
Work in process, May 1 ($10,000 of transferred-in costs, $488 of direct materials, and $5,530 of conversion costs)	$16,018
Transferred in from Forming Department in May	38,400
Direct materials used in May	6,400
Direct labour incurred in May	4,300
Manufacturing overhead allocated in May	20,000
Conversion costs incurred in May	24,300

Required:

Prepare the production cost reports for Forming Department and Finishing Department using the weighted average method.

讲解： 为生产瓷砖，Drimo Tile 需要两个流程：①Forming；②Finishing。先讲解 Forming Department 生产成本报告的编写步骤。

第1步：分析产品流转 （见说明4-1）。

5 月 1 日，Forming Department 的在制品库存为 2 000 块瓷砖；5 月份，Forming Department 开始生产 18 000 块瓷砖，完工并转至 Finishing Department 16 000 块瓷砖；5 月 31 日，Forming Department 的在制品库存为 4 000 块瓷砖。

说明 4 - 1：分析 Forming Department 产品流转	
Units to account for：	
Work in process，May 1	2,000
Started in production in May	18,000
Total physical units to account for	20,000
Units accounted for：	
Completed and transferred out in May	16,000
Work in process，May 31	4,000
Total physical units accounted for	20,000

第 2 步：计算各种直接材料与加工成本的约当产量 （见说明4-2）。

5 月份，Forming Department 完工并转至 Finishing Department 16 000 块瓷砖。对于完工瓷砖，从直接材料和加工成本方面均已完成100%。5 月 31 日，Forming De-partment 的在制品库存为 4 000 块瓷砖。对于尚未完工的 4 000 块瓷砖，基于直接材料已完成25%，约当产量为 1 000 块瓷砖 （4 000 × 25% = 1 000）；基于加工成本已完工55%，约当产量为 2 200 块瓷砖 （4 000 × 55% = 2 200）。从直接材料方面，约当产量为 17 000 块瓷砖 （16 000 + 1 000 = 17 000）；从加工成本方面，约当产量为 18 200 块瓷砖 （16 000 + 2 200 = 18 200）。

请注意：在加权平均法中，不使用在制品期初库存的完工程度 （百分比）。例如 Forming Department 的在制品月初库存为 2 000 块瓷砖，其中直接材料已完工100%，加工成本仅完工10%。

说明 4 - 2：计算 Forming Department 约当产量					
		Percent Complete		Equivalent Units	
	Physical Units	Direct Materials Percent Complete	Conversion Percent Complete	Direct Materials	Conversion
Units to account for：					

带你到北美学习
管理会计
Take You to
North America
to Learn
Managerial Accounting

Work in process, May 1	2,000	100%	10%			
Started in production in May	18,000					
Total physical units to account for	20,000					
Units accounted for:						
Completed and transferred out in May	16,000				16,000	16,000
Work in process, May 31	4,000	25%	55%		1,000	2,200
Total physical units accounted for	20,000					
Total equivalent units					17,000	18,200

第 3 步：计算单件产品成本 （见说明 4-3）。

5 月 1 日，Forming Department 的在制品账目余额为 $4 800，其中直接材料成本为 $800，加工成本为 $4 000；同月，Forming Department 产生成本 $38 400，其中直接材料成本为 $6 000，加工成本为 $32 400；5 月份的需核算总成本（total cost to account for）为 $43 200，其中直接材料成本为 $6 800，加工成本为 $36 400。从直接材料方面，约当产量为 17 000 块瓷砖，因此每块瓷砖的直接材料成本为 $0.40（$6 800 ÷ 17 000 = $0.40）；从加工成本方面，约当产量为 18 200 块瓷砖，所以每块瓷砖的加工成本为 $2（$36 400 ÷ 18 200 = $2）。每块瓷砖成本为 $2.40（$0.40 + $2 = $2.40）。

说明 4-3：计算 Forming Department 单件产品成本	Direct Materials	Conversion	Total
Work in process, May 1	$800	$4,000	$4,800
Costs incurred in May	6,000	32,400	38,400
Total costs to account for	$6,800	$36,400	$43,200
Equivalent units	÷ 17,000	÷ 18,200	
Costs per equivalent unit	$0.40	$2.00	$2.40

第 4 步：将成本计入完工产品、在制品期末库存 （见说明 4-4）。

5 月份，Forming Department 完工并转至 Finishing Department 瓷砖 16 000 块，每块瓷砖成本为 $2.40，完工的 16 000 块瓷砖成本为 $38 400（$2.40 × 16 000 = $38 400）。

5 月 31 日，Forming Department 的在制品库存为 4 000 块瓷砖。对于尚未完工的 4 000 块瓷砖，基于直接材料，约当产量为 1 000 块瓷砖，每块瓷砖的直接材料成本

为 $0.40，因此在制品账目月末余额中的直接材料成本为 $400（$0.40 × 1 000 = $400）；基于加工成本，约当产量为 2 200 块瓷砖，每块瓷砖的加工成本为 $2，因此在制品账目月末余额中的加工成本为 $4 400（$2 × 2 200 = $4 400）。Forming Department 的在制品账目月末余额为 $4 800（$400 + $4 400 = $4 800）。

完工的 16 000 块瓷砖成本为 $38 400，在制品账目月末余额为 $4 800，因此已核实总成本（total cost accounted for）为 $43 200（$38 400 + $4 800 = $43 200）。

说明 4‑4：分析 Forming Department 总成本		
Costs of units completed and transferred out to Finishing Department in May		$38,400
Costs remaining in May 31 work in process inventory		
Direct materials	$400	
Conversion	4,400	
Total costs of May 31 work in process inventory		4,800
Total costs accounted for		$43,200

"说明 4‑5"所示为 Forming Department 生产成本报告。

说明 4‑5：Forming Department 生产成本报告					
Forming Department Production Cost Report（Weighted Average Method） For the month ended by May 31					
		Percent Complete		Equivalent Units	
	Physical Units	Direct Materials Percent Complete	Conversion Percent Complete	Direct Materials	Conversion
Units to account for:					
Work in process, May 1	2,000	100%	10%		
Started in production in May	18,000				
Total physical units to account for	20,000				
Units accounted for:					
Completed and transferred out in May	16,000			16,000	16,000
Work in process, May 31	4,000	25%	55%	1,000	2,200
Total physical units accounted for	20,000				
Total equivalent units				17,000	18,200

带你到北美学习
管理会计
Take You to
North America
to Learn
Managerial Accounting

	Direct Materials	Conversion	Total
Work in process, May 1	$800	$4,000	$4,800
Costs incurred in May	6,000	32,400	38,400
Total costs to account for	$6,800	$36,400	$43,200
Equivalent units	÷ 17,000	÷ 18,200	
Costs per equivalent unit	$0.40	$2.00	$2.40
Costs of units completed and transferred out to Finishing Department in May			$38,400
Costs remaining in May 31 work in process inventory			
Direct materials		$400	
Conversion		4,400	
Total costs of May 31 work in process inventory			4,800
Total costs accounted for			$43,200

接下来，讲解 Finishing Department 生产成本报告的编写步骤。

第 1 步：分析产品流转（见说明 4-6）。

5 月 1 日，Finishing Department 的在制品库存为 4 000 块瓷砖；5 月份，Finishing Department 从 Forming Department 转入 16 000 块瓷砖，完工 15 000 块瓷砖，并将这些完工瓷砖转至制成品库存；5 月 31 日，Finishing Department 的在制品库存为 5 000 块瓷砖。

说明 4-6：分析 Finishing Department 产品流转	
Units to account for:	
Work in process, May 1	4,000
Transferred in during May	16,000
Total physical units to account for	20,000
Units accounted for:	
Completed and transferred out in May	15,000
Work in process, May 31	5,000
Total physical units accounted for	20,000

第 2 步：计算各种直接材料与加工成本的约当产量（见说明 4-7）。

5 月 1 日，Finishing Department 的在制品库存为 4 000 块瓷砖，说明这些瓷砖已于 4 月份在 Forming Department 完工，否则不能转至 Finishing Department 进行加工；5 月份，Finishing Department 从 Forming Department 转入 16 000 块瓷砖，说明这些瓷砖已在 Forming Department 完工。换言之，无论是在制品月末库存的 5 000 块瓷砖，还是 5 月份完工的 15 000 块瓷砖，只要在 Finishing Department 进行加工的瓷砖均已在 Forming Department 完工，所以基于转入成本（transferred-in cost）已完成 100%，约当产量为 20 000 块瓷砖（15 000 + 5 000 = 20 000）。

5 月份，Finishing Department 完工 15 000 块瓷砖。对于完工的 15 000 块瓷砖，基于直接材料和加工成本均已完工 100%。5 月 31 日，Finishing Department 的在制品库存为 5 000 块瓷砖。对于尚未完工的 5 000 块瓷砖，基于直接材料已完成 36%，约当产量为 1 800 块瓷砖（5 000 × 36% = 1 800）；基于加工成本已完工 80%，约当产量为 4 000 块瓷砖（5 000 × 80% = 4 000）。从直接材料方面，约当产量为 16 800 块瓷砖（15 000 + 1 800 = 16 800）；从加工成本方面，约当产量为 19 000 块瓷砖（15 000 + 4 000 = 19 000）。

请注意：在加权平均法中，不使用在制品期初库存的完工程度（百分比）。例如 Finishing Department 的在制品月初库存为 4 000 块瓷砖，基于直接材料仅完工 20%，加工成本已完工 70%。

说明 4-7：计算 Finishing Department 约当产量						
		Percent Complete		Equivalent Units		
	Physical Units	Direct Materials Percent Complete	Conversion Percent Complete	Transferred-in	Direct Materials	Conversion
Units to account for：						
Work in process, May 1	4,000	20%	70%			
Transferred in during May	16,000					
Total physical units to account for	20,000					
Units accounted for：						
Completed and transferred out in May	15,000			15,000	15,000	15,000
Work in process, May 31	5,000	36%	80%	5,000	1,800	4,000

带你到北美学习
管理会计
Take You to
North America
to Learn
Managerial Accounting

Total physical units accounted for	20,000					
Total equivalent units				20,000	16,800	19,000

第3步：计算单件产品成本（见说明4-8）。

5月1日，Finishing Department 的在制品账目余额为 $16 018，其中转入成本为 $10 000，直接材料成本为 $488，加工成本为 $5 530；同月，Finishing Department 产生成本 $69 100，其中转入成本为 $38 400，直接材料成本为 $6 400，加工成本为 $24 300；5月份的需核算总成本为 $85 118，其中转入成本为 $48 400，直接材料成本为 $6 888，加工成本为 $29 830。从转入成本方面，约当产量为 20 000 块瓷砖，因此每块瓷砖的转入成本为 $2.42（$48 400 ÷ 20 000 = $2.42）；从直接材料方面，约当产量为 16 800 块瓷砖，因此每块瓷砖的直接材料成本为 $0.41（$6 888 ÷ 16 800 = $0.41）；从加工成本方面，约当产量为 19 000 块瓷砖，因此每块瓷砖的加工成本为 $1.57（$29 830 ÷ 19 000 = $1.57）。每块瓷砖成本为 $4.40（$2.42 + $0.41 + $1.57 = $4.40）。

说明4-8：计算 Finishing Department 单件产品成本

	Transferred-in	Direct Materials	Conversion	Total
Work in process, May 1	$10,000	$488	$5,530	$16,018
Costs incurred in May	38,400	6,400	24,300	69,100
Total costs to account for	$48,400	$6,888	$29,830	$85,118
Equivalent units	÷ 20,000	÷ 16,800	÷ 19,000	
Costs per equivalent unit	$2.42	$0.41	$1.57	$4.40

第4步：将成本计入完工产品、在制品期末库存（见说明4-9）。

5月份，Finishing Department 完工 15 000 块瓷砖，这些完工的瓷砖将转至制成品库存，每块瓷砖成本为 $4.40，完工的 15 000 块瓷砖成本为 $66 000（$4.40 × 15 000 = $66 000）。

5月31日，Finishing Department 的在制品库存为 5 000 块瓷砖。对于尚未完工的 5 000 块瓷砖，基于转入成本，约当产量为 5 000 块瓷砖，每块瓷砖的转入成本为 $2.42，因此在制品账目月末余额中的转入成本为 $12 100（$2.42 × 5 000 = $12 100）；基于直接材料，约当产量为 1 800 块瓷砖，每块瓷砖的直接材料成本为 $0.41，因此在制品账目月末余额中的直接材料成本为 $738（$0.41 × 1 800 =

$738）；基于加工成本，约当产量为 4 000 块瓷砖，每块瓷砖的加工成本为 $ 1. 57，因此在制品账目月末余额中的加工成本为 $ 6 280 （ $ 1. 57 × 4 000 = $ 6 280）。Finishing Department 的在制品账目月末余额为 $ 19 118 （ $ 12 100 + $ 738 + $ 6 280 = $ 19 118）。

完工的 15 000 块瓷砖成本为 $ 66 000，在制品账目月末余额为 $ 19 118，因此已核实总成本为 $ 85 118 （ $ 66 000 + $ 19 118 = $ 85 118）。

说明 4 - 9：分析 Finishing Department 总成本		
Costs of units completed and transferred out to finished goods inventory		$ 66,000
Costs remaining in May 31 work in process inventory		
Transferred - in	$ 12,100	
Direct materials	738	
Conversion	6,280	
Total costs of May 31 work in process inventory		19,118
Total costs accounted for		$ 85,118

"说明 4 - 10" 所示为 Finishing Department 生产成本报告。

说明 4 - 10：Finishing Department 生产成本报告						
Finishing Department Production Cost Report（Weighted Average Method） For the month ended by May 31						
		Percent Complete		Equivalent Units		
	Physical Units	Direct Materials Percent Complete	Conversion Percent Complete	Transferred - in	Direct Materials	Conversion
Units to account for：						
Work in process, May 1	4,000	20%	70%			
Transferred in during May	16,000					
Total physical units to account for	20,000					
Units accounted for：						
Completed and transferred out in May	15,000			15,000	15,000	15,000

带你到北美学习
管理会计
Take You to
North America
to Learn
Managerial Accounting

Work in process, May 31	5,000	36%	80%	5,000	1,800	4,000
Total physical units accounted for	20,000					
Total equivalent units				20,000	16,800	19,000

	Transferred-in	Direct Materials	Conversion	Total
Work in process, May 1	$10,000	$488	$5,530	$16,018
Costs incurred in May	38,400	6,400	24,300	69,100
Total costs to account for	$48,400	$6,888	$29,830	$85,118
Equivalent units	÷ 20,000	÷ 16,800	÷ 19,000	
Costs per equivalent unit	$2.42	$0.41	$1.57	$4.40

Costs of units completed and transferred out to finished goods inventory		$66,000
Costs remaining in May 31 work in process inventory		
Transferred-in	$12,100	
Direct materials	738	
Conversion	6,280	
Total costs of May 31 work in process inventory		19,118
Total costs accounted for		$85,118

4.4　分步成本计算系统中的日记账分录

The Journal Entries Required in a Process Costing System

在了解分批成本计算法的成本流转和生产成本报告的编写之后，通过"案例4-3"，学习使用日记账分录记录分批成本计算法中涉及的成本流转。

案例4-3

Drimo Tile produces ceramic tiles using two sequential production departments：Forming Department and Finishing Department. During May, the following information was created for Drimo Tile's first production process department, Forming Department：

Forming Department For the month ended by May 31	
Information about units:	
Work in process, May 1 (100% complete as to direct materials, 10% complete as to conversion costs)	2,000
Started in production in May	18,000
Completed and transferred to Finishing Department in May	16,000
Work in process, May 31 (25% complete as to direct materials, 55% complete as to conversion costs)	4,000
Information about costs:	
Work in process, May 1 ($800 of direct materials and $4,000 of conversion costs)	$4,800
Direct materials (DM) used in May	6,000
Direct labour (DL) incurred in May	2,400
Manufacturing overhead (MOH) allocated in May	30,000
Conversion costs incurred in May	32,400

During May, Drimo Tile reported the following information about Finishing Department:

Finishing Department For the month ended by May 31	
Information about units:	
Work in process, May 1 (20% complete as to direct materials, 70% complete as to conversion costs)	4,000
Transferred in from Forming Department in May	16,000
Completed and transferred out to finished goods inventory in May	15,000
Work in process, May 31 (36% complete as to direct materials, 80% complete as to conversion costs)	5,000
Information about costs:	
Work in process, May 1 ($10,000 of transferred-in costs, $488 of direct materials, and $5,530 of conversion costs)	$16,018
Transferred in from Forming Department in May	38,400
Direct materials used in May	6,400
Direct labour incurred in May	4,300
Manufacturing overhead allocated in May	20,000
Conversion costs incurred in May	24,300

带你到北美学习
管理会计
Take You to
North America
to Learn
Managerial Accounting

Required：

Prepare the journal entries to record the transactions incurred in Forming Department and Finishing Department.

讲解： 首先，讲解如何完成 Forming Department 所涉及的日记账分录。

5 月份，Forming Department 所用直接材料成本为 $6 000。在加工开始之后，生产所用直接材料将从原材料库存移入在制品库存，因此 Forming Department 的在制品库存账目增长 $6 000，原材料库存账目减少 $6 000。日记账分录借方和贷方分别记录 Forming Department 的在制品库存账目（work in process inventory – forming）和原材料库存账目（raw materials inventory）。

Work in process inventory – Forming	6,000	
Raw materials inventory		6,000
（To record direct materials used by the Forming in May）		

5 月份，Forming Department 承担直接人工成本 $2 400，这些直接人工成本计入在制品库存账目，因此 Forming Department 的在制品库存账目增长 $2 400，应付工资账目增长 $2 400。日记账分录借方和贷方分别记录 Forming Department 的在制品库存账目（work in process inventory – forming）和应付工资账目（wages payable）。

Work in process inventory – Forming	2,400	
Wages payable		2,400
（To record direct labour incurred in the Forming in May）		

5 月份，Forming Department 的分摊制造费用为 $30 000，这些分摊制造费用计入在制品库存账目，因此 Forming Department 的在制品库存账目增长 $30 000，制造费用账目减少 $30 000。日记账分录借方和贷方分别记录 Forming Department 的在制品库存账目（work in process inventory – forming）和制造费用账目（manufacturing overhead）。

Work in process inventory – Forming	30,000	
Manufacturing overhead		30,000
（To record manufacturing overhead allocated to the Forming in May）		

5 月份，Forming Department 完工并转至 Finishing Department 16 000 块瓷砖，每块瓷砖成本为 $2.40，完工的 16 000 块瓷砖成本为 $38 400（ $2.40 × 16 000 = $38 400）。Finishing Department 的在制品库存账目增长 $38 400，Forming Depart-

ment 的在制品库存账目减少 ＄38 400。日记账分录借方和贷方分别记录 Finishing Department 的在制品库存账目（work in process inventory – finishing）和 Forming Department 的在制品库存账目（work in process inventory – forming）。

Work in process inventory – Finishing	38,400	
Work in process inventory – Forming		38,400
（To record transfer of costs out of the Forming and into the Finishing)		

过账上述日记账分录信息之后，Forming Department 的在制品库存账目月末余额（＄4 800）与"说明 4-4"中 Forming Department 的在制品库存账目月末余额（＄4 800）相吻合（见图 4-5）。

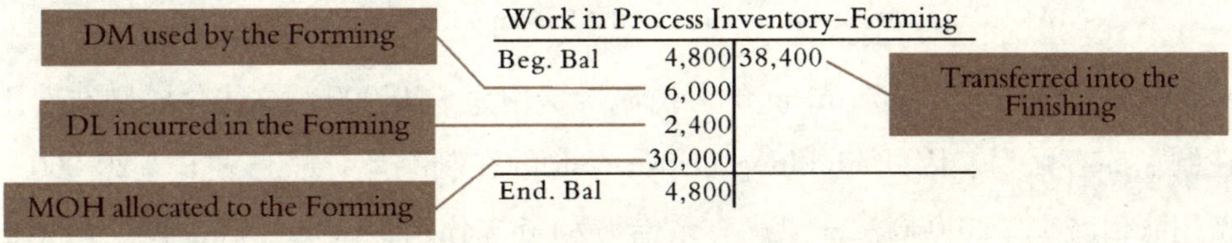

图 4 – 5　**Forming Department 的在制品库存账目**

接下来，讲解如何记录 Finishing Department 所涉及的日记账分录。

5 月份，Forming Department 完工并转至 Finishing Department 16 000 块瓷砖，每块瓷砖成本为 ＄2.40，完工的 16 000 块瓷砖成本为 ＄38 400（＄2.40 × 16 000 = ＄38 400）。Finishing Department 的在制品库存账目增长 ＄38 400，Forming Department 的在制品库存账目减少 ＄38 400，日记账分录借方和贷方分别记录 Finishing Department 的在制品库存账目（work in process inventory – finishing）和 Forming Department 的在制品库存账目（work in process inventory – forming）。

Work in process inventory – Finishing	38,400	
Work in process inventory – Forming		38,400
（To record transfer of costs out of the Forming and into the Finishing)		

5 月份，Finishing Department 所用直接材料成本为 ＄6 400。在加工开始之后，生产所用直接材料将从原材料库存移入在制品库存，因此 Finishing Department 的在制品库存账目增长 ＄6 400，原材料库存账目减少 ＄6 400。日记账分录借方和贷方分别记录 Finishing Department 的在制品库存账目（work in process inventory – finishing）和原材料库存账目（raw materials inventory）。

带你到北美学习
管理会计
Take You to
North America
to Learn
Managerial Accounting

Work in process inventory – Finishing	6,400	
Raw materials inventory		6,400
(To record direct materials used by the Finishing in May)		

5 月份，Finishing Department 承担直接人工成本 $4 300，这些直接人工成本计入在制品库存账目，因此 Finishing Department 的在制品库存账目增长 $4 300，应付工资账目增长 $4 300。日记账分录借方和贷方分别记录 Finishing Department 的在制品库存账目（work in process inventory – finishing）和应付工资账目（wages payable）。

Work in process inventory – Finishing	4,300	
Wages payable		4,300
(To record direct labour incurred in the Finishing in May)		

5 月份，Finishing Department 的分摊制造费用为 $20 000，这些分摊制造费用计入在制品库存账目，因此 Finishing Department 的在制品库存账目增长 $20 000，制造费用账目减少 $20 000。日记账分录借方和贷方分别记录 Finishing Department 的在制品库存账目（work in process inventory – finishing）和制造费用账目（manufacturing overhead）。

Work in process inventory – Finishing	20,000	
Manufacturing overhead		20,000
(To record manufacturing overhead allocated to the Finishing in May)		

5 月份，Finishing Department 完工 15 000 块瓷砖，这些完工的瓷砖将转至制成品库存，每块瓷砖成本为 $4.40，完工的 15 000 块瓷砖成本为 $66 000（$4.40 × 15 000 = $66 000）。制成品库存账目增长 $66 000，Finishing Department 的在制品库存账目减少 $66 000。日记账分录借方和贷方分别记录制成品库存账目（finished goods inventory）和 Finishing Department 的在制品库存账目（work in process inventory – finishing）。

Finished goods inventory	66,000	
Work in process inventory – Finishing		66,000
(To record transfer of costs out of the Finishing and into finished goods inventory)		

过账上述日记账分录信息之后，Finishing Department 的在制品库存账目月末余额（$19 118）与"说明4-9"中 Finishing Department 的在制品库存账目月末余额

（ $19 118 ）相吻合（见图4-6）。

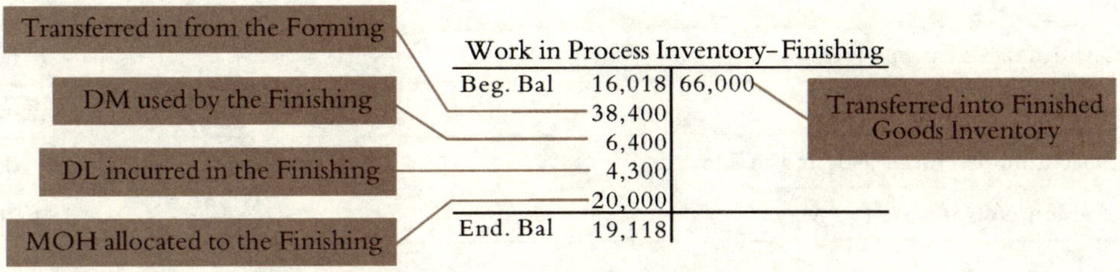

图4-6 **Finishing Department** 的在制品库存账目

4.5 先进先出法

First-In, First-Out Method

使用先进先出法编写生产成本报告也需要如下四步：①分析产品流转；②计算各种直接材料与加工成本的约当产量（equivalent unit）；③计算单件产品成本；④将成本计入完工产品、在制品期末库存（ending work in process inventory）。通过"案例4-4"，掌握先进先出法的应用。

案例4-4

Drimo Tile produces ceramic tiles using two sequential production departments: Forming Department and Finishing Department. During May, the following information was created for Drimo Tile's first production process department, Forming Department:

Forming Department For the month ended by May 31	
Information about units:	
Work in process, May 1 (100% complete as to direct materials, 10% complete as to conversion costs)	2,000
Started in production in May	18,000
Completed and transferred to Finishing Department in May	16,000
Work in process, May 31 (25% complete as to direct materials, 55% complete as to conversion costs)	4,000
Information about costs:	

带你到北美学习
管理会计
Take You to
North America
to Learn
Managerial Accounting

Work in process, May 1 ($800 of direct materials and $4,000 of conversion costs)	$4,800
Direct materials used in May	6,000
Direct labour incurred in May	2,400
Manufacturing overhead allocated in May	30,000
Conversion costs incurred in May	32,400

Required：

Prepare the production cost report for Forming Department using the first-in, first-out (FIFO) method.

讲解：

第1步：分析产品流转 （见说明4-11）。

5月1日，Forming Department 的在制品库存为2 000 块瓷砖；5月份，Forming Department 开始生产18 000 块瓷砖，完工并转至 Finishing Department 16 000 块瓷砖；5月31日，Forming Department 的在制品库存为4 000 块瓷砖。

请注意：无论运用加权平均法，还是使用先进先出法，产品流转是相同的。

说明4-11：分析 Forming Department 产品流转	
Units to account for：	
Work in process, May 1	2,000
Started in production in May	18,000
Total physical units to account for	20,000
Units accounted for：	
Completed and transferred out in May	16,000
Work in process, May 31	4,000
Total physical units accounted for	20,000

第2步：计算各种直接材料与加工成本的约当产量 （见说明4-12）。

请注意：在先进先出法中，需要使用在制品期初库存的完工程度（百分比）。5月1日，Forming Department 的在制品库存为2 000 块瓷砖。对于尚未完工的2 000 块瓷砖，基于直接材料已完成100%，约当产量为2 000 块瓷砖（2 000 × 100% = 2 000）；基于加工成本已完工10%，约当产量为200 块瓷砖（2 000 × 10% = 200）。

5月份，Forming Department 完工并转至 Finishing Department 16 000 块瓷砖。对于完工的16 000 块瓷砖，从直接材料和加工成本方面均已完成100%。5月31日，

Forming Department 的在制品库存为 4 000 块瓷砖。对于尚未完工的 4 000 块瓷砖,基于直接材料已完工 25%,约当产量为 1 000 块瓷砖(4 000 × 25% = 1 000);基于加工成本已完工 55%,约当产量为 2 200 块瓷砖(4 000 × 55% = 2 200)。从直接材料方面,约当产量总额为 17 000 块瓷砖(16 000 + 1 000 = 17 000);从加工成本方面,约当产量总额为 18 200 块瓷砖(16 000 + 2 200 = 18 200)。

从直接材料方面,约当产量总额为 17 000 块瓷砖,月初库存的约当产量为 2 000 块瓷砖,因此 5 月份新增约当产量 15 000 块瓷砖。从加工成本方面,约当产量总额为 18 200 块瓷砖,月初库存的约当产量为 200 块瓷砖,所以 5 月份新增约当产量 18 000 块瓷砖。

说明 4 - 12:计算 Forming Department 约当产量					
		Percent Complete		Equivalent Units	
	Physical Units	Direct Materials Percent Complete	Conversion Percent Complete	Direct Materials	Conversion
Units to account for:					
Work in process, May 1	2,000	100%	10%		
Started in production in May	18,000				
Total physical units to account for	20,000				
Units accounted for:					
Completed and transferred out in May	16,000			16,000	16,000
Work in process, May 31	4,000	25%	55%	1,000	2,200
Total physical units accounted for	20,000				
Total equivalent units				17,000	18,200
Equivalent units shown in May 1 work in process				(2,000①)	(200②)
New equivalent units completed in May only				15,000	18,000
① 2,000 × 100% = 2,000;② 2,000 × 10% = 200					

第 3 步:计算单件产品成本 (见说明 4 - 13)。

5 月 1 日,Forming Department 的在制品账目余额为 $4 800,其中直接材料成本为 $800,加工成本为 $4 000。Forming Department 的在制品账目月初余额($4 800)是 4 月份产生的成本,因此计算 5 月份新增产品的单件成本时,无需考

带你到北美学习
管理会计
Take You to
North America
to Learn
Managerial Accounting

虑在制品账目月初余额。

5 月份，Forming Department 产生成本 $38 400，其中直接材料成本为 $6 000，加工成本为 $32 400。从直接材料方面，5 月份新增约当产量 15 000 块瓷砖，每块瓷砖的直接材料成本为 $0.40（$6 000 ÷ 15 000 = $0.40）；从加工成本方面，5 月份新增约当产量 18 000 块瓷砖，每块瓷砖的加工成本为 $1.80（$32 400 ÷ 18 000 = $1.80）。因此，每块瓷砖成本为 $2.20（$0.40 + $1.80 = $2.20）。

说明 4 - 13：计算 Forming Department 单件产品成本			
	Direct Materials	Conversion	Total
Work in process，May 1			$4,800
Costs incurred in May	$6,000	$32,400	38,400
Total costs to account for			$43,200
Equivalent units for May only	÷ 15,000	÷ 18,000	
Costs per equivalent unit	$0.40	$1.80	$2.20

第 4 步：将成本计入完工产品、在制品期末库存（见说明 4-14）。

5 月 1 日，Forming Department 的在制品库存为 2 000 块瓷砖；5 月份，Forming Department 开始生产 18 000 块瓷砖，完工并转至 Finishing Department 16 000 块瓷砖；5 月 31 日，Forming Department 的在制品库存为 4 000 块瓷砖。

5 月 1 日，Forming Department 的在制品库存为 2 000 块瓷砖，在制品账目余额为 $4 800，说明为生产这 2 000 块瓷砖，Forming Department 在 4 月份产生成本 $4 800。根据先进先出法，Forming Department 首先完成在制品月初库存的 2 000 块瓷砖。对于尚未完工的 2 000 块瓷砖，基于直接材料已完工 100%，基于加工成本仅完成 10%。5 月份，为完成这 2 000 块瓷砖，Forming Department 应从加工成本方面完成余下 90% 的加工流程，相当于 1 800 块瓷砖（2 000 × 90% = 1 800）；每块瓷砖的加工成本为 $1.80，为完成这 2 000 块瓷砖，产生成本 $3 240（$1.80 × 1 800 = $3 240）。因此，为生产这 2 000 块瓷砖，共计产生成本 $8 040（$4 800 + $3 240 = $8 040）。

5 月份，Forming Department 开始生产并完成 14 000 块瓷砖（16 000 – 2 000 = 14 000）。每块瓷砖成本为 $2.20，因此 14 000 块瓷砖成本为 $30 800（$2.20 × 14 000 = $30 800）。5 月份，Forming Department 完工并转至 Finishing Department 16 000 块瓷砖（2 000 + 14 000 = 16 000），共计产生成本 $38 840（$8 040 +

$30 800 = $38 840)。

5 月31 日，Forming Department 的在制品库存为4 000 块瓷砖。对于尚未完工的 4 000 块瓷砖，基于直接材料仅完成25% ，约当产量为1 000 块瓷砖（4 000 × 25% = 1 000），每块瓷砖的直接材料成本为 $0.40，因此在制品账目月末余额中的直接材料成本为 $400（$0.40 × 1 000 = $400）；基于加工成本仅完成55% ，约当产量为2 200 块瓷砖（4 000 × 55% = 2 200），每块瓷砖的加工成本为 $1.80，所以在制品账目月末余额中的加工成本为 $3 960（$1.80 × 2 200 = $3 960）。Forming Department 的在制品账目月末余额为 $4 360。

完工的16 000 块瓷砖成本为 $38 840，在制品账目月末余额为 $4 360，因此已核实总成本为 $43 200（$38 840 + $4 360 = $43 200）。

说明4-14：分析 Forming Department 总成本		
Costs of units completed and transferred out to Finishing Department in May		
Costs of May 1 work in process inventory	$4,800	
Costs incurred to complete May 1 work in process inventory	3,240	
Costs incurred to produce units that were both started and completed in May	30,800	
Total costs of units completed and transferred out to Finishing Departmentin May		$38,840
Costs remaining in May 31 work in process inventory		
Direct materials	400	
Conversion	3,960	
Total costs of May 31 work in process inventory		4,360
Total costs accounted for		$43,200

"说明4-15" 所示为 Forming Department 生产成本报告。

带你到北美学习
管理会计
Take You to
North America
to Learn
Managerial Accounting

说明 4 - 15：Forming Department 生产成本报告

Forming Department
Production Cost Report (FIFO Method)
For the month ended by May 31

	Physical Units	Direct Materials Percent Complete	Conversion Percent Complete	Direct Materials	Conversion
		Percent Complete		**Equivalent Units**	
Units to account for:					
Work in process, May 1	2,000	100%	10%		
Started in production in May	18,000				
Total physical units to account for	20,000				
Units accounted for:					
Completed and transferred out in May	16,000			16,000	16,000
Work in process, May 31	4,000	25%	55%	1,000	2,200
Total physical units accounted for	20,000				
Total equivalent units				17,000	18,200
Equivalent units shown in May 1 work in process				(2,000)	(200)
New equivalent units completed in May only				15,000	18,000

	Direct Materials	Conversion	Total
Work in process, May 1			$4,800
Costs incurred in May	$6,000	$32,400	38,400
Total costs to account for			$43,200
Equivalent units for May only	÷ 15,000	÷ 18,000	
Costs per equivalent unit	$0.40	$1.80	$2.20

Costs of units completed and transferred out to Finishing Department in May		
Costs of May 1 work in process inventory	$4,800	
Costs incurred to complete May 1 work in process inventory	3,240	

Costs incurred to produce units that were both started and completed in May	<u>30,800</u>	
Total costs of units completed and transferred out to Finishing Department in May		$38,840
Costs remaining in May 31 work in process inventory		
Direct materials	400	
Conversion	<u>3,960</u>	
Total costs of May 31 work in process inventory		4,360
Total costs accounted for		<u>$43,200</u>

带你到北美学习
管理会计
Take You to
North America
to Learn
Managerial Accounting

例题综述
Summary of Examples

例题 4 – 1

All of the following statements are correct except for which of the following?

A. Costs are accumulated by departments when using a process costing system.

B. Units produced are indistinguishable from each other in a process costing system.

C. Process costing has the same basic purposes as job costing.

D. Process costing would be appropriate for a customized cabinet market.

讲解： 为确定产品成本，大部分制造商使用如下两种产品成本计算法：①分步成本计算法（process costing）；②分批成本计算法（job costing）。虽然两种产品成本计算法的使用条件和计算方法不同，但它们的目的相同，即确定生产一种产品的成本。生产独特、客户定制、小批量商品的企业使用分批成本计算法，而通过一系列统一生产流程，生产大量完全相同产品的企业使用分步成本计算法。

答案： D

例题 4 – 2

A manufacturer uses a weighted average process costing system. All direct materials at the manufacturer are added at the beginning of its production processes. The equivalent units for direct materials at the manufacturer would be _____.

A. the units started plus the units in beginning work in process inventory

B. the units completed and transferred out plus the units in beginning work in process inventory

C. the units started plus the units in ending work in process inventory

D. the units started and completed plus the units in ending work in process inventory

讲解： 在生产开始之际，从直接材料方面，在制品期初库存、给定财务周期开始生产的产品均已完工 100%，因此约当产量等于实际产量。

答案： A

例题 4 - 3

An equivalent unit for conversion costs is equal to _____.

A. an equivalent unit for material costs

B. the amount of conversion costs needed to produce one unit

C. the amount of conversion costs necessary to start one unit into work in process

D. half of conversion costs necessary to produce one unit

讲解： 约当产量指在制品按完工程度折合为制成品的数量，比如 2 件平均完工 50% 的在制品，相当于 1 件制成品。约当产量（equivalent unit）等于在制品数量（number of partially completed goods）乘以完工程度（percentage of process completed）。

答案： B

例题 4 - 4

When using a weighted average process costing, the computation of costs per equivalent unit includes _____.

A. the costs incurred during the current period only

B. the costs incurred during the current period plus the costs in beginning work in process inventory

C. the costs incurred during the current period plus the costs in ending work in process inventory

D. the costs incurred during the current period plus all of the costs incurred in the previous period

讲解： 见"说明 4-3"。

答案： B

例题 4 - 5

All of the following statements about process costing are true except for which of the following?

A. Process costing is appropriate for those production processes where similar units are produced in a continuous flow.

B. Equivalent units for materials and equivalent units for conversion costs are same.

带你到北美学习
管理会计
Take You to
North America
to Learn
Managerial Accounting

C. Units in beginning work in process inventory plus units started into production should equal units in ending work in process inventory plus units completed.

D. Each process will have its own work in process inventory account.

讲解： 约当产量指在制品按完工程度折合为制成品的数量。约当产量（equivalent unit）等于在制品数量（number of partially completed goods）乘以完工程度（percentage of process completed）。即便在制品数量相同，但直接材料和加工成本的完工程度可能不同，因此两者的约当产量可能不同。

答案： B

例题 4 - 6

The journal entry to record the transfer of units from Department A to the next processing department, Department B, includes a debit to _____.

A. Work in Process Inventory for Dept. B and a credit to Raw Materials Inventory

B. Work in Process Inventory for Dept. A and a credit to Work in Process Inventory for Dept. B

C. Work in Process Inventory for Dept. B and a credit to Work in Process Inventory for Dept. A

D. Finished Goods Inventory and a credit to Work in Process Inventory for Dept. A

讲解： Department A 将完工产品转至下一个生产流程，即 Department B，因此 Department B 的在制品库存账目增长，Department A 的在制品库存账目减少。日记账分录借方和贷方分别记录 Department B 的在制品库存账目（work in process inventory – department B）和 Department A 的在制品库存账目（work in process inventory – department A）。

答案： C

例题 4 - 7

In general, transferred-in costs include _____.

A. costs incurred in the previous period

B. costs incurred in all prior periods

C. costs incurred in the previous process

D. costs incurred in all prior processes

讲解： 转入成本（transferred-in cost）指先前所有生产流程产生的成本。

答案： D

例题 4 - 8

A company uses a weighted average method in its process costing system. The May 1 work in process inventory in a particular department consisted of 16,000 units, which were 50% complete with respect to conversion costs. The company recorded 59,000 equivalent units of production for conversion costs for May in that department. There were 12,000 units in that department's work in process inventory on May 31, which were 75% complete with respect to conversion costs. A total of 50,000 units were completed and transferred out of the department during the month. The number of units started during May in the department was _____.

A. 42,000 units

B. 46,000 units

C. 29,000 units

D. 54,000 units

讲解： 5 月 1 日的在制品库存为 16 000 件产品，5 月份完工 50 000 件产品，5 月 31 日的在制品库存为 12 000 件产品，因此 5 月份开始生产 46 000 件产品（12 000 + 50 000 - 16 000 = 46 000）。

答案： B

例题 4 - 9

Bottling Department had 20,000 units in the work in process inventory on June 1. During June, 110,000 units were started into production. 30,000 units were left in the work in process inventory on June 30.

Required：

Summarize the physical flow of units in a schedule.

讲解： 6 月 1 日的在制品库存为 20 000 件产品，6 月份开始生产 110 000 件产品，6 月 30 日的在制品库存为 30 000 件产品，因此 6 月份完工 100 000 件产品（20 000 + 110 000 - 30 000 = 100 000）。

带你到北美学习
管理会计
Take You to
North America
to Learn
Managerial Accounting

答案:

Units to account for:	
Work in process, June 1	20,000
Started in production in June	110,000
Total physical units to account for	130,000
Units accounted for:	
Completed and transferred out in June	100,000
Work in process, June 30	30,000
Total physical units accounted for	130,000

例题 4 - 10

Packaging Department had the following information at March 31:

	Physical Units	Equivalent Units	
		Direct Materials	Conversion
Units accounted for:			
Completed and transferred out in March	115,000		
Work in process, March 31	15,000		
Total physical units accounted for	130,000		
Total equivalent units			

All direct materials are added at the end of the conversion process. The units in the ending work in process inventory were only 30% of the way through the conversion process.

Required:

Complete the schedule by computing the total equivalent units for direct materials and conversion costs in March.

讲解: 3 月 31 日,Packaging Department 的在制品库存为 15 000 件产品。对于尚未完工的 15 000 件产品,基于直接材料已完成 100% ,约当产量为 15 000 件产品;基于加工成本仅完工 30% ,约当产量为 4 500 件产品 (15 000 × 30% = 4 500)。

3 月份,Packaging Department 完工并转至下一个生产流程 115 000 件产品。对于完工的 115 000 件产品,从直接材料和加工成本方面均已完工 100% 。

从直接材料方面,约当产量为 130 000 件产品 (115 000 + 15 000 = 130 000);从加工成本方面,约当产量为 119 500 件产品 (115 000 + 4 500 = 119 500)。

答案：

	Physical Units	Equivalent Units	
		Direct Materials	Conversion
Units accounted for:			
Completed and transferred out in March	115,000	115,000	115,000
Work in process, March 31	15,000	15,000	4,500
Total physical units accounted for	130,000		
Total equivalent units		130,000	119,500

例题 4 - 11

The Assembly Department of ZAP Surge Protectors began with no work in process inventory in September. During the month, the production that incurred $ 39,860 ($ 9,900 of direct materials and $ 29,960 of direct labour) was started on 23,000 units. The Assembly Department completed and transferred to the Testing Department a total of 15,000 units. The ending work in process inventory was 37.50% complete as to direct materials and 80% complete as to conversion costs.

Required:

1. Compute the equivalent units for direct materials and conversion costs using the weighted average method.

2. Compute the costs per equivalent unit using the weighted average method.

3. Assign the costs to the units completed and transferred out and to the ending work in process inventory using the weighted average method.

4. Present the journal entries to record the use of direct materials and direct labour in the Assembly Department. Also, record the journal entry for the costs transferred out of the Assembly Department to the Testing Department.

5. Post the journal entries to Work in Process Inventory – Assembly. What is the ending balance of this account?

1. Compute the equivalent units for direct materials and conversion costs using the weighted average method.

带你到北美学习
管理会计
Take You to
North America
to Learn
Managerial Accounting

讲解：9 月 1 日，Assembly Department 的在制品库存为 0 件产品；9 月份，Assembly Department 开始生产 23 000 件产品，完工 15 000 件产品，并将这些产品转至 Testing Department；9 月 30 日，Assembly Department 的在制品库存为 8 000 件产品（0 + 23 000 – 15 000 = 8 000）。

9 月份，Assembly Department 完工 15 000 件产品，并将这些完工产品转至 Testing Department。对于完工的 15 000 件产品，从直接材料和加工成本方面均已完成 100%。

9 月 30 日，Assembly Department 的在制品库存为 8 000 件产品。对于尚未完工的 8 000 件产品，基于直接材料已完成 37.50%，约当产量为 3 000 件产品（8 000 × 37.50% = 3 000）；基于加工成本已完成 80%，约当产量为 6 400 件产品（8 000 × 80% = 6 400）。

从直接材料方面，约当产量为 18 000 件产品（15 000 + 3 000 = 18 000）；从加工成本方面，约当产量为 21 400 件产品（15 000 + 6 400 = 21 400）。

答案：

	Physical Units	Percent Complete		Equivalent Units	
		Direct Materials Percent Complete	Conversion Percent Complete	Direct Materials	Conversion
Units to account for:					
Work in process, September 1	0				
Started in production in September	23,000				
Total physical units to account for	23,000				
Units accounted for:					
Completed and transferred out in September	15,000			15,000	15,000
Work in process, September 30	8,000	37.50%	80%	3,000	6,400
Total physical units accounted for	23,000				
Total equivalent units				18,000	21,400

2. Compute the costs per equivalent unit using the weighted average method.

讲解： 9 月 1 日，Assembly Department 的在制品账目余额为 $0；9 月份，Assembly Department 产生成本 $39 860，其中直接材料成本为 $9 900，直接人工成本（加工成本）为 $29 960；9 月份的需核算总成本为 $39 860，其中直接材料成本为 $9 900，直接人工成本（加工成本）为 $29 960。从直接材料方面，约当产量为 18 000件产品，因此单件产品的直接材料成本为 $0.55（$9 900 ÷ 18 000 = $0.55）；从加工成本方面，约当产量为 21 400 件产品，所以单件产品的加工成本为 $1.40（$29 960 ÷ 21 400 = $1.40）。单件产品成本为 $1.95（$0.55 + $1.40 = $1.95）。

答案：

	Direct Materials	Conversion	Total
Work in process，September 1	$0	$0	$0
Costs incurred in September	9,900	29,960	39,860
Total costs to account for	$9,900	$29,960	$39,860
Equivalent units	÷ 18,000	÷ 21,400	
Costs per equivalent unit	$0.55	$1.40	$1.95

3. Assign the costs to the units completed and transferred out and to the ending work in process inventory using the weighted average method.

讲解： 9 月份，Assembly Department 完工 15 000 件产品，单件产品成本为 $1.95，完工的 15 000 件产品成本为 $29 250。9 月 30 日，Assembly Department 的在制品库存为 8 000 件产品。对于尚未完工的 8 000 件产品，基于直接材料，约当产量为 3 000件产品，单件产品的直接材料成本为 $0.55，因此在制品账目月末余额中的直接材料成本为 $1 650（$0.55 × 3 000 = $1 650）；从加工成本方面，约当产量为 6 400 件产品，单件产品的加工成本为 $1.40，因此在制品账目月末余额中的加工成本为 $8 960（$1.40 × 6 400 = $8 960）。Assembly Department 的在制品账目月末余额为 $10 610（$1 650 + $8 960 = $10 610）。

完工的 15 000 件产品的成本为 $29 250，在制品账目月末余额为 $10 610，因此已核实总成本为 $39 860（$29 250 + $10 610 = $39 860）。

答案:

Costs of units completed and transferred out to Assembly Department in September		$29,250
Costs remaining in September 30 work in process inventory		
Direct materials	$1,650	
Conversion	8,960	
Total costs of September 30 work in process inventory		10,610
Total costs accounted for		$39,860

4. Present the journal entries to record the use of direct materials and direct labour in the Assembly Department. Also, record the journal entry for the costs transferred out of the Assembly Department to the Testing Department.

讲解一: 9 月份, Assembly Department 所用直接材料成本为 $9 900。在加工开始之后, 生产所用直接材料将从原材料库存移入在制品库存, 因此 Assembly Department 的在制品库存账目增长 $9 900, 原材料库存账目减少 $9 900。日记账分录借方和贷方分别记录 Assembly Department 的在制品库存账目 (work in process inventory – assembly) 和原材料库存账目 (raw materials inventory)。

答案一:

Work in process inventory – Assembly	9,900	
Raw materials inventory		9,900

讲解二: 9 月份, Assembly Department 承担直接人工成本 $29 960, 这些直接人工成本计入在制品库存, 因此 Assembly Department 的在制品库存账目增长 $29 960, 应付工资账目增长 $29 960。日记账分录借方和贷方分别记录 Assembly Department 的在制品库存账目 (work in process inventory – assembly) 和应付工资账目 (wages payable)。

答案二:

Work in process inventory – Assembly	29,960	
Wages payable		29,960

讲解三: 9 月份, Assembly Department 将完工的 15 000 件产品转至 Testing Department, 单件产品成本为 $1.95, 因此完工的 15 000 件产品的成本为 $29 250。Testing Department 的在制品库存账目增长 $29 250，Assembly Department 的在制品库存账目减少 $29 250。日记账分录借方和贷方分别记录 Testing Department 的在制品库存账目（work in process inventory – testing）和 Assembly Department 的在制品库存账目（work in process inventory – assembly）。

答案三：

Work in process inventory – Testing	29,250	
Work in process inventory – Assembly		29,250

5. Post the journal entries to Work in Process Inventory – Assembly. What is the ending balance of this account?

Work in Process Inventory–Assembly

Beg. Bal	0	29,250
	9,900	
	29,960	
End. Bal	10,610	

答案： The ending balance of Work in Process Inventory – Assembly is $10,610.

例题 4 - 12

Colour Corporation prepares and packages paints. Colour Corporation has two departments: Blending Department and Packaging Department. Direct materials are added at the beginning of the blending process and at the end of the packaging process. Conversion costs are added evenly throughout each process. Data from the month of May for the Blending Department are as follows:

Blending Department For the month ended by May 31	
Information about units:	
Work in process, May 1	0
Started in production in May	8,000
Completed and transferred to Packaging Department in May	6,000
Work in process, May 31 (30% complete as to conversion costs)	2,000
Information about costs:	

带你到北美学习
管理会计
Take You to
North America
to Learn
Managerial Accounting

Work in process, May 1	$0
Direct materials used in May	4,800
Direct labour incurred in May	800
Manufacturing overhead allocated in May	1,840

Required:

1. Prepare the production cost report for the Blending Department using the weighted average method.

2. Present the journal entries to record the use of direct materials and direct labour and the manufacturing overhead allocated to the Blending Department. Also, record the journal entry for the costs of the litres completed and transferred out to the Packaging Department.

3. Post the journal entries to Work in Process Inventory – Blending. What is the ending balance of this account?

1. Prepare the production cost report for the Blending Department using the weighted average method.

讲解： 5 月 1 日，Blending Department 的在制品库存为 0 升涂料；5 月份，Blending Department 开始生产 8 000 升涂料，完工 6 000 升涂料并将这些完工涂料转至 Packaging Department；5 月 31 日，Blending Department 的在制品库存为 2 000 升涂料（0 + 8 000 - 6 000 = 2 000）。

5 月份，Blending Department 完工 6 000 升涂料，并将这些完工涂料转至 Packaging Department。对于完工的 6 000 升涂料，从直接材料和加工成本方面均已完成 100%。

5 月 31 日，Blending Department 的在制品库存为 2 000 升涂料。对于尚未完工的 2 000 升涂料，基于直接材料已完成 100%，约当产量为 2 000 升涂料（2 000 × 100% = 2 000）；基于加工成本已完工 30%，约当产量为 600 升涂料（2 000 × 30% = 600）。

从直接材料方面，约当产量为 8 000 升涂料（6 000 + 2 000 = 8 000）；从加工成本方面，约当产量为 6 600 升涂料（6 000 + 600 = 6 600）。

		Percent Complete		Equivalent Units	
	Physical Units	Direct Materials Percent Complete	Conversion Percent Complete	Direct Materials	Conversion
Units to account for:					
Work in process, May 1	0				
Started in production in May	8,000				
Total physical units to account for	8,000				
Units accounted for:					
Completed and transferred out in May	6,000			6,000	6,000
Work in process, May 31	2,000	100%	30%	2,000	600
Total physical units accounted for	8,000				
Total equivalent units				8,000	6,600

5 月 1 日，Blending Department 的在制品账目余额为 $0；5 月份，Blending Department 产生成本 $7 440，其中直接材料成本为 $4 800，加工成本为 $2 640（$800 + $1 840 = $2 640）；5 月份的需核算总成本为 $7 440，其中直接材料成本为 $4 800，加工成本为 $2 640。从直接材料方面，约当产量为 8 000 升涂料，每升涂料的直接材料成本为 $0.60（$4 800 ÷ 8 000 = $0.60）；从加工成本方面，约当产量为 6 600 升涂料，每升涂料的加工成本为 $0.40（$2 640 ÷ 6 600 = $0.40）。因此，每升涂料成本为 $1（$0.60 + $0.40 = $1）。

	Direct Materials	Conversion	Total
Work in process, May 1	$0	$0	$0
Costs incurred in May	4,800	2,640	7,440
Total costs to account for	$4,800	$2,640	$7,440
Equivalent units	÷ 8,000	÷ 6,600	
Costs per equivalent unit	$0.60	$0.40	$1.00

5 月份，Blending Department 完工 6 000 升涂料，每升涂料成本为 $1，完工的 6 000 升涂料成本为 $6 000。5 月 31 日，Blending Department 的在制品库存为 2 000 升涂料。对于尚未完工的 2 000 升涂料，基于直接材料，约当产量为 2 000 升涂料，每升涂料的直接材料成本为 $0.60，在制品账目月末余额中的直接材料成本为 $1 200（$0.60 × 2 000 = $1 200）；基于加工成本，约当产量为 600 升涂料，每升

带你到北美学习
管理会计
Take You to
North America
to Learn
Managerial Accounting

涂料的加工成本为 $0.40，在制品账目月末余额中的加工成本为 $240（$0.40 ×
600 = $240）。Blending Department 的在制品账目月末余额为 $1 440（$1 200 +
$240 = $1 440）。

完工的 6 000 升涂料成本为 $6 000，在制品账目月末余额为 $1 440，因此已核
实总成本为 $7 440（$6 000 + $1 440 = $7 440）。

Costs of units completed and transferred out to Packaging Department in May		$6,000
Costs remaining in May 31 work in process inventory		
Direct materials	$1,200	
Conversion	240	
Total costs of May 31 work in process inventory		1,440
Total costs accounted for		$7,440

答案：

Blending Department
Production Cost Report（Weighted Average Method）
For the month ended by May 31

	Physical Units	Direct Materials Percent Complete	Conversion Percent Complete	Direct Materials	Conversion
		Percent Complete		**Equivalent Units**	
Units to account for:					
Work in process, May 1	0				
Started in production in May	8,000				
Total physical units to account for	8,000				
Units accounted for:					
Completed and transferred out in May	6,000			6,000	6,000
Work in process, May 31	2,000	100%	30%	2,000	600
Total physical units accounted for	8,000				
Total equivalent units				8,000	6,600

	Direct Materials	Conversion	Total
Work in process, May 1	$0	$0	$0

Costs incurred in May	4,800	2,640	7,440
Total costs to account for	$4,800	$2,640	$7,440
Equivalent units	÷ 8,000	÷ 6,600	
Costs per equivalent unit	$0.60	$0.40	$1.00
Costs of units completed and transferred out to Packaging Department in May			$6,000
Costs remaining in May 31 work in process inventory			
Direct materials		$1,200	
Conversion		240	
Total costs of May 31 work in process inventory			1,440
Total costs accounted for			$7,440

2. Present the journal entries to record the use of direct materials and direct labour and the manufacturing overhead allocated to the Blending Department. Also, record the journal entry for the costs of the litres completed and transferred out to the Packaging Department.

讲解一： 5 月份，Blending Department 所用直接材料成本为 $4 800。在加工开始之后，生产所用直接材料将从原材料库存移入在制品库存，因此 Blending Department 的在制品库存账目增长 $4 800，原材料库存账目减少 $4 800。日记账分录借方和贷方分别记录 Blending Department 的在制品库存账目（work in process inventory – blending）和原材料库存账目（raw materials inventory）。

答案一：

Work in process inventory – Blending	4,800	
Raw materials inventory		4,800

讲解二： 5 月份，Blending Department 承担直接人工成本 $800，这些直接人工成本计入在制品库存，因此 Blending Department 的在制品库存账目增长 $800，应付工资账目增长 $800。日记账分录借方和贷方分别记录 Blending Department 的在制品库存账目（work in process inventory – blending）和应付工资账目（wages payable）。

带你到北美学习
管理会计
Take You to
North America
to Learn
Managerial Accounting

答案二：

Work in process inventory – Blending	800	
Wages payable		800

讲解三： 5 月份，Blending Department 的分摊制造费用为 $1 840，因此 Blending Department 的在制品库存账目增长 $1 840，制造费用账目减少 $1 840。日记账分录借方和贷方分别记录 Blending Department 的在制品库存账目（work in process inventory – blending）和制造费用账目（manufacturing overhead）。

答案三：

Work in process inventory – Blending	1,840	
Manufacturing overhead		1,840

讲解四： 5 月份，Blending Department 将完工的 6 000 升涂料转至 Packaging Department，每升涂料成本为 $1，完工的 6 000 升涂料成本为 $6 000。Packaging Department 的在制品库存账目增长 $6 000，Blending Department 的在制品库存账目减少 $6 000，日记账分录借方和贷方分别记录 Packaging Department 的在制品库存账目（work in process inventory – packaging）和 Blending Department 的在制品库存账目（work in process inventory – blending）。

答案四：

Work in process inventory – Packaging	6,000	
Work in process inventory – Blending		6,000

3. Post the journal entries to Work in Process Inventory – Blending. What is the ending balance of this account?

```
         Work in Process Inventory–Blending
Beg. Bal          0 | 6,000
              4,800 |
                800 |
              1,840 |
            _____|
End. Bal      1,440 |
```

答案： The ending balance of Work in Process Inventory – Blending is $1,440.

专业名词汇编
Glossary of Accounting Terms

订单成本计算法	job-order costing	分步成本计算法	process costing
分批成本计算法	job costing	加工成本	conversion cost
加权平均法	weighted average method	生产成本报告	production cost report
完工程度	percentage of process completed	先进先出法	first-in, first-out method
需核算总成本	total cost to account for	已核实总成本	total cost accounted for
约当产量	equivalent unit	直接材料	direct materials
直接人工	direct labour	制造成本	manufacturing cost
制造费用	manufacturing overhead	转入成本	transferred-in cost

成本习性与边际贡献收益表

Cost Behaviour and Contribution
Margin Income Statement

带你到北美学习
管理会计
Take You to
North America
to Learn
Managerial Accounting

5.1 变动成本

Variable Costs

变动成本指在相关范围内，成本总额的变化与活动作业量的变化呈正比关系的成本。换言之，在相关范围内，当制造商增加产量时，变动成本总额随之呈正比增加；当制造商降低产量时，变动成本总额随之呈正比减少。

假设一家咖啡店每天最多出售 5 000 杯咖啡，每杯咖啡的售价为 $2，每只纸杯的成本为 $0.50，每日店面租金为 $200。2017 年 3 月 9 日，咖啡店出售了 800 杯咖啡，赚取销售额 $1 600，纸杯成本总额为 $400，店面租金为 $200；3 月 10 日，咖啡店出售了 1 000 杯咖啡，赚取销售额 $2 000，纸杯成本总额为 $500，店面租金为 $200；3 月 11 日，咖啡店出售了 1 200 杯咖啡，赚取销售额 $2 400，纸杯成本总额为 $600，店面租金为 $200。每只纸杯的成本（$0.50）恒定不变，而纸杯成本总额随咖啡销量的变动而变化，因此纸杯成本属于变动成本。我们可以得出结论：在相关范围内，虽然变动成本总额与活动作业量呈正比关系，但单位变动成本保持不变。

如何运用数学等式（mathematical equation）表述纸杯成本总额与咖啡销量之间的正比关系，即变动成本等式？变动成本总额（total variable cost）等于单位变动成本（variable cost per unit）乘以活动作业量（volume of activity），因此变动成本等式为 $y = vx$，y 代表变动成本总额（total variable cost），v 代表单位变动成本，x 代表活动作业量（见图 5-1）。

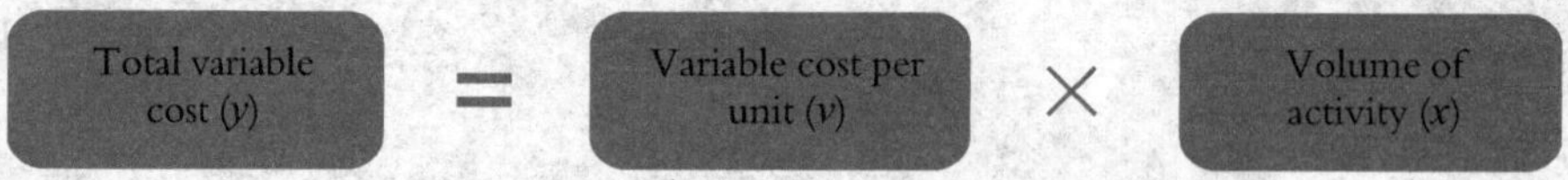

$$\boxed{\text{Total variable cost } (y)} = \boxed{\text{Variable cost per unit } (v)} \times \boxed{\text{Volume of activity } (x)}$$

图 5 - 1 变动成本计算公式

变动成本图像也称变动成本线（variable cost line），如图 5-2 所示。变动成本线始于坐标原点（origin），没有截距（intercept），变动成本线的斜率（slope）为单位变动成本；x 轴代表活动作业量，y 轴代表变动成本总额。如果没有出售咖啡，咖啡店不产生任何变动成本（纸杯成本），因此变动成本线始于坐标原点。每只纸杯的成本为 $0.50，即单位变动成本，说明变动成本线的斜率为 $0.50。2017 年 3 月 10 日，咖啡店出售了 1 000 杯咖啡，每只纸杯的成本为 $0.50，因此纸杯成本总额（变动成本总额）为 $500。变动成本线经过坐标点（1 000，$500），表示 3 月 10

日的咖啡销量与变动成本总额。

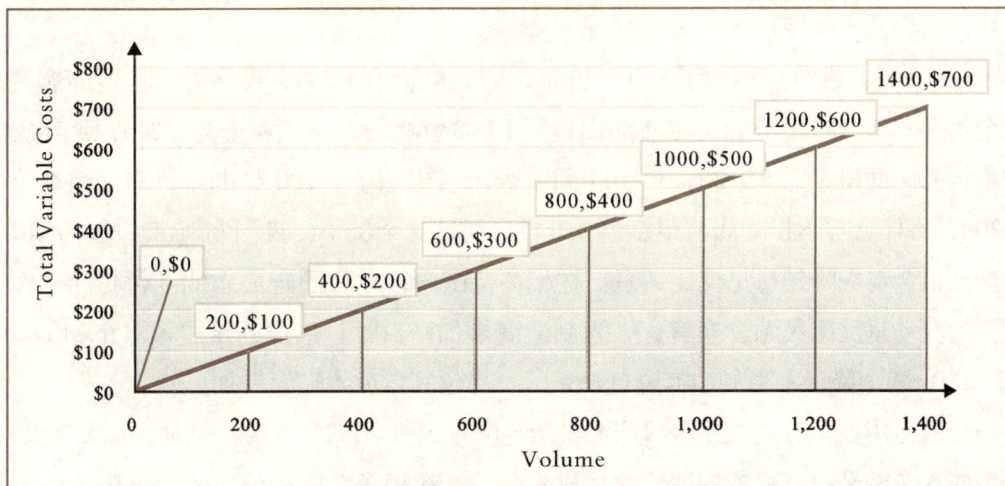

图 5 - 2　变动成本线

"说明 5 -1"为变动成本的重要特性。

说明 5 - 1：变动成本重要特性
（1）在相关范围内，变动成本总额与活动作业量呈正比关系； （2）在相关范围内，单位变动成本保持不变，单位变动成本是变动成本线的斜率； （3）变动成本线通常始于坐标原点、没有截距，即当活动作业量为 0 时，变动成本总额也为 $0； （4）变动成本等式为 $y = vx$，y 代表变动成本总额，v 代表单位变动成本，x 代表活动作业量。

5.2　固定成本
Fixed Costs

与变动成本不同，固定成本指在相关范围内，成本总额不随活动作业量变动而变化的成本。换言之，在相关范围内，固定成本总额（total fixed cost）恒定不变。假设一家咖啡店每天最多出售 5 000 杯咖啡，每杯咖啡的售价为 $2，每只纸杯的成本为 $0.50，每日店面租金为 $200。2017 年 3 月 9 日，咖啡店出售了 800 杯咖啡，赚取销售额 $1 600，纸杯成本总额为 $400，店面租金为 $200；3 月 10 日，咖啡店出售了 1 000 杯咖啡，赚取销售额 $2 000，纸杯成本总额为 $500，店面租金为 $200；3 月 11 日，咖啡店出售了 1 200 杯咖啡，赚取销售额 $2 400，纸杯成本总额为 $600，店面租金为 $200。纸杯成本总额随咖啡销量的变动而呈正比变化，因

带你到北美学习
管理会计
Take You to
North America
to Learn
Managerial Accounting

此纸杯成本属于变动成本，而每日店面租金为 $200，不随咖啡销量的变动而变化，故店面租金属于固定成本。

3 月 9 日，咖啡店出售了 800 杯咖啡，店面租金为 $200，每杯咖啡承担的店面租金为 $0.25；3 月 10 日，咖啡店出售了 1 000 杯咖啡，店面租金为 $200，每杯咖啡承担的店面租金为 $0.20；3 月 11 日，咖啡店出售了 1 200 杯咖啡，店面租金为 $200，每杯咖啡承担的店面租金为 $0.17。通过这个例子，我们发现每杯咖啡承担的店面租金与咖啡销量呈反比关系。在相关范围内，单位固定成本的变化与活动作业量的变动呈反比关系。换言之，当制造商增加产量时，单位固定成本（fixed cost per unit）随之降低；当制造商降低产量时，单位固定成本随之增加。

如何运用数学等式表述每日店面租金与咖啡销量之间的关系，即固定成本等式？固定成本总额是给定财务周期的固定成本金额，在相关范围内恒定不变，因此固定成本等式为 $y = f$，y 代表固定成本总额（total fixed cost），f 代表给定财务周期的固定成本金额，如图 5-3 所示。

| Total fixed cost (y) | = | Fixed cost over a period of time (f) |

图 5 - 3　固定成本计算等式

固定成本图像以水平线（horizontal line）呈现，也称固定成本线（fixed cost line），如图 5-4 所示。固定成本线不始于坐标原点（origin），斜率（slope）为 0；固定成本线与 y 轴相交，与 y 轴的交点是 y 轴截距（intercept），即固定成本总额；x

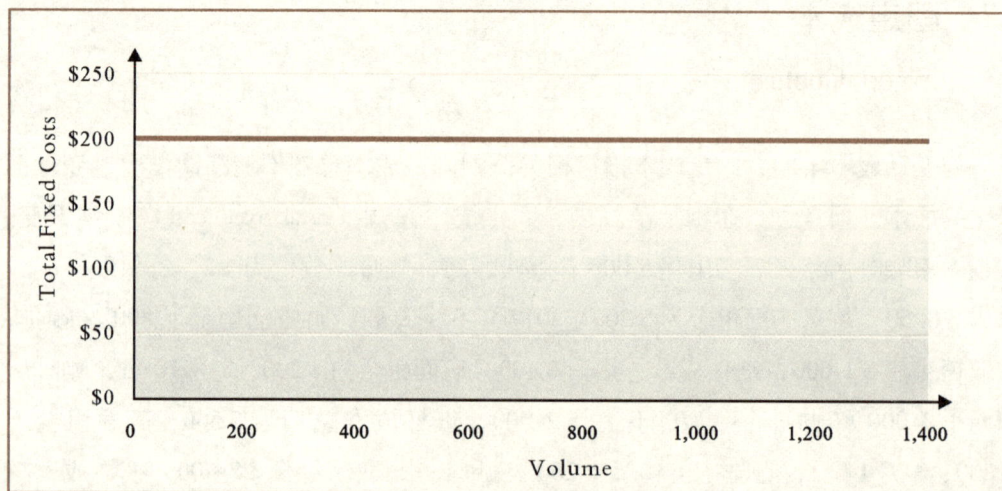

图 5 - 4　固定成本线

轴代表活动作业量，y 轴代表固定成本总额。因为就算没有出售咖啡，咖啡店依旧承担固定成本（每日店面租金），所以固定成本线不始于坐标原点。只要咖啡量在相关范围内，即 $0 \leqslant x \leqslant 5\,000$，店面租金都是 $\$200$，因此固定成本线是一条与 y 轴交于坐标（0，$\$200$）的水平线。

"说明 5-2" 为固定成本的重要特性。

5.3　混合成本

Mixed Costs

混合成本（mixed cost）指在相关范围内，成本总额随活动作业量的变动而变化，但成本总额变化与活动作业量的变动不呈正比关系的成本。混合成本既包含固定成本，又包含变动成本。换言之，在相关范围内，当制造商增加产量时，混合成本总额随之增长，但混合成本总额的变化与制造商产量的变动不呈正比关系。继续用咖啡店的例子来说明，纸杯成本总额随咖啡销量的变动而呈正比变化，属于变动成本；每日店面租金为 $\$200$，不随咖啡销量的变动而变化，属于固定成本；每日成本总额随活动作业量的变动而变化，但它们之间不呈正比关系，属于混合成本。

2017 年 3 月 9 日，咖啡店出售 800 杯咖啡，产生成本 $\$600$，因此每杯咖啡承担的成本为 $\$0.75$；3 月 10 日，咖啡店出售 1 000 杯咖啡，产生成本 $\$700$，因此每杯咖啡承担的成本为 $\$0.70$；3 月 11 日，咖啡店出售 1 200 杯咖啡，产生成本 $\$800$，因此每杯咖啡承担的成本为 $\$0.67$。当咖啡销量增加时，每杯咖啡承担的成本降低，而当咖啡销量降低时，每杯咖啡承担的成本增加。在相关范围内，单位混合成本的变化与活动作业量的变动呈反比关系。换言之，当制造商增加产量时，单位混合成本（mixed cost per unit）随之降低；当制造商降低产量时，单位混合成本随之增加。

混合成本既包含固定成本，又包含变动成本，即混合成本总额等于变动成本总额与固定成本总额之和。混合成本等式为 $y = vx + f$，y 代表混合成本总额（total

带你到北美学习
管理会计
Take You to
North America
to Learn
Managerial Accounting

mixed cost)，v 代表单位变动成本（variable cost per unit），x 代表活动作业量（volume of activity），f 代表固定成本总额，如图 5-5 所示。

$$\text{Total mixed cost} \ (y) = \text{Total variable cost} \ (vx) + \text{Total fixed cost} \ (f)$$

图 5-5　混合成本计算公式

通过混合成本等式，我们进一步分析，为什么混合成本总额随活动作业量的变动而变化，但混合成本总额的变化与活动作业量的变动不呈正比关系？为什么单位混合成本的变化与活动作业量的变动呈反比关系？

在相关范围内，变动成本总额的变化与活动作业量的变动呈正比关系，而固定成本总额不随活动作业量的变动而变化。混合成本中的变动成本部分使混合成本总额随活动作业量的变动而变化，但混合成本中的固定成本部分使混合成本总额的变化与活动作业量的变动不呈正比关系。

在相关范围内，单位固定成本的变化与活动作业量的变动呈反比关系。换言之，当制造商增加产量时，单位固定成本随之降低；当制造商降低产量时，单位固定成本随之增加。混合成本中的固定成本部分使单位混合成本的变化与活动作业量的变动呈反比关系。

混合成本既包含固定成本，又包含变动成本，所以混合成本图像既具有变动成本图像的特点，又具有固定成本图像的特点，如图 5-6 所示。混合成本线不始于坐标系原点；混合成本线与 y 轴相交，与 y 轴的交点是 y 轴截距，即固定成本总额（total fixed cost）；混合成本线的斜率为单位变动成本（variable cost per unit）；x 轴代表活动作业量（volume of activity），y 轴代表混合成本总额（total mixed cost）。如果没有出售咖啡，咖啡店依旧承担固定成本（每日店面租金），因此混合成本线与 y 轴交于坐标点（0，$\$200$），即 y 轴截距；每只纸杯的成本为 $\$0.50$，即单位变动成本，混合成本线的斜率为 $\$0.50$。

2017 年 3 月 10 日，咖啡店出售 1 000 杯咖啡，店面租金（固定成本）为 $\$200$，纸杯成本（变动成本）为 $\$500$，共计产生成本（混合成本）$\$700$。混合成本线经过坐标点（1 000，$\$700$），表示 3 月 10 日的咖啡销量与混合成本总额。

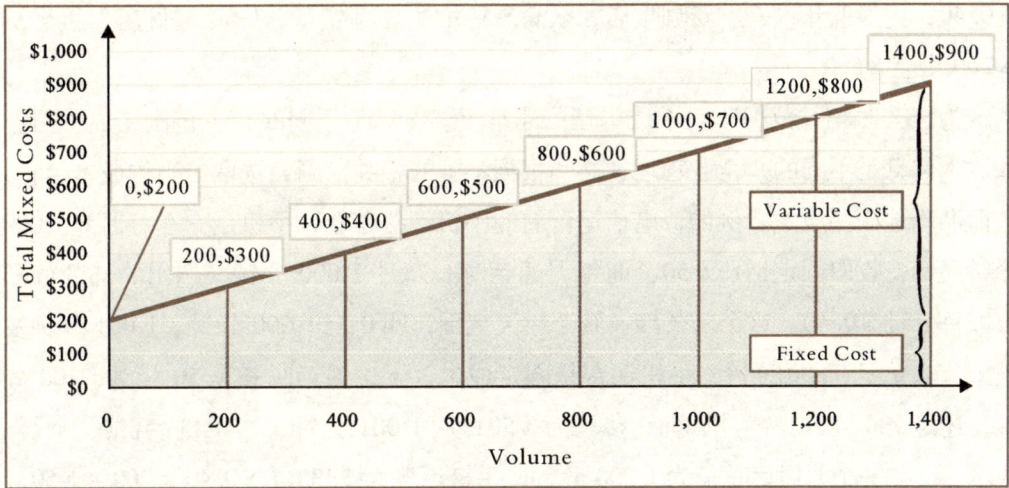

图 5 - 6　混合成本线

"说明 5 -3"为混合成本的重要特性。

说明 5 - 3：混合成本重要特性
（1）混合成本中的变动成本部分使混合成本总额随活动作业量的变动而变化，但混合成本中的固定成本部分使混合成本总额的变化与活动作业量的变动不呈正比关系； （2）混合成本中的固定成本部分使单位混合成本的变化与活动作业量的变动呈反比关系； （3）混合成本线不始于坐标系原点；混合成本线与 y 轴相交，与 y 轴的交点是 y 轴截距，即固定成本总额；混合成本线的斜率为单位变动成本； （4）混合成本等式为 $y = vx + f$，y 代表混合成本总额，v 代表单位变动成本，x 代表活动作业量，f 代表固定成本总额。

5.4　相关范围

Relevant Range

在讲解变动成本、固定成本和混合成本的重要特性时，均提到了一个前提，即"在相关范围内"。相关范围指活动作业量的特定值域。在相关范围内，单位变动成本（variable cost per unit）与固定成本总额（total fixed cost）恒定不变；然而，如果活动作业量的值域改变，即相关范围改变，单位变动成本与固定成本总额也随之改变。假设一家咖啡店每天最多出售 5 000 杯咖啡，每杯咖啡的售价为 \$2，每只纸杯的成本为 \$0.50，每日店面租金为 \$200。由于几家大型企业总部的新址搬迁至这家咖啡店附近，所以咖啡店的咖啡销量猛增，经常突破 5 000 杯。为此，咖啡店老板决定：与纸杯供应商协商，每天采购更多的纸杯，所以每只纸杯的成本可以降至

带你到北美学习
管理会计
Take You to
North America
to Learn
Managerial Accounting

$0.40；在附近开设一家新咖啡店，以满足猛增的咖啡销量，因此每日店面租金从
$200 增至 $500。

为什么"相关范围"对于成本预测非常重要？对于不同的相关范围，成本习性
和成本信息是不同的，企业管理者必须根据不同的相关范围，选取恰当的成本信息，
进而准确地预测成本。例如，电信运营商的手机话费套餐，手机用户在每月前 1 000
分钟通话，收取固定话费 $50，而每月通话时长超过 1 000 分钟，超出的部分额外
收取每分钟 $0.40。这个例子涉及两个相关范围，即 0 至 1 000 分钟、1 001 分钟及
以上。从 0 至 1 000 分钟，手机话费是固定成本，无论通话时长是 50 分钟、100 分
钟，还是 900 分钟，每月手机话费均为 $50；从 1 001 分钟起，手机话费属于混合
成本，比如一个月通话时长为 1 200 分钟，手机话费为 $130（$0.40 × 200 + $50 =
$130）（见图 5-7）。

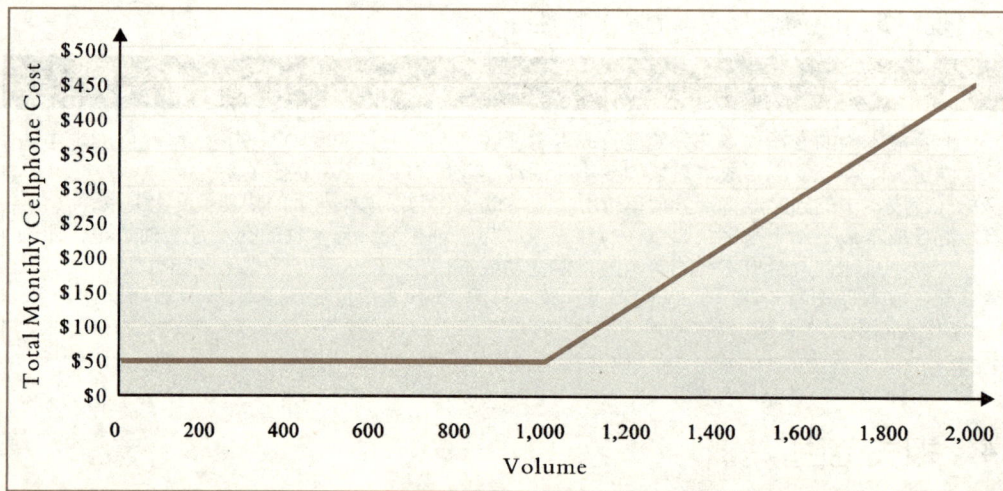

图 5 - 7　每月手机话费

5.5　确定成本等式

Determining the Cost Equation

我们一般使用如下两种方法确定成本等式：①高低点法（high-low method）；
②回归分析法（regression analysis method）。两种方法之间的区别：高低点法使用历
史数据中的两组数据确定成本等式，而回归分析法使用所有历史数据确定成本等式。
理论上，回归分析法在两者中更佳。

5.5.1 高低点法

High-Low Method

如何使用高低点法确定成本等式？相比于回归分析法，高低点法是一种非常简单的成本等式确定方法，仅使用最高与最低活动作业量数据。通过"案例5-1"，学习采用高低点法确定成本等式。

案例 5 - 1

A corporation is trying to predict its manufacturing overhead for the upcoming year. Its management is debating the high-low method versus the regression analysis method. The corporation has gathered the following information about the manufacturing overhead and its associated cost driver（machine hour）in each of the past six months：

Month	Manufacturing Overhead	Machine Hours
April	$ 22,000	12,250
May	22,860	12,510
June	21,600	11,280
July	21,800	11,410
August	21,250	10,980
September	21,930	11,670

Required：

1. What is the cost equation if the high-low method is used to estimate manufacturing overhead?

2. Using the high-low method, predict total manufacturing overhead if the corporation uses 12,000 hours.

讲解： 首先，需要确定最高与最低活动作业量。最高活动作业量是机器运转 12 510 小时，最低活动作业量是机器运转 10 980 小时。机器运转 12 510 小时对应的制造费用为 $ 22 860，机器运转 10 980 小时对应的制造费用为 $ 21 250。

Month	Manufacturing Overhead	Machine Hours
April	$ 22,000	12,250
May	22,860	12,510

带你到北美学习
管理会计
Take You to
North America
to Learn
Managerial Accounting

Month	Manufacturing Overhead	Machine Hours
June	21,600	11,280
July	21,800	11,410
August	21,250	10,980
September	21,930	11,670

上述两组数据可以形成如下二元一次方程组，自变量（x）代表机器运转时长，因变量（y）代表制造费用。

$$\begin{cases} \$22\ 860 = 12\ 510v + f \ (\text{High}) \\ \$21\ 250 = 10\ 980v + f \ (\text{Low}) \end{cases}$$

通过计算得出，单位变动成本（v）约为 \$1.05，固定成本总额（f）约为 \$9 695.88，因此成本等式为 $y = \$1.05x + \$9\ 695.88$。

再计算机器运转 12 000 小时产生的制造费用。将 12 000（x）代入成本等式（$y = \$1.05x + \$9\ 695.88$），得出制造费用（$y$）为 \$22 295.88。

5.5.2 回归分析法

Regression Analysis Method

回归分析法是一种运用所有历史数据确定成本等式的统计方法。与高低点法不同，回归分析法使用所有历史数据，因此可以提供更精确的成本等式，以求最佳匹配历史数据。通过"案例 5-2"，学习采用回归分析法确定成本等式。

案例 5 - 2

A corporation is trying to predict its manufacturing overhead for the upcoming year. Its management is debating the high-low method versus the regression analysis method. The corporation has gathered the following information about the manufacturing overhead and its associated cost driver (machine hour) in each of the past six months:

Month	Manufacturing Overhead	Machine Hours
April	\$22,000	12,250
May	22,860	12,510
June	21,600	11,280

Month	Manufacturing Overhead	Machine Hours
July	21,800	11,410
August	21,250	10,980
September	21,930	11,670

Required:

1. What is the cost equation if the regression analysis method is used to estimate manufacturing overhead?

2. Using the regression analysis method, predict total manufacturing overhead if the corporation uses 12,000 hours.

讲解: 我们必须使用 Microsoft Excel 进行回归分析, 以确定成本等式 ($y = vx + f$)。如图 5-8 所示, 回归分析结果提供了许多数据, 但对于确定成本等式, 仅需三类数据: Intercept, X Variable 1, R-Square。

Intercept 是混合成本线与坐标系 y 轴的交点, 即 y 轴截距, 呈现混合成本等式中的固定成本总额 (f)。

X Variable 1 是混合成本线的斜率, 代表混合成本等式中的单位变动成本 (v)。

R-Square 反映回归线 (regression line) 匹配历史数据的程度, 因此 R-Square 数据也被称为 goodness-of-fit 数据。R-Square 的值域为 0~1。在管理会计学中, R-Square 体现了成本等式中的活动作业量 (x) 与成本 (y) 之间的关联程度, 提供给企业管理者非常有用的信息。一般来说, 如果 R-Square 接近于 0, 说明活动作业量 (x) 与成本 (y) 之间几乎无关联; 如果 R-Square 等于 1, 说明活动作业量 (x) 与成本 (y) 之间具有完美关联。R-Square 数值越大, 说明活动作业量 (x) 与成本 (y) 之间的关联越强。从企业管理者角度出发, 当 R-Square 大于 0.80 时, 请放心使用成本等式; 当 R-Square 大于 0.50、小于 0.80 时, 请谨慎使用成本等式; 当 R-Square 小于 0.50 时, 说明活动作业量 (x) 与成本 (y) 之间关系很弱, 建议管理者不要使用成本等式, 应重新进行成本分析 (cost analysis), 以寻找更合适、更精确的成本分摊基础 (cost allocation base), 即成本动因 (cost driver)。

从图 5-8 可获知, Intercept 约为 12 116.14, 说明成本等式中的 f 约为 $12 116.14; X Variable 1 约为 0.84, 说明成本等式中的 v 约为 $0.84; R-Square 约为 0.838 4, 说明可以放心使用成本等式 ($y = $0.84x + $12 116.14$), 预测在相关范围内机器运转时长 (x) 带来的制造费用 (y)。

带你到北美学习
管理会计
Take You to
North America
to Learn
Managerial Accounting

计算机器运转 12 000 小时产生的制造费用。将 12 000（x）代入成本等式（$y = $0.84x + $12 116.14$），得出制造费用（y）为 $22 196.14。

SUMMARY OUTPUT					
Regression Statistics					
Multiple R	0.915617656				
R Square	0.838355692				
Adjusted R Square	0.797944615				
Standard Error	242.4610086				
Observations	6				
ANOVA					
	df	SS	MS	F	Significance F
Regression	1	1219583.971	1219583.971	20.74569042	0.010380153
Residual	4	235149.3628	58787.3407		
Total	5	1454733.333			
	Coefficients	Standard Error	t Stat	P-value	Lower 95%
Intercept	12116.14007	2151.800921	5.630697503	0.004894245	6141.782938
X Variable 1	0.837990864	0.183982001	4.554743727	0.010380153	0.327174938

图 5 - 8　**Microsoft Excel 回归分析结果**

5.6　边际贡献收益表

Contribution Margin Income Statement

无论是在《带你到北美学习财务会计》一书，还是本书前四章，所涉及的收益表均以成本功能（cost function）进行成本分类，如售出商品成本（cost of goods sold）、经营费用（operating expense）、市场费用（marketing expense）、折旧费用（depreciation expense）等，这类收益表被称为传统收益表（traditional income statement）。毛利润（gross profit）是传统收益表的分界线。毛利润以上部分体现与生产或采购环节有关的成本，如售出商品成本；毛利润以下部分体现与研发、设计、采购、市场营销、配送和客户服务环节有关的成本，如经营费用、市场费用、折旧费用等（见说明 5-4）。

传统收益表很难为企业管理者提供有价值的成本习性信息，因为这类收益表不能将成本分为变动成本或固定成本。虽然传统收益表对投资人（investor）和债权人（creditor）等外部使用者很有价值，但内部使用者一般需要成本习性信息，进而对企业进行规划并制定决策，因此传统收益表对内部使用者帮助有限。

说明 5-4：传统收益表

<table>
<tr><th colspan="3">Traditional Income Statement
For the year ended by December 31</th></tr>
<tr><td>Sales revenue</td><td></td><td>$ 987,000</td></tr>
<tr><td>Cost of goods sold</td><td></td><td>(665,000)</td></tr>
<tr><td>Gross profit</td><td></td><td>322,000</td></tr>
<tr><td>Operating expenses</td><td></td><td></td></tr>
<tr><td>Selling and marketing expenses</td><td>$ 61,000</td><td></td></tr>
<tr><td>Website maintenance expense</td><td>56,000</td><td></td></tr>
<tr><td>Other operating expenses</td><td>17,000</td><td></td></tr>
<tr><td>Total operating expenses</td><td></td><td>(134,000)</td></tr>
<tr><td>Operating income</td><td></td><td>$188,000</td></tr>
</table>

为向内部使用者提供有价值的成本习性信息，企业必须编写边际贡献收益表（contribution margin income statement）。财务会计报告准则要求，企业不可以使用边际贡献收益表对外公布财务信息，所以边际贡献收益表仅对内部使用者有益。边际贡献收益表以成本习性（变动成本或固定成本）进行成本分类，而非成本功能。通过"案例5-3"，学习边际贡献收益表的编写。

案例 5-3

As a small retail business, Pets specializes in the sale of accessories. The business is owned by a sole proprietor and operated out of her home. The actual results for last year were as follows:

<table>
<tr><th colspan="3">Pets
Income Statement
For the year ended by December 31</th></tr>
<tr><td>Sales revenue</td><td></td><td>$ 987,000</td></tr>
<tr><td>Cost of goods sold</td><td></td><td>(665,000)</td></tr>
<tr><td>Gross profit</td><td></td><td>322,000</td></tr>
<tr><td>Operating expenses</td><td></td><td></td></tr>
<tr><td>Selling and marketing expenses</td><td>$ 61,000</td><td></td></tr>
<tr><td>Website maintenance expense</td><td>56,000</td><td></td></tr>
</table>

带你到北美学习
管理会计
Take You to
North America
to Learn
Managerial Accounting

Other operating expenses	17,000	
Total operating expenses		(134,000)
Operating income		$188,000

For internal planning and decision-making purposes, the owner of Pets would like to translate the traditional income statement into the contribution margin format. Since Pets is a retailer, the cost of goods sold was variable. A large portion of the selling and marketing expenses consisted of freight-out charges ($19,000), which were also variable. Only 20% of the remaining selling and marketing expenses and 25% of the website maintenance expense were variable. 90% of the other operating expenses were fixed.

Required:

Based on these information, prepare Pets' contribution margin income statement for last year.

讲解：　首先，根据成本习性（变动成本或固定成本）进行成本分类。Cost of goods sold 属于变动成本，Selling and marketing expenses 中价值为 $19 000 的 Freight-out charges 属于变动成本，20% 的剩余 Selling and marketing expenses 也属于变动成本，即价值为 $27 400 的 Selling and marketing expenses 属于变动成本（$19 000 + ($61 000 – $19 000) × 20% = $27 400），价值为 $33 600 的 Selling and marketing expenses 属于固定成本（$61 000 – $27 400 = $33 600）。25% 的 Website maintenance expenses 属于变动成本，即价值为 $14 000 的 Website maintenance expenses 归为变动成本（$56 000 × 25% = $14 000），价值为 $42 000 的 Website maintenance expenses 归为固定成本（$56 000 × 75% = $42 000）。90% 的 Other operating expenses 属于固定成本，即价值为 $15 300 的 Other operating expenses 属于固定成本（$17 000 × 90% = $15 300），价值为 $1 700 的 Other operating expenses 属于变动成本（$17 000 × 10% = $1 700）。

其次，贡献毛利（contribution margin）是边际贡献收益表的分界线。贡献毛利以上部分是变动成本，以下部分是固定成本。贡献毛利等于销售额（sales revenue）减去变动成本（variable cost）。

最后，单独讲解售出商品成本（cost of goods sold）。零售商一般从批发商手中采购商品，并将商品出售给消费者。对于零售商，售出商品成本属于变动成本；而对于制造商，售出商品成本是一种混合成本。因此，涉及"售出商品成本"时，一定要具体问题、具体分析，千万不要将售出商品成本默认为变动成本。

Pets Contribution Margin Income Statement For the year ended by December 31		
Sales revenue		$987,000
Variable expenses		
Cost of goods sold	$665,000	
Variable selling and marketing expenses	27,400	
Variable website maintenance expense	14,000	
Variable other operating expenses	1,700	(708,100)
Contribution margin		278,900
Fixed expenses		
Fixed selling and marketing expenses	33,600	
Fixed website maintenance expense	42,000	
Fixed other operating expenses	15,300	(90,900)
Operating income		$188,000

5.7 对比变动成本法与归纳成本法
Contrasting Variable Costing and Absorption Costing

为制定内部管理决策，管理者应使用变动成本法（variable costing）编写边际贡献收益表。变动成本法将直接材料成本、直接人工成本、变动性制造费用计入产品成本（product cost），固定性制造费用计入期间成本（period cost）。变动成本法的支持者认为，虽然固定性制造费用给予制造商生产能力，但无论是否生产产品，制造商在每个财务周期均产生固定性制造费用，因此固定性制造费用属于期间成本，而非产品成本。

为向投资人（investor）和债权人（creditor）等外部使用者提供有价值的信息，财务会计报告准则要求管理者使用归纳成本法（absorption costing）编写传统收益表。根据归纳成本法，直接材料成本、直接人工成本、变动性制造费用、固定性制造费用计入产品成本。归纳成本法的支持者认为，如果没有固定性制造费用，制造商不能生产产品，因此固定性制造费用也应计入产品成本。在讲解本书前四章时，我们将固定性制造费用计入产品成本。

带你到北美学习
管理会计
Take You to
North America
to Learn
Managerial Accounting

　　无论变动成本法，还是归纳成本法，直接材料成本、直接人工成本和变动性制造费用均计入产品成本，而非制造成本（non-manufacturing cost）则计入期间成本（见说明5-5）。

说明5-5：对比归纳成本法与变动成本法		
	Absorption Costing	Variable Costing
Product Costs	Direct materials Direct labour Variable manufacturing overhead *Fixed manufacturing overhead*	Direct materials Direct labour Variable manufacturing overhead
Period Costs	Variable non-manufacturing costs Fixed non-manufacturing costs	*Fixed manufacturing overhead* Variable non-manufacturing costs Fixed non-manufacturing costs
Focus	*External reporting*	*Internal reporting*
Income Statement Format	*Traditional income statement*	*Contribution margin income statement*

　　通过以下案例，进一步分析归纳成本法与变动成本法之间的区别。

案例5-4

GG Corporation produces and sells a single product. The corporation has provided the following data about September 2014：

Units in finished goods inventory at August 31, 2014	500 units
Units produced during September	2,100 units
Units sold during September	1,900 units
Selling price per unit	$75
Direct materials per unit	$25
Direct labour per unit	$13
Variable manufacturing overhead per unit	$6
Sales commissions per unit	$8
Fixed manufacturing overhead each month	$37,500
Fixed administrative and depreciation expenses each month	$22,000

Although sales volume varies, the corporation has same production volume each month. Additionally, variable costs per unit and total fixed costs are consistent from month to month.

Required：

1. Prepare a traditional（absorption costing）income statement in good form for September.

2. Prepare a contribution margin income statement in good form for September.

讲解： 根据归纳成本法，单件产品成本为 $ 61.86，而根据变动成本法，单件产品成本为 $ 44。两种成本计算法的结果为什么会产生 $ 17.86 的差异？因为固定性制造费用（fixed manufacturing overhead）在归纳成本法中计入产品成本（product cost），而在变动成本法中则属于期间成本（period cost）。2014 年 9 月，GG Corporation 生产 2 100 件商品，产生固定性制造费用 $ 37 500，因此单件产品的固定性制造费用约为 $ 17.86 （ $ 37 500 ÷ 2 100 ≈ $ 17.86）。

	Absorption Costing	Variable Costing
Direct materials	$ 25.00	$ 25.00
Direct labour	13.00	13.00
Variable manufacturing overhead	6.00	6.00
Fixed manufacturing overhead	17.86	
Unit costs	$ 61.86	$ 44.00

如果使用归纳成本法（absorption costing），必须编写传统收益表体现财务信息。传统收益表依据成本功能（cost function）进行成本分类，如制造成本（manufacturing cost）和非制造成本（non-manufacturing cost）。毛利润（gross profit）是传统收益表的分界线。毛利润以上部分是制造成本，以下部分是非制造成本，即经营费用。毛利润等于销售额（sales revenue）减去售出商品成本（cost of goods sold）。

根据 "案例 5-4" 信息，2014 年 8 月 31 日，GG Corporation 拥有 500 件库存商品；经过 2014 年 9 月，生产 2 100 件商品，出售 1 900 件商品；2014 年 9 月 30 日，企业拥有 700 件库存商品。根据归纳成本法，单件商品成本为 $ 61.86，因此 2014 年 8 月 31 日的制成品库存账目余额为 $ 30 930 （ $ 61.86 × 500 = $ 30 930），制成商品成本为 $ 129 906 （ $ 61.86 × 2 100 = $ 129 906），售出商品成本为 $ 117 534 （ $ 61.86 × 1 900 = $ 117 534），2014 年 9 月 30 日的制成品库存账目余额为 $ 43 302 （ $ 61.86 × 700 = $ 43 302）。

2014 年 9 月，GG Corporation 出售 1 900 件商品，单件售价为 $ 75，销售额为 $ 142 500。销售额（ $ 142 500）减去售出商品成本（ $ 117 534）等于毛利润

带你到北美学习
管理会计
Take You to
North America
to Learn
Managerial Accounting

（＄24 966）。

2014 年 9 月，GG Corporation 出售 1 900 件商品，单件商品的销售佣金为 ＄8，产生销售佣金费用 ＄15 200；此外，GG Corporation 在同月还产生行政管理费用 ＄22 000。销售佣金费用和行政管理费用属于经营费用，因此经营费用总额为 ＄37 200。毛利润（＄24 966）减去经营费用总额（＄37 200）等于经营亏损（＄12 234）。

GG Corporation Income Statement（Absorption Costing） For the month ended by September 30，2014		
Sales revenue		＄142,500
Cost of goods sold：		
Beginning finished goods inventory	＄30,930	
Cost of goods manufactured	129,906	
Cost of goods available for sale	160,836	
Ending finished goods inventory	(43,302)	(117,534)
Gross profit		24,966
Operating expenses		
Sales commissions expense	15,200	
Administrative and depreciation expenses	22,000	(37,200)
Operating income		（＄12,234）

GG Corporation 希望预测出，如果销售额增长 10%，对经营收益产生的影响。因为传统收益表未将成本分为固定成本或变动成本，这限制了传统收益表在企业内部的使用，所以传统收益表很难为 GG Corporation 提供有效的关于"销售额增长 10%"的预测信息。由于归纳成本法和传统收益表的局限性，为了内部报告和决策制定，企业管理者更偏爱变动成本法和边际贡献收益表。

根据"案例 5-4"信息，2014 年 8 月 31 日，GG Corporation 拥有 500 件库存商品；2014 年 9 月，企业生产 2 100 件商品，出售 1 900 件商品；2014 年 9 月 30 日，企业拥有 700 件库存商品。根据变动成本法，单件商品成本为 ＄44，因此 2014 年 8 月 31 日的制成品库存账目余额为 ＄22 000（＄44 × 500 ＝ ＄22 000），变动性制成商品成本为 ＄92 400（＄44 × 2 100 ＝ ＄92 400），变动性售出商品成本为 ＄83 600（＄44 × 1 900 ＝ ＄83 600），2014 年 9 月 30 日的制成品库存账目余额为 ＄30 800（＄44 × 700 ＝ ＄30 800）；此外，单件商品的销售佣金为 ＄8，为出售 1 900 件商品，

GG Corporation 产生变动性销售佣金费用 $ 15 200。变动性制成商品成本和变动性销售佣金费用均属于变动成本，所以变动成本总额为 $ 98 800。

2014 年 9 月，GG Corporation 出售 1 900 件商品，单件售价为 $ 75，销售额为 $ 142 500。销售额（$ 142 500）减去变动成本总额（$ 98 800）等于贡献毛利（$ 43 700）。

固定性制造费用为 $ 37 500，固定性行政管理费用为 $ 22 000，因此固定成本总额为 $ 59 500。贡献毛利（$ 43 700）减去固定成本总额（$ 59 500）等于经营亏损（$ 15 800）。

GG Corporation Income Statement (Variable Costing) For the month ended by September 30, 2014		
Sales revenue		$ 142,500
Variable expenses		
Variable cost of goods sold:		
Beginning finished goods inventory	$ 22,000	
Variable cost of goods manufactured	92,400	
Variable cost of goods available for sale	114,400	
Ending finished goods inventory	(30,800)	
Variable cost of goods sold	83,600	
Sales commissions expense	15,200	(98,800)
Contribution margin		43,700
Fixed expenses		
Fixed manufacturing overhead	37,500	
Fixed administrative and depreciation expenses	22,000	(59,500)
Operating income		($ 15,800)

根据归纳成本法和传统收益表，经营亏损为 $ 12 234，而根据变动成本法和边际贡献收益表，经营亏损为 $ 15 800。为什么归纳成本法和变动成本法造成数值不同的经营收益或经营亏损？企业管理者如何对账两种成本计算法产生的、数值不同的经营收益或经营亏损？

变动成本法将固定性制造费用计入期间成本（period cost），而归纳成本法将固定性制造费用计入产品成本（product cost）。

带你到北美学习
管理会计
Take You to
North America
to Learn
Managerial Accounting

	Absorption Costing	Variable Costing
Direct materials	$ 25.00	$ 25.00
Direct labour	13.00	13.00
Variable manufacturing overhead	6.00	6.00
Fixed manufacturing overhead	17.86	
Unit costs	$ 61.86	$ 44.00

根据"案例5-4"信息,2014年8月31日,GG Corporation 拥有500件库存商品;2014年9月,企业生产2 100件商品,出售1 900件商品;2014年9月30日,企业拥有700件库存商品。相比于2014年8月31日的500件库存商品,9月30日的库存商品增长200件,增至700件。根据变动成本法,单件商品成本为$44,200件新增库存商品成本为$8 800;根据归纳成本法,单件商品成本为$61.86,200件新增库存商品成本为$12 372,说明归纳成本法将新增200件库存商品的固定性制造费用$3 572($17.86×200=$3 572)计入产品成本,并出现在资产负债表的制成品库存账目,而非收益表中的一种费用。

反观变动成本法,新增200件库存商品的固定性制造费用($3 572)计入期间成本,体现于收益表,而非资产负债表的制成品库存账目。相比于归纳成本法,变动成本法多支出费用$3 572,造成变动成本法的经营亏损($15 800)比归纳成本法的经营亏损($12 234)多$3 566。

同学们可能会疑惑:为什么变动成本法多支出费用$3 572,反而多亏损$3 566,而非$3 572?这是计算单件商品的固定性制造费用($37 500÷2 100=$17.857 143≈$17.86)保留小数所致。

我们总结一下,通过给定财务周期,如果生产商品数量大于出售商品数量,库存商品数量增加,归纳成本法的经营收益高于变动成本法的经营收益;如果生产商品数量小于出售商品数量,库存商品数量降低,归纳成本法的经营收益低于变动成本法的经营收益。

例题综述
Summary of Examples

例题 5 - 1

A company uses a regression analysis to predict total manufacturing overhead based on monthly direct labour hours incurred. In the regression analysis output, the fixed cost component is represented by the _____.

A. R - Square coefficient

B. X variable 1 coefficient

C. intercept coefficient

D. None of the above

讲解： Intercept 是混合成本线与坐标系 y 轴的交点，即 y 轴截距，呈现混合成本等式中的固定成本总额（f）。

X Variable 1 是混合成本线的斜率，代表混合成本等式中的单位变动成本（v）。

R - Square 反映了回归线（regression line）匹配历史数据的程度，因此 R - Square 也经常被称为 goodness - of - fit 数据。R - Square 的值域为 0 ~ 1。在管理会计学中，R - Square 体现了成本等式中的活动作业量（x）与成本（y）之间的关联程度。

答案： C

例题 5 - 2

In a contribution margin income statement, _____.

A. variable costs are above the gross profit line, fixed costs are below the gross profit line

B. variable manufacturing and non - manufacturing costs are above the gross profit line

C. fixed manufacturing and non - manufacturing costs are below the contribution margin line

D. variable manufacturing costs are above the contribution margin line, variable non - manufacturing costs are below the contribution margin line

讲解： 贡献毛利（contribution margin）是边际贡献收益表的分界线。贡献毛利以上部分是变动成本，以下部分是固定成本。贡献毛利等于销售额（sales revenue）减去变动成本（variable cost）。

答案： C

带你到北美学习
管理会计
Take You to
North America
to Learn
Managerial Accounting

例题 5 - 3

Within the relevant range, which of the following statements is true with respect to the fixed cost per unit?

A. It will increase as production increases.

B. It will decrease as production decreases.

C. It will increase as production decreases.

D. It will remain the same as production changes.

讲解： 固定成本有如下四点特性：①在相关范围内，固定成本总额不随生产作业活动的变动而变化；②在相关范围内，单位固定成本的变化与活动作业量的变动呈反比关系；③固定成本线不始于坐标原点，没有斜率；④固定成本线与 y 轴相交，与 y 轴的交点是 y 轴截距，即固定成本总额；⑤固定成本等式为 $y=f$，y 代表固定成本总额，f 代表给定财务周期的固定成本金额。

答案： C

例题 5 - 4

Which of the following statements is true with respect to the correct difference between absorption costing and variable costing?

A. In periods when sales exceed production, the variable costing operating income will be higher than the absorption costing operating income.

B. In periods when production exceeds sales, the absorption costing operating income will be lower than the variable costing operating income.

C. In periods when sales exceed production, absorption costing holds back the higher value of ending inventory compared with variable costing.

D. In periods when production exceeds sales, variable costing holds back the higher value of ending inventory compared with absorption costing.

讲解： 通过给定财务周期，如果生产商品数量大于出售商品数量，库存商品数量增加，那么归纳成本法的经营收益高于变动成本法的经营收益；如果生产商品数量小于出售商品数量，库存商品数量降低，那么归纳成本法的经营收益低于变动成本法的经营收益。

答案： A

例题 5 - 5

In an absorption costing income statement, the cost of goods sold _____.

A. includes fixed and variable non-manufacturing costs incurred

B. includes only fixed manufacturing overhead incurred

C. includes fixed and variable manufacturing overhead incurred

D. includes fixed and variable manufacturing costs incurred

讲解： 变动成本法（variable costing）将直接材料成本、直接人工成本、变动性制造费用计入产品成本（product cost），固定性制造费用计入期间成本（period cost），而归纳成本法（absorption costing）将直接材料成本、直接人工成本、变动性制造费用和固定性制造费用计入产品成本。

答案： D

例题 5 - 6

The manager at Mulch Company has been trying to calculate the portion of the company's manufacturing overhead that is fixed and the portion that is variable. Over the past year, the number of yards of mulch processed was the highest in July, the monthly manufacturing overhead totaled $6,000 for 25,000 yards of mulch processed. The lowest number of yards of mulch processed in the last twelve months occurred in October, the monthly manu-facturing overhead totaled $4,000 for 15,000 yards of mulch processed. Using the high-low method, Calculate the Mulch's fixed costs per month.

A. $1,000

B. $0.20

C. $4,000

D. $2,000

E. None of the above

讲解： 首先，需要确定最高与最低活动作业量。最高活动作业量是处理 25 000 码覆盖物，最低活动作业量是处理 15 000 码覆盖物；$25 000 码覆盖物对应的制造费用为 $6 000，15 000 码覆盖物对应的制造费用为 $4 000。

这两组数据可以形成如下二元一次方程组，自变量（x）代表处理的覆盖物，因变量（y）代表制造费用。

带你到北美学习
管理会计
Take You to
North America
to Learn
Managerial Accounting

$$\begin{cases} \$ 6\ 000 = 25\ 000v + f \ (\text{High}) \\ \$ 4\ 000 = 15\ 000v + f \ (\text{Low}) \end{cases}$$

通过计算得出，单位变动成本（v）为 $\$0.20$，固定成本总额（$f$）为 $\$1\ 000$。

答案： A

例题 5 - 7

The owner of Burger Stand is concerned because the stand has been averaging only 3,000 burger sales per month, the stand and its staffs can make 6,000 burgers per month. The variable costs of each burger are $\$2.50$. The monthly fixed costs are $\$7,500$. The owner wants some cost information about different volumes so that he can make operating decisions.

Required：

Fill in the following table to provide the information the owner wants.

Monthly sales in units	2,500 units	3,000 units	5,000 units
Total fixed costs			
Total variable costs			
Total costs			
Fixed costs per unit			
Variable costs per unit			
Average costs per unit			

讲解： 变动成本（variable cost）指在相关范围内，成本总额的变化与活动作业量的变动呈正比关系的成本。换言之，在相关范围内，当制造商增加产量时，变动成本总额随之呈正比增加；当制造商降低产量时，变动成本总额随之呈正比减少。在相关范围内，单位变动成本保持不变。

与变动成本不同，固定成本（fixed cost）指在相关范围内，成本总额不随活动作业量的变动而变化的成本。换言之，在相关范围内，固定成本总额恒定不变。在相关范围内，单位固定成本的变化与活动作业量的变动呈反比关系。当制造商增加产量时，单位固定成本随之降低；当制造商降低产量时，单位固定成本随之增加。

答案：

Monthly sales in units	2,500 units	3,000 units	5,000 units
Total fixed costs	$7,500	$7,500	$7,500
Total variable costs	6,250	7,500	12,500
Total costs	$13,750	$15,000	$20,000
Fixed costs per unit	$3.00	$2.50	$1.50
Variable costs per unit	2.50	2.50	2.50
Average costs per unit	$5.50	$5.00	$4.00

例题 5 - 8

Acme Mailboxes produces decorative mailboxes. The company's average costs per unit are $23.43 when it produces 1,400 mailboxes.

Required：

1. What are the total costs of producing 1,400 mailboxes?

2. If $15,000 of the total costs are fixed, what are the variable costs of producing each mailbox?

3. Write Acme Mailboxes' cost equation.

4. If the plant manager uses the average costs per unit to predict total costs, what would his forecast be for producing 1,700 mailboxes?

5. If the plant manager uses the cost equation to predict total costs, what would his forecast be for producing 1,700 mailboxes?

6. What is the dollar difference between your answers to Part 4. and Part 5.? Which approach to forecasting costs is appropriate? Why?

1. What are the total costs of producing 1,400 mailboxes?

讲解： Acme Mailboxes 生产 1 400 个邮箱，单个邮箱成本为 $23.43，总成本为 $32 802。

答案： The total costs of producing 1,400 mailboxes are $32,802.

2. If $15,000 of the total costs are fixed, what are the variable costs of producing each mailbox?

带你到北美学习
管理会计
Take You to
North America
to Learn
Managerial Accounting

讲解： 总成本为 $32 802，固定成本总额为 $15 000，变动成本总额为 $17 802。Acme Mailboxes 生产 1 400 个邮箱，产生变动成本 $17 802，因此单个邮箱的变动成本约为 $12.72（$17 802 ÷ 1 400 ≈ $12.72）。

答案： The variable costs of producing each mailbox are approximately $12.72.

3. Write Acme Mailboxes' cost equation.

讲解： 固定成本总额（f）为 $15 000，单个邮箱的变动成本（$v$）为 $12.72，成本等式为 $y = $12.72x + $15 000$。

答案： The cost equation is $y = $12.72x + $15,000$.

4. If the plant manager uses the average costs per unit to predict total costs, what would his forecast be for producing 1,700 mailboxes?

讲解： Acme Mailboxes 生产 1 700 个邮箱，单个邮箱成本为 $23.43，总成本为 $39 831。

答案： The estimated total costs of producing 1,700 mailboxes based on the average costs per unit are $39,831.

5. If the plant manager uses the cost equation to predict total costs, what would his forecast be for producing 1,700 mailboxes?

讲解： 将 1 700（x）代入成本等式（$y = $12.72x + $15 000$），得出总成本（y）为 $36 624。

答案： The expected total costs of producing 1,700 mailboxes are $36,624.

6. What is the dollar difference between your answers to Part 4. and Part 5.? Which approach to forecasting costs is appropriate? Why?

答案： The plant manager's forecast would be $3,207（$39,831 - $36,624 = $3,207$）too high if he uses the average costs per unit to predict costs. The average costs per unit are a mixed cost that will change as volume changes. If the manager uses the average costs per unit to predict costs, he is erroneously assuming that the average costs per unit do not change at different volumes. The manager should use the cost equation to predict costs since it correctly takes into account the variable and fixed costs of producing mailboxes.

例题 5 - 9

Production Volume	Total Costs
100	$ 4,800
200	6,100
250	8,000
300	8,500
400	14,000
480	21,000
500	20,500

Required:

1. Using the high-low method, determine the cost equation to estimate total costs.

2. Determine the estimated total costs of producing 410 units.

1. Using the high-low method, determine the cost equation to estimate total costs.

讲解： 首先，需要确定最高与最低活动作业量。最高活动作业量为 500 件商品，最低活动作业量为 100 件商品；500 件商品对应的总成本为 $ 20 500，100 件商品对应的总成本为 $ 4 800。

Production Volume	Total Costs
100	$ 4,800
200	6,100
250	8,000
300	8,500
400	14,000
480	21,000
500	20,500

这两组数据可以形成如下二元一次方程组，自变量（x）代表产量，因变量（y）代表总成本，

$$\begin{cases} \$ 20\ 500 = 500v + f\ (\text{High}) \\ \$ 4\ 800 = 100v + f\ (\text{Low}) \end{cases}$$

通过计算得出，单位变动成本（v）为 $ 39.25，固定成本总额（f）为 $ 875，成本等式为 $y = \$ 39.25x + \$ 875$。

带你到北美学习
管理会计
Take You to
North America
to Learn
Managerial Accounting

答案： Using the high-low method, the cost equation is $y = \$39.25x + \$875$.

2. Determine the estimated total costs of producing 410 units.

讲解： 将 410（x）代入成本等式（$y = \$39.25x + \$875$），得出总成本（$y$）为 $\$16\,967.50$。

答案： The estimated total costs of producing 410 units are $\$16,967.50$.

例题 5 - 10

The Lakeshore Hotel's guest days of occupancy and custodial supplies expense over the last seven months were as follows:

Month	Guest Days	Custodial Supplies Expense
March	8,000	$\$7,500$
April	12,500	8,250
May	15,000	10,500
June	20,500	12,000
July	24,000	13,500
August	19,000	10,750
September	14,500	9,750

Required：

1. Using the high-low method, determine the cost equation to estimate custodial supplies expense.

2. Using the cost equation derived in Part 1, estimate the custodial supplies expense in a month expected to have 11,000 guest days.

1. Using the high-low method, determine the cost equation to estimate custodial supplies expense.

讲解： 首先，需要确定最高与最低居住天数。最高居住天数为 24 000 天，最低居住天数为 8 000 天；24 000 天对应的办公用品费用为 $\$13\,500$，8 000 天对应的办公用品费用为 $\$7\,500$。

Month	Guest Days	Custodial Supplies Expense
March	8,000	$7,500
April	12,500	8,250
May	15,000	10,500
June	20,500	12,000
July	24,000	13,500
August	19,000	10,750
September	14,500	9,750

这两组数据可以形成如下二元一次方程组，自变量（x）代表客户居住天数，因变量（y）代表办公用品费用。

$$\begin{cases} \$13\ 500 = 24\ 000v + f\ (\text{High}) \\ \$7\ 500 = 8\ 000v + f\ (\text{Low}) \end{cases}$$

通过计算得出，单位变动成本（v）为 $0.375，固定成本总额（$f$）为 $4 500，成本等式为 $y = \$0.375x + \$4\ 500$。

答案： Using the high-low method, the cost equation is $y = \$0.375x + \$4,500$.

2. Using the cost equation derived in Part 1, estimate the custodial supplies expense in a month expected to have 11,000 guest days.

讲解： 将 11 000（x）代入成本等式（$y = \$0.375x + \$4\ 500$），得出办公用品费用（$y$）为 $8 625。

答案： Using the cost equation derived in Part 1, the custodial supplies expense expected to have 11,000 guest days is $8,625.

例题 5 - 11

Schultz Company, which uses the high-low method to analyze cost behavior patterns, has determined that the machine hours used can best predict the company's total costs. The company's cost and machine hour usage data for the first six months of the year are as follows：

带你到北美学习
管理会计
Take You to
North America
to Learn
Managerial Accounting

Month	Total Costs	Machine Hours
January	$3,420	1,090
February	3,720	1,160
March	3,590	1,040
April	3,760	1,200
May	4,600	1,310
June	4,086	1,440

Required:

1. What are the variable costs per machine hour?

2. What are the fixed costs each month?

3. If Schultz Company uses 1,220 machine hours in a month, what will its total costs be?

1. What are the variable costs per machine hour?

2. What are the fixed costs each month?

讲解： 首先，需要确定机器的最高与最低运转时间。机器最高运转时长为 1 440 小时，最低运转时长为 1 040 小时；1 440 小时对应的总成本为 $4 086，1 040 小时对应的总成本为 $3 590。

Month	Total Costs	Machine Hours
January	$3,420	1,090
February	3,720	1,160
March	3,590	1,040
April	3,760	1,200
May	4,600	1,310
June	4,086	1,440

这两组数据可以形成如下二元一次方程组，自变量 (x) 代表机器运转时长，因变量 (y) 代表总成本。

$$\begin{cases} \$4\ 086 = 1\ 440v + f \ (\text{High}) \\ \$3\ 590 = 1\ 040v + f \ (\text{Low}) \end{cases}$$

通过计算得出，单位变动成本 (v) 为 $1.24，固定成本总额 ($f$) 为 $2 300.40。

答案： Using the high-low method, the variable costs per machine hour are $1.24, the fixed costs each month are $2,300.40.

3. If Schultz Company uses 1,220 machine hours in a month, what will its total costs be?

讲解： 单位变动成本 (v) 为 $1.24，固定成本总额 ($f$) 为 $2 300.40，则成本等式为 $y = $1.24x + $2 300.40。将 1 220 ($x$) 代入成本等式，得出总成本 ($y$) 为 $3 813.20。

答案： If Schultz Company uses 1,220 machine hours in a month, its total costs will be $3,813.20.

例题 5 - 12

To plan for the future, Asokan, a pancake restaurant, needs to figure out its cost behaviour patterns. The restaurant has the following information about its operating costs and the number of pancakes served:

Month	Pancakes	Total Operating Costs
July	3,600	$2,340
August	3,900	2,390
September	3,200	2,320
October	3,300	2,270
November	3,850	2,560
December	3,620	2,530

Required：

1. Use the high-low method to determine Asokan's operating cost equation.

2. Use your answer from Part 1 to predict total operating costs if Asokan serves 4,000 pancakes in one month.

3. Can you predict total operating costs if Asokan serves 10,000 pancakes a month? Explain.

1. Use the high-low method to determine Asokan's operating cost equation.

讲解： 首先，需要确定 pancake 的最高与最低产量，最高产量为 3 900 个，最低产量为 3 200 个；3 900 个 pancake 对应的经营费用为 $2 390，3 200 个 pancake 对应的

带你到北美学习
管理会计
Take You to
North America
to Learn
Managerial Accounting

经营费用为 $2 320。

Month	Pancakes	Total Operating Costs
July	3,600	$2,340
August	3,900	2,390
September	3,200	2,320
October	3,300	2,270
November	3,850	2,560
December	3,620	2,530

这两组数据可以形成如下二元一次方程组，自变量（x）代表 pancake 产量，因变量（y）代表经营费用。

$$\begin{cases} \$2\ 390 = 3\ 900v + f\ (\text{High}) \\ \$2\ 320 = 3\ 200v + f\ (\text{Low}) \end{cases}$$

通过计算得出，单位变动成本（v）为 $0.10，固定成本总额（$f$）为 $2 000，成本等式为 $y = \$0.10x + \$2\ 000$。

答案：Using the high-low method, the operating cost equation is $y = \$0.10x + \$2,000$.

2. Use your answer from Part 1 to predict total operating costs if Asokan serves 4,000 pancakes in one month.

讲解：将 4 000（x）代入成本等式（$y = \$0.10x + \$2\ 000$），得出经营费用（$y$）为 $2 400。

答案：If Asokan serves 4,000 pancakes in one month, the total operating costs are $2,400.

3. Can you predict total operating costs if Asokan serves 10,000 pancakes a month? Explain.

答案：The current production volume range of Asokan is from 3,200 to 3,900 pancakes. If Asokan sells 10,000 pancakes in one month, the restaurant might be operating outside of its current relevant range. Asokan should not predict costs using the current cost equation for any production volumes that fall outside of its relevant range since cost behaviour patterns may change at higher or lower production volumes.

例题 5 - 13

To control costs, a company compiled the following data to analyze its utilities cost.

Month	Machine Hours	Utilities Cost
January	3,150	$2,250
February	3,000	2,100
March	3,750	2,400
April	4,250	2,600
May	5,500	3,000
June	7,200	3,800
July	9,000	4,500
August	8,750	4,300

Required:

1. Using the high-low method, calculate the fixed and variable components of the utilities cost and express this as an equation in the form $y = vx + f$.

2. Assuming September's machine hours are expected to be 7,600 hours, what is the expected utilities cost for September using the equation you calculated in Part 1.

3. Using the regression analysis method, calculate the fixed and variable components of the utilities cost and express this as an equation in the form $y = vx + f$.

4. Explain why there is a difference between the equation calculated in Part 1 and the equation calculated in Part 3.

1. Using the high-low method, calculate the fixed and variable components of the utilities cost and express this as an equation in the form $y = vx + f$.

讲解： 首先，需要确定机器的最高与最低运转时间。机器最高运转时长为 9 000 小时，机器最低运转时长为 3 000 小时；机器运转 9 000 小时对应的水电费用为 $4 500，机器运转 3 000 小时对应的水电费用为 $2 100。

Month	Machine Hours	Utilities Cost
January	3,150	$2,250
February	3,000	2,100
March	3,750	2,400

带你到北美学习
管理会计
Take You to
North America
to Learn
Managerial Accounting

April	4,250	2,600
May	5,500	3,000
June	7,200	3,800
July	9,000	4,500
August	8,750	4,300

这两组数据可以形成如下二元一次方程组，自变量（x）代表机器运转时长，因变量（y）代表水电费用。

$$\begin{cases} \$4\,500 = 9\,000v + f \ (\text{High}) \\ \$2\,100 = 3\,000v + f \ (\text{Low}) \end{cases}$$

通过计算得出，单位变动成本（v）为 $\$0.40$，固定成本总额（$f$）为 $\$900$，成本等式为 $y = \$0.40x + \$900$。

答案： Using the high-low method, the cost equation is $y = \$0.40x + \$900$.

2. Assuming September's machine hours are expected to be 7,600 hours, what is the expected utilities cost for September using the equation you calculated in Part 1.

讲解： 将 7 600（x）代入成本等式（$y = \$0.40x + \$900$），得出水电费用（$y$）为 $\$3\,940$。

答案： If September's machine hours are expected to be 7,600 hours, the expected utilities cost for September is $\$3,940$.

3. Using the regression analysis method, calculate the fixed and variable components of the utilities cost and express this as an equation in the form $y = vx + f$.

讲解： 我们必须使用 Microsoft Excel 进行回归分析，进而确定成本等式（$y = vx + f$）。回归分析结果提供了许多数据，但对于确定成本等式，我们仅需三类数据：Intercept，X Variable 1，R-Square。Intercept 约为 954.47，说明成本等式中的 f 约为 $\$954.47$；X Variable 1 约为 0.39，说明成本等式中的 v 约为 $\$0.39$；R-Square 约为 0.996 6，说明可以放心使用成本等式（$y = \$0.39x + \$954.47$），预测在相关范围内机器运转时长（$x$）产生的水电费用（$y$）。

SUMMARY OUTPUT					
Regression Statistics					
Multiple R	0.998296931				
R Square	0.996596762				
Adjusted R Square	0.996029555				
Standard Error	60.06043107				
Observations	8				
ANOVA					
	df	SS	MS	F	Significance F
Regression	1	6338043.968	6338043.968	1757.026687	1.23334E-08
Residual	6	21643.53228	3607.25538		
Total	7	6359687.5			
	Coefficients	Standard Error	t Stat	P-value	Lower 95%
Intercept	954.4688503	55.82865288	17.09639766	2.56274E-06	817.861058
X Variable 1	0.388211865	0.009261464	41.91690216	1.23334E-08	0.36554988

答案： Using the regression analysis method, the cost equation is $y = \$0.39x + \$954.47$.

4. Explain why there is a difference between the equation calculated in Part 1 and the equation calculated in Part 3.

答案： The high-low method is an easy way to estimate the variable and fixed components of a mixed cost. The high-low method determines a cost equation through the highest and lowest volume data points, however, the regression analysis method is a statistical procedure for determining the cost equation that best fit the data by using all of the data points, not just the highest and lowest volume data points. Therefore, the regression analysis method is usually more accurate than the high-low method.

例题 5 - 14

Power Inc. manufactures snowboards. As a part of the production planning process, the company is trying to determine the appropriate cost driver for applying manufacturing overhead to products. The company have narrowed it down to two choices: machine hours used and number of units produced.

Regression outputs for the two possible choices are as follows:

带你到北美学习
管理会计
Take You to
North America
to Learn
Managerial Accounting

SUMMARY OUTPUT Using Machine Hours					
Regression Statistics					
Multiple R	0.97054108				
R Square	0.94194999				
Adjusted R Square	0.93832186				
Standard Error	70691.6844				
Observations	18				
ANOVA					
	df	SS	MS	F	Significance F
Regression	1	1.30E+12	1.30E+12	259.624408	2.60E-11
Residual	16	79957027944	5.00E+09		
Total	17	1.38E+12			
	Coefficients	Standard Error	t Stat	P-value	
Intercept	598523.577	71550.13708	8.3650934	3.09E-07	
X Variable 1	80.0939223	4.970805872	16.112865	2.60E-11	

SUMMARY OUTPUT Using Number of Units					
Regression Statistics					
Multiple R	0.9568683				
R Square	0.915597				
Adjusted R Square	0.9103218				
Standard Error	85240.535				
Observations	18				
ANOVA					
	df	SS	MS	F	Significance F
Regression	1	1.26E+12	1.26E+12	173.5667	5.26E-10
Residual	16	1.16E+11	7.27E+09		
Total	17	1.38E+12			
	Coefficients	Standard Error	t Stat	P-value	
Intercept	617205.7	86062.55382	7.171594	2.22E-06	
X Variable 1	23.276393	1.766780138	13.17447	5.26E-10	

Required:

1. What is the cost equation if machine hours are used as the volume (cost driver)?

2. Predict total manufacturing overhead using machine hours as the volume (cost driver) if Power Inc. uses 18,000 machine hours.

3. What is the cost equation if units produced are used as the volume (cost driver)?

4. Predict total manufacturing overhead using units produced as the volume (cost driver) if Power Inc. produces 65,000 units.

5. Which volume (cost driver) is a better predictor of total manufacturing overhead? Why?

1. What is the cost equation if machine hours are used as the volume (cost driver)?

讲解： Intercept 约为 598 523.58，说明成本等式中的 f 约为 \$598 523.58；X Variable 1约为 80.09，说明成本等式中的 v 约为 \$80.09；R-Square 约为 0.941 9，说明可以放心使用成本等式（$y = \$80.09x + \$598 523.58$），预测在相关范围内机器运转时长（$x$）产生的制造费用（$y$）。

SUMMARY OUTPUT Using Machine Hours					
Regression Statistics					
Multiple R	0.97054108				
R Square	0.94194999				
Adjusted R Square	0.93832186				
Standard Error	70691.6844				
Observations	18				
ANOVA					
	df	SS	MS	F	Significance F
Regression	1	1.30E+12	1.30E+12	259.624408	2.60E-11
Residual	16	799957027944	5.00E+09		
Total	17	1.38E+12			
	Coefficients	Standard Error	t Stat	P-value	
Intercept	598523.577	71550.13708	8.3650934	3.09E-07	
X Variable 1	80.0939223	4.970805872	16.112865	2.60E-11	

答案： If machine hours are used as the volume (cost driver), the cost equation is $y = \$80.09x + \$598,523.58$.

2. Predict total manufacturing overhead using machine hours as the volume (cost driver) if Power Inc. uses 18,000 hours.

讲解： 将18 000（x）代入成本等式（$y = \$80.09x + \$598 523.58$），得出制造费用（$y$）为 \$2 040 143.58。

答案： If Power Inc. uses 18,000 machine hours, the total manufacturing overhead is \$2,040,143.58.

3. What is the cost equation if units produced are used as the volume (cost driver)?

讲解： Intercept 约为 617 205.70，说明成本等式中的 f 约为 \$617 205.70；X Variable 1 约为 23.28，说明成本等式中的 v 约为 \$23.28；R-Square 约为 0.915 6，说明

带你到北美学习
管理会计
Take You to
North America
to Learn
Managerial Accounting

可以放心使用成本等式（$y = \$23.28x + \$617\ 205.70$），预测在相关范围内产量（$x$）带来的制造费用（$y$）。

SUMMARY OUTPUT	Using Number of Units				
Regression Statistics					
Multiple R	0.9568683				
R Square	0.915597				
Adjusted R Square	0.9103218				
Standard Error	85240.535				
Observations	18				
ANOVA					
	df	SS	MS	F	Significance F
Regression	1	1.26E+12	1.26E+12	173.5667	5.26E-10
Residual	16	1.16E+11	7.27E+09		
Total	17	1.38E+12			
	Coefficients	Standard Error	t Stat	P-value	
Intercept	617205.7	86062.55382	7.171594	2.22E-06	
X Variable 1	23.276393	1.766780138	13.17447	5.26E-10	

答案：If units produced are used as the volume (cost driver), the cost equation is $y = \$23.28x + \$617,205.70$.

4. Predict total manufacturing overhead using units produced as the volume (cost driver) if Power Inc. produces 65,000 units.

讲解：将 65 000（x）代入成本等式（$y = \$23.28x + \$617\ 205.70$），得出制造费用（$y$）为 $\$2\ 130\ 405.70$。

答案：If Power Inc. produces 65,000 units, the total manufacturing overhead is $\$2,130,405.70$.

5. Which volume (cost driver) is a better predictor of total manufacturing overhead? Why?

答案：Because the R-Square for the machine hours model is 0.9419, but the R-Square for the units produced model is 0.9156, so the machine hour as the appropriate cost driver for applying manufacturing overhead to products appears to be the better choice in this case.

例题 5 – 15

The following data are related to the sales and production of Welch Corporation for last year：

Units in beginning inventory	0 units
Units produced during year	10,000 units
Units sold during year	9,000 units
Units in ending inventory	1,000 units
Selling price per unit	$ 50
Variable manufacturing costs per unit	$ 24
Variable selling and administrative expenses per unit	$ 4
Fixed manufacturing costs each year	$ 50,000
Fixed selling and administrative expenses each year	$ 8,000

Required：

1. Prepare an absorption costing income statement for last year.

2. Calculate the value of the ending inventory under absorption costing.

3. Prepare a variable costing income statement for last year.

4. Calculate the value of the ending inventory under variable costing.

1. Prepare an absorption costing income statement for last year.

讲解： 变动成本法（variable costing）将直接材料成本、直接人工成本、变动性制造费用计入产品成本（product cost），固定性制造费用计入期间成本（period cost），而归纳成本法（absorption costing）将直接材料成本、直接人工成本、变动性制造费用和固定性制造费用计入产品成本。

Welch Corporation 生产了 10 000 件商品，产生固定性制造费用 $ 50 000，因此单件商品承担的固定性制造费用为 $ 5。根据归纳成本法，单件商品成本为 $ 29，而根据变动成本法，单件商品成本为 $ 24。

	Absorption Costing	Variable Costing
Variable manufacturing costs	$ 24	$ 24
Fixed manufacturing costs	5	
Unit costs	$ 29	$ 24

去年年初，Welch Corporation 没有库存商品；去年，企业生产 10 000 件商品，

带你到北美学习
管理会计
Take You to
North America
to Learn
Managerial Accounting

出售 9 000 件商品；去年年底，企业库存 1 000 件商品。

我们知道，如果使用归纳成本法，必须编写传统收益表。根据归纳成本法，单件商品成本为 $29，因此制成品库存账目年初余额为 $0（$29 × 0 = $0），制成商品成本为 $290 000（$29 × 10 000 = $290 000），售出商品成本为 $261 000（$29 × 9 000 = $261 000），制成品库存账目年末余额为 $29 000（$29 × 1 000 = $29 000）。

Welch Corporation 出售 9 000 件商品，单件售价为 $50，销售额为 $450 000。销售额（$450 000）减去售出商品成本（$261 000）等于毛利润（$189 000）。

去年，Welch Corporation 出售 9 000 件商品，单件商品的销售与行政管理费用为 $4，产生变动性销售与行政管理费用 $36 000；此外，企业还产生固定性销售与行政管理费用 $8 000。销售与行政管理费用属于经营费用，因此经营费用总额为 $44 000。毛利润（$189 000）减去经营费用总额（$44 000）等于经营收益（$145 000）。

答案：

Welch Corporation Income Statement（Absorption Costing） For the year ended by December 31，2016		
Sales revenue		$450,000
Cost of goods sold：		
Beginning finished goods inventory	$0	
Cost of goods manufactured	290,000	
Cost of goods available for sale	290,000	
Ending finished goods inventory	(29,000)	(261,000)
Gross profit		189,000
Operating expenses		
Selling and administrative expenses		(44,000)
Operating income		$145,000

2. Calculate the value of the ending inventory under absorption costing.

讲解： 根据归纳成本法，单件商品成本为 $29。去年年底，Welch Corporation 拥有 1 000 件库存商品，因此制成品库存账目年末余额为 $29 000。

答案： The value of the ending inventory under absorption costing is $29,000.

3. Prepare a variable costing income statement for last year.

讲解： Welch Corporation 生产 10 000 件商品，产生固定性制造费用 $ 50 000，因此单件商品的固定性制造费用为 $ 5。根据归纳成本法，单件商品成本为 $ 29，而根据变动成本法，单件商品成本为 $ 24。

去年年初，Welch Corporation 没有库存商品；去年，企业生产 10 000 件商品，出售 9 000 件商品；去年年底，企业库存 1 000 件商品。

我们知道，如果使用变动成本法，必须编写边际贡献收益表。根据变动成本法，单件商品成本为 $ 24，因此制成品库存账目年初余额为 $ 0（$ 24 × 0 = $ 0），变动性制成商品成本为 $ 240 000（$ 24 × 10 000 = $ 240 000），变动性售出商品成本为 $ 216 000（$ 24 × 9 000 = $ 216 000），制成品库存账目年末余额为 $ 24 000（$ 24 × 1 000 = $ 24 000）；此外，单件商品的销售与行政管理费用为 $ 4，为出售 9 000 件商品，Welch Corporation 产生变动性销售与行政管理费用 $ 36 000。变动性售出商品成本、变动性销售与行政管理费用均属于变动成本，因此变动成本总额为 $ 252 000（$ 216 000 + $ 36 000 = $ 252 000）。

Welch Corporation 出售 9 000 件商品，单件售价为 $ 50，销售额为 $ 450 000。销售额（$ 450 000）减去变动成本总额（$ 252 000）等于贡献毛利（$ 198 000）。

固定性制造成本为 $ 50 000，固定性销售与行政管理费用为 $ 8 000，固定成本总额为 $ 58 000。贡献毛利（$ 198 000）减去固定成本总额（$ 58 000）等于经营收益（$ 140 000）。

答案：

Welch Corporation Income Statement（Variable Costing） For the year ended by December 31，2016		
Sales revenue		$ 450,000
Variable expenses		
Variable cost of goods sold：		
Beginning finished goods inventory	$ 0	
Variable cost of goods manufactured	240,000	
Variable cost of goods available for sale	240,000	
Ending finished goods inventory	(24,000)	
Variable cost of goods sold	216,000	
Variable selling and administrative expenses	36,000	(252,000)

带你到北美学习
管理会计
Take You to
North America
to Learn
Managerial Accounting

Contribution margin		198,000
Fixed expenses		
Fixed manufacturing costs	50,000	
Fixed selling and administrative expenses	8,000	(58,000)
Operating income		$140,000

4. Calculate the value of the ending inventory under variable costing.

讲解： 根据变动成本法，单件商品成本为 $24。去年年底，Welch Corporation 库存 1 000 件商品，因此制成品库存账目年末余额为 $24 000。

答案： The value of the ending inventory under variable costing is $24,000.

例题 5 - 16

Guitars Company produces guitars for beginning guitar students. The company produced 2,000 guitars in May (the first month of its operations). At the month-end, 600 guitars remained unsold. There was no inventory in raw materials or work in process. The guitars were sold for $122.50 each. The costs incurred in May were as follows:

Direct materials used	$85,000
Direct labour	55,000
Variable manufacturing overhead	30,000
Fixed manufacturing overhead	48,000
Variable selling and administrative expenses	10,000
Fixed selling and administrative expenses	15,000

The company prepares an absorption costing (traditional) income statement for its bankers. Also, the company would like to prepare a contribution margin income statements for its own management.

Required:

Determine the following amounts that would appear on these statements for May:

1. The gross profit.

2. The contribution margin.

3. The total expenses shown below the gross profit line.

4. The total expenses shown below the contribution margin line.

5. The ending inventory in dollars under absorption costing.

6. The ending inventory in dollars under variable costing.

7. The operating income for each of the two statements.

1. The gross profit.

讲解： 为生产 2 000 把吉他，Guitars Company 承担直接材料成本 $85 000、直接人工成本 $55 000、变动性制造费用 $30 000、固定性制造费用 $48 000，因此每把吉他的直接材料成本为 $42.50，直接人工成本为 $27.50，变动性制造费用为 $15，固定性制造费用为 $24（$48 000 ÷ 2 000 = 24）。根据归纳成本法，每把吉他成本为 $109；而根据变动成本法，每把吉他成本为 $85。

	Absorption Costing	Variable Costing
Direct materials	$42.50	$42.50
Direct labour	27.50	27.50
Variable manufacturing overhead	15.00	15.00
Fixed manufacturing overhead	24.00	——
Unit costs	$109.00	$85.00

5 月初，Guitars Company 没有库存吉他；5 月份，生产 2 000 把吉他，出售 1 400 把吉他；5 月底，企业库存 600 把吉他。

如果使用归纳成本法，必须编写传统收益表计算毛利润（gross profit）。Guitars Company 出售 1 400 把吉他，每把吉他售价为 $122.50，销售额为 $171 500。根据归纳成本法，每把吉他成本为 $109，售出商品成本为 $152 600（$109 × 1 400 = $152 600）。销售额（$171 500）减去售出商品成本（$152 600）等于毛利润（$18 900）。

答案： The gross profit in May was $18,900.

2. The contribution margin.

讲解： 如果使用变动成本法，必须编写边际贡献收益表计算贡献毛利（contribution margin）。根据变动成本法，每把吉他成本为 $85。Guitars Company 出售 1 400 把吉他，因此变动性售出商品成本为 $119 000（$85 × 1 400 = $119 000）；此外，Guitars Company 产生变动性销售与行政管理费用 $10 000。变动性制成商品成本、

带你到北美学习
管理会计
Take You to
North America
to Learn
Managerial Accounting

变动性销售与行政管理费用属于变动成本，因此变动成本总额为 $ 129 000。Guitars Company 出售 1 400 把吉他，每把吉他售价为 $ 122. 50，销售额为 $ 171 500。销售额（ $ 171 500）减去变动成本总额（ $ 129 000）等于贡献毛利（ $ 42 500）。

答案： The contribution margin in May was $ 42,500.

3. The total expenses shown below the gross profit line.

讲解： 5 月份，Guitars Company 不但产生变动性销售与行政管理费用 $ 10 000，而且还产生固定性销售与行政管理费用 $ 15 000。销售与行政管理费用属于经营费用，因此经营费用总额为 $ 25 000。

答案： The total expenses shown below the gross profit line were $ 25,000.

4. The total expenses shown below the contribution margin line.

讲解： 固定性制造成本为 $ 48 000，固定性销售与行政管理费用为 $ 15 000，因此固定成本总额为 $ 63 000。

答案： The total expenses shown below the contribution margin line were $ 63,000.

5. The ending inventory in dollars under absorption costing.

讲解： 5 月初，Guitars Company 没有库存吉他；5 月份，生产 2 000 把吉他，出售 1 400 把吉他；5 月底，企业库存 600 把吉他。根据归纳成本法，每把吉他成本为 $ 109，吉他库存账目月末余额为 $ 65 400。

答案： The dollar value of ending inventory under absorption costing was $ 65,400.

6. The ending inventory in dollars under variable costing.

讲解： 5 月初，Guitars Company 没有库存吉他；5 月份，生产 2 000 把吉他，出售 1 400 把吉他；5 月底，企业库存 600 把吉他。根据变动成本法，每把吉他成本为 $ 85，吉他库存账目月末余额为 $ 51 000。

答案： The dollar value of ending inventory under variable costing was $ 51,000.

7. The operating income for each of the two statements.

讲解： 在传统收益表中，毛利润（ $ 18 900）减去经营费用总额（ $ 25 000）等于经营亏损（＄6 100）；在边际贡献收益表中，贡献毛利（＄42 500）减去固定成本总额（＄63 000）等于经营亏损（＄20 500）。

答案： The operating loss in the traditional income statement was ＄6,100. The operating loss in the contribution margin income statement was ＄20,500.

例题 5 - 17

The annual data pertain to Swim Clearly, a manufacturer of swimming goggles, is provided below. Swim Clearly has no beginning inventories.

Selling price per goggle	＄42
Variable manufacturing costs per goggle	＄20
Sales commissions per goggle	＄5
Fixed manufacturing overhead each year	＄1,935,000
Fixed operating expenses each year	＄265,000
Number of goggles produced	215,000 units
Number of goggles sold	200,000 units

Required:

1. Prepare both an absorption costing income statement and a variable costing income statement for Swim Clearly for the year.

2. Which statement shows the higher operating income? Why? Reconcile the difference between the two statements.

1. Prepare both an absorption costing income statement and a variable costing income statement for Swim Clearly for the year.

讲解一： Swim Clearly 生产 215 000 副泳镜，产生固定性制造费用 ＄1 935 000，因此每副泳镜的固定性制造费用为 ＄9。根据归纳成本法，单件商品成本为 ＄29，而根据变动成本法，单件商品成本为 ＄20。

	Absorption Costing	Variable Costing
Variable manufacturing costs	＄20	＄20
Fixed manufacturing overhead	9	-
Unit costs	＄29	＄20

带你到北美学习
管理会计
Take You to
North America
to Learn
Managerial Accounting

年初，Swim Clearly 没有库存泳镜；本年度，企业生产 215 000 副泳镜，出售 200 000 副泳镜；年底，企业库存 15 000 副泳镜。

如果使用归纳成本法，必须编写传统收益表。根据归纳成本法，每副泳镜的成本为 $29，因此制成品库存账目年初余额为 $0（$29 × 0 = $0），制成商品成本为 $6 235 000（$29 × 215 000 = $6 235 000），售出商品成本为 $5 800 000（$29 × 200 000 = $5 800 000），制成品库存账目年末余额为 $435 000（$29 × 15 000 = $435 000）。

Swim Clearly 出售 200 000 副泳镜，每副售价为 $42，销售额为 $8 400 000。销售额（$8 400 000）减去售出商品成本（$5 800 000）等于毛利润（$2 600 000）。

本年度，Swim Clearly 出售 200 000 副泳镜，每副泳镜的销售佣金费用为 $5，产生销售佣金费用 $1 000 000；此外，还产生固定性经营费用 $265 000。销售佣金费用、固定性经营费用均属于经营费用，因此经营费用总额为 $1 265 000。毛利润（$2 600 000）减去经营费用总额（$1 265 000）等于经营收益（$1 335 000）。

答案一：

Swim Clearly Income Statement（Absorption Costing） For the year ended by December 31		
Sales revenue		$8,400,000
Cost of goods sold：		
Beginning finished goods inventory	$0	
Cost of goods manufactured	6,235,000	
Cost of goods available for sale	6,235,000	
Ending finished goods inventory	(435,000)	(5,800,000)
Gross profit		2,600,000
Operating expenses		
Sales commissions expense	1,000,000	
Fixed operating expenses	265,000	(1,265,000)
Operating income		$1,335,000

讲解二： 如果使用变动成本法，必须编写边际贡献收益表。根据变动成本法，每副泳镜的成本为 $20，因此制成品库存账目年初余额为 $0（$20 × 0 = $0），变动性制成商品成本为 $4 300 000（$20 × 215 000 = $4 300 000），变动性售出商品成本为 $4 000 000（$20 × 200 000 = $4 000 000），制成品库存账目年末余额为

$300 000（$20 × 15 000 = $300 000）；此外，每副泳镜的销售佣金费用为$5，为出售200 000副泳镜，Swim Clearly 产生变动性销售佣金费用$1 000 000。变动性售出商品成本、变动性销售佣金费用均属于变动成本，因此变动成本总额为$5 000 000。

Swim Clearly 出售200 000副泳镜，每副售价为$42，销售额为$8 400 000。销售额（$8 400 000）减去变动成本总额（$5 000 000）等于贡献毛利（$3 400 000）。

固定性制造费用为$1 935 000，固定性经营费用为$265 000，固定成本总额为$2 200 000。贡献毛利（$3 400 000）减去固定成本总额（$2 200 000）等于经营收益（$1 200 000）。

答案二：

Swim Clearly Income Statement（Variable Costing） For the year ended by December 31		
Sales revenue		$8,400,000
Variable expenses		
Variable cost of goods sold:		
Beginning finished goods inventory	$0	
Variable cost of goods manufactured	4,300,000	
Variable cost of goods available for sale	4,300,000	
Ending finished goods inventory	(300,000)	
Variable cost of goods sold	4,000,000	
Sales commissions expense	1,000,000	(5,000,000)
Contribution margin		3,400,000
Fixed expenses		
Fixed manufacturing overhead	1,935,000	
Fixed operating expenses	265,000	(2,200,000)
Operating income		$1,200,000

2. Which statement shows the higher operating income? Why? Reconcile the difference between the two statements.

讲解： 通过给定财务周期，如果生产商品数量大于出售商品数量，库存商品数量增加，那么归纳成本法的经营收益高于变动成本法的经营收益；如果生产商品数量小于出售商品数量，库存商品数量降低，那么归纳成本法的经营收益低于变动成本法

带你到北美学习
管理会计
Take You to
North America
to Learn
Managerial Accounting

的经营收益。

答案： Absorption costing defers $135,000 of fixed manufacturing overhead as an asset in ending inventory (15,000 goggles × $9 fixed manufacturing overhead per goggle), so the absorption costing operating income is higher than the variable costing operating income. In contrast, variable costing expenses all of the fixed manufacturing overhead during the year, which expenses $135,000 more costs during the year, so the variable costing operating income is $135,000 less than the absorption costing operating income ($1,335,000 − $1,200,000 = $135,000).

Absorption costing operating income	$1,335,000
Fixed manufacturing overhead released from beginning inventory	0
Fixed manufacturing overhead deferred to ending inventory	(135,000)
Variable costing operating income	$1,200,000

例题 5 - 18

Pizza Company produces frozen pizzas, which it sells for $10 each. The company uses the first-in, first-out inventory costing method and it computes a new monthly fixed manufacturing overhead rate based on the actual number of meals produced in that month. All costs and production levels are exactly as planned. The following data are from Pizza Company's first two-month operations:

	July	August
Sales volume	1,500 units	1,800 units
Production volume	2,100 units	1,500 units
Variable manufacturing costs per pizza	$6	$6
Sales commissions per pizza	$1.50	$1.50
Fixed manufacturing overhead each month	$1,050	$1,050
Fixed marketing and administrative expenses each month	$900	$900

Required:

1. Compute the product costs per meal produced under absorption costing and variable costing. Do this first for July and then for August.

2. Prepare the monthly income statements for July and for August under absorption costing and variable costing.

3. Is operating income higher under absorption costing or variable costing in July? In August? Explain the difference in operating income based on absorption costing versus variable costing.

1. Compute the product costs per meal produced under absorption costing and variable costing. Do this first for July and then for August.

讲解： 根据题目信息，7 月份，Pizza Company 生产 2 100 张比萨，产生固定性制造费用 $1 050，因此每张比萨的固定性制造费用为 $0.50；8 月份，Pizza Company 生产 1 500 张比萨，产生固定性制造费用 $1 050，因此每张比萨的固定性制造费用为 $0.70。每张比萨的变动性制造费用为 $6。

根据变动成本法，7 月份与 8 月份的每张比萨成本均为 $6，而根据归纳成本法，7 月份的每张比萨成本为 $6.50（$6 + $0.50 = $6.50），8 月份的每张比萨成本为 $6.70（$6 + $0.70 = $6.70）。

答案：

	July		August	
	Absorption	Variable	Absorption	Variable
Variable manufacturing costs	$6.00	$6.00	$6.00	$6.00
Fixed manufacturing overhead	0.50	———	0.70	———
Unit costs	$6.50	$6.00	$6.70	$6.00

2. Prepare the monthly income statements for July and for August under absorption costing and variable costing.

讲解一： 根据题目信息，Pizza Company 使用先进先出存货成本计算法。7 月初，Pizza Company 开始营业，因此比萨库存为 0 张；7 月份，生产 2 100 张比萨，出售 1 500 张比萨；7 月底，比萨库存为 600 张。

如果使用变动成本法，必须编写边际贡献收益表。根据变动成本法，7 月份的每张比萨成本为 $6，因此 7 月初的比萨库存账目余额为 $0（$6 × 0 = $0），变动性制成商品成本为 $12 600（$6 × 2 100 = $12 600），变动性售出商品成本为

带你到北美学习

管理会计

Take You to
North America
to Learn
Managerial Accounting

$9 000（$6 × 1 500 = $9 000），7 月末的比萨库存账目余额为 $3 600（$6 × 600 = $3 600）；此外，每张比萨的销售佣金为 $1.50，为出售 1 500 张比萨，Pizza Company 产生销售佣金费用 $2 250。变动性售出商品成本、销售佣金费用均属于变动成本，因此变动成本总额为 $11 250（$9 000 + $2 250 = $11 250）。

7 月份，Pizza Company 出售 1 500 张比萨，每张售价为 $10，销售额为 $15 000。销售额（$15 000）减去变动成本总额（$11 250）等于贡献毛利（$3 750）。

固定性制造费用为 $1 050，固定性市场与行政费用为 $900，固定成本总额为 $1 950。贡献毛利（$3 750）减去固定成本总额（$1 950）等于经营收益（$1 800）。

答案一：

Pizza Company Income Statement (Variable Costing) For the year ended by July 31		
Sales revenue		$ 15,000
Variable expenses		
Variable cost of goods sold：		
Beginning finished goods inventory	$ 0	
Variable cost of goods manufactured	12,600	
Variable cost of goods available for sale	12,600	
Ending finished goods inventory	(3,600)	
Variable cost of goods sold	9,000	
Sales commissions expense	2,250	(11,250)
Contribution margin		3,750
Fixed expenses		
Fixed manufacturing overhead	1,050	
Fixed marketing and administrative expenses	900	(1,950)
Operating income		$ 1,800

讲解二：根据题目信息，Pizza Company 使用先进先出存货成本计算法。8 月初，比萨库存为 600 张；8 月份，生产 1 500 张比萨，出售 1 800 张比萨；8 月末，比萨库存为 300 张。

如果使用变动成本法，必须编写边际贡献收益表。根据变动成本法，8 月份的每张比萨成本为 $6，因此 8 月初的比萨库存账目余额为 $3 600（$6 × 600 =

$3 600），变动性制成商品成本为 $9 000（$6 × 1 500 = $9 000），变动性售出商品成本为 $10 800（$6 × 1 800 = $10 800），8 月末的比萨库存账目余额为 $1 800（$6 × 300 = $1 800）；此外，每张比萨的销售佣金为 $1.50，为出售 1 800 张比萨，Pizza Company 产生销售佣金费用 $2 700。变动性售出商品成本、销售佣金费用均属于变动成本，因此变动成本总额为 $13 500。

8 月份，Pizza Company 出售 1 800 张比萨，每张售价为 $10，销售额为 $18 000。销售额（$18 000）减去变动成本总额（$13 500）等于贡献毛利（$4 500）。

固定性制造费用为 $1 050，固定性市场与行政费用为 $900，固定成本总额为 $1 950。贡献毛利（$4 500）减去固定成本总额（$1 950）等于经营收益（$2 550）。

答案二：

Pizza Company Income Statement (Variable Costing) For the year ended by August 31		
Sales revenue		$18,000
Variable expenses		
Variable cost of goods sold：		
Beginning finished goods inventory	$3,600	
Variable cost of goods manufactured	9,000	
Variable cost of goods available for sale	12,600	
Ending finished goods inventory	(1,800)	
Variable cost of goods sold	10,800	
Sales commissions expense	2,700	(13,500)
Contribution margin		4,500
Fixed expenses		
Fixed manufacturing overhead	1,050	
Fixed marketing and administrative expenses	900	(1,950)
Operating income		$2,550

讲解三： 根据题目信息，Pizza Company 使用先进先出存货成本计算法。7 月初，Pizza Company 开始营业，因此比萨库存为 0 张；7 月份，生产 2 100 张比萨，出售 1 500张比萨；7 月底，比萨库存为 600 张。

如果使用归纳成本法，必须编写传统收益表。根据归纳成本法，7 月份的每张

带你到北美学习
管理会计
Take You to
North America
to Learn
Managerial Accounting

比萨成本为 $6.50，因此 7 月初的比萨库存账目余额为 $0（$6.50 × 0 = $0），制成商品成本为 $13 650（$6.50 × 2 100 = $13 650），售出商品成本为 $9 750（$6.50 × 1 500 = $9 750），7 月末的比萨库存账目余额为 $3 900（$6.50 × 600 = $3 900）。

7 月份，Pizza Company 出售 1 500 张比萨，每张售价为 $10，销售额为 $15 000。销售额（$15 000）减去售出商品成本（$9 750）等于毛利润（$5 250）。

7 月份，Pizza Company 出售 1 500 张比萨，每张比萨的销售佣金为 $1.50，产生销售佣金费用 $2 250，市场与行政费用为 $900。销售佣金费用、市场与行政费用均属于经营费用，因此经营费用总额为 $3 150。毛利润（$5 250）减去经营费用总额（$3 150）等于经营收益（$2 100）。

答案三：

<table>
<tr><td colspan="3">Pizza Company
Income Statement（Absorption Costing）
For the year ended by July 31</td></tr>
<tr><td>Sales revenue</td><td></td><td>$15,000</td></tr>
<tr><td>Cost of goods sold:</td><td></td><td></td></tr>
<tr><td>Beginning finished goods inventory</td><td>$0</td><td></td></tr>
<tr><td>Cost of goods manufactured</td><td>13,650</td><td></td></tr>
<tr><td>Cost of goods available for sale</td><td>13,650</td><td></td></tr>
<tr><td>Ending finished goods inventory</td><td>(3,900)</td><td>(9,750)</td></tr>
<tr><td>Gross profit</td><td></td><td>5,250</td></tr>
<tr><td>Operating expenses</td><td></td><td></td></tr>
<tr><td>Sales commissions expense</td><td>2,250</td><td></td></tr>
<tr><td>Marketing and administrative expenses</td><td>900</td><td>(3,150)</td></tr>
<tr><td>Operating income</td><td></td><td>$2,100</td></tr>
</table>

讲解四： 根据题目信息，Pizza Company 使用先进先出存货成本计算法。8 月初，比萨库存为 600 张；8 月份，生产 1 500 张比萨，出售 1 800 张比萨；8 月末，比萨库存为 300 张。

如果使用归纳成本法，必须编写传统收益表。根据归纳成本法，8 月份的每张比萨成本为 $6.70。8 月初的比萨库存账目余额为 $3 900（$6.50 × 600 = $3 900），8 月份制成商品成本为 $10 050（$6.70 × 1 500 = $10 050），8 月末的比萨库存账目余额为 $2 010（$6.70 × 300 = $2 010），因此 8 月份售出商品成本

为 $ 11 940（ $ 3 900 + $ 10 050 − $ 2 010 = $ 11 940）。

8 月份，Pizza Company 出售 1 800 张比萨，每张售价为 $ 10，销售额为 $ 18 000。销售额（ $ 18 000）减去售出商品成本（ $ 11 940）等于毛利润（ $ 6 060）。

8 月份，Pizza Company 出售 1 800 张比萨，每张比萨的销售佣金为 $ 1. 50，产生销售佣金费用 $ 2 700，市场与行政费用为 $ 900。销售佣金费用、市场与行政费用均属于经营费用，因此经营费用总额为 $ 3 600。毛利润（ $ 6 060）减去经营费用总额（ $ 3 600）等于经营收益（ $ 2 460）。

答案四：

Pizza Company Income Statement (Absorption Costing) For the year ended by August 31		
Sales revenue		$ 18,000
Cost of goods sold:		
Beginning finished goods inventory	$ 3,900	
Cost of goods manufactured	10,050	
Cost of goods available for sale	13,950	
Ending finished goods inventory	(2,010)	(11,940)
Gross profit		6,040
Operating expenses		
Sales commissions expense	2,700	
Marketing and administrative expenses	900	(3,600)
Operating income		$ 2,460

3. Is operating income higher under absorption costing or variable costing in July? In August? Explain the difference in operating income based on absorption costing versus variable costing.

讲解： 在给定财务周期，如果生产商品数量大于出售商品数量，库存商品数量增加，那么归纳成本法的经营收益高于变动成本法的经营收益；如果生产商品数量小于出售商品数量，库存商品数量降低，那么归纳成本法的经营收益低于变动成本法的经营收益。

答案： In July, production exceeds sales, so the absorption costing operating income exceeds the variable costing operating income. Absorption costing defers some of July's fixed

带你到北美学习
管理会计
Take You to
North America
to Learn
Managerial Accounting

manufacturing overhead in the 600 units of ending inventory, these costs will not be expensed until those units are sold. Deferring some of July's fixed manufacturing overhead to the future increases July's absorption costing operating income.

In August, fewer units are produced than are sold, so the absorption costing operating income is less than the variable costing operating income. As inventory declines, July's fixed manufacturing overhead that absorption costing assigned to that inventory are expensed in August, which decreases August's absorption costing operating income.

■ 专业名词汇编
Glossary of Accounting Terms

变动成本	variable cost	变动成本法	variable costing
变动成本线	variable cost line	变动成本总额	total variable cost
产品成本	product cost	成本等式	cost equation
成本动因	cost driver	成本分摊基础	cost allocation base
成本分析	cost analysis	成本功能	cost function
单位变动成本	variable cost per unit	单位固定成本	fixed cost per unit
单位混合成本	mixed cost per unit	非制造成本	non-manufacturing cost
高低点法	high-low method	贡献毛利	contribution margin
固定成本	fixed cost	固定成本线	fixed cost line
固定成本总额	total fixed cost	归纳成本法	absorption costing
回归线	regression line	混合成本	mixed cost
混合成本线	mixed cost line	混合成本总额	total mixed cost
毛利润	gross profit	期间成本	period cost
活动作业量	volume of activity	市场费用	marketing expense
售出商品成本	cost of goods sold	对外公布财务报告	external reporting
相关范围	relevant range	销售额	sales revenue
经营费用	operating expense	折旧费用	depreciation expense
直接材料	direct materials	直接人工	direct labour
制造成本	manufacturing cost		
边际贡献收益表	contribution margin income statement		
变动性制造费用	variable manufacturing overhead		
变动性售出商品成本	variable cost of goods sold		
变动性制成商品成本	variable cost of goods manufactured		
传统收益表	traditional income statement		
固定性制造费用	fixed manufacturing overhead		
回归分析法	regression analysis method		

本量利分析

Cost-Volume-Profit Analysis

带你到北美学习
管理会计
Take You to
North America
to Learn
Managerial Accounting

6.1 单位贡献毛利
Unit Contribution Margin

边际贡献收益表以成本习性（变动成本或固定成本）进行成本分类，而非成本功能（cost function），因此为提供有价值的成本习性信息和本量利信息，企业管理者更愿意使用边际贡献收益表（contribution margin income statement）。贡献毛利（contribution margin）是边际贡献收益表的分界线，贡献毛利以上部分是变动成本，以下部分是固定成本。

贡献毛利等于销售额（sales revenue）减去变动成本（variable cost），即贡献毛利指销售额超过变动成本之后的剩余部分，所以贡献毛利也是在支付变动成本之后的剩余销售额。贡献毛利可以表现为单位贡献毛利（unit contribution margin）或边际贡献率（contribution margin ratio）。

单位贡献毛利等于商品售价（selling price）减去单位变动成本（variable cost per unit）。

案例 6 - 1

Kitchen Appliances Company manufactures two products: toaster oven and bread machine. The following data are available:

	Toaster Oven	Bread Machine
Selling price	$ 100	$ 200
Variable costs	30	150

The company can manufacture three toaster ovens per machine hour and two bread machines per machine hour. The company's production capacity is 1,200 machine hours per month.

Required:

What is the unit contribution margin for bread machine?

讲解： 面包机售价为 $ 200，单位变动成本为 $ 150，因此单位贡献毛利为 $ 50。

6.2 边际贡献率
Contribution Margin Ratio

除了单位贡献毛利（unit contribution margin），边际贡献率也可以体现贡献毛利。边际贡献率指贡献毛利与销售额之间的比率。边际贡献率说明了销售额用于承担固定成本和产生利润的百分比（见说明6-1）。

说明6-1：计算边际贡献率

$$\text{Contribution margin ratio} = \frac{\text{Unit contribution margin}}{\text{Selling price}}$$

$$\text{Contribution margin ratio} = \frac{\text{Contribution margin}}{\text{Sales revenue}}$$

案例6-2

Kitchen Appliances Company manufactures two products: toaster oven and bread machine. The following data are available:

	Toaster Oven	Bread Machine
Selling price	$100	$200
Variable costs	30	150

The company can manufacture three toaster ovens per machine hour and two bread machines per machine hour. The company's production capacity is 1,200 machine hours per month.

Required:

What is the contribution margin ratio for toaster oven?

讲解： 烤箱的售价为 $100，单位变动成本为 $30，因此单位贡献毛利为 $70。单位贡献毛利（$70）除以售价（$100），计算出边际贡献率（70%）。

在边际贡献收益表中，贡献毛利以上部分是变动成本，以下部分是固定成本。销售额（sales revenue）减去变动成本（variable cost）等于贡献毛利（contribution margin），贡献毛利减去固定成本（variable cost）等于经营收益（operating income）。单位贡献毛利和边际贡献率可以预测在相关范围内不同销量产生的经营收益。

带你到北美学习
管理会计
Take You to
North America
to Learn
Managerial Accounting

案例 6 - 3

GigaGo manufactures 1-GB flash drives (jump drives). Price and cost data for a relevant range extending to 200,000 units per month are as follows:

Selling price per unit (current monthly sales volume is 130,000 units)	$20.00
Direct materials per unit	6.20
Direct labour per unit	7.00
Variable manufacturing overhead per unit	2.00
Variable selling and administrative expenses per unit	1.80
Fixed manufacturing overhead each month	102,300
Fixed selling and administrative expenses each month	187,800

Required:

1. What would the company's monthly operating income be if it sold 160,000 units?

2. What would the company's monthly operating income be if it had a sales revenue of $4,000,000?

讲解: U 盘售价为 $20,单位变动成本为 $17 ($6.20 + $7 + $2 + $1.80 = $17),因此单位贡献毛利为 $3 ($20 – $17 = $3)。单位贡献毛利 ($3)除以售价 ($20),计算出边际贡献率 (15%)。

U 盘的销量为 160 000 件,售价为 $20,销售额为 $3 200 000。销售额 ($3 200 000)乘以边际贡献率 (15%)等于贡献毛利 ($480 000)。

固定性制造费用为 $102 300,固定性销售与行政管理费用为 $187 800,因此固定成本总额为 $290 100。贡献毛利 ($480 000)减去固定成本 ($290 100)等于经营收益 ($189 900)。

Sales revenue	$3,200,000
Contribution margin ratio	×15%
Contribution margin	$480,000
Fixed costs	(290,100)
Operating income	$189,900

根据"第 2 问"信息,U 盘销售额为 $4 000 000。销售额 ($4 000 000)乘以边际贡献率 (15%)等于贡献毛利 ($600 000)。

固定性制造费用为 $102 300,固定性销售与行政管理费用为 $187 800,因此固

定成本总额为 $290 100。贡献毛利（$600 000）减去固定成本（$290 100）等于经营收益（$309 900）。

Sales revenue	$4,000,000
Contribution margin ratio	×15%
Contribution margin	$600,000
Fixed costs	(290,100)
Operating income	$309,900

6.3　确定收支平衡点

Determining the Breakeven Point

收支平衡点是使经营收益为 0 的销量或销售额。换言之，如果销量或销售额高于收支平衡点，将产生经营收益（operating income）；如果销量或销售额低于收支平衡点，将造成经营亏损（operating loss）。我们使用如下三种方法确定收支平衡点：

（1）收益表法（income statement approach）；

（2）单位贡献毛利法（unit contribution margin approach）；

（3）边际贡献率法（contribution margin ratio approach）。

6.3.1　收益表法

Income Statement Approach

收益表法是从边际贡献收益表衍生而来的。在边际贡献收益表中，销售额（sales revenue）减去变动成本（variable cost）等于贡献毛利（contribution margin），贡献毛利减去固定成本等于经营收益（operating income）（见说明 6-2）。

说明 6-2：收益表法

Operating income = Sales revenue – Variable costs – Fixed costs
Operating income =
  （Sales price per unit × Units sold）–（Variable costs per unit × Units sold）– Fixed costs

收支平衡点意味着，经营收益为 0，因此当计算收支平衡点销量或销售额时，我们需要将经营收益设为 0。

带你到北美学习
管理会计
Take You to
North America
to Learn
Managerial Accounting

案例 6 - 4

GigaGo manufactures 1-GB flash drives (jump drives). Price and cost data for a relevant range extending to 200,000 units per month are as follows:

Selling price per unit (current monthly sales volume is 130,000 units)	$20.00
Direct materials per unit	6.20
Direct labour per unit	7.00
Variable manufacturing overhead per unit	2.00
Variable selling and administrative expenses per unit	1.80
Fixed manufacturing overhead each month	102,300
Fixed selling and administrative expenses each month	187,800

Required:

1. What is the breakeven point in units?

2. What is the breakeven point in dollars?

讲解: 固定性制造费用为 $102 300，固定性销售与行政管理费用为 $187 800，因此固定成本总额为 $290 100。U 盘售价为 $20，单位变动成本为 $17。将上述数据代入收益表法的公式，计算出收支平衡点销量为 96 700 个。收支平衡点销量为 96 700个，U 盘售价为 $20，因此收支平衡点销售额为 $1 934 000。

6.3.2 单位贡献毛利法

Unit Contribution Margin Approach

通过收益表法的公式，我们可以衍生出单位贡献毛利法（见说明6-3）。单位贡献毛利法的主要目的在于确定收支平衡点销量。

说明6-3: 单位贡献毛利法

$$\text{Sales in units} = \frac{\text{Fixed costs} + \text{Operating income}}{\text{Unit contribution margin}}$$

根据"案例6-4"信息，U 盘售价为 $20，单位变动成本为 $17，因此单位贡献毛利为 $3。固定性制造费用为 $102 300，固定性销售与行政管理费用为 $187 800，因此固定成本总额为 $290 100。将上述数据代入单位贡献毛利法的公式，计算出收支平衡点销量为96 700 个（（$290 100 + $0）÷ $3 = 96 700）。

6.3.3 边际贡献率法

Contribution Margin Ratio Approach

通过收益表法公式，我们还可以衍生出边际贡献率法（见说明6-4）。边际贡献率法的主要目的在于确定收支平衡点销售额。

说明6-4：边际贡献率法

$$\text{Sales in dollars} = \frac{\text{Fixed costs} + \text{Operating income}}{\text{Contribution margin ratio}}$$

根据"案例6-4"信息，U盘售价为 $20，单位变动成本为 $17，因此单位贡献毛利为 $3。单位贡献毛利（$3）除以售价（$20），计算出边际贡献率（15%）。固定性制造费用为 $102 300，固定性销售与行政管理费用为 $187 800，因此固定成本总额为 $290 100。将上述数据代入边际贡献率法的公式，计算出收支平衡点销售额为 $1 934 000（（$290 100 + $0）÷15% = $1 934 000）。

我们也可以使用单位贡献毛利法和边际贡献率法，确定获得目标利润（target profit）所需的销量或销售额。

案例6 – 5

GigaGo manufactures 1-GB flash drives (jump drives). Price and cost data for a relevant range extending to 200,000 units per month are as follows:

Selling price per unit (current monthly sales volume is 130,000 units)	$20.00
Direct materials per unit	6.20
Direct labour per unit	7.00
Variable manufacturing overhead per unit	2.00
Variable selling and administrative expenses per unit	1.80
Fixed manufacturing overhead each month	102,300
Fixed selling and administrative expenses each month	187,800

Required：

How many units would the company have to sell to earn a target monthly profit of $260,100?

讲解： U盘售价为 $20，单位变动成本为 $17，因此单位贡献毛利为 $3。固定性制造费用为 $102 300，固定性销售与行政管理费用为 $187 800，因此固定成本为

带你到北美学习
管理会计
Take You to
North America
to Learn
Managerial Accounting

$290 100。目标利润为 $260 100。将上述数据代入单位贡献毛利法的公式，计算出赚取目标利润（$260 100）所需的销量为 183 400 个 U 盘。

6.4 本量利分析在商业环境中的应用
The Application of CVP Analysis in Business Conditions

在如今瞬息万变的市场环境下，企业管理者不得不面对成本增长、行业竞争者带来的价格压力以及商业环境的改变等各种局面。许多企业管理者通过本量利分析（CVP analysis）进行敏感性分析（sensitivity analysis）。敏感性分析是一种假设分析法，比如实际产品售价或成本发生改变，分析这些改变对企业产品销量产生的影响。

接下来，从改变售价、变动成本、固定成本、产品销售组合等四个方面，了解企业运用本量利分析应对商业环境变化。

6.4.1 改变售价
Changing Sales Price

通过"案例6-6"，分析在单位变动成本和固定成本恒定不变的前提下，产品售价改变对于单位贡献毛利和达到目标利润或收支平衡点所需的产品销量的影响。

案例6-6

GigaGo manufactures 1-GB flash drives (jump drives). Price and cost data for a relevant range extending to 200,000 units per month are as follows:

Selling price per unit (current monthly sales volume is 130,000 units)	$20.00
Direct materials per unit	6.20
Direct labour per unit	7.00
Variable manufacturing overhead per unit	2.00
Variable selling and administrative expenses per unit	1.80
Fixed manufacturing overhead each month	102,300
Fixed selling and administrative expenses each month	187,800

Required：

1. If selling price increases by 10% , how many units will the company have to sell each month to break even?

2. If selling price decreases by 10% , how many units will the company have to sell each month to break even?

讲解： 在 U 盘涨价之前，售价为 $ 20，单位变动成本为 $ 17，因此单位贡献毛利为 $ 3。固定性制造费用为 $ 102 300，固定性销售与行政管理费用为 $ 187 800，因此固定成本总额为 $ 290 100。将上述数据代入单位贡献毛利法公式，计算出收支平衡点销量为 96 700 个（（ $ 290 100 + $ 0） ÷ $ 3 = 96 700）。

如果价格上涨 10% ，U 盘售价为 $ 22，单位变动成本仍为 $ 17，因此单位贡献毛利为 $ 5（ $ 22 – $ 17 = $ 5）。固定成本总额仍为 $ 290 100。将上述数据代入单位贡献毛利法公式，计算出收支平衡点销量为 58 020 个（（ $ 290 100 + $ 0） ÷ $ 5 = 58 020）。

如果价格下调 10% ，U 盘售价为 $ 18，单位变动成本仍为 $ 17，因此单位贡献毛利为 $ 1（ $ 18 – $ 17 = $ 1）。固定成本总额仍为 $ 290 100。将上述数据代入单位贡献毛利法公式，计算出收支平衡点销量为 290 100 个（（ $ 290 100 + $ 0） ÷ $ 1 = 290 100）。

从"案例 6-6"可知，在单位变动成本和固定成本恒定不变的前提下，如果产品售价增长，单位贡献毛利随之增加，达到目标利润或收支平衡点所需的产品销量最终降低；如果产品售价降低，单位贡献毛利随之减少，达到目标利润或收支平衡点所需的产品销量最终增加（见图 6-1）。

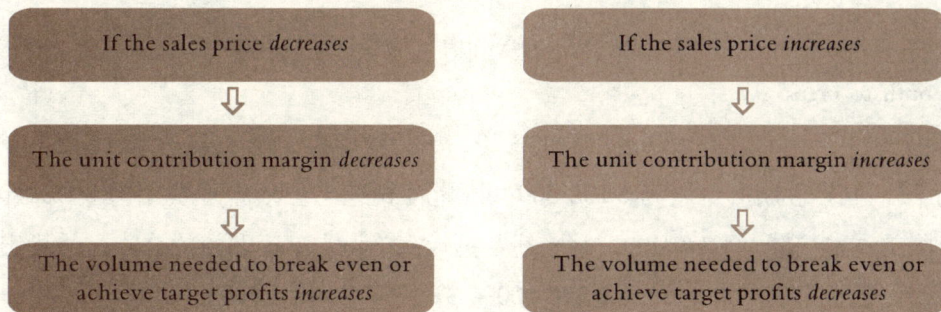

If the sales price *decreases*	If the sales price *increases*
⇩	⇩
The unit contribution margin *decreases*	The unit contribution margin *increases*
⇩	⇩
The volume needed to break even or achieve target profits *increases*	The volume needed to break even or achieve target profits *decreases*

图 6 – 1　售价改变引起的变化

带你到北美学习
管理会计
Take You to
North America
to Learn
Managerial Accounting

6.4.2 改变变动成本

Changing Variable Costs

通过"案例6-7",分析在产品售价和固定成本恒定不变的前提下,单位变动成本改变对于单位贡献毛利和达到目标利润或收支平衡点所需的产品销量的影响。

案例6 – 7

GigaGo manufactures 1-GB flash drives (jump drives). Price and cost data for a relevant range extending to 200,000 units per month are as follows:

Selling price per unit (current monthly sales volume is 130,000 units)	$20.00
Direct materials per unit	6.20
Direct labour per unit	7.00
Variable manufacturing overhead per unit	2.00
Variable selling and administrative expenses per unit	1.80
Fixed manufacturing overhead each month	102,300
Fixed selling and administrative expenses each month	187,800

Required:

1. The management is currently in contract negotiations with the labour union. If direct labour costs per unit increase by $1, how many units will the company have to sell each month to break even?

2. The management is currently in contract negotiations with the labour union. If direct labour costs per unit decrease by $1, how many units will the company have to sell each month to break even?

讲解: 与工会协商之前,U 盘售价为 $20,单位变动成本为 $17,因此单位贡献毛利为 $3。固定性制造费用为 $102 300,固定性销售与行政管理费用为 $187 800,因此固定成本总额为 $290 100。将上述数据代入单位贡献毛利法的公式,计算出收支平衡点销量为 96 700 个(($290 100 + $0) ÷ $3 = 96 700)。

与工会协商之后,单位直接人工成本上调 $1,增至 $8($7 + $1 = $8),因此单位变动成本增至 $18($6.20 + $8 + $2 + $1.80 = $18)。U 盘售价仍为 $20,因此单位贡献毛利为 $2($20 - $18 = $2)。固定成本总额仍为 $290 100。

将上述数据代入单位贡献毛利法的公式，计算出收支平衡点销量为 145 050 个
（（＄290 100＋＄0）÷ ＄2 = 145 050）。

如果单位直接人工成本下调＄1，降至＄6（＄7 – ＄1 = ＄6），则单位变动成
本降至＄16（＄6.20＋＄6＋＄2＋＄1.80 = ＄16）。U 盘售价仍为＄20，因此单位
贡献毛利为＄4（＄20 – ＄16 = ＄4）。固定成本总额仍为＄290 100。将上述数据代
入单位贡献毛利法的公式，计算出收支平衡点销量为72 525个（（＄290 100＋＄0）÷
＄4 = 72 525）。

从"案例6-7"可知，在产品售价和固定成本恒定不变的前提下，如果上调单
位变动成本，单位贡献毛利随之降低，达到目标利润或收支平衡点所需的产品销量
最终增加；如果下调单位变动成本，单位贡献毛利随之增加，达到目标利润或收支
平衡点所需的产品销量最终降低（见图6-2）。

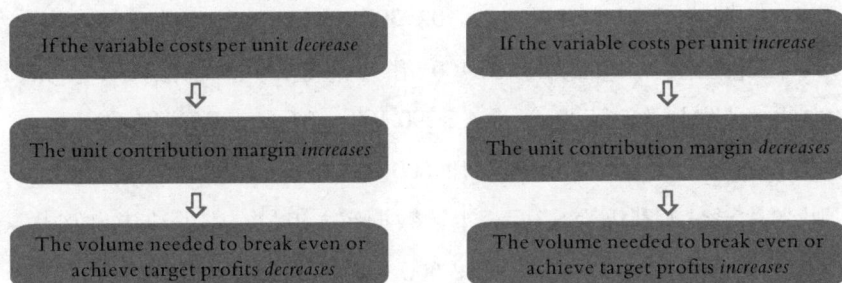

图6-2 变动成本改变引起的变化

6.4.3 改变固定成本
Changing Fixed Costs

通过"案例6-8"，分析在产品售价和单位变动成本恒定不变的前提下，固定成
本改变对于达到目标利润或收支平衡点所需的产品销量的影响。

案例6-8

GigaGo manufactures 1-GB flash drives (jump drives). Price and cost data for a relevant
range extending to 200,000 units per month are as follows:

Selling price per unit (current monthly sales volume is 130,000 units)	＄20.00
Direct materials per unit	6.20

带你到北美学习
管理会计
Take You to
North America
to Learn
Managerial Accounting

Direct labour per unit	7.00
Variable manufacturing overhead per unit	2.00
Variable selling and administrative expenses per unit	1.80
Fixed manufacturing overhead each month	102,300
Fixed selling and administrative expenses each month	187,800

Required：

1. If fixed costs increase by ＄22,500 each month, how many units will the company have to sell each month to break even?

2. If fixed costs decrease by ＄22,500 each month, how many units will the company have to sell each month to break even?

讲解： 在固定成本改变之前，U 盘售价为＄20，单位变动成本为＄17，因此单位贡献毛利为＄3。固定性制造费用为＄102 300，固定性销售与行政管理费用为＄187 800，因此固定成本总额为＄290 100。将上述数据代入单位贡献毛利法的公式，计算出收支平衡点销量为96 700 个（（＄290 100 ＋＄0）÷＄3 ＝ 96 700）。

固定成本增加＄22 500，增至＄312 600。U 盘售价为＄20，单位变动成本为＄17，因此单位贡献毛利仍为＄3。将上述数据代入单位贡献毛利法的公式，计算出收支平衡点销量为104 200 个（（＄312 600 ＋＄0）÷＄3 ＝ 104 200）。

固定成本减少＄22 500，降至＄267 600。U 盘售价仍为＄20，单位变动成本仍为＄17，单位贡献毛利仍为＄3。将上述数据代入单位贡献毛利法的公式，计算出收支平衡点销量为89 200 个（（＄267 600 ＋＄0）÷＄3 ＝ 89 200）。

从"案例6-8"可知，在产品售价和单位变动成本恒定不变的前提下，如果增加固定成本，达到目标利润或收支平衡点所需的产品销量也随之增加；如果降低固定成本，达到目标利润或收支平衡点所需的产品销量也随之降低（见图6-3）。

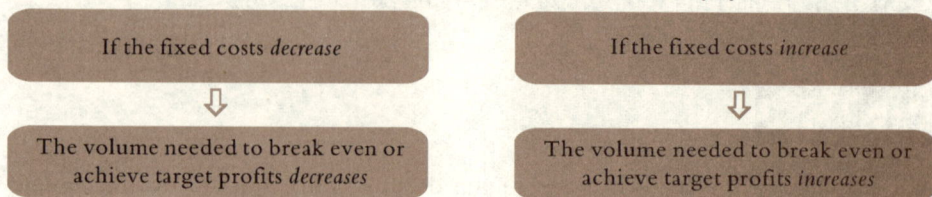

If the fixed costs *decrease*	If the fixed costs *increase*
⇩	⇩
The volume needed to break even or achieve target profits *decreases*	The volume needed to break even or achieve target profits *increases*

图 6 – 3　固定成本改变引起的变化

6.4.4 改变产品销售组合
Changing the Sales Mix of Products

无论是介绍单位贡献毛利、边际贡献率和确定收支平衡点，还是介绍应用本量利法分析商业环境变化，我们均假设企业仅出售一种产品；如果从出售一种产品变为出售两种或多种产品，企业应如何计算达到目标利润或收支平衡点所需的产品销量。"案例6-9"将解答这一问题。

案例 6 - 9

GigaGo manufactures 1-GB flash drives (jump drives). Price and cost data for a relevant range extending to 200,000 units per month are as follows：

Selling price per unit (current monthly sales volume is 130,000 units)	$20.00
Direct materials per unit	6.20
Direct labour per unit	7.00
Variable manufacturing overhead per unit	2.00
Variable selling and administrative expenses per unit	1.80
Fixed manufacturing overhead each month	102,300
Fixed selling and administrative expenses each month	187,800

Required：

Let's say GigaCo adds a second line of 2-GB flash drives. A package of 2-GB flash drives will sell for $45 and its variable costs per unit will be $28. The expected sales mix is six of the smaller flash drives for each larger flash drive. Given this sales mix, how many of each type of flash drives will GigaCo need to sell to reach its target monthly profit of $260,100？

讲解： 对于出售一种产品，在确定达到目标利润或收支平衡点所需的产品销量时，企业需要使用单位贡献毛利（unit contribution margin），而对于出售两种或多种产品，在确定达到目标利润或收支平衡点所需的产品销量时，需要使用加权平均单位贡献毛利（weighted average contribution margin per unit）。与单位贡献毛利不同，计算加权平均单位贡献毛利时，需要考虑产品的销售组合（sales mix）。

根据"案例6-9"信息，1-GB U 盘售价为 $20，单位变动成本为 $17，因此单位贡献毛利为 $3。2-GB U 盘售价为 $45，单位变动成本为 $28，所以单位贡献

带你到北美学习
管理会计
Take You to
North America
to Learn
Managerial Accounting

毛利为 $17。

当出售 6 个 1-GB U 盘时，GigaGo 出售 1 个 2-GB U 盘。6 个 1-GB U 盘与 1 个 2-GB U 盘构成的销售组合的贡献毛利为 $35（$3 × 6 + $17 × 1 = $35），因此加权平均单位贡献毛利为 $5（$35 ÷ 7 = $5）（见说明6-5）。

说明6-5：计算加权平均单位贡献毛利	1-GB Flash Drive	2-GB Flash Drive	Total
Selling price	$20	$45	
Variable costs	(17)	(28)	
Contribution margin	$3	$17	
Sales mix	× 6	× 1	7
Contribution margin	$18	$17	$35
Weighted average contribution margin per unit			$5

固定性制造费用为 $102 300，固定性销售与行政管理费用为 $187 800，所以固定成本总额为 $290 100。加权平均单位贡献毛利为 $5，目标利润为 $260 100。将上述数据代入单位贡献毛利法的公式，计算出赚取目标利润所需的销量为110 040个。

$$\text{Sales in units} = \frac{(\text{Fixed costs} + \text{Operating income})}{\text{Weighted average contribution margin per unit}}$$

$$= \frac{(\$290\ 100 + \$260\ 100)}{\$5} = 110\ 040$$

在销售组合中，1-GB U 盘占 6/7，2-GB U 盘占 1/7，因此为赚取目标利润（$260 100），1-GB U 盘销量为 94 320 个（110 040 ×（6/7）= 94 320），2-GB U 盘销量为 15 720 个（110 040 ×（1/7）= 15 720）。

1-GB U 盘售价为 $20，销量为 94 320 个，因此销售额为 $1 886 400。2-GB U 盘售价为 $45，销量为 15 720 个，因此销售额为 $707 400。为赚取目标利润（$260 100）所需的销售额为 $2 593 800（$1 886 400 + $707 400 = $2 593 800）。

6.5 两种风险衡量指标
Two Indicators of Measuring Risk

企业风险取决于许多因素，诸如经济环境、企业所在行业环境、企业当前产品销量、固定成本和变动成本所占总成本的比例等。这里介绍两种企业普遍使用的风险衡量指标：安全边际（margin of safety）和经营杠杆（operating leverage）。

6.5.1 安全边际
Margin of Safety

安全边际指实际或预期销售额超出收支平衡点销售额的多余部分。通过使用安全边际，企业管理者可以评估企业当前运营风险和新商业计划风险等。安全边际数值越大，则商业计划风险越低；安全边际数值越小，则商业计划风险越高。"说明 6-6"列出了与安全边际有关的计算公式。

说明 6-6：计算安全边际

Margin of safety in units = Expected or Actual sales in units − Breakeven sales in units

Margin of safety in dollars = Expected or Actual sales in dollars − Breakeven sales in dollars

$$\text{Margin of safety as a percentage} = \frac{\text{Margin of safety in units}}{\text{Expected or Actual sales in units}}$$

$$\text{Margin of safety as a percentage} = \frac{\text{Margin of safety in dollars}}{\text{Expected or Actual sales in dollars}}$$

通过"案例 6-10"，学习使用安全边际评估企业风险。

案例 6 - 10

GigaGo manufactures 1 - GB flash drives（jump drives）. Price and cost data for a relevant range extending to 200,000 units per month are as follows：

Selling price per unit（current monthly sales volume is 130,000 units）	$ 20.00
Direct materials per unit	6.20
Direct labour per unit	7.00
Variable manufacturing overhead per unit	2.00
Variable selling and administrative expenses per unit	1.80
Fixed manufacturing overhead each month	102,300
Fixed selling and administrative expenses each month	187,800

Required：

1. What is the company's margin of safety in dollars?

2. What is the company's margin of safety as a percentage of sales?

带你到北美学习
管理会计
Take You to
North America
to Learn
Managerial Accounting

讲解： U 盘售价为 $ 20，单位变动成本为 $ 17，因此单位贡献毛利为 $ 3。固定性制造费用为 $ 102 300，固定性销售与行政管理费用为 $ 187 800，因此固定成本总额为 $ 290 100。将上述数据代入边际贡献率法的公式，计算出收支平衡点销售额为 $ 1 934 000（（$ 290 100 + $ 0）÷ 15% = $ 1 934 000）。

实际销售额为 $ 2 600 000（$ 20 × 130 000 = $ 2 600 000），收支平衡点销售额为 $ 1 934 000，因此安全边际额（margin in safety in dollars）为 $ 666 000（$ 2 600 000 - $ 1 934 000 = $ 666 000），说明企业在产生经营亏损之前，销售额还可降低 $ 666 000。

由安全边际额和实际销售额计算出的安全边际率（margin in safety as a percentage）约为 25.62%（$ 666 000 ÷ $ 2 600 000 ≈ 25.62%），说明企业在产生经营亏损之前，销售额还可降低约 25.62%。

6.5.2 经营杠杆

Operating Leverage

大部分企业既要承担固定成本，又要产生变动成本。经营杠杆可用于说明固定成本和变动成本所占总成本的比例。企业经营杠杆过高，说明企业承担相对多的固定成本、相对少的变动成本；企业经营杠杆过低，说明企业承担相对少的固定成本、相对多的变动成本。"说明 6-7"列出了与经营杠杆有关的公式。

说明 6-7：计算经营杠杆

$$\text{Operating leverage} = \frac{\text{Contribution margin}}{\text{Operating income}} = \frac{(\text{Sales revenue} - \text{Variable costs})}{\text{Operating income}}$$

$$= \frac{(\text{Fixed costs} + \text{Operating income})}{\text{Operating income}}$$

$$\text{Operating leverage} = \frac{\text{Percentage in operating income}}{\text{Percentage in sales revenue}}$$

从经营杠杆公式可知，经营杠杆过高，则边际贡献率过大；换言之，如果企业销售额出现下滑趋势，经营收益将大幅下跌，而如果企业销售额呈现上升趋势，经营收益也随之大幅上涨。当企业经营杠杆过高时，如果销售额出现下滑趋势，企业将面临更大风险，而如果销售额呈现上升趋势，企业将获得更大收益。

经营杠杆过低，则边际贡献率过小。当企业经营杠杆过低时，如果销售额出现下滑趋势，企业将面临更小风险，而如果销售额呈现上升趋势，企业将获得更小收益。

经营杠杆最低值为 1。当经营杠杆为 1 时，企业不承担任何固定成本。换言之，只要企业出售商品，便可赚取经营收益；企业不出售商品，经营收益为 0，达到收支平衡点，因此不承担任何风险。

案例 6 – 11

GigaGo manufactures 1-GB flash drives（jump drives）. Price and cost data for a relevant range extending to 200,000 units per month are as follows：

Selling price per unit（current monthly sales volume is 130,000 units）	$20.00
Direct materials per unit	6.20
Direct labour per unit	7.00
Variable manufacturing overhead per unit	2.00
Variable selling and administrative expenses per unit	1.80
Fixed manufacturing overhead each month	102,300
Fixed selling and administrative expenses each month	187,800

Required：

1. What is the company's current operating leverage factor（round to two decimals）？

2. If sales volume increases by 7%, by what percentage will operating income increase？

讲解： U 盘销量为 130 000 台，售价为 $20，单位变动成本为 $17，所以销售额为 $2 600 000，变动成本为 $2 210 000。销售额（$2 600 000）减去变动成本（$2 210 000）等于贡献毛利（$390 000）。固定性制造费用为 $102 300，固定性销售与行政管理费用为 $187 800，因此固定成本总额为 $290 100。贡献毛利（$390 000）减去固定成本（$290 100）等于经营收益（$99 900）。

销售额为 $2 600 000，变动成本为 $2 210 000，经营收益为 $99 900，因此经营杠杆约为 3.90（（$2 600 000 – $2 210 000）÷ $99 900≈3.90）。

如果产品销量增长 7%，经营收益将增长 27.30%（7% × 3.90 = 27.30%）。

带你到北美学习
管理会计
Take You to
North America
to Learn
Managerial Accounting

例题综述
Summary of Examples

例题 6 - 1

In July, Akron Laser Wash sold 200 deluxe car washes for $15 per customer. Variable costs are $9 per wash, fixed costs are $1,000 per month. What is the contribution margin ratio?

A. $1,200

B. $200

C. 40%

D. 60%

讲解： 一次汽车清洗的价格为 $15，单位变动成本为 $9，因此单位贡献毛利为 $6。单位贡献毛利（$6）除以售价（$15）等于边际贡献率（40%）。

答案： C

例题 6 - 2

An operating leverage factor of 2 implies that for every _____.

A. 1% percentage change in contribution margin, operating income will change by 2%

B. 1% percentage change in sales volume, operating income will change by 2%

C. 2% percentage change in sales volume, contribution margin will change by 1%

D. 2% percentage change in contribution margin, operating income will change by 1%

讲解： 当经营杠杆为 2 时，如果产品销量增长 1%，经营收益将增长 2%；如果产品销量降低 1%，经营收益将随之降低 2%。

答案： B

例题 6 - 3

Low operating leverage implies _____.

A. higher level of fixed cost, lower level of variable cost, and lower risk of operating loss

B. higher level of fixed cost, lower level of variable cost, and higher risk of operating loss

C. lower level of fixed cost, higher level of variable cost, and higher risk of operating loss

D. lower level of fixed cost, higher level of variable cost, and lower risk of operating loss

讲解： 经营杠杆过低，则边际贡献率过小。当企业经营杠杆过低时，如果销售额出现下滑趋势，企业将面临更小风险，而如果销售额呈现上升趋势，企业将获得更小收益。

答案： D

例题 6-4

The income statement format that is required for internal users is _____.

A. a relevant costing income statement

B. an incremental income statement

C. an absorption costing income statement

D. a contribution margin income statement

讲解： 为向内部使用者提供有价值的成本习性信息，企业不得不编写边际贡献收益表（contribution margin income statement）。边际贡献收益表以成本习性（变动成本或固定成本）分类成本，而非成本功能。

答案： D

例题 6-5

Kitchen Appliances Company manufactures two products: toaster oven and bread machine. The following data are available:

	Toaster Oven	Bread Machine
Selling price	$ 100	$ 200
Variable costs	30	150

The company can manufacture three toaster ovens per machine hour and two bread machines per machine hour. The company's production capacity is 1,200 machine hours per month. What is the contribution margin ratio for bread machine?

A. 233.33%

B. 70.00%

C. 30.00%

D. 130.00%

带你到北美学习
管理会计
Take You to
North America
to Learn
Managerial Accounting

E. None of the above

讲解： 面包机售价为 $200，单位变动成本为 $150，因此单位贡献毛利为 $50。单位贡献毛利（$50）除以售价（$200）等于边际贡献率（25%）。

答案： E

例题 6 - 6

Motor Company produces heated motorcycle gloves. The company has fixed costs of $125,000 per month and variable costs of $75 per pair. Each pair sells for $125. How many pairs will the company have to sell to generate an operating income of $100,000?

A. 4,000

B. 5,200

C. 4,500

D. 2,500

E. None of the above

讲解： 手套售价为 $125，单位变动成本为 $75，因此单位贡献毛利为 $50。固定成本总额为 $125 000，经营收益为 $100 000。将上述数据代入单位贡献毛利法的公式，计算出赚取经营收益（$100 000）所需的销量为 4 500 副手套。

答案： C

例题 6 - 7

Checkerbox Company has a predicted operating income of $97,500. Its variable expenses are $42,000 and its fixed expenses are $96,000. The company has a unit contribution margin of $15.

Required：

1. Calculate the required sales in units to achieve the predicted operating income.

2. Calculate the required sales in units to achieve the predicted operating income if the company's fixed expenses increase from $96,000 to $192,000.

1. Calculate the required sales in units to achieve the predicted operating income.

讲解： 单位贡献毛利为 $15，固定成本为 $96 000，预计经营收益为 $97 500。将上述数据代入单位贡献毛利法的公式，计算出赚取经营收益（$97 500）所需的销量为 12 900 件产品（（$97 500 + $96 000）÷ $15 = 12 900）。

答案：To achieve the predicted operating income, the required sales in units is 12,900 units.

2. Calculate the required sales in units to achieve the predicted operating income if the company's fixed expenses increase from $96,000 to $192,000.

讲解：单位贡献毛利为 $15，预计经营收益为 $97 500，固定成本增至 $192 000。将上述数据代入单位贡献毛利法的公式，计算出赚取经营收益（$97 500）所需的销量为 19 300 件产品（（$97 500 + $192 000）÷ $15 = 19 300）。

答案：To achieve the predicted operating income, the required sales in units is 19,300 units.

例题 6 – 8

Nova Scotia does not have a Chinese restaurant, and Brian and Nui Soon are contemplating opening one. Brian has noticed a restaurant for lease. The restaurant has seven tables, each of which can have four seats. Tables can be moved together for a large party. Nui is planning two seatings per evening, and the restaurant will be open 50 weeks per year. The Soons have drawn up the following estimates：

Average revenue per meal	$40
Average costs per meal	12
Chef's and dishwasher's salaries expense each year	50,400
Rent expense each month	4,000
Cleaning expense each month	800
Replacement expense of dishes, cutlery, and glasses each month	300
Utilities, advertising and telephone expenses each month	1,900

Required：

1. Compute the breakeven number of meals and sales revenue for the restaurant.

2. Compute the number of meals and the amount of sales revenue needed to earn an operating income of $75,600 for the year.

带你到北美学习

管理会计

Take You to
North America
to Learn
Managerial Accounting

3. How many meals must the Soons serve each night to earn their target operating income of ＄75,600? Should the couple open the restaurant?

1. Compute the breakeven number of meals and sales revenue for the restaurant.

讲解： 每餐售价为＄40，单位变动成本为＄12，单位贡献毛利为＄28。固定成本总额为＄134 400（（＄4 000＋＄800＋＄300＋＄1 900）×12＋＄50 400＝＄134 400），因此收支平衡点销量为4 800餐（（＄134 400＋＄0）÷＄28＝4 800）。每餐售价为＄40，收支平衡点销量为4 800餐，收支平衡点销售额为＄192 000。

答案： The breakeven number of meals for the restaurant is 4,800 meals and the breakeven sales revenue is ＄192,000.

2. Compute the number of meals and the amount of sales revenue needed to earn an operating income of ＄75,600 for the year.

讲解： 每餐售价为＄40，单位变动成本为＄12，单位贡献毛利为＄28。固定成本总额为＄134 400，经营收益为＄75 600，因此赚取经营收益（＄75 600）所需的销量为7 500餐（（＄134 400＋＄75 600）÷＄28＝7 500）。每餐售价为＄40，销量为7 500餐，赚取经营收益（＄75 600）所需的销售额为＄300 000。

答案： To earn an operating income of ＄75,600 for the year, the number of meals is 7,500 meals and the amount of sales revenue needed is ＄300,000.

3. How many meals must the Soons serve each night to earn their target operating income of ＄75,600? Should the couple open the restaurant?

讲解： 赚取经营收益（＄75 600）所需的销量为7 500餐。这家餐厅一年运营50周，每周5天，共计250天，因此餐厅每晚仅需提供30餐（7 500 meals÷250 days＝30 meals per day）。餐厅每晚可以提供56餐（7 tables×4 meals per table×2 seatings per evening＝56 meals），因此这对夫妇可以通过开设这家餐厅赚取目标经营收益（＄75 600）。

答案： To earn their target operating income of ＄75,600, the Soons must serve 30 meals each night. The target operating income of ＄75,600 appears to be realistic if the restaurant can attract customers. The restaurant has adequate seating for 56 meals per night (7 tables ×

4 meals per table × 2 seatings per evening = 56 meals), and the Soons only need to serve 30 meals a night to achieve their target operating income. The key to earn this income is attracting enough diners to the restaurant. If Brian and Nui Soon believe that they can operate at 54% (30/56≈53.57%) of capacity or more, they should open the restaurant.

例题 6 – 9

Happy Feet has variable costs of $6.50 per pair, which is then sold for $11 per pair. Monthly fixed costs are $18,000, current sales in units is 12,000 pairs per month.

Required:

1. Calculate the breakeven sales in units.

2. Calculate Happy Feet's margin of safety in units and dollars.

3. Calculate Happy Feet's margin of safety as a percentage.

4. Calculate Happy Feet's operating leverage factor.

5. Using the operating leverage factor you calculated above, calculate Happy Feet's percentage change in operating income decline if sales revenue falls by 20%.

1. Calculate the breakeven sales in units.

讲解： 袜子售价为 $11，单位变动成本为 $6.50，单位贡献毛利为 $4.50。固定成本总额为 $18 000，因此收支平衡点销量为 4 000 双袜子（（$18 000 + $0）÷ $4.50 = 4 000）。

答案： The breakeven sales in units is 4,000 socks.

2. Calculate Happy Feet's margin of safety in units and dollars.

讲解： 实际销量为 12 000 双，收支平衡点销量为 4 000 双，因此安全边际量为 8 000双。袜子售价为 $11，所以安全边际额为 $88 000。

答案： The margin of safety in units is 8,000 socks and the margin of safety in dollars is $88,000.

3. Calculate Happy Feet's margin of safety as a percentage.

讲解： 袜子售价为 $11，实际销量为 12 000 双，实际销售额为 $132 000。安全边

带你到北美学习
管理会计
Take You to
North America
to Learn
Managerial Accounting

际额为 $88 000，实际销售额为 $132 000，安全边际率约为 66.67% （$88 000 ÷ $132 000 ≈ 66.67%）。

答案： The margin of safety as a percentage is about 66.67%.

4. Calculate Happy Feet's operating leverage factor.

讲解： 袜子售价为 $11，单位变动成本为 $6.50，实际销量为 12 000 双，因此实际销售额为 $132 000，变动成本为 $78 000。销售额（$132 000）减去变动成本（$78 000）等于贡献毛利（$54 000），贡献毛利（$54 000）减去固定成本（$18 000）等于经营收益（$36 000）。计算得出经营杠杆为 1.50 （（$132 000 − $78 000）÷ $36 000 = 1.50）。

答案： The operating leverage factor is 1.50.

5. Using the operating leverage factor you calculated above, calculate Happy Feet's percentage change in operating income decline if sales revenue falls by 20%.

讲解： 当经营杠杆为 1.50 时，如果销售额降低 20%，则经营收益随之降低 30%。

答案： The operating income will decline by 30%.

例题 6 - 10

Mac Company is the distributor for two products: Model Z50 and Model Z99. The company's fixed expenses are $980,000 per month. The monthly sales revenue and contribution margin ratio data for the two products are as follows:

	Model Z50	Model Z99
Sales revenue	$1,400,000	$600,000
Contribution margin ratio	65%	60%

Required:

1. Prepare a contribution margin income statement for the company.

2. Calculate the breakeven point for the company based on its current sales mix.

3. If sales revenue increases by $100,000 per month, by how much would you expect operating income to increase? State your assumptions.

1. Prepare a contribution margin income statement for the company.

讲解： Model Z50 的销售额为 $1 400 000，Model Z99 的销售额为 $600 000，所以企业销售额为 $2 000 000。Model Z50 和 Model Z99 的边际贡献率分别为 65% 和 60%，因此 Model Z50 和 Model Z99 的贡献毛利分别为 $910 000（$1 400 000 × 65% = $910 000）和 $360 000（$600 000 × 60% = $360 000），企业贡献毛利为 $1 270 000。企业固定成本总额为 $980 000。贡献毛利（$1 270 000）减去固定成本（$980 000）等于经营收益（$290 000）。

答案：

Mac Company Contribution Margin Income Statement			
	Model Z50	Model Z99	Total
Sales revenue	$1,400,000	$600,000	
Contribution margin ratio	× 65%	× 60%	
Contribution margin	$910,000	$360,000	$1,270,000
Fixed costs			(980,000)
Operating income			$290,000

2. Calculate the breakeven point for the company based on its current sales mix.

讲解： 企业销售额为 $2 000 000，贡献毛利为 $1 270 000，所以边际贡献率为 63.50%（$1 270 000 ÷ $2 000 000 = 63.50%）。固定成本总额为 $980 000，因此收支平衡点销售额约为 $1 543 307.09（（$980 000 + $0）÷ 63.50% ≈ $1 543 307.09）。

答案： Based on the current sales mix, the breakeven point for the company as a whole is about $1,543,307.09.

3. If sales revenue increases by $100,000 per month, by how much would you expect operating income to increase? State your assumptions.

讲解： 企业边际贡献率为 63.50%。如果销售额增长 $100 000，贡献毛利随之增长 $63 500。固定成本总额没有改变，因此经营收益也随之增长 $63 500。如果使用边际贡献率法预测销售额变化对于企业经营收益的影响，我们必须假设商品售价、单位变动成本和商品销售组合均未改变。

答案： If sales revenue increases by $100,000 per month, the expected operating income

带你到北美学习
管理会计
Take You to
North America
to Learn
Managerial Accounting

would increase by $63,500. In order to use the contribution margin ratio to predict the expected operating income based on the increase in sales, the sales price, variable cost per unit, and sales mix are not changed.

例题 6 - 11

Sporting Goods is a retailer of sporting equipment. Last year, Sporting Goods' sales revenue totaled $6,400,000. Total expenses were $2,800,000. Of this amount, approximately $1,792,000 were variable, while the remainder were fixed. Since Sporting Goods offers thousands of different products, its managers prefer to calculate the breakeven point in terms of dollars rather than units.

Required:

1. What is Sporting Goods' current operating income (prepare a contribution margin income statement)?

2. What is Sporting Goods' contribution margin ratio?

3. What is Sporting Goods' breakeven point in dollars? What does it mean? (Hint: The contribution margin ratio calculated in Part 2 is already weighted by Sporting Goods' actual sales mix.)

4. Sporting Goods' top management is deciding whether to embark on a $190,000 advertisement campaign. The marketing firm has projected annual sales volume to increase by 20% as a result of this campaign. Assuming that the projection is correct, how would this advertising campaign affect Sporting Goods' annual operating income?

1. What is Sporting Goods' current operating income (prepare a contribution margin format income statement)?

讲解: 销售额（$6 400 000）减去变动成本（$1 792 000）等于贡献毛利（$4 608 000），贡献毛利（$4 608 000）减去固定成本（$1 008 000）等于经营收益（$3 600 000）。

答案：

Sporting Goods Contribution Margin Income Statement	
Sales revenue	$6,400,000
Variable costs	(1,792,000)
Contribution margin	4,608,000
Fixed costs	(1,008,000)
Operating income	$3,600,000

2. What is Sporting Goods' contribution margin ratio?

讲解： 销售额为 $6 400 000，贡献毛利为 $4 608 000，边际贡献率为72%。

答案： The contribution margin ratio for Sporting Goods is 72%.

3. What is Sporting Goods' breakeven point in dollars? What does it mean? (Hint: The contribution margin ratio calculated in Part 2 is already weighted by Sporting Goods' actual sales mix.)

讲解： 固定成本总额为 $1 008 000，边际贡献率为72%，因此收支平衡点销售额为 $1 400 000（（$1 008 000 + $0）÷ 72% = $1 400 000）。当销售额低于 $1 400 000 时，企业将出现经营亏损；当销售额高于 $1 400 000 时，企业将获取经营收益。

答案： Sporting Goods' breakeven point in dollars is $1,400,000. Sporting Goods will have to generate $1,400,000 in sales revenue in order to breakeven.

4. Sporting Goods' top management is deciding whether to embark on a $190,000 advertisement campaign. The marketing firm has projected annual sales volume to increase by 20% as a result of this campaign. Assuming that the projection is correct, how would this advertising campaign affect Sporting Goods' annual operating income?

讲解： 在产品售价、单位变动成本、单位贡献毛利保持不变的前提下，如果产品销量增长20%，意味着销售额、变动成本总额和贡献毛利均增长20%。贡献毛利原先为 $4 608 000，因此增长 $921 600（$4 608 000 × 20% = $921 600）。为使产品销量增长20%，企业支付广告费用 $190 000，因此固定成本总额增长 $190 000。贡献毛利增长 $921 600，固定成本总额增长 $190 000，所以经营收益增长 $731 600

带你到北美学习
管理会计
Take You to
North America
to Learn
Managerial Accounting

（ $ 921\ 600 - $ 190\ 000 = $ 731\ 600$ ）。

答案： Due to this advertising campaign, the company's annual operating income will increase by $ 731,600$.

例题 6 - 12

Peter Company's most recent contribution margin income statement is as follows:

	Total	Unit
Sales revenue (30,000 units)	$ 150,000	$ 5
Variable expenses	(90,000)	(3)
Contribution margin	60,000	$ 2
Fixed expenses	(50,000)	
Operating income	$ 10,000	

Required:

Prepare a new contribution margin income statement under each of the following independent cases.

1. Selling price decreases by $ 0.50$ and number of units sold increases by 20% .

2. Selling price increases by $ 0.50$, fixed expenses increase by $ 15,000$, and number of units sold decreases by 5% .

3. Selling price increases by 15% , variable expenses per unit increase by $ 0.40$, and number of units sold decreases by 10% .

1. Selling price decreases by $ 0.50$ and number of units sold increases by 20% .

答案：

	Total	Unit
Sales revenue (30,000 units × (1 + 20%) = 36,000 units)	$ 162,000	$ 4.50
Variable expenses	(108,000)	(3.00)
Contribution margin	54,000	$ 1.50
Fixed expenses	(50,000)	
Operating income	$ 4,000	

2. Selling price increases by $0.50, fixed expenses increase by $15,000, and number of units sold decreases by 5%.

答案：

	Total	Unit
Sales revenue (30,000 units × (1 - 5%) = 28,500 units)	$156,750	$5.50
Variable expenses	(85,500)	(3.00)
Contribution margin	71,250	$2.50
Fixed expenses	(65,000)	
Operating income	$6,250	

3. Selling price increases by 15%, variable expenses per unit increase by $0.40, and number of units sold decreases by 10%.

答案：

	Total	Unit
Sales revenue (30,000 units × (1 - 10%) = 27,000 units)	$155,250	$5.75
Variable expenses	(91,800)	(3.40)
Contribution margin	63,450	$2.35
Fixed expenses	(50,000)	
Operating income	$13,450	

例题 6 - 13

The Alumni Association is planning its annual dinner and dance event. The dinner and dance committee would like to charge $55 per person for the evening's activities. This committee has assembled the following expected costs for the event：

Dinner per person	$28
Favours and programs per person	2
Bands	4,000
Rental of ballroom	1,900
Professional entertainment during intermission	2,000
Tickets and advertising	2,300

带你到北美学习
管理会计
Take You to
North America
to Learn
Managerial Accounting

Required：

1. Calculate the breakeven number of tickets for the event.

2. Assume that only 300 people attended the event last year. If the same number of people attend this year, what price per ticket must be charged to break even?

3. If the association anticipates that 600 people will attend this year's event. What is the margin of safety in dollars?

1. Calculate the breakeven number of tickets for the event.

讲解： 入场券价格为 $55，单位变动成本为 $30（$28 + $2 = $30），单位贡献毛利为 $25。固定成本总额为 $10 200（$4 000 + $1 900 + $2 000 + $2 300 = $10 200），因此收支平衡点销量为408张（（$10 200 + $0）÷ $25 = 408）。入场券价格为 $55，收支平衡点销量为408张，所以收支平衡点销售额为 $22 440。

答案： The breakeven point in dollars is $22,440 and the breakeven point in units is 408 persons.

2. Assume that only 300 people attended the event last year. If the same number of people attend this year, what price per ticket must be charged to break even?

讲解： 仅300人参加晚宴，单位变动成本为 $30（$28 + $2 = $30），固定成本总额为 $10 200（$4 000 + $1 900 + $2 000 + $2 300 = $10 200）。将上述数据代入收益表法的公式，计算出收支平衡点的入场券价格为 $64。

答案： If only 300 people attend the dinner and dance event this year, the ticket price charged should be $64 to break even.

3. If the association anticipates that 600 people will attend this year's event. What is the margin of safety in dollars?

讲解： 如果600人参加晚宴，入场券价格为 $55，预期销售额为 $33 000，收支平衡点销售额为 $22 440，因此安全边际额为 $10 560（$33 000 − $22 440 = $10 560）。

答案： The margin of safety in dollars is $10,560.

例题 6 – 14

Campus Service Company imprints desk calendars. Each carton of calendars is sold for $ 12. 25. The company has fixed expenses of $ 1,155,000 each month. Variable expenses amount to $ 4 per carton of calendars. These variable expenses can be broken down into cost of goods sold (65%) and variable operating expenses (35%).

Required:

1. Use the income statement equation approach to calculate the number of cartons of calendars that Campus Service Company must sell each month to break even.

2. Use the contribution margin ratio formula to calculate the dollar amount of monthly sales revenue that Campus Service Company needs to earn $ 250,000 in operating income.

3. Assuming Campus Service Company sold 460,000 cartons of calendars in June, prepare a contribution margin income statement for June.

4. What was the June's margin of safety in dollars? What was the operating leverage factor at this level of sales?

5. By what percentage will operating income change if July's sales volume is 10% higher? Prove your answer.

1. Use the income statement equation approach to calculate the number of cartons of calendars that Campus Service Company must sell each month to break even.

讲解： 日历售价为 $ 12. 25，单位变动成本为 $ 4，固定成本总额为 $ 1 155 000。将上述数据代入收益表法的公式，计算出收支平衡点销量为 140 000 台日历。

答案： The breakeven point in units is 140,000 cartons.

2. Use the contribution margin ratio formula to calculate the dollar amount of monthly sales revenue that Campus Service Company needs to earn $ 250,000 in operating income.

讲解： 日历售价为 $ 12. 25，单位变动成本为 $ 4，所以单位贡献毛利为 $ 8. 25，边际贡献率约为 67. 35% （ $ 8. 25 ÷ $ 12. 25 ≈ 67. 35% ）。固定成本总额为 $ 1 155 000。将上述数据代入边际贡献率法的公式，计算出获取经营收益（ $ 250 000）所需的销售额约为 $ 2 086 117. 30 （ （ $ 1 155 000 + $ 250 000) ÷ 67. 35% ≈ $ 2 086 117. 30）。

带你到北美学习

管理会计

Take You to
North America
to Learn
Managerial Accounting

答案： In order to earn an operating income of $250,000, the monthly sales revenue should be approximately $2,086,117.30.

3. Assuming Campus Service Company sold 460,000 cartons of calendars in June, prepare a contribution margin income statement for June.

讲解： 6 月份日历销量为 460 000 台，日历售价为 $12.25，单位变动成本为 $4，因此销售额为 $5 635 000，变动成本总额为 $1 840 000。固定成本总额为 $1 155 000。销售额（$5 635 000）减去变动成本（$1 840 000）等于贡献毛利（$3 795 000），贡献毛利（$3 795 000）减去固定成本（$1 155 000）等于经营收益（$2 640 000）。

答案：

Campus Service Company Contribution Margin Income Statement For the month ended by June 30	
Sales revenue	$5,635,000
Variable costs	(1,840,000)
Contribution margin	3,795,000
Fixed costs	(1,155,000)
Operating income	$2,640,000

4. What was the June's margin of safety in dollars? What was the operating leverage factor at this level of sales?

讲解： 6 月份销售额为 $5 635 000，收支平衡点销售额为 $1 715 000，因此安全边际额为 $3 920 000（$5 635 000 − $1 715 000 = $3 920 000）。当 6 月份销售额为 $5 635 000 时，贡献毛利为 $3 795 000，经营收益为 $2 640 000，经营杠杆约为 1.44（$3 795 000 ÷ $2 640 000 = 1.437 5 ≈ 1.44）。

答案： The June's margin of safety in dollars was $3,920,000. The operating leverage factor at this level of sales was about 1.44.

5. By what percentage will operating income change if July's sales volume is 10% higher? Prove your answer.

讲解： 当经营杠杆为 1.44 时，如果 6 月份销量增长 10%，则经营收益随之增长 14.40% 。

日历售价、单位变动成本、单位贡献毛利均未变化，分别为 $12.25，$4 和 $8.25。如果 6 月份销量增长 10%，当月销售额、变动成本总额、贡献毛利均随之增长 10%，即销售额增长 $563 500，变动成本总额增长 $184 000，贡献毛利增长 $379 500。贡献毛利增长 $379 500，固定成本总额未改变，因此经营收益增长 $379 500，涨幅约为 14.40% （ $379 500 ÷ $2 640 000 = 14.375% ≈ 14.40% ）。

答案： If July's sales volume is 10% higher, the operating income will increase by 14.40% .

Increase in sales revenue	$ 563,500
Increase in variable costs	(184,000)
Increase in contribution margin	379,500
Increase in fixed costs	(0)
Increase in operating income	$ 379,500
Percentage increase in operating income	14.40%

带你到北美学习
管理会计
Take You to
North America
to Learn
Managerial Accounting

专业名词汇编
Glossary of Accounting Terms

安全边际	margin of safety	安全边际额	margin of safety in dollars
安全边际量	margin of safety in units	边际贡献率	contribution margin ratio
变动成本	variable cost	成本功能	cost function
成本习性	cost behaviour	单位变动成本	variable cost per unit
单位贡献毛利	unit contribution margin	贡献毛利	contribution margin
经营杠杆	operating leverage	收益表法	income statement approach
销售组合	sales mix		
安全边际率	margin in safety as a percentage		
边际贡献率法	contribution margin ratio approach		
边际贡献收益表	contribution margin income statement		
本量利分析	cost–volume–profit（CVP）analysis		
单位贡献毛利法	unit contribution margin approach		
加权平均单位贡献毛利	weighted average contribution margin per unit		

总预算

Master Budget

带你到北美学习
管理会计
Take You to
North America
to Learn
Managerial Accounting

7.1 运用预算

Using Budgets

通过预算，企业管理者履行规划、监督、控制等方面的职责。预算是一种不间断进行的循环：为制定战略决策，企业首先制定长期战略，一般涉及企业未来 5 ~ 10 年的战略目标；一旦建立长期目标，企业管理层需要设计核心战略（key strategy）以实现既定目标；根据企业核心战略决策，管理者出台详细规划并组织实施；通过绩效报告（performance report），管理者将企业实际运营与预算进行对比，并对规划提出反馈意见；反馈可以帮助企业管理者采取矫正措施（corrective action），必要时需要调整企业战略目标与核心战略决策，这也是新一轮循环的开始。

7.2 制定预算

Preparing Budgets

在制定企业长期战略目标与核心战略决策之后，企业管理者需要根据企业战略目标与核心战略决策出台企业规划（预算）。许多企业以先前预算数据或实际数据作为未来预算的起点，这些数据主要取自过去的收益表和资产负债表，而为了体现新产品、新客户、新行业政策、同行业竞争者导致的市场份额变化、制造成本变化、经济通胀等因素，这些数据需要做出适当修改才能作为未来预算的基础。

企业一般在给定财务周期的前两个季度，制定未来一年的预算，而有的企业使用滚动预算（rolling budget）。滚动预算是一种持续更新的预算，比如 2017 年 1 月的企业运营结束，2018 年 1 月的企业预算会自动生成。滚动预算的优势在于企业管理者永远拥有未来 12 个月的预算。

7.3 预算的作用

The Benefits of Budgeting

预算一般有如下三种作用：①推动企业管理者履行规划职责；②促进协调与合作；③激励员工，评估企业实际绩效。

（1）企业管理者一般忙于企业日常运营，而无暇顾及企业未来规划。预算可以促使管理者在企业未来发展上投入更多时间和精力，而非仅考虑企业日常运营。

（2）预算可以协调企业价值链的各个环节，促使企业管理者考虑价值链中各环节的相互关系与作用。例如，一家制造商未来 10 年的战略目标是推出一款新产品。根据这一战略决策，企业研发团队开始研发新产品；一旦新产品研制成功，设计和生产团队将考虑大规模生产这款新产品；市场团队开始设计足够吸引人的标识、别具匠心的产品推广活动；为配合新产品上市，配送团队调整当前配送系统；客服团队考虑解决新产品带来的客户投诉与产品维修。预算有助于企业各环节之间的协调与合作（见 P10 图 1-3）。

（3）预算可以激励员工，评估企业实际绩效。预算提供了大多数企业管理者试图实现的预定目标；但是，如果预算太难或太易实现，均很难起到激励员工的作用。因此为了激励员工，企业预算应制定在合理范围内。预算也提供了评估企业实际绩效的标准。在财务周期结束之际，通过绩效报告，企业管理者可以对比实际收入与预算收入、实际费用与预算费用之间的差异，评估企业实际运营情况与企业规划的适合程度。

7.4　制定总预算

Preparing Master Budget

总预算（master budget）是制定企业整体规划的文件。总预算包括编写预算财务报表（budgeted financial statement）需要的所有辅助性预算（supporting budget）。图 7-1 所示为制造商总预算的辅助性预算以及编写辅助性预算的先后顺序。

经营预算（operating budget）指企业日常运营所需的预算。如图 7-1 所示，销售预算（sales budget）是经营预算的起点，决定经营预算的其他辅助性预算；在完成销售预算之后，制造商准备生产预算（production budget），生产预算提供了产品产量的预算数据；一旦确定产品产量，制造商便可制定直接材料预算（direct materials budget）、直接人工预算（direct labour budget）和制造费用预算（manufacturing overhead budget）；在完成与生产有关的预算之后，制造商编写经营费用预算（operating expenses budget）。上述这些经营预算的辅助性预算均是编写预算收益表（budgeted income statement）所需的数据。

带你到北美学习
管理会计
Take You to
North America
to Learn
Managerial Accounting

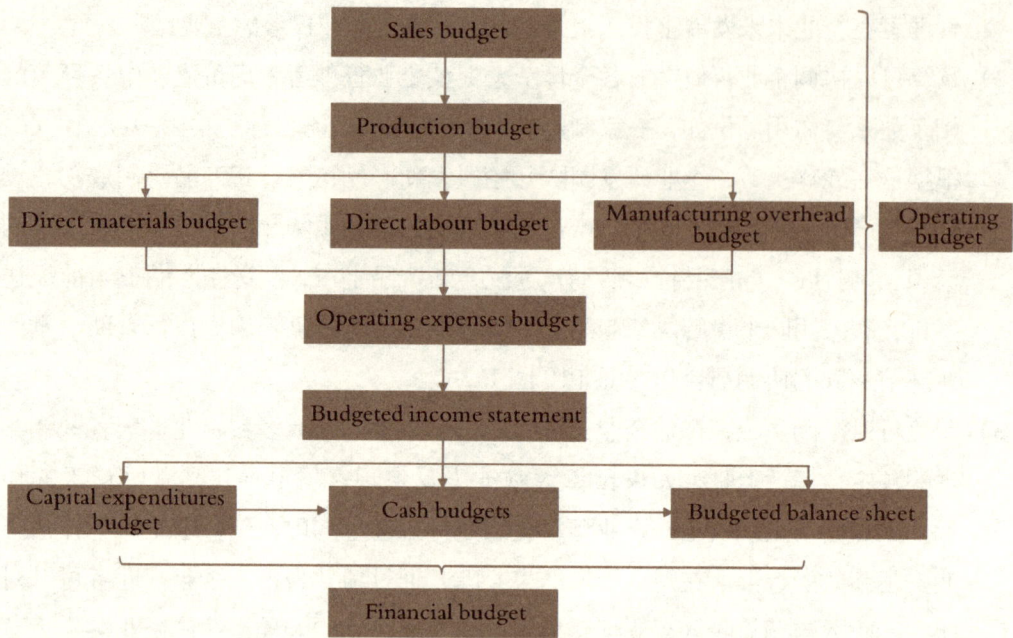

图 7 - 1 制造商总预算

财务预算（financial budget）包括资本支出预算（capital expenditure budget）、现金预算（cash budget）、预算资产负债表（budgeted balance sheet）。资本支出预算说明企业采购新物业、厂房与设备（property, plant, and equipment）的规划。现金预算说明企业日常运营是否有可用现金、企业是否有额外资金用于投资以及企业是否需要借贷。预算资产负债表用于预测企业未来财务周期的财务状况。

7.4.1 制定经营预算

Preparing Operating Budgets

通过"案例7-1"，学习制定总预算的辅助性预算。

案例 7 - 1

QWE Manufacturing is preparing its market budget for the first quarter of the year. The data pertain to QWE Manufacturing's operations are as follows:

Current assets as of December 31（prior year）	
Cash	$ 4,500

Accounts receivable	98,000
Inventory	15,320
Property, plant, and equipment, net	121,500
Accounts payable	23,536
Capital stock	196,884
Retained earnings	22,920

a. Actual sales revenue in December was $140,000. Selling price per unit is projected to remain stable at $20 per unit throughout the budget period. Sales in units for the first five months of the upcoming year is budgeted to be as follows:

Number of units to be sold in January	8,000
Number of units to be sold in February	9,200
Number of units to be sold in March	9,900
Number of units to be sold in April	9,700
Number of units to be sold in May	8,500

b. Sales is 30% cash and 70% credit. All credit sales is collected in the month following sales.

c. QWE Manufacturing has a new policy that states that each month's ending inventory of finished goods should be 25% of the following month's sales in units.

d. Of each month's direct materials (DM) purchases, 20% are paid for in the month of purchases, while the remainder are paid for in the month following purchases. Two kilograms of direct materials are needed per unit at $2 per kilogram. The ending inventory of direct materials should be 10% of next month's production needs.

e. QWE Manufacturing is fairly automated, so very little direct labour (DL) is required. Each unit requires only 0.10 DL hour. Direct labourers are paid $30 per hour. Direct labour is paid in the month in which it is incurred.

f. Monthly manufacturing conversion costs are $5,000 for factory rent, $3,000 for other fixed manufacturing expenses, and $1.20 for variable manufacturing overhead per unit. No depreciation is included in these figures. All expenses are paid in the month in which they are incurred.

g. Computer equipment for the administrative offices will be purchased in the upcoming quarter. In January, QWE Manufacturing will purchase equipment for $5,000 in

271

带你到北美学习
管理会计
Take You to
North America
to Learn
Managerial Accounting

cash, while February's cash expenditure will be $12,000 and March's cash expenditure will be $16,000.

h. Sales commissions are budgeted to be $1 per unit sold plus salaries for the general and administrative employees of $1,000 per month. All operating expenses are paid in the month in which they are incurred.

i. Depreciation on the building and equipment for the general and administrative offices is budgeted to be $1,600 each month, which includes depreciation on new acquisitions.

j. QWE Manufacturing has a new policy that the ending cash balance in each month must be at least $100,000. It has a line of credit of $100,000 with a local bank. The interest rate on these loans is 1% per month simple interest (not compounded). QWE Manufacturing pays down on the line of credit balance if it has excess funds at the end of the quarter. The company also pays the accumulated interest at the end of the quarter on the funds borrowed during the quarter.

k. The company's income tax rate is projected to be 30% of operating income less interest expense. The company must file its income tax return within six months of its fiscal year end. Payments for its estimated income tax liability are typically due quarterly, or monthly if it does not qualify for quarterly payments. QWE Manufacturing has a December 31 fiscal year end and meet the criteria for quarterly payments, the income tax return is not due until June 30; however, the first payment is due by April 15. As a result, QWE Manufacturing will not pay any income taxes in the first quarter of the year.

l. The total production volume for the coming year budgeted to be 120,000 units.

Required:

1. Prepare a sales budget for January, February, and March, and for the first quarter in total.

2. Prepare a production budget for January, February, and March, and for the first quarter in total.

3. Prepare a direct materials budget for January, February, and March, and for the first quarter in total.

4. Prepare a direct labour budget for January, February, and March, and for the first quarter in total.

5. Prepare a manufacturing overhead budget for January, February, and March, and for the first quarter in total.

6. Prepare an operating expenses budget for January, February, and March, and for the first quarter in total.

7. Prepare a budgeted income statement for the first quarter in total ended by March 31.

8. Prepare a capital expenditures budget for January, February, and March, and for the first quarter in total.

9. Prepare a combined cash budget for January, February, and March, and for the first quarter in total.

10. Prepare a partial budgeted balance sheet at March 31. Follow the same format as the original balance sheet provided at December 31.

7.4.1.1 销售预算 (Sales Budget)

销售预算是总预算的起点。预期销售额 (expected sales revenue) 等于预计销量 (expected sales in units) 乘以预期售价 (expected sales price) (见图 7-2)。

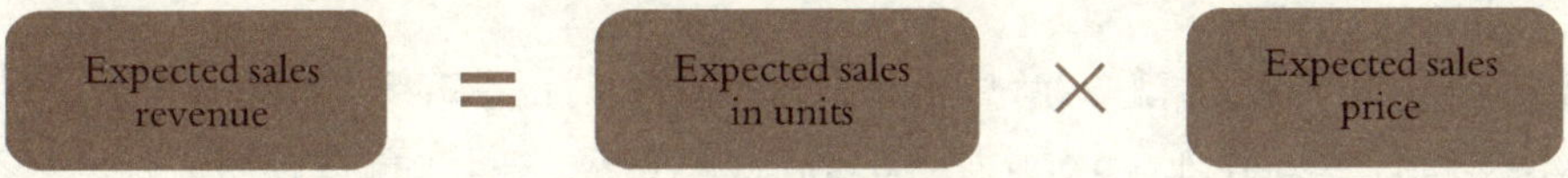

图 7 - 2　销售预算计算公式

根据 "案例 7-1" 信息,1～3 月份的预计产品销量分别为 8 000 件、9 200 件和 9 900 件,1 季度的预计产品销量为 27 100 件,产品价格为 $20,因此 1～3 月份的预期销售额分别为 $160 000,$184 000 和 $198 000,1 季度的预期销售额为 $542 000。现金销售占销售额的 30%,赊销占销售额的 70% (见说明 7-1)。

说明 7 - 1: 销售预算				
QWE Manufacturing Sales Budget For the quarter ended by March 31				
	January	February	March	1st Quarter
Sales in units	8,000	9,200	9,900	27,100
Sales price	× $20	× $20	× $20	× $20
Sales revenue	$160,000	$184,000	$198,000	$542,000

带你到北美学习
管理会计
Take You to
North America
to Learn
Managerial Accounting

Type of Sale：				
Cash sales（30%）	$48,000	$55,200	$59,400	$162,600
Credit sales（70%）	112,000	128,800	138,600	379,400
Sales revenue	$160,000	$184,000	$198,000	$542,000

7.4.1.2 生产预算（Production Budget）

为保障产品供应，大部分制造商保留一部分制成品作为期末库存或安全库存（safety stock），以备不时之需。预计产品销量加上预期产品期末库存（desired units in ending inventory）等于产品需求总量（total units needed），产品需求总量减去产品期初库存（units in beginning inventory）等于产品产量（units to produce）（见图7-3）。

| Expected sales in units | **+** | Desired units in ending inventory | **=** | Total units needed |
| Total units needed | **−** | Units in beginning inventory | **=** | Units to produce |

图 7 – 3 生产预算计算公式

根据"案例7-1"信息，产品月末库存等于下月销量的25%。1~4月份的预计产品销量分别为8 000件、9 200件、9 900件和9 700件，因此去年12月末、今年1月末、2月末和3月末的产品库存分别为2 000件、2 300件、2 475件和2 425件。

1月份预计产品销量（8 000）加上1月末产品库存（2 300）等于1月份产品需求总量（10 300），1月份产品需求总量（10 300）减去1月初产品库存（2 000）等于1月份产品产量（8 300）。1月初产品库存（2 000）等于去年12月末产品库存（2 000）。

2月份预计产品销量（9 200）加上2月末产品库存（2 475）等于2月份产品需求总量（11 675），2月份产品需求总量（11 675）减去2月初产品库存（2 300）等于2月份产品产量（9 375）。2月初产品库存（2 300）等于1月末产品库存（2 300）。

3月份预计产品销量（9 900）加上3月末产品库存（2 425）等于3月份产品需求总量（12 325），3月份产品需求总量（12 325）减去3月初产品库存（2 475）等于3月份产品产量（9 850）。3月初产品库存（2 475）等于2月末产品库存（2 475）。

1 季度预计产品销量（27 100）加上 1 季度末产品库存（2 425）等于 1 季度产品需求总量（29 525），1 季度产品需求总量（29 525）减去 1 季度初产品库存（2 000）等于 1 季度产品产量（27 525）。

1 季度包括 1 月份、2 月份和 3 月份，因此 1 季度初产品库存也是 1 月初产品库存，1 季度末产品库存也是 3 月末产品库存（见说明 7-2）。

说明 7-2：生产预算				
QWE Manufacturing Production Budget For the quarter ended by March 31				
	January	February	March	1st Quarter
Sales in units	8,000	9,200	9,900	27,100
Desired units in ending inventory	2,300	2,475	2,425	2,425
Total units needed	10,300	11,675	12,325	29,525
Units in beginning inventory	(2,000)	(2,300)	(2,475)	(2,000)
Units to produce	8,300	9,375	9,850	27,525

7.4.1.3 直接材料预算（Direct Materials Budget）

根据生产预算，QWE Manufacturing 可以制定直接材料预算（direct materials budget）。生产所需直接材料（direct materials needed for production）加上预期直接材料期末库存（desired ending direct materials inventory）等于直接材料需求总量（total direct materials needed），直接材料需求总量减去直接材料期初库存（beginning direct materials inventory）等于直接材料采购量（direct materials to purchase）（见图 7-4）。

根据"案例 7-1"信息，QWE Manufacturing 期望，单件产品需要 2 千克直接材料，因此为生产 1～3 月份的 8 300 件、9 375 件和 9 850 件产品，QWE Manufacturing 在 1～3 月份分别需要直接材料 16 600 千克、18 750 千克和 19 700 千克。

直接材料月末库存等于下月生产所需直接材料的 10%，因此去年 12 月末、今年 1 月末和 2 月末的直接材料库存分别为 1 660 千克、1 875 千克和 1 970 千克。我们还需要计算，今年 3 月末的直接材料库存；为获知今年 3 月末的直接材料库存，必须计算 4 月份生产所需的直接材料数量。

带你到北美学习
管理会计
Take You to
North America
to Learn
Managerial Accounting

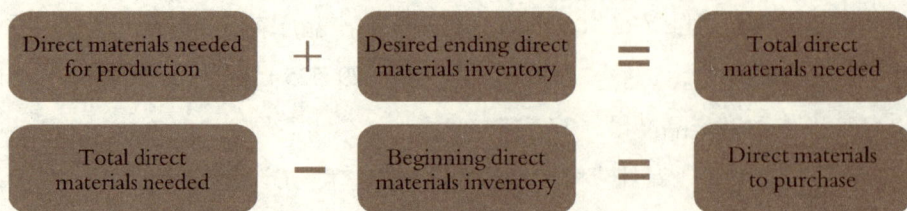

| Direct materials needed for production | + | Desired ending direct materials inventory | = | Total direct materials needed |
| Total direct materials needed | − | Beginning direct materials inventory | = | Direct materials to purchase |

图 7 - 4　直接材料预算计算公式

4 月初产品库存（2 425）等于 3 月末产品库存（2 425），4 月末产品库存（2 125）等于 5 月份产品销量（8 500）的 25%。4 月份预计产品销量（9 700）加上 4 月末产品库存（2 125）等于 4 月份产品需求总量（11 825），4 月份产品需求总量（11 825）减去 4 月初产品库存（2 425）等于 4 月份产品产量（9 400）。4 月份产品产量为 9 400 件，单件产品需要 2 千克直接材料，因此 4 月份生产所需直接材料 18 800 千克。我们知道，直接材料月末库存等于下月生产所需直接材料的 10%，4 月份生产所需直接材料 18 800 千克，因此 3 月末直接材料库存为 1 880 千克。

1 月份生产所需直接材料（16 600）加上 1 月末直接材料库存（1 875）等于 1 月份直接材料需求总量（18 475），1 月份直接材料需求总量（18 475）减去 1 月初直接材料库存（1 660）等于 1 月份直接材料采购量（16 815）。1 月初直接材料库存（1 660）等于去年 12 月末直接材料库存（1 660）。

2 月份生产所需直接材料（18 750）加上 2 月末直接材料库存（1 970）等于 2 月份直接材料需求总量（20 720），2 月份直接材料需求总量（20 720）减去 2 月初直接材料库存（1 875）等于 2 月份直接材料采购量（18 845）。2 月初直接材料库存（1 875）等于 1 月末直接材料库存（1 875）。

3 月份生产所需直接材料（19 700）加上 3 月末直接材料库存（1 880）等于 3 月份直接材料需求总量（21 580），3 月份直接材料需求总量（21 580）减去 3 月初直接材料库存（1 970）等于 3 月份直接材料采购量（19 610）。3 月初直接材料库存（1 970）等于 2 月末直接材料库存（1 970）。

1 季度生产所需直接材料（55 050）加上 1 季度末直接材料库存（1 880）等于 1 季度直接材料需求总量（56 930），1 季度直接材料需求总量（56 930）减去 1 季度初直接材料库存（1 660）等于 1 季度直接材料采购量（55 270）。

1 季度包括 1 月份、2 月份和 3 月份，因此 1 季度初直接材料库存也是 1 月初直接材料库存，1 季度末直接材料库存也是 3 月末直接材料库存。

我们计算出，1～3 月份的直接材料采购量分别为 16 815 千克、18 845 千克和

19 610千克，每千克直接材料的价格为＄2，因此 QWE Manufacturing 在1～3月份分别采购价值为＄33 630，＄37 690 和＄39 220 的直接材料，1 季度采购价值为＄110 540的直接材料（见说明7-3）。

说明 7-3：直接材料预算				
QWE Manufacturing Direct Materials Budget For the quarter ended by March 31				
	January	February	March	1st Quarter
Units to be produced	8,300	9,375	9,850	27,525
Kilograms of DM needed per unit	× 2	× 2	× 2	× 2
DM needed for production	16,600	18,750	19,700	55,050
Desired ending DM inventory	1,875	1,970	1,880	1,880
Total DM needed	18,475	20,720	21,580	56,930
Beginning DM inventory	(1,660)	(1,875)	(1,970)	(1,660)
DM to purchase	16,815	18,845	19,610	55,270
Cost per kilogram	× ＄2	× ＄2	× ＄2	× ＄2
Total cost of DM purchases	＄33,630	＄37,690	＄39,220	＄110,540

7.4.1.4 直接人工预算 （Direct Labour Budget）

根据1～3月份产品产量，QWE Manufacturing 制定直接人工预算（direct labour budget）。产品产量（units to be produced）乘以单件产品所需直接人工工时（direct labour hours needed per unit）等于生产所需直接人工工时，生产所需直接人工工时（direct labour hours needed for production）乘以直接人工工资率（direct labour rate）等于直接人工成本总额（total direct labour cost）（见图7-5）。

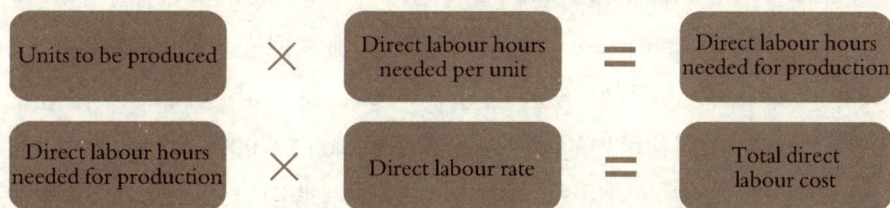

图 7-5 直接人工预算计算公式

根据生产预算，1～3月份的产品产量分别为 8 300 件、9 375 件和 9 850 件。根据"案例7-1"信息，单件产品耗费直接人工工时 0.10 小时，因此为生产 1～3 月

带你到北美学习
管理会计
Take You to
North America
to Learn
Managerial Accounting

份的 8 300 件、9 375 件和 9 850 件产品，QWE Manufacturing 在1 ~ 3月份分别耗费直接人工工时 830 小时、937.50 小时和 985 小时，1 季度耗费直接人工工时 2 752.50小时。直接人工工资率为 $30，所以在1 ~ 3月份分别产生直接人工成本 $24 900，$28 125和$29 550，1 季度产生直接人工成本 $82 575（见说明7-4）。

说明7-4：直接人工预算

QWE Manufacturing
Direct Labour Budget
For the quarter ended by March 31

	January	February	March	1st Quarter
Units to be produced	8,300	9,375	9,850	27,525
Direct labour hours needed per unit	× 0.10	× 0.10	× 0.10	× 0.10
Direct labour hours needed for production	830	937.50	985	2,752.50
Direct labour rate	× $30	× $30	× $30	× $30
Total direct labour cost	$24,900	$28,125	$29,550	$82,575

7.4.1.5 制造费用预算 （Manufacturing Overhead Budget）

制造费用预算（manufacturing overhead budget）高度依赖成本习性（cost behaviour）。一些制造费用属于变动成本（variable cost），而另一些制造费用属于固定成本（fixed cost），还有一些制造费用属于混合成本（mixed cost）。对于属于混合成本的制造费用，必须先将这些制造费用区分为变动性制造费用（variable manufacturing overhead）和固定性制造费用（fixed manufacturing overhead）。

根据"案例7-1"信息，每月厂房租金为 $5 000，每月其他固定性制造费用为 $3 000，单件产品的变动性制造费用为 $1.20。根据生产预算，1 ~ 3月份的产品产量分别为 8 300 件、9 375 件和 9 850 件。为生产1 ~ 3月份的 8 300 件、9 375 件和 9 850件产品，QWE Manufacturing 在1 ~ 3月份分别承担变动性制造费用 $9 960，$11 250 和 $11 820。每月厂房租金为 $5 000，每月其他固定性制造费用为 $3 000，因此在1 ~ 3月份承担的固定性制造费用均为 $8 000。

1 月份的变动性制造费用为 $9 960，固定性制造费用为 $8 000，因此制造费用为 $17 960；2 月份的变动性制造费用为 $11 250，固定性制造费用为 $8 000，因此制造费用为 $19 250；3 月份的变动性制造费用为 $11 820，固定性制造费用为 $8 000，因此制造费用为 $19 820。1 季度的变动性制造费用为 $33 030（$9 960 +

$ 11 250 + $ 11 820 = $ 33 030），固定性制造费用为 $ 24 000（ $ 8 000 + $ 8 000 + $ 8 000 = $ 24 000），因此制造费用为 $ 57 030（见说明 7-5）。

说明7-5：制造费用预算				
QWE Manufacturing Manufacturing Overhead Budget For the quarter ended by March 31				
	January	February	March	1st Quarter
Units to be produced	8,300	9,375	9,850	27,525
Variable manufacturing overhead	$9,960	$11,250	$11,820	$33,030
Fixed manufacturing overhead				
Factory rent	5,000	5,000	5,000	15,000
Other fixed manufacturing overhead	3,000	3,000	3,000	9,000
Total fixed manufacturing overhead	8,000	8,000	8,000	24,000
Total manufacturing overhead	$17,960	$19,250	$19,820	$57,030

7. 4. 1. 6 经营费用预算 （Operating Expenses Budget）

企业在价值链生产环节产生的成本被视为产品成本（product cost），而在价值链其他五个环节（研发、设计、市场营销、配送和客户服务）产生的成本则被视为期间成本（period cost），期间成本也被称为经营费用（operating expense）或销售、常规与行政费用（selling, general, and administrative expense）。

与制造费用相同，经营费用预算（operating expenses budget）同样依赖于成本习性（cost behaviour）。一些经营费用属于变动成本（variable cost），而另一些经营费用属于固定成本（fixed cost），还有一些经营费用属于混合成本（mixed cost）。对于属于混合成本的经营费用，必须先将这些经营费用区分为变动性经营费用（variable operating expense）和固定性经营费用（fixed operating expense）。

根据"案例7-1"信息，每月行政办公人员薪资为 $ 1 000，每月行政办公场所与设备产生的折旧费用为 $ 1 600，单件产品的销售佣金为 $ 1。根据销售预算，1～3月份的产品销量分别为 8 000 件、9 200 件和 9 900 件。为出售1～3月份的 8 000 件、9 200件和9 900件产品，QWE Manufacturing 在1～3月份分别承担销售佣金费用 $ 8 000，$ 9 200 和 $ 9 900。每月行政办公人员薪资为 $ 1 000，每月行政办公场所与设备产生的折旧费用为 $ 1 600，因此企业在1～3月份承担的固定性经营费用均为

带你到北美学习
管理会计
Take You to
North America
to Learn
Managerial Accounting

$2 600。

1 月份的变动性经营费用为 $8 000，固定性经营费用为 $2 600，因此经营费用为 $10 600；2 月份的变动性经营费用为 $9 200，固定性经营费用为 $2 600，因此经营费用为 $11 800；3 月份的变动性经营费用为 $9 900，固定性经营费用为 $2 600，因此经营费用为 $12 500。1 季度的变动性经营费用为 $27 100（$8 000 + $9 200 + $9 900 = $27 100），固定性经营费用为 $7 800（$2 600 + $2 600 + $2 600 = $7 800），因此经营费用为 $34 900（见说明7-6）。

说明7-6：经营费用预算

QWE Manufacturing
Operating Expenses Budget
For the quarter ended by March 31

	January	February	March	1st Quarter
Sales in units	8,000	9,200	9,900	27,100
Variable operating expense				
Sales commissions expense	$8,000	$9,200	$9,900	$27,100
Fixed operating expenses				
Salaries expense	1,000	1,000	1,000	3,000
Depreciation expense	1,600	1,600	1,600	4,800
Total fixed operating expenses	2,600	2,600	2,600	7,800
Total operating expenses	$10,600	$11,800	$12,500	$34,900

7.4.1.7 预算收益表（Budgeted Income Statement）

除了使用预算数据（budgeted data），而非真实数据（actual data），编写预算收益表（budgeted income statement）与编写收益表的方法和步骤完全相同。根据"案例7-1"信息，产品售价为 $20，1～3 月份的预计产品销量分别为 8 000 件、9 200 件和 9 900 件，1 季度的预计产品销量为 27 100 件，因此 1～3 月份的预期销售额分别为 $160 000，$184 000 和 $198 000，1 季度的预期销售额为 $542 000。

1 季度，QWE Manufacturing 出售 27 100 件产品，1 件产品的预算制造成本为 $9（见说明 7-7），因此售出商品成本为 $243 900。1 季度的预期销售额为 $542 000，售出商品成本为 $243 900，因此毛利润为 $298 100（$542 000 − $243 900 = $298 100）。

说明 7-7：计算单件产品的预算制造成本	
Direct materials（2 kilograms per unit × $2 per kilogram）	$4.00
Direct labour（0.10 DL hour per unit × $30 per DL hour）	3.00
Variable manufacturing overhead	1.20
Fixed manufacturing overhead	0.80[1]
Unit costs	$9.00

[1] 每月固定性制造费用为 $8 000，因此每年固定性制造费用为 $96 000（$8 000 × 12 = $96 000）；未来一年的预计产品产量为 120 000 件，所以单件产品的固定性制造费用为 $0.80（$96 000 ÷ 120 000 = $0.80）。

从"说明7-6"可知，1季度的经营费用为 $34 900，毛利润（$298 100）减去经营费用（$34 900）等于经营收益（263 200）。从"说明7-17"可知，1季度的利息费用为 $400，经营收益（263 200）减去利息费用（$400）等于税前收益（$262 800）。根据"案例7-1"信息，所得税税率为30%；税前收益（$262 800）乘以所得税税率（30%）等于所得税费用（$78 840），税前收益（$262 800）减去所得税费用（$78 840）等于净收益（$183 960）（见说明7-8）。

说明 7-8：预算收益表	
QWE Manufacturing Budgeted Income Statement For the quarter ended by March 31	
Sales revenue	$542,000
Cost of goods sold	(243,900)
Gross profit	298,100
Operating expenses	(34,900)
Operating income	263,200
Interest expense	(400)
Income before taxes	262,800
Income taxes（30% tax rate）	(78,840)
Net income	$183,960

带你到北美学习
管理会计
Take You to
North America
to Learn
Managerial Accounting

7.4.2 制定财务预算

Preparing Financial Budgets

财务预算（financial budget）包括资本支出预算（capital expenditure budget）、现金预算（cash budget）、预算资产负债表（budgeted balance sheet）。资本支出预算说明企业采购新物业、厂房与设备（property, plant, and equipment）的规划。现金预算说明企业日常运营是否有可用现金、企业是否有额外资金用于投资以及企业是否需要借贷。预算资产负债表用于预测企业未来财务周期的财务状况。

7.4.2.1 资本支出预算 （Capital Expenditures Budget）

资本支出预算说明企业采购新物业、厂房与设备的规划。如果资本投资预算数额巨大，将严重影响折旧费用（depreciation expense）、利息费用（interest expense）和股息支付（dividend payment），所以企业需要尽早制定资本支出预算。

根据"案例7-1"信息，1月份，QWE Manufacturing 购买价值为 $5 000 的计算机；2月份，购买价值为 $12 000 的计算机；3月份，购买价值为 $16 000 的计算机；1季度购买总价值为 $33 000 的计算机（见说明7-9）。

说明 7 - 9：资本支出预算				
QWE Manufacturing Capital Expenditures Budget For the quarter ended by March 31				
	January	February	March	1st Quarter
New investments in computer equipment	$5,000	$12,000	$16,000	$33,000

7.4.2.2 现金预算 （Cash Budget）

现金预算说明企业日常运营是否有可用现金、企业是否有额外资金用于投资以及企业是否需要借贷。在制定现金预算之前，我们需要制定现金收取预算（cash collections budget）和现金支付预算（cash payments budget）。

根据"案例7-1"信息，去年12月份的销售额为 $140 000。根据销售预算（见说明7-1），1~3月份的预计产品销量分别为 8 000 件、9 200 件和 9 900 件，1季度的预计产品销量为 27 100 件。产品售价为 $20，因此1~3月份的预期销售额分别为 $160 000，$184 000 和 $198 000，1季度的预期销售额为 $542 000。

　　根据"案例 7-1"信息，现金销售占销售额的 30%，赊销占销售额的 70%；现金销售在当月收取，赊销将在下月收取，如 1 月份的现金销售在 1 月份收取，1 月份的赊销将在 2 月份收取。

　　去年 12 月份的现金销售额为 $\$ 42\,000$，赊销额为 $\$ 98\,000$；今年 1 月份的现金销售额为 $\$ 48\,000$，赊销额为 $\$ 112\,000$；今年 2 月份的现金销售额为 $\$ 55\,200$，赊销额为 $\$ 128\,800$；今年 3 月份的现金销售额为 $\$ 59\,400$，赊销额为 $\$ 138\,600$。

　　1 月份，QWE Manufacturing 收取去年 12 月份、金额为 $\$ 98\,000$ 的赊销以及今年 1 月份、金额为 $\$ 48\,000$ 的现金销售，共计 $\$ 146\,000$；2 月份，企业收取今年 1 月份、金额为 $\$ 112\,000$ 的赊销以及今年 2 月份、金额为 $\$ 55\,200$ 的现金销售，共计 $\$ 167\,200$；3 月份，企业收取今年 2 月份、金额为 $\$ 128\,800$ 的赊销以及今年 3 月份、金额为 $\$ 59\,400$ 的现金销售，共计 $\$ 188\,200$。1 季度，QWE Manufacturing 收取现金 $\$ 501\,400$（见说明 7-10）。

<table>
<tr><td colspan="5">说明 7-10：现金收取预算</td></tr>
<tr><td colspan="5">QWE Manufacturing
Cash Collections Budget
For the quarter ended by March 31</td></tr>
<tr><td></td><td>January</td><td>February</td><td>March</td><td>1st Quarter</td></tr>
<tr><td>Cash sales</td><td>$48,000</td><td>$55,200</td><td>$59,400</td><td>$162,600</td></tr>
<tr><td>Collections on credit sales：</td><td></td><td></td><td></td><td></td></tr>
<tr><td>　December credit sales</td><td>98,000</td><td></td><td></td><td>98,000</td></tr>
<tr><td>　January credit sales</td><td></td><td>112,000</td><td></td><td>112,000</td></tr>
<tr><td>　February credit sales</td><td></td><td></td><td>128,800</td><td>128,800</td></tr>
<tr><td>Total cash collections</td><td>$146,000</td><td>$167,200</td><td>$188,200</td><td>$501,400</td></tr>
</table>

　　根据"案例 7-1"信息，QWE Manufacturing 在当月支付直接材料采购钱款的 20%，在下月支付剩余采购钱款（80%）。根据直接材料预算（见说明 7-3），企业在 1～3 月份分别采购价值为 $\$ 33\,630$，$\$ 37\,690$ 和 $\$ 39\,220$ 的直接材料。例如，为支付 1 月份采购的、价值为 $\$ 33\,630$ 的直接材料，QWE Manufacturing 在 1 月份支付现金 $\$ 6\,726$（$\$ 33\,630 \times 20\% = \$ 6\,726$），2 月份支付现金 $\$ 26\,904$（$\$ 33\,630 \times 80\% = \$ 26\,904$）；此外，1 月份，企业还需要支付去年 12 月份的直接材料采购钱款，所以首先需要计算去年 12 月份的直接材料采购量。

　　根据"案例 7-1"信息，去年 12 月份产品销售额为 $\$ 140\,000$，产品售价为

带你到北美学习
管理会计
Take You to
North America
to Learn
Managerial Accounting

＄20，因此产品销量为 7 000 件。QWE Manufacturing 期望，产品月末库存等于下月销量的 25%。1 月份预计产品销量为 8 000 件，因此去年 12 月末产品库存为 2 000 件；去年 12 月份产品销量为 7 000 件，所以去年 11 月末产品库存为 1 750 件。去年 12 月初产品库存（1 750）等于去年 11 月末产品库存（1 750）。我们知道，去年 12 月初产品库存为 1 750 件，去年 12 月份产品销量为 7 000 件，去年 12 月末产品库存为 2 000 件，因此去年 12 月份产品产量为 7 250 件（7 000 + 2 000 – 1 750 = 7 250）。

QWE Manufacturing 期望，单件产品需要 2 千克直接材料，直接材料月末库存等于下月生产所需直接材料的 10%。1 月份生产所需直接材料为 16 600 千克，因此去年 12 月末直接材料库存为 1 660 千克。为生产去年 12 月份的 7 250 件产品，需要直接材料 14 500 千克，所以去年 11 月末直接材料库存为 1 450 千克。去年 12 月初直接材料库存（1 450）等于去年 11 月末直接材料库存（1 450）。我们知道，去年 12 月初直接材料库存为 1 450 千克，去年 12 月份所需直接材料为 14 500 千克，去年 12 月末直接材料库存为 1 660 千克，去年 12 月份直接材料采购量为 14 710 千克（14 500 + 1 660 – 1 450 = 14 710）。每千克直接材料的价格为 ＄2，因此 QWE Manufacturing 在去年 12 月份采购价值为 ＄29 420 的直接材料。

根据"案例 7-1"信息，QWE Manufacturing 在当月支付直接材料采购钱款的 20%，在下月支付剩余采购钱款（80%）。1 月份，QWE Manufacturing 支付去年 12 月份采购的、价值为 ＄23 536 的直接材料以及今年 1 月份采购的、价值为 ＄6 726 的直接材料，共计现金 ＄30 262；2 月份，企业支付今年 1 月份采购的、价值为 ＄26 904的直接材料以及今年 2 月份采购的、价值为 ＄7 538 的直接材料，共计现金 ＄34 442；3 月份，企业支付今年 2 月份采购的、价值为 ＄30 152 的直接材料以及今年 3 月份采购的、价值为 ＄7 844 的直接材料，共计现金 ＄37 996。为采购直接材料，QWE Manufacturing 在 1 季度支付现金 ＄102 700（见说明 7-11）。

说明 7-11：采购直接材料的现金支付预算

	January	February	March	1st Quarter
Cash payments for December DM purchases	＄23,536			＄23,536
Cash payments for January DM purchases	6,726	＄26,904		33,630
Cash payments for February DM purchases		7,538	＄30,152	37,690
Cash payments for March DM purchases			7,844	7,844
Total cash payments for DM purchases	＄30,262	＄34,442	＄37,996	＄102,700

根据直接人工预算（见说明 7-4），1 ~ 3 月份的直接人工成本分别为 $24 900，$28 125 和 $29 550，1 季度的直接人工成本为 $82 575。根据"案例 7-1"信息，QWE Manufacturing 在当月支付所承担的直接人工成本，因此 1 ~ 3 月份分别支付直接人工成本 $24 900，$28 125 和 $29 550，1 季度支付直接人工成本 $82 575（见说明 7-12）。

说明 7-12：直接人工的现金支付预算

	January	February	March	1st Quarter
Cash payments for direct labour	$24,900	$28,125	$29,550	$82,575

根据制造费用预算（见说明 7-5），1 ~ 3 月份的制造费用分别为 $17 960，$19 250 和 $19 820，1 季度的制造费用为 $57 030。根据"案例 7-1"信息，QWE Manufacturing 在当月支付所承担的制造费用，因此 1 ~ 3 月份分别支付制造费用 $17 960，$19 250 和 $19 820，1 季度支付制造费用 $57 030（见说明 7-13）。

说明 7-13：制造费用的现金支付预算

	January	February	March	1st Quarter
Cash payments for manufacturing overhead	$17,960	$19,250	$19,820	$57,030

根据经营费用预算（见说明 7-6），1 ~ 3 月份的经营费用分别为 $10 600，$11 800 和 $12 500，1 季度的经营费用为 $34 900。根据"案例 7-1"信息，QWE Manufacturing 的经营费用包含折旧费用，折旧费用属于非现金费用，因此折旧费用不呈现于现金支付预算。每月行政办公场所与设备产生的折旧费用为 $1 600，即 1 季度行政办公场所与设备产生的折旧费用为 $4 800，因此 QWE Manufacturing 在 1 ~ 3 月份分别支付经营费用 $9 000，$10 200 和 $10 900，在 1 季度支付经营费用 $30 100（见说明 7-14）。

请注意：折旧费用（depreciation expense）和坏账费用（bad debt expense）均属于非现金费用（non-cash expense），非现金费用不出现在现金支付预算（cash payments budget）。

说明 7-14：经营费用的现金支付预算

	January	February	March	1st Quarter
Operating expenses	$10,600	$11,800	$12,500	$34,900
Depreciation expense	(1,600)	(1,600)	(1,600)	(4,800)

带你到北美学习
管理会计
Take You to
North America
to Learn
Managerial Accounting

Cash payments for operating expenses	$9,000	$10,200	$10,900	$30,100

根据预算收益表（见说明 7-8），1 季度的所得税费用为 $78 840。根据"案例 7-1"信息，QWE Manufacturing 将于 4 月 15 日支付这笔所得税费用，因此 1～3 月份支付的所得税费用为 $0（见说明 7-15）。

说明 7-15：所得税费用的现金支付预算

	January	February	March	1st Quarter
Cash payments for income taxes	$0	$0	$0	$0

至此，完成了现金支付预算（cash payments budget）的各类辅助性预算的准备工作，即资本支出预算（见说明 7-9）、采购直接材料的现金支付预算（见说明 7-11）、直接人工的现金支付预算（见说明 7-12）、制造费用的现金支付预算（见说明 7-13）、经营费用的现金支付预算（见说明 7-14）和所得税费用的现金支付预算（见说明 7-15）。将这些辅助性预算汇总，便可制定现金支付预算（见说明 7-16）。

说明 7-16：现金支付预算

QWE Manufacturing
Cash Payments Budget
For the quarter ended by March 31

	January	February	March	1st Quarter
Cash payments for direct material purchases	$30,262	$34,442	$37,996	$102,700
Cash payments for direct labour	24,900	28,125	29,550	82,575
Cash payments for manufacturing overhead	17,960	19,250	19,820	57,030
Cash payments for operating expenses	9,000	10,200	10,900	30,100
Cash payments for capital expenditures	5,000	12,000	16,000	33,000
Cash payments for income taxes	0	0	0	0
Total cash payments	$87,122	$104,017	$114,266	$305,405

在完成现金收取预算与现金支付预算之后，我们可以制定现金预算。现金账目期初余额（beginning cash balance）加上财务周期收取的现金（cash collections for the fiscal period）等于可用现金总额，可用现金总额（total cash available）减去财务周期支付的现金（cash payments for the fiscal period）等于融资前现金账目期末余额（ending cash balance before financing）（见图 7-6）。

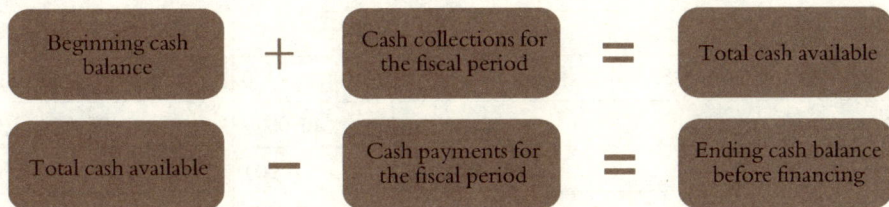

图7-6 现金预算计算公式

　　1 月初现金账目余额为 $4 500，1 月份收取现金 $146 000、支付现金 $87 122，所以 1 月末融资前现金账目余额为 $63 378。根据"案例 7-1"信息，QWE Manufacturing 出台新政策，即月末现金账目余额不能低于 $100 000，因此需要借款 $40 000，使 1 月末现金账目余额达到 $103 378，不低于现金账目余额最低限（$100 000）。

　　2 月初现金账目余额为 $103 378，2 月份收取现金 $167 200、支付现金 $104 017，2 月末融资前现金账目余额为 $166 561，比现金账目余额最低限（$100 000）超出 $66 561，因此偿还 1 月份借款 $40 000，并支付利息费用 $400（$40 000 × 1% = $400）。2 月末融资前现金账目余额为 $166 561，2 月份偿还借款 $40 000，支付利息费用 $400，所以 2 月末现金账目余额为 $126 161。

　　3 月初现金账目余额为 $126 161，3 月份收取现金 $188 200、支付现金 $114 266，因此 3 月末融资前现金账目余额为 $200 095。

　　1 季度初现金账目余额为 $4 500，1 季度收取现金 $501 400、支付现金 $305 405，所以 1 季度末融资前现金账目余额为 $200 495。1 季度末融资前现金账目余额为 $200 495，1 月份借款 $40 000，2 月份偿还这笔借款，并支付利息费用 $400，所以 1 季度末现金账目余额为 $200 095（见说明 7-17）。

说明 7 - 17：现金预算

QWE Manufacturing Cash Budget For the quarter ended by March 31				
	January	February	March	1st Quarter
Beginning cash balance	$4,500	$103,378	$126,161	$4,500
Cash collections（见说明 7-10）	146,000	167,200	188,200	501,400
Total cash available	150,500	270,578	314,361	505,900
Cash payments（见说明 7-16）	(87,122)	(104,017)	(114,266)	(305,405)
Ending cash balance before financing	63,378	166,561	200,095	200,495

带你到北美学习
管理会计
Take You to
North America
to Learn
Managerial Accounting

Financing：				
Borrowings	40,000	0	0	40,000
Repayments	0	(40,000)	0	(40,000)
Interest payments	0	(400)	0	(400)
Ending cash balance	$ 103,378	$ 126,161	$ 200,095	$ 200,095

7. 4. 2. 3 预算资产负债表 （Budgeted Balance Sheet）

预算资产负债表用于预测企业未来财务周期的财务状况。根据"案例 7-1"信息，去年 12 月 31 日的现金账目余额为 $ 4 500，而现金预算（见说明 7-17）说明，3 月 31 日的现金账目余额为 $ 200 095。

去年 12 月份的销售额为 $ 140 000，其中赊销额为 $ 98 000，这与去年 12 月 31 日的应收账款账目余额（$ 98 000）吻合；今年 3 月份的销售额为 $ 198 000，其中赊销额为 $ 138 600，因此 3 月 31 日的应收账款账目余额为 $ 138 600。

库存账目包含直接材料库存和产品库存。3 月 31 日，QWE Manufacturing 库存 1 880 千克直接材料、2 425 件产品。每千克直接材料的价格为 $ 2，单件产品的成本为 $ 9，因此 1 880 千克直接材料的成本为 $ 3 760，2 425 件产品的成本为 $ 21 825。3 月 31 日的库存账目余额为 $ 25 585（$ 3 760 + $ 21 825 = $ 25 585）。

物业、厂房与设备账面净值等于物业、厂房与设备成本减去物业、厂房与设备累计折旧。1 季度，QWE Manufacturing 购买价值为 $ 33 000 的新物业、厂房与设备，物业、厂房与设备产生的折旧费用为 $ 4 800，因此物业、厂房与设备成本增长 $ 33 000，物业、厂房与设备累计折旧增长 $ 4 800，物业、厂房与设备账面净值增长 $ 28 200（$ 33 000 − $ 4 800 = $ 28 200）。去年 12 月 31 日的物业、厂房与设备账面净值为 $ 121 500，物业、厂房与设备账面净值于 1 季度增长 $ 28 200，因此 3 月 31 日的物业、厂房与设备账面净值为 $ 149 700（$ 121 500 + $ 28 200 = $ 149 700）。

根据"案例 7-1"信息，QWE Manufacturing 当月支付直接材料采购钱款的 20%，下月支付剩余采购钱款（80%）。去年 12 月份直接材料采购量为 14 710 千克（14 500 + 1 660 − 1 450 = 14 710），每千克直接材料的价格为 $ 2，因此去年 12 月份采购价值为 $ 29 420 的直接材料，但仅支付其中价值为 $ 5 884 的直接材料，尚未支付价值为 $ 23 536 的直接材料，这与去年 12 月 31 日的应付账款账目余额（$ 23 536）吻合。

今年 3 月份的直接材料采购量为 19 610 千克，每千克直接材料的价格为 $2，因此今年 3 月份采购价值为 $39 220 的直接材料，但仅支付其中价值为 $7 844 的直接材料（$39 220 × 20% = $7 844），尚未支付价值为 $31 376 的直接材料（$39 220 × 80% = $31 376），即 3 月 31 日的应付账款账目余额为 $31 376。

1 季度，QWE Manufacturing 产生所得税费用 $78 840（见说明 7-8），但尚未支付，因此 3 月 31 日的资产负债表应出现这笔尚未支付的所得税费用，应付所得税账目余额为 $78 840。

QWE Manufacturing 在 1 月份借款 $40 000，2 月份偿还这笔借款并支付利息费用 $400（见说明 7-17），因此 1 季度不产生任何应付贷款（loan payable）和应付利息（interest payable）。

QWE Manufacturing 在 1～3 月份支付了当月产生的直接人工成本（见说明 7-12）、制造费用（见说明 7-13）和经营费用（见说明 7-14），因此这些成本与费用不带来任何负债。

QWE Manufacturing 在 1 季度没有购回股票，也未发行新股票，因此股份资本账目余额没有变化，即 3 月 31 日的股份资本账目余额仍为 $196 884。

留存收益账目期初余额加上财务周期赚取的净收益（net income），减去相同财务周期宣布的股息（dividend），等于留存收益账目期末余额。去年 12 月 31 日的留存收益账目余额为 $22 920，1 季度赚取净收益（$183 960）、未宣布股息，因此 3 月 31 日的留存收益账目余额为（$22 920 + $183 960 − $0 = $206 880）（见说明 7-18）。

说明 7-18：预算资产负债表

QWE Manufacturing Budgeted Balance Sheet At March 31	
Assets	
Current assets	
Cash	$200,095
Accounts receivable	138,600
Inventory	25,585
Total current assets	364,280
Property, plant, and equipment, net	149,700
Total assets	$513,980

带你到北美学习
管理会计
Take You to
North America
to Learn
Managerial Accounting

Liabilities and Shareholders' Equity	
Liabilities	
Accounts payable	$ 31,376
Income taxes payable	78,840
Total liabilities	110,216
Shareholders' equity	
Capital stock	196,884
Retained earnings	206,880
Total shareholders' equity	403,764
Total liabilities and shareholders' equity	$ 513,980

例题综述

Summary of Examples

例题 7 - 1

Budgets are _____.

A. future oriented

B. only used by large corporations

C. prepared by a controller for his or her whole corportaion

D. required by International Financial Reporting Standards or Accounting Standards for Private Enterprises

讲解： 通过预算，企业管理者履行规划（planning）、监督（directing）、控制（controlling）等方面的职责。预算是一种不间断进行的循环：为制定战略决策，企业首先制定长期战略，一般涉及企业未来 5～10 年的战略目标；一旦建立长期目标，企业管理层需要设计核心战略（key strategy）以实现既定目标；根据企业核心战略决策，管理者出台详细规划并组织实施；通过绩效报告（performance report），管理者将企业实际运营与预算进行对比，并对规划提出反馈意见；反馈可以帮助管理者采取矫正措施（corrective action），必要时需要调整企业战略目标与核心战略决策，这也是新一轮循环的开始。

答案： A

例题 7 - 2

Mac's Convenience expects to receive which of the following benefits when it uses the budgeting process?

A. The budget helps managers foresee and avoid potential problems before they occur.

B. The budget motivates employees to achieve Mac's sales growth and cost reduction goals.

C. The budget provides Mac's managers with a benchmark against which to compare actual results for performance evaluation.

D. All of the above

讲解： 预算一般有如下三种作用：①推动企业管理者履行规划职能；②促进协调与合作；③激励员工，评估企业实际绩效。

带你到北美学习
管理会计
Take You to
North America
to Learn
Managerial Accounting

答案： D

例题 7 - 3

Which of the following is the starting point for the master budget?

A. The sales budget

B. The production budget

C. The direct materials budget

D. The operating expenses budget

讲解： 如图 7-2 所示。

答案： A

例题 7 - 4

The income statement is a part of which element of a company's master budget?

A. The operating budget

B. The financial budget

C. The cash budget

D. The capital expenditures budget

讲解： 如图 7-2 所示。

答案： A

例题 7 - 5

The starting point for a direct labour budget for a manufacturer is the _____.

A. sales budget

B. cash budget

C. production budget

D. direct materials budget

讲解： 如图 7-2 所示。

答案： C

例题 7 - 6

The following budgets are all financial budgets except for the _____.

A. combined cash budget

B. budgeted balance sheet

C. capital expenditures budget

D. budgeted income statement

讲解： 如图 7-2 所示。

答案： D

例题 7 - 7

Which of the following expenses would never appear in a cash budget?

A. Supplies expense

B. Depreciation expense

C. Interest expense

D. Marketing expense

讲解： 折旧费用（depreciation expense）和坏账费用（bad debt expense）均属于非现金费用（non-cash expense），非现金费用不出现在现金支付预算（cash payments budget）。

答案： B

例题 7 - 8

Green Corporation produces self-watering planters for use in upscale retail establishments. Sales projections for the first five months of the upcoming year show the estimated number of planters to be sold each month to be as follows：

Number of planters to be sold in January	3,300
Number of planters to be sold in February	3,100
Number of planters to be sold in March	3,500
Number of planters to be sold in April	4,800
Number of planters to be sold in May	4,600

The inventory at the start of the upcoming year was 330 planters. The desired inventory of

带你到北美学习
管理会计
Take You to
North America
to Learn
Managerial Accounting

planters at the end of each month should be equal to 10% of the following month's budget-ed sales. Each planter requires four kilograms of polypropylene (a type of plastic). The company wants to have 30% of the polypropylene required for next month's production on hand at the end of each month. The polypropylene costs $0.30 per kilogram.

Required:

1. Prepare a production budget for each month in the first quarter of the upcoming year, including production in units for each month and for the first quarter.

2. Prepare a direct materials (DM) budget for polypropylene for each month in the first quarter of the upcoming year, including the kilograms of polypropylene required and the total costs of polypropylene to be purchased.

1. Prepare a production budget for each month in the first quarter of the upcoming year, including production in units for each month and for the first quarter.

讲解：　根据题目信息，播种机月末库存等于下月销量的 10%。1~4月份的播种机预计销量分别为 3 300 台、3 100 台、3 500 台和 4 800 台，因此去年 12 月末、今年 1 月末、2 月末和 3 月末的播种机库存分别为 330 台、310 台、350 台和 480 台。

1 月份播种机预计销量（3 300）加上 1 月末播种机库存（310）等于 1 月份播种机需求总量（3 610），1 月份播种机需求总量（3 610）减去 1 月初播种机库存（330）等于 1 月份播种机产量（3 280）。1 月初播种机库存（330）等于去年 12 月末播种机库存（330）。

2 月份播种机预计销量（3 100）加上 2 月末播种机库存（350）等于 2 月份播种机需求总量（3 450），2 月份播种机需求总量（3 450）减去 2 月初播种机库存（310）等于 2 月份播种机产量（3 140）。2 月初播种机库存（310）等于 1 月末播种机库存（310）。

3 月份播种机预计销量（3 500）加上 3 月末播种机库存（480）等于 3 月份播种机需求总量（3 980），3 月份播种机需求总量（3 980）减去 3 月初播种机库存（350）等于 3 月份播种机产量（3 630）。3 月初播种机库存（350）等于 2 月末播种机库存（350）。

1 季度播种机预计销量（9 900）加上 1 季度末播种机库存（480）等于 1 季度播种机需求总量（10 380），1 季度播种机需求总量（10 380）减去 1 季度初播种机库存（330）等于 1 季度播种机产量（10 050）。

　　1 季度包括 1 月份、2 月份和 3 月份，因此 1 季度初播种机库存也是 1 月初播种机库存，1 季度末播种机库存也是 3 月末播种机库存。

答案：

Green Corporation Production Budget For the quarter ended by March 31				
	January	February	March	1st Quarter
Sales in units	3,300	3,100	3,500	9,900
Desired units in ending inventory	310	350	480	480
Total units needed	3,610	3,450	3,980	10,380
Units in beginning inventory	(330)	(310)	(350)	(330)
Units to produce	3,280	3,140	3,630	10,050

2. Prepare a direct materials（DM）budget for polypropylene for each month in the first quarter of the upcoming year, including the kilograms of polypropylene required and the total costs of polypropylene to be purchased.

讲解： 根据题目信息，每台播种机需要 4 千克塑料，塑料月末库存等于下月生产所需塑料的 30%。根据生产预算，1 ~ 3 月份的播种机产量分别为 3 280 台、3 140 台和 3 630 台，因此 1 ~ 3 月份分别需要塑料 13 120 千克、12 560 千克和 14 520 千克，去年 12 月末、今年 1 月末和 2 月末的塑料库存分别为 3 936 千克、3 768 千克和 4 356 千克。我们还需要计算今年 3 月末的塑料库存。为了获知今年 3 月末的塑料库存，必须计算 4 月份生产所需塑料的数量。

　　4 月初播种机库存（480）等于 3 月末播种机库存（480），4 月末播种机库存（460）等于 5 月份播种机销量（4 600）的 10%。4 月份播种机预计销量（4 800）加上 4 月末播种机库存（460）等于 4 月份播种机需求总量（5 260），4 月份播种机需求总量（5 260）减去 4 月初播种机库存（480）等于 4 月份播种机产量（4 780）。4 月份播种机产量为 4 780 台，每台播种机需要 4 千克塑料，因此 4 月份需要塑料 19 120 千克。我们知道，塑料月末库存等于下月生产所需塑料的 30%，所以 3 月末塑料库存为 5 736 千克。

　　1 月份生产所需塑料（13 120）加上 1 月末塑料库存（3 768）等于 1 月份塑料

需求总量（16 888），1 月份塑料需求总量（16 888）减去 1 月初塑料库存（3 936）等于 1 月份塑料采购量（12 952）。1 月初塑料库存（3 936）等于去年 12 月末塑料库存（3 936）。

2 月份生产所需塑料（12 560）加上 2 月末塑料库存（4 356）等于 2 月份塑料需求总量（16 916），2 月份塑料需求总量（16 916）减去 2 月初塑料库存（3 768）等于 2 月份塑料采购量（13 148）。2 月初塑料库存（3 768）等于 1 月末塑料库存（3 768）。

3 月份生产所需塑料（14 520）加上 3 月末塑料库存（5 736）等于 3 月份塑料需求总量（20 256），3 月份塑料需求总量（20 256）减去 3 月初塑料库存（4 356）等于 3 月份塑料采购量（15 900）。3 月初塑料库存（4 356）等于 2 月末塑料库存（4 356）。

1 季度生产所需塑料（40 200）加上 1 季度末塑料库存（5 736）等于 1 季度塑料需求总量（45 936），1 季度塑料需求总量（45 936）减去 1 季度初塑料库存（3 936）等于 1 季度塑料采购量（42 000）。

1 季度包括 1 月份、2 月份和 3 月份，因此 1 季度初塑料库存也是 1 月初塑料库存，1 季度末塑料库存也是 3 月末塑料库存。

计算得出，1～3 月份的塑料采购量分别为 12 952 千克、13 148 千克和 15 900 千克，每千克塑料价格为 $0.30，所以 1～3 月份分别采购价值为 $3 885.60，$3 944.40 和 $4 770 的塑料。

答案：

Green Corporation Direct Materials Budget For the quarter ended by March 31				
	January	February	March	1st Quarter
Units to be produced	3,280	3,140	3,630	10,050
Kilograms of DM required per unit	× 4	× 4	× 4	× 4
DM required for production	13,120	12,560	14,520	40,200
Desired ending DM inventory	3,768	4,356	5,736	5,736
Total DM required	16,888	16,916	20,256	45,936
Beginning DM inventory	(3,936)	(3,768)	(4,356)	(3,936)
DM to purchase	12,952	13,148	15,900	42,000

Cost per kilogram	× $0.30	× $0.30	× $0.30	× $0.30
Total cost of DM purchases	$3,885.60	$3,944.40	$4,770	$12,600

例题 7 − 9

Pasta Company produces a hand-processed pasta that is made with organic flour. A batch of pasta requires five pounds of organic flour. The organic flour costs $2.40 per pound. The company needs to have 30% of the following month's production needs of organic flour in the ending inventory of each month. The production budget of batches of pasta from April to July is as follows:

Number of batches of pasta to be produced in April	600
Number of batches of pasta to be produced in May	750
Number of batches of pasta to be produced in June	800
Number of batches of pasta to be produced in July	700

Required:

Prepare a direct materials budget for organic flour for each month in the second quarter and for the second quarter in total, including both the quantity and cost of flour to be purchased in each month.

讲解: 根据题目信息, 4 ~ 7 月份的 pasta 产量分别为 600 批、750 批、800 批和 700 批, 每批 pasta 需要 5 磅有机面粉, 因此 4 ~ 7 月份分别需要有机面粉 3 000 磅、3 750磅、4 000 磅和 3 500 磅。有机面粉月末库存等于下月生产所需有机面粉的 30%, 因此 3 月末、4 月末、5 月末和 6 月末的有机面粉库存分别为 900 磅、1 125 磅、1 200 磅和 1 050 磅。

4 月份生产所需有机面粉 (3 000) 加上 4 月末有机面粉库存 (1 125) 等于 4 月份有机面粉需求总量 (4 125), 4 月份有机面粉需求总量 (4 125) 减去 4 月初有机面粉库存 (900) 等于 4 月份有机面粉采购量 (3 225)。4 月初有机面粉库存 (900) 等于 3 月末有机面粉库存 (900)。

5 月份生产所需有机面粉 (3 750) 加上 5 月末有机面粉库存 (1 200) 等于 5 月份有机面粉需求总量 (4 950), 5 月份有机面粉需求总量 (4 950) 减去 5 月初有机面粉库存 (1 125) 等于 5 月份有机面粉采购量 (3 825)。5 月初有机面粉库存 (1 125) 等于 4 月末有机面粉库存 (1 125)。

带你到北美学习

管理会计

Take You to
North America
to Learn
Managerial Accounting

6 月份生产所需有机面粉 (4 000) 加上 6 月末有机面粉库存 (1 050) 等于 6 月份有机面粉需求总量 (5 050), 6 月份有机面粉需求总量 (5 050) 减去 6 月初有机面粉库存 (1 200) 等于 6 月份有机面粉采购量 (3 850)。6 月初有机面粉库存 (1 200) 等于 5 月末有机面粉库存 (1 200)。

2 季度生产所需有机面粉 (10 750) 加上 2 季度末有机面粉库存 (1 050) 等于 2 季度有机面粉需求总量 (11 800), 2 季度有机面粉需求总量 (11 800) 减去 2 季度初有机面粉库存 (900) 等于 2 季度有机面粉采购量 (10 900)。

2 季度包括 4 月份、5 月份和 6 月份, 因此 2 季度初有机面粉库存也是 4 月初有机面粉库存, 2 季度末有机面粉库存也是 6 月末有机面粉库存。

计算得出, 4～6 月份的有机面粉采购量分别为 3 225 磅、3 825 磅和 3 850 磅, 每磅有机面粉的价格为 $2.40, 因此 4～6 月份分别采购价值为 $7 740, $9 180 和 $9 240 的有机面粉。

答案:

Pasta Company Direct Materials Budget For the quarter ended by June 30	April	May	June	2nd Quarter
Batches to be produced	600	750	800	2,150
Pounds of direct materials needed per batch	× 5	× 5	× 5	× 5
Direct materials needed for production	3,000	3,750	4,000	10,750
Desired ending direct materials inventory	1,125	1,200	1,050	1,050
Total direct materials needed	4,125	4,950	5,050	11,800
Beginning direct materials inventory	(900)	(1,125)	(1,200)	(900)
Direct materials to purchase	3,225	3,825	3,850	10,900
Cost per pound	× $2.40	× $2.40	× $2.40	× $2.40
Total cost of direct material purchases	$7,740	$9,180	$9,240	$26,160

例题 7 - 10

One of the products that Josey Corporation produces and sells is SillyDough. A container of SillyDough requires three kilograms of C45 (direct materials). As a student of managerial accounting, you have been asked to assist the company management by preparing a direct materials budget for July, August and September.

The company is very interested in maintaining adequate inventories and has advised you of the following information:

a. The desired finished goods inventory (container of SillyDough) at the end of each month must equal 7,000 containers plus 30% of the next month's sales volume of Silly-Dough.

b. The desired C45 in the ending inventory of each month must equal 50% of the following month's production needs for C45.

c. The ending inventory of C45 for June was 64,500 kilograms.

d. Each kilogram of C45 costs $2.50.

The sales budget for SillyDough for July through to December is as follows:

Number of containers to be sold in July	40,000
Number of containers to be sold in August	50,000
Number of containers to be sold in September	65,000
Number of containers to be sold in October	35,000
Number of containers to be sold in November	20,000
Number of containers to be sold in December	10,000

Required:

1. Prepare a production budget for SillyDough for July, August, September, and October.

2. Prepare a direct materials (DM) budget showing the quantity as well as the purchases in dollars for July, August, and September and for the third quarter in total.

1. Prepare a production budget for SillyDough for July, August, September and October.

讲解: 根据销售预算, 7～11 月份的容器销量分别为 40 000 个、50 000 个、65 000 个、35 000 个和 20 000 个, 容器月末库存等于下月销量的 30% 外加 7 000 个, 因此 6 月末、7 月末、8 月末、9 月末和 10 月末的容器库存分别为 19 000 个、22 000 个、26 500 个、17 500 个和 13 000 个。

7 月份容器预计销量 (40 000) 加上 7 月末容器库存 (22 000) 等于 7 月份容器需求总量 (62 000), 7 月份容器需求总量 (62 000) 减去 7 月初容器库存 (19 000) 等于 7 月份容器产量 (43 000)。7 月初容器库存 (19 000) 等于 6 月末容器库存 (19 000)。

带你到北美学习
管理会计
Take You to
North America
to Learn
Managerial Accounting

8月份容器预计销量（50 000）加上8月末容器库存（26 500）等于8月份容器需求总量（76 500），8月份容器需求总量（76 500）减去8月初容器库存（22 000）等于8月份容器产量（54 500）。8月初容器库存（22 000）等于7月末容器库存（22 000）。

9月份容器预计销量（65 000）加上9月末容器库存（17 500）等于9月份容器需求总量（82 500），9月份容器需求总量（82 500）减去9月初容器库存（26 500）等于9月份容器产量（56 000）。9月初容器库存（26 500）等于8月末容器库存（26 500）。

10月份容器预计销量（35 000）加上10月末容器库存（13 000）等于10月份容器需求总量（48 000），10月份容器需求总量（48 000）减去10月初容器库存（17 500）等于10月份容器产量（30 500）。10月初容器库存（17 500）等于9月末容器库存（17 500）。

答案：

Josey Corporation Production Budget For the months ended by July 31, August 31, September 30, and October 31				
	July	August	September	October
Sales in units	40,000	50,000	65,000	35,000
Desired units in ending inventory	22,000	26,500	17,500	13,000
Total units needed	62,000	76,500	82,500	48,000
Units in beginning inventory	(19,000)	(22,000)	(26,500)	(17,500)
Units to produce	43,000	54,500	56,000	30,500

2. Prepare a direct materials (DM) budget showing the quantity as well as the purchases in dollars for July, August, and September and for the third quarter in total.

讲解： 根据生产预算，7~10月份的容器产量分别为43 000个、54 500个、56 000个和30 500个，单个容器需要3千克直接材料（C45），因此7~10月份分别需要直接材料129 000千克、163 500千克、168 000千克和91 500千克。直接材料月末库存等于下月生产所需直接材料的50%，因此6月末、7月末、8月末和9月末的直接材料库存分别为64 500千克、81 750千克、84 000千克和45 750千克。

7月份生产所需直接材料（129 000）加上7月末直接材料库存（81 750）等于7月份直接材料需求总量（210 750），7月份直接材料需求总量（210 750）减去7月初直接材料库存（64 500）等于7月份直接材料采购量（146 250）。7月初直接材料库存（64 500）等于 6 月末直接材料库存（64 500）。

8 月份生产所需直接材料（163 500）加上 8 月末直接材料库存（84 000）等于 8 月份直接材料需求总量（247 500），8 月份直接材料需求总量（247 500）减去 8 月初直接材料库存（81 750）等于 8 月份直接材料采购量（165 750）。8 月初直接材料库存（81 750）等于 7 月末直接材料库存（81 750）。

9 月份生产所需直接材料（168 000）加上 9 月末直接材料库存（45 750）等于 9 月份直接材料需求总量（213 750），9 月份直接材料需求总量（213 750）减去 9 月初直接材料库存（84 000）等于 9 月份直接材料采购量（129 750）。9 月初直接材料库存（84 000）等于 8 月末直接材料库存（84 000）。

3 季度生产所需直接材料（460 500）加上 3 季度末直接材料库存（45 750）等于 3 季度直接材料需求总量（506 250），3 季度直接材料需求总量（506 250）减去 3 季度初直接材料库存（64 500）等于 3 季度直接材料采购量（441 750）。

3 季度包括 7 月份、8 月份和 9 月份，因此 3 季度初直接材料库存也是 7 月初直接材料库存，3 季度末直接材料库存也是 9 月末直接材料库存。

计算得出，7～9 月份的直接材料采购量分别为 146 250 千克、165 750 千克和 129 750 千克，每千克直接材料的价格为 $2.50，因此在 7～9 月份分别采购价值为 $365 625，$414 375 和 $324 375 的直接材料。

答案：

Josey Corporation Direct Materials Budget For the quarter ended by September 30	July	August	September	3rd Quarter
Units to be produced	43,000	54,500	56,000	153,500
Kilograms of DM required per unit	× 3	× 3	× 3	× 3
DM required for production	129,000	163,500	168,000	460,500
Desired ending DM inventory	81,750	84,000	45,750	45,750
Total DM required	210,750	247,500	213,750	506,250
Beginning DM inventory	(64,500)	(81,750)	(84,000)	(64,500)
DM to purchase	146,250	165,750	129,750	441,750
Cost per kilogram	× $2.50	× $2.50	× $2.50	× $2.50
Total cost of DM purchases	$365,625	$414,375	$324,375	$1,104,375

带你到北美学习
管理会计
Take You to
North America
to Learn
Managerial Accounting

例题 7 - 11

Logo Corporation buys logo-imprinted merchandise and then sells it to university book-stores. Sales revenue is expected to be ＄2,006,000 in September, ＄2,240,000 in October, ＄2,381,000 in the November, and ＄2,570,000 in December. Logo Corporation sets its price to earn an average 40% gross profit on sales revenue. The company does not want inventory to fall below ＄420,000 plus 15% of the next month's cost of goods sold.

Required：

Prepare an inventory, purchases, and cost of goods sold budget for October and November.

讲解一： 毛利润占销售额的40%，因此售出商品成本占销售额的60%。9 月份销售额为 ＄2 006 000，预计售出商品成本为 ＄1 203 600；10 月份销售额为 ＄2 240 000，预计售出商品成本为 ＄1 344 000；11 月份销售额为 ＄2 381 000，预计售出商品成本为 ＄1 428 600；12 月份销售额为 ＄2 570 000，预计售出商品成本为 ＄1 542 000。

答案一：

<table>
<tr><td colspan="3" align="center">Logo Corporation
Cost of Goods Sold Budget
For the months ended by October 31 and November 30</td></tr>
<tr><td></td><td>October</td><td>November</td></tr>
<tr><td>Sales revenue</td><td>＄2,240,000</td><td>＄2,381,000</td></tr>
<tr><td>Cost of goods sold (60% of sales revenue)</td><td>1,344,000</td><td>1,428,600</td></tr>
</table>

讲解二： 商品库存账目月末余额等于下月售出商品成本的15% 外加 ＄420 000。9 ~ 12 月份的预计售出商品成本分别为 ＄1 203 600，＄1 344 000，＄1 428 600 和 ＄1 542 000，因此 8 月末、9 月末、10 月末和 11 月末的商品库存账目余额分别为 ＄600 540，＄621 600，＄634 290 和 ＄651 300。

答案二：

<table>
<tr><td colspan="3" align="center">Logo Corporation
Inventory Budget
For the months ended by October 31 and November 30</td></tr>
<tr><td></td><td>October</td><td>November</td></tr>
<tr><td>Cost of goods sold (COGS)</td><td>＄1,344,000</td><td>＄1,428,600</td></tr>
<tr><td>Ending inventory in dollars (＄420,000 + COGS × 15%)</td><td>634,290</td><td>651,300</td></tr>
</table>

讲解三： 商品库存账目月初余额加上购买商品成本（cost of goods purchased）等于可供销售商品成本（cost of goods available for sale），可供销售商品成本减去售出商品

成本（cost of goods sold）等于商品库存账目月末余额。根据上述计算关系推导出，商品库存账目月末余额加上售出商品成本等于可供销售商品成本，可供销售商品成本减去商品库存账目月初余额等于购买商品成本。

10 月末库存账目余额（$634 290）加上 10 月份预计售出商品成本（$1 344 000）等于 10 月份可供销售商品成本（$1 978 290），10 月份可供销售商品成本（$1 978 290）减去 10 月初库存账目余额（$621 600）等于 10 月份预计购买商品成本（$1 356 690）。10 月初库存账目余额（$621 600）等于 9 月末库存账目余额（$621 600）。

11 月末库存账目余额（$651 300）加上 11 月份预计售出商品成本（$1 428 600）等于 11 月份可供销售商品成本（$2 079 900），11 月份可供销售商品成本（$2 079 900）减去 11 月初库存账目余额（$634 290）等于 11 月份预计购买商品成本（$1 445 610）。11 月初库存账目余额（$634 290）等于 10 月末库存账目余额（$634 290）。

答案三：

Logo Corporation Purchases Budget For the months ended by October 31 and November 30		
	October	November
Ending inventory in dollars	$634,290	$651,300
Cost of goods sold	1,344,000	1,428,600
Cost of goods available for sale	1,978,290	2,079,900
Beginning inventory in dollars	(621,600)	(634,290)
Cost of goods purchased	$1,356,690	$1,445,610

例题 7 - 12

The Elliot Corporation sells hammocks. On June 30, 70 hammocks were in the ending inventory and accounts receivable account had a balance of $12,000. The sales budget of hammocks from April to July is as follows:

Accounts receivable, June 30	$12,000
Number of hammocks to be sold in July	350 units
Number of hammocks to be sold in August	420 units

带你到北美学习
管理会计
Take You to
North America
to Learn
Managerial Accounting

| Number of hammocks to be sold in September | 370 units |
| Number of hammocks to be sold in October | 300 units |

The corporation has a new policy that the ending inventory of hammocks should be equal to 20% of the number of hammocks to be sold in the following month. The corporation sells the hammocks for $100 each. The corporation's collection history shows that 40% of sales in a month is paid by customers in the month of sales, while the remainder is collected in the following month.

Required:

1. Prepare a hammock purchases budget for July, August, and September.

2. Prepare a cash collections budget for July, August, and September.

1. Prepare a hammock purchases budget for July, August, and September.

讲解: 商品月初库存加上商品采购量等于可供销售商品数量,可供销售商品数量减去商品销量等于商品月末库存。根据上述计算关系推导出,商品月末库存加上商品销量等于可供销售商品数量,可供销售商品数量减去商品月初库存等于商品采购量。

根据题目信息,7~10 月份的吊床销量分别为350 个、420 个、370 个和300 个,吊床月末库存等于下月销量的20%,因此6 月末、7 月末、8 月末和9 月末的吊床库存分别为70 个、84 个、74 个和60 个。

7 月末吊床库存(84)加上7 月份吊床预计销量(350)等于7 月份可供销售吊床数量(434),7 月份可供销售吊床数量(434)减去7 月初吊床库存(70)等于7 月份吊床预计采购量(364)。7 月初吊床库存(70)等于6 月末吊床库存(70)。

8 月末吊床库存(74)加上8 月份吊床预计销量(420)等于8 月份可供销售吊床数量(494),8 月份可供销售吊床数量(494)减去8 月初吊床库存(84)等于8 月份吊床预计采购量(410)。8 月初吊床库存(84)等于7 月末吊床库存(84)。

9 月末吊床库存(60)加上9 月份吊床预计销量(370)等于9 月份可供销售吊床数量(430),9 月份可供销售吊床数量(430)减去9 月初吊床库存(74)等于9 月份吊床预计采购量(356)。9 月初吊床库存(74)等于8 月末吊床库存(74)。

答案:

Elliot Corporation Purchases Budget For the months ended by July 31, August 31 and September 30	July	August	September
Units in ending inventory	84	74	60
Number of units sold	350	420	370
Number of units available for sale	434	494	430
Units in beginning inventory	(70)	(84)	(74)
Number of units purchased	364	410	356

2. Prepare a cash collections budget for July, August, and September.

讲解: 根据题目信息,7 ~ 9 月份的吊床预计销量分别为 350 个、420 个和 370 个,吊床售价为 $100,因此7 ~ 9 月份的预期销售额分别为 $35 000,$42 000 和 $37 000。现金销售占销售额的 40%,赊销占销售额的 60%,现金销售在当月收取,赊销将在下月收取,比如7 月份现金销售在 7 月份收取,7 月份赊销将在 8 月份收取。

6 月 30 日,应收账款账目余额为 $12 000,说明 6 月份的赊销额为 $12 000。7 月份的现金销售额为 $14 000、赊销额为 $21 000,8 月份的现金销售额为 $16 800、赊销额为 $25 200,9 月份的现金销售额为 $14 800、赊销额为 $22 200。

7 月份,企业收取 6 月份的赊销 $12 000 以及 7 月份的现金销售 $14 000,共计 $26 000;8 月份,企业收取 7 月份的赊销 $21 000 以及 8 月份的现金销售 $16 800,共计 $37 800;9 月份,企业收取 8 月份的赊销 $25 200 以及 9 月份的现金销售 $14 800,共计 $40 000。

答案:

Elliot Corporation Cash Collections Budget For the months ended by July 31, August 31 and September 30	July	August	September
Cash sales	$14,000	$16,800	$14,800
Collections on credit sales:			
June credit sales	12,000		

带你到北美学习
管理会计
Take You to
North America
to Learn
Managerial Accounting

July credit sales		21,000	
August credit sales			25,200
Total cash collections	$ 26,000	$ 37,800	$ 40,000

例题 7 - 13

You recently began a job as an accounting internship at Backyard Capitals. Your first task was to help reconstruct the cash budget for February and March. Backyard Capitals eliminates any cash deficiency by borrowing the exact amount needed from a local bank, where the interest rate is 6%. Backyard Capitals pays interest on its outstanding debt at the end of each month. The company also repays all borrowed amounts at the end of the month as cash becomes available.

Required:

Complete the following cash budget.

Backyard Capitals Cash Budget For the months ended by February 28 and March 31		
	February	March
Beginning cash balance	$ 16,500	
Cash collections		$ 80,000
Cash from the sale of plant assets	0	1,900
Cash available	106,500	
Cash payments:		
Purchases of inventory		41,000
Operating expenses	47,400	
Total payments	(98,300)	
Ending cash balance before financing		23,700
Minimum cash balance desired	(21,000)	(21,000)
Cash excess (deficiency)		
Financing of cash deficiency:		
Borrowings (at the end of each month)		
Principal repayments (at the end of each month)		
Interest payments		

Total effects of financing		
Ending cash balance		

讲解： 现金账目期初余额加上财务周期收取的现金等于可用现金总额，可用现金总额减去财务周期支付的现金等于融资前现金账目期末余额。

2 月初现金账目余额为 $ 16 500，2 月份出售厂房而获取现金 $ 0，2 月份可用现金总额为 $ 106 500，因此 Backyard Capitals 在 2 月份收取现金 $ 90 000（ $ 106 500 – $ 16 500 = $ 90 000）。

2 月份，Backyard Capitals 支付现金 $ 98 300，其中经营费用占 $ 47 400，因此为购买商品支付现金 $ 50 900（ $ 98 300 – $ 47 400 = $ 50 900）。

2 月份可用现金总额为 $ 106 500，2 月份支付现金 $ 98 300，因此 2 月末融资前现金账目余额为 $ 8 200。由于现金账目余额最低限为 $ 21 000，所以产生现金赤字 $ 12 800。为填补现金赤字，需要在 2 月份借款 $ 12 800；在借款 $ 12 800 之后，2 月末现金账目余额为 $ 21 000（ $ 8 200 + $ 12 800 = $ 21 000），即 3 月初现金账目余额。

3 月初现金账目余额为 $ 21 000，3 月份共计收取现金 $ 81 900（ $ 80 000 + $ 1 900 = $ 81 900），因此 3 月份可用现金总额为 $ 102 900（ $ 21 000 + $ 81 900 = $ 102 900）。

3 月份可用现金总额为 $ 102 900，融资前现金账目期末余额为 $ 23 700，因此企业在 3 月份支付现金 $ 79 200，其中购买商品占 $ 41 000，经营费用占 $ 38 200（ $ 79 200 – $ 41 000 = $ 38 200）。

3 月末融资前现金账目余额为 $ 23 700，现金账目余额最低限为 $ 21 000，产生现金盈余 $ 2 700（ $ 23 700 – $ 21 000 = $ 2 700），因此支付 2 月份借款产生的利息费用，并偿还一部分 2 月份借款。

2 月份借款金额为 $ 12 800，年利率为 6%，借款时长为 1 个月，因此利息费用为 $ 64（ $ 12 800 × 6% × 1/12 = $ 64）。3 月末现金盈余为 $ 2 700，支付利息费用 $ 64，因此偿还 2 月份借款 $ 2 636（ $ 2 700 – $ 64 = $ 2 636）。

带你到北美学习
管理会计
Take You to
North America
to Learn
Managerial Accounting

答案：

<table>
<tr><td colspan="3">Backyard Capitals
Cash Budget
For the months ended by February 28 and March 31</td></tr>
<tr><td></td><td>February</td><td>March</td></tr>
<tr><td>Beginning cash balance</td><td>$ 16,500</td><td>$ 21,000</td></tr>
<tr><td>Cash collections</td><td>90,000</td><td>80,000</td></tr>
<tr><td>Cash from the sale of plant assets</td><td>0</td><td>1,900</td></tr>
<tr><td>Cash available</td><td>106,500</td><td>102,900</td></tr>
<tr><td>Cash payments：</td><td></td><td></td></tr>
<tr><td>　　Purchases of inventory</td><td>50,900</td><td>41,000</td></tr>
<tr><td>　　Operating expenses</td><td>47,400</td><td>38,200</td></tr>
<tr><td>　　　　Total payments</td><td>(98,300)</td><td>(79,200)</td></tr>
<tr><td>Ending cash balance before financing</td><td>8,200</td><td>23,700</td></tr>
<tr><td>　　Minimum cash balance desired</td><td>(21,000)</td><td>(21,000)</td></tr>
<tr><td>　　Cash excess (deficiency)</td><td>(12,800)</td><td>2,700</td></tr>
<tr><td>　　Financing of cash deficiency：</td><td></td><td></td></tr>
<tr><td>　　　　Borrowings (at the end of each month)</td><td>12,800</td><td>0</td></tr>
<tr><td>　　　　Principal repayments (at the end of each month)</td><td>0</td><td>(2,636)</td></tr>
<tr><td>　　　　Interest payments</td><td>0</td><td>(64)</td></tr>
<tr><td>Total effects of financing</td><td>12,800</td><td>(2,700)</td></tr>
<tr><td>Ending cash balance</td><td>$ 21,000</td><td>$ 21,000</td></tr>
</table>

例题 7 - 14

The budget committee of Office Supplier has assembled the following data. As the business manager, you must prepare a budgeted income statement for May and June.

a . Sales in April was $ 42,000. You forecast that monthly sales will increase 12% in May and 3% in June.

b . Office Supplier maintains an inventory of $ 8,000 plus 30% of the sales revenue budgeted for the following month. Monthly purchases average 50% of the sales revenue in that same month. The actual inventory on April 30 was $ 15,000. The sales budget for July is $ 45,000.

c. Monthly salaries amount to $6,000. Monthly sales commissions equal 12% of the sales for that same month.

d. Other monthly expenses are as follows:

Rent expense	$2,200
Depreciation expense	300
Insurance expense	100
Income taxes expense	20% of operating income

Required:

Prepare a budgeted income statement for May and June, showing cost of goods sold.

讲解: 根据题目信息, 4 月份销售额为 $42 000。相比于 4 月份销售额, 5 月份销售额增长 12%, 增至 $47 040 ($42 000 × (1 + 12%) = $47 040); 相比于 5 月份销售额, 6 月份销售额增长 3%, 增至 $48 451 ($47 040 × (1 + 3%) = $48 451)。

商品库存账目月末余额等于下月销售额的 30% 外加 $8 000, 每月购买商品成本等于当月销售额的 50%。

4 月 30 日的商品库存账目余额为 $15 000, 即 5 月初商品库存账目余额, 5 月份购买价值为 $23 520 的商品 ($47 040 × 50% = $23 520), 5 月末商品库存账目余额为 $22 535 ($8 000 + $48 451 × 30% = $22 535)。5 月初商品库存账目余额 ($15 000) 加上 5 月份购买商品成本 ($23 520) 等于 5 月份可供销售商品成本 ($38 520), 5 月份可供销售商品成本 ($38 520) 减去 5 月末商品库存账目余额 ($22 535) 等于 5 月份售出商品成本 ($15 985)。

6 月初商品库存账目余额 ($22 535) 等于 5 月末商品库存账目余额 ($22 535), 6 月份购买价值为 $24 226 的商品 ($48 451 × 50% = $24 226), 6 月末商品库存账目余额为 $21 500 ($8 000 + $45 000 × 30% = $21 500)。6 月初商品库存账目余额 ($22 535) 加上 6 月份购买商品成本 ($24 226) 等于 6 月份可供销售商品成本 ($46 761), 6 月份可供销售商品成本 ($46 761) 减去 6 月末商品库存账目余额 ($21 500) 等于 6 月份售出商品成本 ($25 261)。

5 月份销售额 ($47 040) 减去 5 月份售出商品成本 ($15 985) 等于 5 月份毛利润 ($31 055)。6 月份销售额 ($48 451) 减去 6 月份售出商品成本 ($25 261) 等于 6 月份毛利润 ($23 190)。

每月销售佣金费用等于当月销售额的 12%。5 月份销售额为 $47 040, 因此销

带你到北美学习
管理会计
Take You to
North America
to Learn
Managerial Accounting

售佣金费用为 $5 645（ $47 040 × 12% = $5 645）；6 月份销售额为 $48 451，所以销售佣金费用为 $5 814（ $48 451 × 12% = $5 814）。每月薪水费用为 $6 000，租金费用为 $2 200，折旧费用为 $300，保险费用为 $100。根据上述信息与数据，5 月份经营费用为 $14 245，6 月份经营费用为 $14 414。

5 月份毛利润（ $31 055）减去 5 月份经营费用（ $14 245）等于 5 月份经营收益（ $16 810）。6 月份毛利润（ $23 190）减去 6 月份经营费用（ $14 414）等于 6 月份经营收益（ $8 776）。

企业所得税税率为 20%。5 月份经营收益为 $16 810，因此 5 月份所得税费用为 $3 362（ $16 810 × 20% = $3 362）；6 月份经营收益为 $8 776，所以 6 月份所得税费用为 $1 755（ $8 776 × 20% = $1 755）。

5 月份经营收益（ $16 810）减去 5 月份所得税费用（ $3 362）等于 5 月份净收益（ $13 448）。6 月份经营收益（ $8 776）减去 6 月份所得税费用（ $1 755）等于 6 月份净收益（ $7 021）。

答案：

Office Supplier Budgeted Income Statement For the months ended by May 31 and June 30		May		June
Sales revenue		$47,040		$48,451
Cost of goods sold		(15,985)		(25,261)
Gross profit		31,055		23,190
Operating expenses				
Rent expense	$2,200		$2,200	
Depreciation expense	300		300	
Insurance expense	100		100	
Salaries expense	6,000		6,000	
Sales commissions expense	5,645		5,814	
Total operating expenses		(14,245)		(14,414)
Operating income		16,810		8,776
Income taxes expense (20% tax rate)		(3,362)		(1,755)
Net income		$13,448		$7,021

例题 7 - 15

Supplies Limited is a merchandising company that sells paper products and school supplies. The company is presently working on budgeting for its cash requirements for the third quarter.

Supplies Limited provided the following information:

a. Budgeted monthly income statements for July through to October are as follows:

	July	August	September	October
Sales	$40,000	$70,000	$50,000	$45,000
Cost of goods sold (60% of sales)	(24,000)	(42,000)	(30,000)	(27,000)
Gross margin	16,000	28,000	20,000	18,000
Sales commissions expense	7,000	12,000	10,500	7,300
Administrative expense	5,600	7,200	6,100	5,900
Total expenses	(12,600)	(19,200)	(16,600)	(13,200)
Operating income	$3,400	$8,800	$3,400	$4,800

b. 20% of sales is cash sales and the remainder is credit sales.

c. Credit sales is collected as follows:

 · 10% in the month of sales

 · 70% in the month following sales

 · 20% in the second month following sales

d. Past monthly sales was $30,000 in May and $36,000 in June.

e. All merchandise purchases are made on account.

f. Merchandise purchases are paid for 50% in the month of purchases and 50% in the month following purchases.

g. The company maintains its ending inventory at 75% of the following month's budgeted cost of goods sold.

h. The ending merchandise inventory for June was $18,000.

i. Included in the administrative expense for each month is $2,000 for depreciation.

j. Land costing $4,500 is expected to be purchased in July.

k. Dividends totaling $1,000 will be paid in September.

l. On June 30, the company's cash balance was $10,000.

m. The minimum monthly cash balance that the company must maintain is $10,000.

带你到北美学习
管理会计
Take You to
North America
to Learn
Managerial Accounting

n. The company has an agreement with its bankers that allows them to borrow $5,000, $10,000, $15,000, or $20,000 per month (increments of $5,000) up to a maximum loan of $40,000. All borrowings are assumed to be occured at the end of each month. Simple interest is charged at the rate of 1% per month.

o. Interest must be paid on the outstanding amount at the end of each quarter. Also, to the extent that loans can be repaid, such repayments are made at the end of each quarter.

p. On June 30, no loans were outstanding.

Required:

1. Prepare a cash collections budget for July, August, and September and for the third quarter in total.

2. Prepare a merchandise purchases budget for July, August, and September and for the third quarter in total.

3. Prepare a cash payments budget for merchandise purchases for July, August, and September and for the third quarter in total.

4. Prepare a combined cash budget for July, August, and September and for the third quarter in total.

5. What amounts would be shown on the balance sheet at September 30 for:

   · Accounts receivable

   · Accounts payable

   · Inventory

   · Cash

   · Loans payable

1. Prepare a cash collections budget for July, August, and September and for the third quarter in total.

讲解： 5~10 月份的销售额分别为 $30 000， $36 000， $40 000， $70 000， $50 000 和 $45 000。现金销售占销售额的20%，赊销占销售额的80%。现金销售和10% 的赊销在当月收取，70% 的赊销下月收取，20% 的赊销 2 个月之后收取，比如 5 月份现金销售在 5 月份收取，10% 的 5 月份赊销额在 5 月份收取，70% 的 5 月份赊销在 6

月份收取，20% 的 5 月份赊销在 7 月份收取。

5 月份销售额为 $30 000，其中现金销售占 $6 000，赊销占 $24 000；6 月份销售额为 $36 000，其中现金销售占 $7 200，赊销占 $28 800；7 月份销售额为 $40 000，其中现金销售占 $8 000，赊销占 $32 000；8 月份销售额为 $70 000，其中现金销售占 $14 000，赊销占 $56 000；9 月份销售额为 $50 000，其中现金销售占 $10 000，赊销占 $40 000；10 月份销售额为 $45 000，其中现金销售占 $9 000，赊销占 $36 000。

7 月份，企业收取 5 月份的赊销 $4 800、6 月份的赊销 $20 160 以及 7 月份的赊销 $3 200、7 月份的现金销售 $8 000，共计 $36 160；8 月份，企业收取 6 月份的赊销 $5 760、7 月份的赊销 $22 400、8 月份的赊销 $5 600 以及 8 月份的现金销售 $14 000，共计 $47 760；9 月份，企业收取 7 月份的赊销 $6 400、8 月份的赊销 $39 200、9 月份的赊销 $4 000 以及 9 月份的现金销售 $10 000，共计 $59 600；3 季度，企业收取现金 $143 520。

答案：

Supplies Limited Cash Collections Budget For the quarter ended by September 30				
	July	August	September	3rd Quarter
Cash sales	$8,000	$14,000	$10,000	$32,000
Collections on credit sales：				
May credit sales	4,800			4,800
June credit sales	20,160	5,760		25,920
July credit sales	3,200	22,400	6,400	32,000
August credit sales		5,600	39,200	44,800
September credit sales			4,000	4,000
Total cash collections	$36,160	$47,760	$59,600	$143,520

2. Prepare a merchandise purchases budget for July, August, and September and for the third quarter in total.

讲解： 商品库存账目月初余额加上购买商品成本（cost of goods purchased）等于可供销售商品成本（cost of goods available for sale），可供销售商品成本减去售出商品成本（cost of goods sold）等于商品库存账目月末余额。根据上述计算关系推导出，商

带你到北美学习
管理会计
Take You to
North America
to Learn
Managerial Accounting

品库存账目月末余额加上售出商品成本等于可供销售商品成本，可供销售商品成本减去商品库存账目月初余额等于购买商品成本。

根据题目信息，商品库存账目月末余额等于下月售出商品成本的 75%。7～10 月份的预计售出商品成本分别为 $24 000，$42 000，$30 000 和 $27 000，因此 6 月末、7 月末、8 月末和 9 月末的商品库存账目余额分别为 $18 000，$31 500，$22 500 和 $20 250。

7 月份预计售出商品成本（$24 000）加上 7 月末商品库存账目余额（$31 500）等于 7 月份可供销售商品成本（$55 500），7 月份可供销售商品成本（$55 500）减去 7 月初商品库存账目余额（$18 000）等于 7 月份购买商品成本（$37 500）。7 月初商品库存账目余额（$18 000）等于 6 月末商品库存账目余额（$18 000）。

8 月份预计售出商品成本（$42 000）加上 8 月末商品库存账目余额（$22 500）等于 8 月份可供销售商品成本（$64 500），8 月份可供销售商品成本（$64 500）减去 8 月初商品库存账目余额（$31 500）等于 8 月份购买商品成本（$33 000）。8 月初商品库存账目余额（$31 500）等于 7 月末商品库存账目余额（$31 500）。

9 月份预计售出商品成本（$30 000）加上 9 月末商品库存账目余额（$20 250）等于 9 月份可供销售商品成本（$50 250），9 月份可供销售商品成本（$50 250）减去 9 月初商品库存账目余额（$22 500）等于 9 月份购买商品成本（$27 750）。9 月初商品库存账目余额（$22 500）等于 8 月末商品库存账目余额（$22 500）。

3 季度预计售出商品成本（$96 000）加上 3 季度末商品库存账目余额（$20 250）等于 3 季度可供销售商品成本（$116 250），3 季度可供销售商品成本（$116 250）减去 3 季度初商品库存账目余额（$18 000）等于 3 季度购买商品成本（$98 250）。

答案：

Supplies Limited Merchandise Purchases Budget For the quarter ended by September 30				
	July	August	September	3rd Quarter
Ending inventory in dollars	$31,500	$22,500	$20,250	$20,250
Cost of goods sold	24,000	42,000	30,000	96,000
Cost of goods available for sale	55,500	64,500	50,250	116,250
Beginning inventory in dollars	(18,000)	(31,500)	(22,500)	(18,000)
Cost of goods purchased	$37,500	$33,000	$27,750	$98,250

3. Prepare a cash payments budget for merchandise purchases for July, August, and September and for the third quarter in total.

讲解： 根据题目信息，每月售出商品成本占当月销售额的 60%，商品库存账目月末余额等于下月售出商品成本的 75%。6 月份销售额为 \$36 000，因此 6 月份售出商品成本为 \$21 600。5 月末商品库存账目余额为 \$16 200，即 6 月初商品库存账目余额。6 月份售出商品成本（\$21 600）加上 6 月末商品库存账目余额（\$18 000）等于 6 月份可供销售商品成本（\$39 600），6 月份可供销售商品成本（\$39 600）减去 6 月初商品库存账目余额（\$16 200）等于 6 月份购买商品成本（\$23 400）。

根据题目信息，50% 的购买商品成本在当月支付，剩余 50% 的购买商品成本将在下月支付。6 月份购买商品成本为 \$23 400，7 月份购买商品成本为 \$37 500，8 月份购买商品成本为 \$33 000，9 月份购买商品成本为 \$27 750。7 月份，企业支付 6 月份购买商品成本 \$11 700、7 月份购买商品成本 \$18 750，共计 \$30 450；8 月份，企业支付 7 月份购买商品成本 \$18 750、8 月份购买商品成本 \$16 500，共计 \$35 250；9 月份，企业支付 8 月份购买商品成本 \$16 500、9 月份购买商品成本 \$13 875，共计 \$30 375。为购买商品，企业在 3 季度支付现金 \$96 075。

答案：

Supplies Limited Cash Payments Budget for Merchandise Purchases For the quarter ended by September 30				
	July	August	September	3rd Quarter
Cost of goods purchased during June	\$11,700			\$11,700
Cost of goods purchased during July	18,750	\$18,750		37,500
Cost of goods purchased during August		16,500	\$16,500	33,000
Cost of goods purchased during September			13,875	13,875
Cash payments for merchandise purchases	\$30,450	\$35,250	\$30,375	\$96,075

4. Prepare a combined cash budget for July, August, and September and for the third quarter in total.

讲解： 已经计算得出，Supplies Limited 在 7 ~ 9 月份分别收取现金 \$36 160，\$47 760 和 \$59 600，在 3 季度收取现金 \$143 520。为购买商品，企业在 7 ~ 9 月份分别支付现金 \$30 450，\$35 250 和 \$30 375，在 3 季度支付现金 \$96 075。

带你到北美学习
管理会计
Take You to
North America
to Learn
Managerial Accounting

根据题目信息，Supplies Limited 在 7 ~ 9 月份分别产生和支付销售佣金费用 $7 000，$12 000 和 $10 500。7 ~ 9 月份的行政管理费用分别为 $5 600，$7 200 和 $6 100，每月行政管理费用包含金额为 $2 000 的折旧费用，因此 7 ~ 9 月份分别支付行政管理费用 $3 600，$5 200 和 $4 100。

为购买土地，Supplies Limited 在 7 月份支付现金 $4 500；此外，企业在 9 月份支付股息 $1 000。

通过计算，企业在 7 ~ 9 月份分别支付现金 $45 550，$52 450 和 $45 975，在 3 季度支付现金 $143 975。

Supplies Limited Cash Payments Budget For the quarter ended by September 30				
	July	August	September	3rd Quarter
Cash payments for merchandise purchases	$30,450	$35,250	$30,375	$96,075
Cash payments for sales commissions	7,000	12,000	10,500	29,500
Cash payments for adiministrative expense	3,600	5,200	4,100	12,900
Cash payments for land	4,500	0	0	4,500
Cash payments for dividends	0	0	1,000	1,000
Total cash payments	$45,550	$52,450	$45,975	$143,975

现金账目期初余额（beginning cash balance）加上财务周期收取的现金（cash collections for the fiscal period）等于可用现金总额，可用现金总额（total cash available）减去财务周期支付的现金（cash payments for the fiscal period）等于融资前现金账目期末余额（ending cash balance before financing）。

7 月初现金账目余额为 $10 000，7 月份收取现金 $36 160、支付现金 $45 550，因此 7 月末融资前现金账目余额为 $610。Supplies Limited 规定，现金账目月末余额不能低于 $10 000，因此需要借款 $10 000，使 7 月末现金账目余额达到 $10 610，超过现金账目余额最低限（$10 000）。

8 月初现金账目余额为 $10 610，8 月份收取现金 $47 760、支付现金 $52 450，8 月末融资前现金账目余额为 $5 920，低于现金账目余额最低限（$10 000），因此 Supplies Limited 在 8 月份仍需借款 $5 000，使 8 月末现金账目余额达到 $10 920。

9 月初现金账目余额为 $10 920，9 月份收取现金 $59 600、支付现金 $45 975，9 月末融资前现金账目余额为 $24 545，远高于现金账目余额最低限（$10 000），因此 Supplies Limited 在 9 月份支付利息费用 $250（$10 000 × 1% × 2 + $5 000 × 1% × 1 = $250），并偿还借款 $10 000。

3 季度初现金账目余额为 $10 000，3 季度收取现金 $143 520、支付现金 $143 975，3 季度末融资前现金账目余额为 $9 545。3 季度末融资前现金账目余额为 $9 545，Supplies Limited 在 7 月份借款 $10 000，在 8 月份借款 $5 000，在 9 月份还款 $10 000、支付利息费用 $250，所以 3 季度末现金账目余额为 $14 295。

答案：

Supplies Limited Cash Budget For the quarter ended by September 30				
	July	August	September	3rd Quarter
Beginning cash balance	$10,000	$10,610	$10,920	$10,000
Cash collections	36,160	47,760	59,600	143,520
Total cash available	46,160	58,370	70,520	153,520
Cash payments	(45,550)	(52,450)	(45,975)	(143,975)
Ending cash balance before financing	610	5,920	24,545	9,545
Financing：				
Borrowings	10,000	5,000	0	15,000
Repayments	0	0	(10,000)	(10,000)
Interest payments	0	0	(250)	(250)
Ending cash balance	$10,610	$10,920	$14,295	$14,295

5. What amounts would be shown on the balance sheet at September 30 for：

· Accounts receivable

· Accounts payable

· Inventory

· Cash

· Loans payable

讲解： 10% 的赊销额当月收取，70% 的赊销额下月收取，20% 的赊销额 2 个月之后收取。8 月份销售额为 $70 000，其中现金销售占 $14 000，赊销占 $56 000；9 月份销售额为 $50 000，其中现金销售为 $10 000，赊销为 $40 000。截至 9 月 30 日，企业尚未收取金额为 $11 200 的 8 月份赊销、金额为 $36 000 的 9 月份赊销，因此

带你到北美学习
管理会计
Take You to
North America
to Learn
Managerial Accounting

9 月 30 日的应收账款账目余额为 $ 47 200（$ 11 200 + $ 36 000 = $ 47 200）。

50% 的购买商品成本当月支付，50% 的购买商品成本下月支付。9 月份购买商品成本为 $ 27 750。截至 9 月 30 日，尚未支付的 9 月份购买商品成本为 $ 13 875，因此 9 月 30 日的应付账款账目余额为 $ 13 875（$ 27 750 × 50% = $ 13 875）。

由商品采购预算可知，9 月 30 日的商品库存账目余额为 $ 20 250。

由现金预算可知，9 月 30 日的现金账目余额为 $ 14 295。

Supplies Limited 在 7 月份借款 $ 10 000，8 月份借款 $ 5 000，9 月份还款 $ 10 000，因此 9 月 30 日的应付贷款账目余额为 $ 5 000。

答案：

Accounts receivable	$ 47,200
Accounts payable	13,875
Inventory	20,250
Cash	14,295
Loans payable	5,000

例题 7 - 16

Printing Corporation has applied for a loan. The Royal Bank has requested a budgeted balance sheet at April 30 and a combined cash budget for April. As the controller of Printing Corporation, you have assembled the following information:

a. On March 31, the equipment balance was $ 52,600, the accumulated depreciation balance was $ 41,700.

b. April capital expenditures budgeted for the cash purchases of new equipment are $ 42,000.

c. April depreciation expense is $ 900.

d. Monthly cost of goods sold equals 65% of the sales for that same month.

e. Other April operating expenses, including income taxes, total $ 14,000, 20% of which are paid in cash and the remainder will be accrued at April 30.

f. On March 31, the shareholders' equity balance was $ 91,700.

g. On March 31, the cash balance was $ 40,100.

h. April budgeted sales is $ 84,000, 60% of which is cash sales, the remainder is credit sales. Half of the credit sales will be collected in April and half in May.

i. April cash collections on March sales are $29,200.

j. April cash payments of March 31 liabilities incurred for March purchases of inventory are $17,600.

k. On March 31, the inventory balance was $29,100.

l. April purchases of inventory are $10,300 for cash and $36,300 on credit. Half of the credit purchases will be paid in April and half in May.

Required：

1. Prepare a combined cash budget for April.

2. Prepare a budgeted balance sheet for Printing Corporation at April 30.

1. Prepare a combined cash budget for April.

讲解： 4 月份销售额为 $84 000，其中现金销售占 60%，赊销占 40%，因此 4 月份现金销售额为 $50 400，赊销额为 $33 600。50% 的 4 月份赊销在 4 月份收取，剩余 50% 的 4 月份赊销将在 5 月份收取，所以在 4 月份，Printing Corporation 收取 3 月份赊销 $29 200、4 月份现金销售 $50 400、4 月份赊销 $16 800（$33 600 × 50% = $16 800），共计 $96 400（$50 400 + $16 800 + $29 200 = $96 400）。

为购买商品，Printing Corporation 在 4 月份支付现金 $10 300，赊账 $36 300。50% 的 4 月份赊账在 4 月份支付，剩余 50% 的 4 月份赊账将在 5 月份支付，因此在 4 月份，企业支付 3 月份购买商品欠下的债务 $17 600、4 月份赊账 $18 150（$36 300 × 50% = $18 150）。

包括所得税费用在内的 4 月份费用为 $14 000。20% 的 4 月份费用在 4 月份支付，剩余 80% 的 4 月份费用将在 5 月份支付，因此 4 月份支付现金 $2 800（$14 000 × 20% = $2 800）。

为购买新设备，Printing Corporation 在 4 月份支付现金 $42 000。

综上所述，4 月份共计支付现金 $90 850（$10 300 + $18 150 + $17 600 + $2 800 + $42 000 = $90 850）。

3 月 31 日的现金账目余额为 $40 100，4 月份收取现金 $96 400、支付现金 $90 850，4 月 30 日的现金账目余额为 $45 650（$40 100 + $96 400 − $90 850 = $45 650）。

带你到北美学习
管理会计
Take You to
North America
to Learn
Managerial Accounting

答案：

Printing Corporation Cash Budget For the month ended by April 30	
Beginning cash balance	$ 40,100
Cash collections	96,400
Total cash available	136,500
Cash payments	(90,850)
Ending cash balance	$ 45,650

2. Prepare a budgeted balance sheet for Printing Corporation at April 30.

讲解： 根据 4 月份现金预算，现金账目余额为 $ 45 650。

　　4 月份销售额为 $ 84 000，其中现金销售占 60%，赊销占 40%，因此 4 月份现金销售额为 $ 50 400，赊销额为 $ 33 600。50% 的 4 月份赊销在 4 月份收取，剩余 50% 的 4 月份赊销在 5 月份收取，所以在 4 月份，Printing Corporation 收取当月现金销售 $ 50 400、赊销 $ 16 800（$ 33 600 × 50% = $ 16 800），尚未收取当月赊销 $ 16 800，因此 4 月 30 日的应收账款账目余额为 $ 16 800。

　　商品库存账目月初余额加上购买商品成本（cost of goods purchased）等于可供销售商品成本（cost of goods available for sale），可供销售商品成本减去售出商品成本（cost of goods sold）等于商品库存账目月末余额。根据题目信息，售出商品成本等于销售额的 65%。4 月份销售额为 $ 84 000，所以 4 月份售出商品成本为 $ 54 600（$ 84 000 × 65% = $ 54 600）。4 月初商品库存账目余额（$ 29 100）加上 4 月份购买商品成本（$ 46 600）等于 4 月份可供销售商品成本（$ 75 700），4 月份可供销售商品成本（$ 75 700）减去 4 月份售出商品成本（$ 54 600）等于 4 月末商品库存账目余额（$ 21 100）。

　　3 月 31 日的设备账目余额为 $ 52 600，4 月份购买价值为 $ 42 000 的新设备，4 月 30 日的设备账目余额为 $ 94 600。

　　3 月 31 日的设备累计折旧账目余额为 $ 41 700，4 月份产生的设备折旧费用为 $ 900，4 月 30 日的设备累计折旧账目余额为 $ 42 600。

　　设备账面净值等于设备成本减去设备累计折旧。4 月 30 日的设备账目余额为 $ 94 600，设备累计折旧账目余额为 $ 42 600，因此 4 月 30 日的设备账面净值为

$ 52 000（$ 94 600 - $ 42 600 = $ 52 000）。

　　为购买商品，4 月份支付现金 $ 10 300，赊账 $ 36 300。50% 的 4 月份赊账在 4 月份支付，剩余 50% 的 4 月份赊账在 5 月份支付，所以在 4 月份，Printing Corporation 支付当月赊账 $ 18 150（$ 36 300 × 50% = $ 18 150），尚未支付当月赊账 $ 18 150，因此 4 月 30 日的应付账款账目余额为 $ 18 150。

　　包括所得税费用在内的 4 月份其他经营费用为 $ 14 000。20% 的 4 月份其他经营费用在 4 月份支付，剩余 80% 的 4 月份其他经营费用在 5 月份支付，所以支付 4 月份其他经营费用 $ 2 800（$ 14 000 × 20% = $ 2 800），尚未支付 4 月份其他经营费用 $ 11 200（$ 14 000 × 80% = $ 11 200），因此 4 月 30 日的应计费用账目余额为 $ 11 200。

　　股东权益分为股份资本（share capital）和留存收益（retained earnings）。留存收益账目期初余额加上财务周期赚取的净收益（net income），减去相同财务周期宣布的股息（dividend），等于留存收益账目期末余额，这说明净收益可以增加留存收益和股东权益，股息可以减少留存收益和股东权益。

　　4 月份销售额（$ 84 000）减去 4 月份售出商品成本（$ 54 600）等于 4 月份毛利润（$ 29 400）。4 月份折旧费用为 $ 900，包括所得税费用在内的 4 月份其他经营费用为 $ 14 000，所以 4 月份费用为 $ 14 900。4 月份毛利润（$ 29 400）减去 4 月份费用（$ 14 900）等于 4 月份净收益（$ 14 500）。

　　根据题目信息，企业在 4 月份未宣布股息。

　　3 月 31 日的股东权益账目余额为 $ 91 700，4 月份赚取净收益 $ 14 500，因此 4 月 30 日的股东权益账目余额为 $ 106 200（$ 91 700 + $ 14 500 - $ 0 = $ 106 200）。

答案：

Printing Corporation Budgeted Balance Sheet At April 30	
Assets	
Current assets	
Cash	$ 45,650
Accounts receivable	16,800
Inventory	21,100
Total current assets	83,550

带你到北美学习
管理会计
Take You to
North America
to Learn
Managerial Accounting

Equipment, net	52,000
Total assets	$ 135,550
Liabilities and Shareholders' Equity	
Liabilities	
Accounts payable	$ 18,150
Accrued expenses	11,200
Total liabilities	29,350
Total shareholders' equity	106,200
Total liabilities and shareholders' equity	$ 135,550

专业名词汇编
Glossary of Accounting Terms

安全库存	safety stock	变动性经营费用	variable operating expense
财务预算	financial budget	产品成本	product cost
产品期初库存	units in beginning inventory	预计销量	expected sales in units
成本习性	cost behaviour	非现金费用	non-cash expense
辅助性预算	supporting budget	股息	dividend
股息支付	dividend payment	固定成本	fixed cost
固定性经营费用	fixed operating expense	滚动预算	rolling budget
核心战略	key strategy	坏账费用	bad debt expense
混合成本	mixed cost	矫正措施	corrective action
经营费用	operating expense	经营费用预算	operating expenses budget
净收益	net income	变动成本	variable cost
可用现金总额	total cash available	利息费用	interest expense
直接人工工资率	direct labour rate	期间成本	period cost
生产预算	production budget	收益表	income statement
产品需求总量	total units needed	现金收取预算	cash collections budget
现金预算	cash budget	现金账目期初余额	beginning cash balance
现金支付预算	cash payments budget	销售佣金	sales commission
销售预算	sales budget	绩效报告	performance report
应付贷款	loan payable	应付利息	interest payable
预算	budget	预算数据	budgeted data
预算资产负债表	budgeted balance sheet	经营预算	operating budget
战略规划	strategic planning	折旧费用	depreciation expense
真实数据	actual data	直接材料预算	direct materials budget
直接人工成本总额	total direct labour cost	直接人工预算	direct labour budget
资产负债表	balance sheet	总预算	master budget
变动性制造费用	variable manufacturing overhead		
预期产品期末库存	desired units in ending inventory		
固定性制造费用	fixed manufacturing overhead		
融资前现金账目期末余额	ending cash balance before financing		
直接材料需求总量	total direct materials needed		

带你到北美学习
管理会计
Take You to
North America
to Learn
Managerial Accounting

预算财务报表	budgeted financial statement
预算收益表	budgeted income statement
制造费用预算	manufacturing overhead budget
财务周期收取的现金	cash collections for the fiscal period
财务周期支付的现金	cash payments for the fiscal period
资本支出预算	capital expenditures budget

标准成本与差异分析

Standard Costs and Variance Analysis

带你到北美学习
管理会计
Take You to
North America
to Learn
Managerial Accounting

8.1　静态与弹性预算
Static and Flexible Budgets

第 7 章介绍了总预算（master budget），总预算是按某一产品数量制定的预算，而非按不同产品数量制定的预算。这种按某一产品数量制定的预算被称为静态预算（static budget），而按不同产品数量制定的预算则被称为弹性预算（flexible budget）。

弹性预算可以协助企业管理者对未来财务周期进行规划，并在财务周期结束之际对企业财务绩效进行评估。企业管理者可以通过弹性预算规划不同产品数量带来的收入和产生的费用。

案例 8 - 1

A company sells its mouse pads for ＄11 each. Its variable costs are ＄5 per pad. Fixed costs are ＄200,000 per month for sales volume up to 60,000 pads. Above 60,000 pads, monthly fixed costs are ＄250,000.

Required：

Prepare a monthly flexible budget for the sales volumes of 40,000 pads, 50,000 pads, and 70,000 pads.

讲解： 鼠标垫单价为 ＄11，单位变动成本为 ＄5。鼠标垫销量低于 60 000 个时，固定费用为 ＄200 000；鼠标垫销量高于 60 000 个时，固定费用为 ＄250 000。根据上述信息，分别制定销量为 40 000 个、50 000 个和 70 000 个鼠标垫的弹性预算（见说明 8-1）。

说明 8 - 1：弹性预算				
	Flexible Budget per Unit	40,000 units	50,000 units	70,000 units
Sales revenue	＄11	＄440,000	＄550,000	＄770,000
Variable costs	5	(200,000)	(250,000)	(350,000)
Fixed costs		(200,000)	(200,000)	(250,000)
Operating income		＄40,000	＄100,000	＄170,000

在财务周期结束之际，企业使用弹性预算评估财务绩效，进而控制成本。为什么企业管理者更愿意将实际结果与弹性预算进行对比，进而评估财务绩效，而非静态预算？因为弹性预算是按不同产品数量制定的预算，而静态预算是按某一产品数

量制定的预算，所以实际结果和弹性预算基于同一产品数量，这会给企业管理者提供更加精确的差异信息，以找到实际结果与预算之间出现差异的真正原因，进而更好地控制企业的未来成本。

8.2 计算销量差异、弹性预算差异和静态预算差异

Computing Sales Volume Variance, Flexible Budget Variance, and Static Budget Variance

差异（variance）指实际结果与预算之间的差值。静态预算与实际结果之间的差值为静态预算差异（static budget variance）。造成静态预算差异的原因包括产品实际数量不同于预算数量、产品实际售价不同于预算售价、产品实际变动成本不同于预算变动成本以及实际固定成本不同于预算固定成本。

静态预算差异分为销量差异（sales volume variance）和弹性预算差异（flexible budget variance）。销量差异指静态预算与按产品实际数量制定的弹性预算之间的差值。销量差异产生的原因：产品实际数量不同于制定静态预算的产品数量。弹性预算差异指按产品实际数量制定的弹性预算与实际结果之间的差值。弹性预算差异产生的原因：产品实际售价不同于预算售价，产品实际变动成本不同于预算变动成本，实际固定成本不同于预算固定成本。

使经营收益增长的差异被视为有利差异（favourable variance），比如实际收入高于预算收入、实际成本低于预算成本；使经营收益降低的差异被视为不利差异（unfavourable variance），比如实际收入低于预算收入、实际成本高于预算成本。

请注意：有利差异和不利差异仅代表对企业经营收益的影响，而非企业经营得"好"与"坏"。

> 案例 8 – 2

A manager received the following incomplete performance report：

	Actual Results	Flexible Budget Variance	Flexible Budget	Sales Volume Variance	Static Budget
Output units	6		6		5

带你到北美学习
管理会计
Take You to
North America
to Learn
Managerial Accounting

	Actual Results	Flexible Budget Variance	Flexible Budget	Sales Volume Variance	Static Budget
Sales revenue	$ 102,000		$ 108,000		$ 90,000
Variable expenses	57,000		60,000		50,000
Fixed expenses	21,000		25,000		25,000
Total expenses	(78,000)		(85,000)		(75,000)
Operating income	$ 24,000		$ 23,000		$ 15,000

Required:

Complete the performance report.

讲解: 销量差异指静态预算与按产品实际数量制定的弹性预算之间的差值。销量差异产生的原因:产品实际数量不同于制定静态预算的产品数量。

根据"案例8-2"信息,产品实际销量为 6 件,而静态预算销量为 5 件,这也是两种预算之间的唯一差异。对于静态预算和按产品实际销量制定的弹性预算,单件产品的预算售价、单件产品的预算变动成本和预算固定成本均相同。单件产品的预算售价为 $18 000,单件产品的预算变动费用为 $10 000,预算固定费用为 $25 000。

相比于静态预算销量(5 件),产品实际销量为 6 件,因此按产品实际销量制定的弹性预算销售额为 $108 000($18 000 × 6 = $108 000),而静态预算销售额为 $90 000($18 000 × 5 = $90 000)。弹性预算销售额高于静态预算销售额 $18 000,这使经营收益增长 $18 000,产生有利差异 $18 000。

按产品实际销量制定的弹性预算变动费用为 $60 000($10 000 × 6 = $60 000),而静态预算变动费用为 $50 000($10 000 × 5 = $50 000)。弹性预算变动费用高于静态预算变动费用 $10 000,这使经营收益降低 $10 000,产生不利差异 $10 000。

按产品实际销量制定的弹性预算固定费用和静态预算固定费用均为 $25 000,没有差异。

按产品实际销量制定的弹性预算费用总额为 $85 000($60 000 + $25 000 = $85 000),而静态预算费用总额为 $75 000($50 000 + $25 000 = $75 000)。弹性预算费用总额高于静态预算费用总额 $10 000,这使经营收益降低 $10 000,产生不利差异 $10 000。

按产品实际销量制定的弹性预算经营收益为 $23 000($108 000 − $85 000 =

$23 000），而静态预算经营收益为 $15 000 （ $90 000 – $75 000 = $15 000），因此产生有利差异 $8 000。

	Flexible Budget	Static Budget	Sales Volume Variance
Output units	<u>6</u>	<u>5</u>	<u>1</u>(F)
Sales revenue	$108,000	$90,000	$18,000(F)
Variable expenses	60,000	50,000	10,000(U)
Fixed expenses	<u>25,000</u>	<u>25,000</u>	<u>0</u>(-)
Total expenses	(85,000)	(75,000)	10,000(U)
Operating income	<u>$23,000</u>	<u>$15,000</u>	<u>$8,000</u>(F)

　　弹性预算差异指按产品实际数量制定的弹性预算与实际结果之间的差值。弹性预算差异产生的原因：产品实际售价不同于预算售价，产品实际变动成本不同于预算变动成本，实际固定成本不同于预算固定成本。

　　根据"案例 8-2"信息，实际销售额为 $102 000，按产品实际销量制定的弹性预算销售额为 $108 000。实际销售额低于弹性预算销售额 $6 000，这使经营收益降低 $6 000，产生不利差异 $6 000。造成此不利差异的原因：产品实际售价为 $17 000 （ $102 000 ÷ 6 = $17 000），而预算售价为 $18 000。

　　实际变动费用为 $57 000，按产品实际销量制定的弹性预算变动费用为 $60 000。实际变动费用低于弹性预算变动费用 $3 000，这使经营收益增长 $3 000，产生有利差异 $3 000。造成此有利差异的原因：单件产品的实际变动费用为 $9 500 （ $57 000 ÷ 6 = $9 500），而单件产品的预算变动费用为 $10 000。

　　实际固定费用为 $21 000，而预算固定费用为 $25 000。实际固定费用低于预算固定费用 $4 000，这使经营收益增长 $4 000，产生有利差异 $4 000。

　　实际费用总额为 $78 000 （ $57 000 + $21 000 = $78 000），而弹性预算费用总额为 $85 000 （ $60 000 + $25 000 = $85 000）。实际费用总额低于弹性预算费用总额 $7 000，这使经营收益增长 $7 000，产生有利差异 $7 000。

　　实际经营收益为 $24 000 （ $102 000 – $78 000 = $24 000），按产品实际销量制定的弹性预算经营收益为 $23 000 （ $108 000 – $85 000 = $23 000），因此产生有利差异 $1 000。

带你到北美学习
管理会计
Take You to
North America
to Learn
Managerial Accounting

	Actual Results	Flexible Budget	Flexible Budget Variance
Output units	6	6	0(–)
Sales revenue	$ 102,000	$ 108,000	$ 6,000(U)
Variable expenses	57,000	60,000	3,000(F)
Fixed expenses	21,000	25,000	4,000(F)
Total expenses	(78,000)	(85,000)	7,000(F)
Operating income	$ 24,000	$ 23,000	$ 1,000(F)

"说明 8-2"所示为绩效报告。

说明 8-2：绩效报告

	Actual Results	Flexible Budget Variance	Flexible Budget	Sales Volume Variance	Static Budget
Output units	6	0(–)	6	1(F)	5
Sales revenue	$ 102,000	$ 6,000(U)	$ 108,000	$ 18,000(F)	$ 90,000
Variable expenses	57,000	3,000(F)	60,000	10,000(U)	50,000
Fixed expenses	21,000	4,000(F)	25,000	0(–)	25,000
Total expenses	(78,000)	7,000(F)	(85,000)	10,000(U)	(75,000)
Operating income	$ 24,000	$ 1,000(F)	$ 23,000	$ 8,000(F)	$ 15,000

8.3 标准成本

Standard Costs

我们可以将一件产品的标准成本（standard cost）视为一件产品的预算。大部分企业使用标准成本制定弹性预算。一件产品的标准成本既包括与生产产品有关的制造成本，又包括与销售产品有关的销售、市场营销和管理成本。本书主要讲解如何计算产品的标准制造成本（standard manufacturing cost）。

为计算一件产品的标准制造成本，首先需要获知生产要素的数量标准（quantity standard）和价格标准（price standard）。生产要素包括直接材料、直接人工和制造费用。一件产品的标准制造成本等于产品生产要素的数量标准乘以价格标准（见图 8-1）。

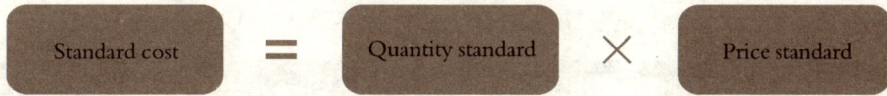

图 8 - 1 标准成本计算公式

通过"案例 8-3",学习计算一件产品的标准直接材料成本、标准直接人工成本、标准变动性制造费用和标准固定性制造费用。

案例 8 - 3

Bottle Company manufactures bottles. The company has the following standards：

Direct materials	1. 30 kg per bottle at a cost of $ 0.40 per kg
Direct labour (DL)	0. 20 hour per bottle at a cost of $ 14.80 per hour
Static budgeted direct labour hours	10,000 hours
Static budgeted number of bottles	52,000 bottles
Static budgeted variable manufacturing overhead	$ 70,500
Static budgeted fixed manufacturing overhead	$ 30,500

Bottle Company allocated manufacturing overhead to production based on standard direct labour hour.

Required：

1. Compute the standard cost of each of the following inputs：direct materials, direct labour, variable manufacturing overhead, and fixed manufacturing overhead.

2. Determine the standard costs of one bottle.

讲解： 生产 1 个瓶子的标准直接材料为 1. 30 千克,每千克直接材料的标准成本为 $ 0.40,因此 1 个瓶子的标准直接材料成本为 $ 0.52。生产 1 个瓶子的标准直接人工工时为 0. 20 小时,每小时标准工资为 $ 14.80,因此 1 个瓶子的标准直接人工成本为 $ 2.96。

在计算标准变动性制造费用之前,需要计算标准变动性制造费用分摊率。标准变动性制造费用分摊率 (standard variable manufacturing overhead rate) 等于预估变动性制造费用总额 (estimated total variable manufacturing overhead) 除以预估分摊基础总额 (estimated total amount of allocation base) (见说明 8-3)。预估变动性制造费用总额为 $ 70 500,分摊基础为直接人工工时 (direct labour hour),预估直接人工工时为 10 000 小时，因此标准变动性制造费用分摊率为 $7.05 per DL hour。

在计算标准固定性制造费用之前，需要计算标准固定性制造费用分摊率。标准固定性制造费用分摊率（standard fixed manufacturing overhead rate）等于预估固定性制造费用总额（estimated total fixed manufacturing overhead）除以预估分摊基础总额（estimated total amount of allocation base）（见说明 8-4）。预估固定性制造费用总额为 $30 500，分摊基础为直接人工工时，预估直接人工工时为 10 000 小时，因此标准固定性制造费用分摊率为 $3.05 per DL hour。

标准制造费用分摊率等于标准变动性制造费用分摊率加上标准固定性制造费用分摊率。标准变动性制造费用分摊率为 $7.05 per DL hour，标准固定性制造费用分摊率为 $3.05 per DL hour，因此标准制造费用分摊率为 $10.10 per DL hour。标准制造费用分摊率（standard manufacturing overhead rate）也等于预估制造费用总额（estimated total manufacturing overhead）除以预估分摊基础总额（estimated total amount of allocation base）（见说明 8-5）。

生产 1 个瓶子的标准直接人工工时为 0.20 小时，所以分摊至 1 个瓶子的标准变动性制造费用为 $1.41（$7.05 × 0.20 = $1.41），标准固定性制造费用为 $0.61（$3.05 × 0.20 = $0.61），标准制造费用为 $2.02（$10.10 × 0.20 = $2.02）。

1 个瓶子的标准直接材料成本为 $0.52，标准直接人工成本为 $2.96，标准变动性制造费用为 $1.41，标准固定性制造费用为 $0.61，因此 1 个瓶子的标准成本为 $5.50。

8.4 分析直接材料差异

Analyzing Direct Material Variances

直接材料是制成品生产过程中使用的主要原材料。直接材料与制成品有直接关系，并易于追溯至制成品，因此直接材料是制成品的实体，如烘烤面包使用的面粉、瓶装饮料使用的瓶子、汽车生产中使用的座椅和发动机等。

为分析直接材料差异，可以将直接材料差异（direct materials variance）分为直接材料价格差异（direct materials price variance）和直接材料效率差异（direct materials efficiency variance）（见图 8-2）。

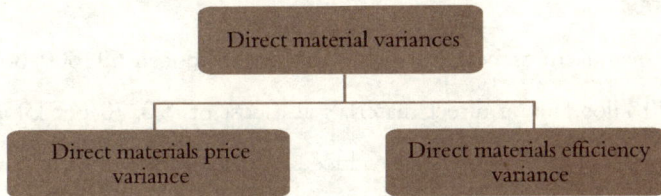

图 8 - 2　直接材料差异分类

直接材料价格差异等于直接材料实际价格与标准价格之间的差值乘以直接材料实际采购量（见说明 8-6）。

说明 8 - 6：计算直接材料价格差异

Direct materials（DM）price variance =
　（Actual DM price − Standard DM price）× Actual quantity of DM purchased

请注意：当直接材料实际价格大于标准价格时，直接材料价格差异为不利差异；而当直接材料实际价格小于标准价格时，直接材料价格差异为有利差异。由于企业采购部门知道直接材料实际价格不同于标准价格的原因，因此采购部门负责解释直接材料价格差异。

直接材料效率差异也称为直接材料数量差异（direct materials quantity variance）或直接材料用量差异（direct materials usage variance）。直接材料效率差异等于直接材料实际使用量与标准量之间的差值乘以直接材料标准价格（见说明 8-7）。

说明 8 - 7：计算直接材料效率差异

Direct materials（DM）efficiency variance =
　（Actual quantity of DM used − Standard quantity of DM）× Standard price per DM

带你到北美学习
管理会计
Take You to
North America
to Learn
Managerial Accounting

请注意：当直接材料实际使用量大于标准量时，直接材料效率差异为不利差异；而当直接材料实际使用量小于标准量时，直接材料效率差异为有利差异。因为企业生产部门有责任确保工人高效使用直接材料，所以生产部门负责解释直接材料效率差异。

有利的直接材料价格差异和直接材料效率差异不能代表部门管理者出色地完成工作，而不利的直接材料价格差异和直接材料效率差异也不能代表部门管理者工作效率低下。为什么？因为差异分析仅是一种调查，而非工作绩效评估。

案例 8 – 4

Bottle Company manufactures bottles. The company produced 69,000 bottles, purchased and used 103,500 kilograms of direct materials at a cost of $ 0. 70 per kilogram. Standards indicate that for the number of bottles produced, the company should have used 89,700 kilograms of direct materials at a cost of $ 0. 40 per kilogram.

Required：

1. Compute the direct materials price variance and the direct materials efficiency variance. Be sure to label each variance as favourable or unfavourable.

2. Compute the flexible budget variance for direct materials. Be sure to label the variance as favourable or unfavourable.

讲解： 为生产 69 000 个瓶子，Bottle Company 采购和使用了 103 500 千克直接材料，因此直接材料的实际采购量和使用量均为 103 500 千克。按产品实际数量制定的直接材料标准量为 89 700 千克。每千克直接材料的实际价格为 $ 0. 70，而标准价格为 $ 0. 40。

每千克直接材料的实际价格为 $ 0. 70，每千克直接材料的标准价格为 $ 0. 40，直接材料实际采购量为 103 500 千克，因此直接材料价格差异为 $ 31 050（（$ 0. 70 – $ 0. 40）× 103 500 = $ 31 050）。每千克直接材料的实际价格超出标准价格 $ 0. 30，即采购 1 千克直接材料，Bottle Company 多支付 $ 0. 30，因此直接材料价格差异为不利差异 $ 31 050。

直接材料实际使用量为 103 500 千克，按产品实际数量制定的直接材料标准量为 89 700 千克，每千克直接材料的标准价格为 $ 0. 40，所以直接材料效率差异为

$ 5 520（（103 500 – 89 700）× $ 0. 40 = $ 5 520）。直接材料实际使用量超出标准量 13 800 千克，即为生产 69 000 个瓶子，Bottle Company 多使用直接材料 13 800 千克，所以直接材料效率差异为不利差异 $ 5 520。

为分析直接材料差异（direct materials variance），可以将直接材料差异分为直接材料价格差异（direct materials price variance）和直接材料效率差异（direct materials efficiency variance）。直接材料效率差异为不利差异 $ 5 520，直接材料价格差异为不利差异 $ 31 050，因此直接材料差异为不利差异 $ 36 570。

Direct materials price variance	$ 31,050(U)
Direct materials efficiency variance	5,520(U)
Direct material variances	$ 36,570(U)

请注意：只有当直接材料实际采购量等于实际使用量时，才可以通过直接材料价格差异加上直接材料效率差异，计算出直接材料差异；而当直接材料实际采购量不等于实际使用量时，就不能通过直接材料价格差异加上直接材料效率差异，计算出直接材料差异。

案例 8 – 5

Bottle Company manufactures bottles. The company produced 69,000 bottles, purchased 103,500 kilograms of direct materials at a cost of $ 0. 70 per kilogram, and used 100,000 kilograms of direct materials. Standards indicate that for the number of bottles produced, the company should have used 89,700 kilograms of direct materials at a cost of $ 0. 40 per kilogram.

Required:

1. Compute the direct materials price variance and the direct materials efficiency variance. Be sure to label each variance as favourable or unfavourable.

2. Compute the flexible budget variance for direct materials. Be sure to label the variance as favourable or unfavourable.

讲解： 为生产 69 000 个瓶子，Bottle Company 采购了 103 500 千克直接材料，使用了 100 000 千克直接材料，因此直接材料实际采购量为 103 500 千克，实际使用量为 100 000 千克。按产品实际数量制定的直接材料标准量为 89 700 千克。每千克直接

带你到北美学习
管理会计
Take You to
North America
to Learn
Managerial Accounting

材料的实际价格为 $ 0. 70，而标准价格为 $ 0. 40。

每千克直接材料的实际价格为 $ 0. 70，每千克直接材料的标准价格为 $ 0. 40，直接材料实际采购量为 103 500 千克，因此直接材料价格差异为 $ 31 050（（ $ 0. 70 – $ 0. 40）× 103 500 = $ 31 050）。每千克直接材料的实际价格超出标准价格 $ 0. 30，即采购 1 千克直接材料，Bottle Company 多支付 $ 0. 30，所以直接材料价格差异为不利差异 $ 31 050。

直接材料实际使用量为 100 000 千克，按产品实际数量制定的直接材料标准量为 89 700 千克，每千克直接材料的标准价格为 $ 0. 40，所以直接材料效率差异为 $ 4 120（（100 000 – 89 700）× $ 0. 40 = $ 4 120）。直接材料实际使用量超出标准量 10 300 千克，即为生产 69 000 个瓶子，Bottle Company 多使用直接材料 10 300 千克，所以直接材料效率差异为不利差异 $ 4 120。

请注意：只有当直接材料实际采购量等于实际使用量时，才可以通过直接材料价格差异加上直接材料效率差异，计算出直接材料差异；而当直接材料实际采购量不等于实际使用量时，就不能通过直接材料价格差异加上直接材料效率差异，计算出直接材料差异。

8.5　分析直接人工差异

Analyzing Direct Labour Variances

工厂中，直接参与将原材料加工为制成品的员工被视为直接人工，如汽车生产厂的机器操作员和技术员、饮料生产厂的装瓶工、面包店的烘焙师等。

为分析直接人工差异，可以将直接人工差异（direct labour variance）分为直接人工工资率差异（direct labour rate variance）和直接人工效率差异（direct labour effi-ciency variance）（见图 8-3）。

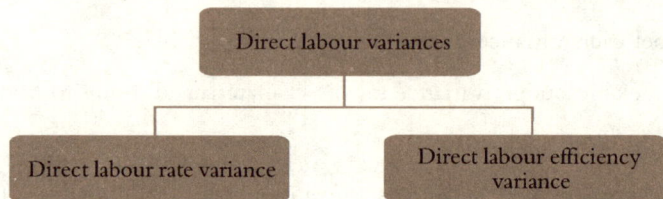

图 8 - 3　直接人工差异分类

直接人工工资率差异等于直接人工实际工资率与标准工资率之间的差值乘以直

接人工实际工时（见说明8-8）。

> **说明 8 - 8：计算直接人工工资率差异**
>
> Direct labour (DL) rate variance =
> (Actual rate per DL hour − Standard rate per DL hour) × Actual DL hours

请注意：当直接人工实际工资率高于标准工资率时，直接人工工资率差异为不利差异；而当直接人工实际工资率低于标准工资率时，直接人工工资率差异为有利差异。由于企业人力资源部门知道直接人工实际工资率不同于标准工资率的原因，因此人力资源部门负责解释直接人工工资率差异。

直接人工效率差异也称为直接人工数量差异（direct labour quantity variance）或直接人工用量差异（direct labour usage variance）。直接人工效率差异等于直接人工实际工时与标准工时之间的差值乘以直接人工标准工资率（见说明8-9）。

> **说明 8 - 9：计算直接人工效率差异**
>
> Direct labour (DL) efficiency variance =
> (Actual DL hours − Standard DL hours) × Standard rate per DL hour

请注意：当直接人工实际工时高于标准工时时，直接人工效率差异为不利差异；而当直接人工实际工时低于标准工时时，直接人工效率差异为有利差异。因为企业生产部门有责任确保工人高效地完成工作，所以生产部门负责解释直接人工效率差异。

有利的直接人工工资率差异和直接人工效率差异不能代表部门管理者出色地完成工作，而不利的直接人工工资率差异和直接人工效率差异也不能代表部门管理者工作效率低下。为什么？因为差异分析仅是一种调查，而非工作绩效评估。

案例 8 - 6

Bottle Company manufactures bottles. The company produced 69,000 bottles and used 0.25 hour of direct labour per bottle at a cost of $12.90 per hour. Standards indicate that for the number of bottles produced, the company should have used 0.20 hour of direct labour per bottle at a cost of $14.80 per hour.

Required：

1. Compute the direct labour price variance and the direct labour efficiency variance. Be sure to label each variance as favourable or unfavourable.

带你到北美学习
管理会计
Take You to
North America
to Learn
Managerial Accounting

2. Compute the flexible budget variance for direct labour. Be sure to label the variance as favourable or unfavourable.

讲解： 为生产 1 个瓶子，需要直接人工工作 0.25 小时，因此直接人工实际工时为 17 250 小时（69 000 × 0.25 = 17 250）。Bottle Company 生产 69 000 个瓶子。按产品实际数量制定的直接人工标准工时为 13 800 小时（69 000 × 0.20 = 13 800）。每小时实际工资率为 $12.90，而标准工资率为 $14.80。

每小时实际工资率为 $12.90，每小时标准工资率为 $14.80，直接人工实际工时为 17 250 小时，因此直接人工工资率差异为 $32 775（（$12.90 – $14.80）× 17 250 = $32 775）。每小时实际工资率低于标准工资率 $1.90，即工人工作 1 小时，Bottle Company 少支付 $1.90，所以直接人工工资率差异为有利差异 $32 775。

直接人工实际工时为 17 250 小时，按产品实际数量制定的直接人工标准工时为 13 800 小时，每小时标准工资率为 $14.80，所以直接人工效率差异为 $51 060（（17 250 – 13 800）× $14.80 = $51 060）。直接人工实际工时超出标准工时 3 450 小时，即为生产 69 000 个瓶子，工人比标准工时多工作 3 450 小时，所以直接人工效率差异为不利差异 $51 060。

为分析直接人工差异（direct labour variance），可以将直接人工差异分为直接人工工资率差异（direct labour rate variance）和直接人工效率差异（direct labour efficiency variance）。直接人工工资率差异为有利差异 $32 775，直接人工效率差异为不利差异 $51 060，因此直接人工差异为不利差异 $18 285。

Direct labour rate variance	$32,775(F)
Direct labour efficiency variance	51,060(U)
Direct labour variances	$18,285(U)

8.6 分析制造费用差异
Analyzing Manufacturing Overhead Variances

制造费用指直接材料成本和直接人工成本以外的制造成本；换言之，制造费用包含了所有间接制造成本（indirect manufacturing cost），一般由三部分组成：①间接材料成本；②间接人工成本；③其他间接制造成本。

制造费用差异（manufacturing overhead variance）指实际制造费用（actual manufacturing overhead）与分摊至生产的标准制造费用（standard manufacturing overhead）之间的差值；换言之，制造费用差异指企业多分摊或少分摊的制造费用。制造费用差异可以分为变动性制造费用差异（variable manufacturing overhead variance）和固定性制造费用差异（fixed manufacturing overhead variance）（见图8-4）。

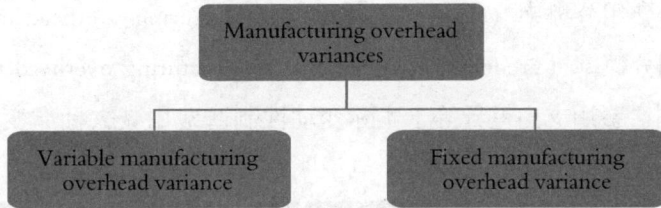

图 8 - 4　制造费用差异分类

请注意：如果实际制造费用大于分摊的标准制造费用，制造费用少分摊，因此制造费用差异为不利差异；而如果实际制造费用小于分摊的标准制造费用，制造费用多分摊，因此制造费用差异为有利差异。

8.6.1 分析变动性制造费用差异
Analyzing Variable Manufacturing Overhead Variances

变动性制造费用（variable manufacturing overhead）指在相关范围内，成本总额变化与活动作业量变动呈正比关系的制造费用。换言之，在相关范围内，当制造商增加产量时，变动性制造费用随之呈正比增长；当制造商降低产量时，变动性制造费用随之呈正比减少。理论上，分析变动性制造费用差异与分析直接材料差异和直接人工差异相似。

为分析变动性制造费用差异，可以将变动性制造费用差异（variable manufacturing overhead variance）分为变动性制造费用支出差异（variable manufacturing overhead spending variance）和变动性制造费用效率差异（variable manufacturing overhead efficiency variance）（见图8-5）。

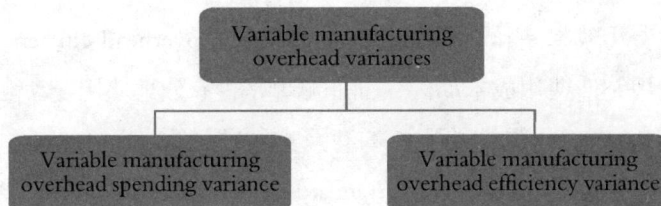

图 8 - 5　变动性制造费用差异分类

带你到北美学习
管理会计
Take You to
North America
to Learn
Managerial Accounting

变动性制造费用支出差异（variable manufacturing overhead spending variance）指实际变动性制造费用（actual variable manufacturing overhead）与按制造费用成本动因实际量制定的预算变动性制造费用之间的差值。按制造费用成本动因实际量制定的预算变动性制造费用等于标准变动性制造费用分摊率乘以制造费用成本动因实际量。标准变动性制造费用分摊率（standard variable manufacturing overhead rate）就是预定变动性制造费用分摊率（predetermined variable manufacturing overhead rate）（见说明8-3）。变动性制造费用支出差异等于实际变动性制造费用减去标准变动性制造费用分摊率乘以制造费用成本动因实际量（见说明8-10）。

说明 8 - 10：计算变动性制造费用支出差异
Variable manufacturing overhead（MOH）spending variance =   Actual variable MOH − Standard variable MOH rate × Actual quantity of cost driver

造成变动性制造费用支出差异的原因：实际变动性制造费用分摊率不同于标准变动性制造费用分摊率（预定变动性制造费用分摊率），使用比预算更多或更少的变动性制造费用，因此变动性制造费用支出差异并不纯粹是一种价格差异（price variance）。

请注意：当实际变动性制造费用高于按制造费用成本动因实际量制定的预算变动性制造费用时，变动性制造费用支出差异为不利差异；而当实际变动性制造费用低于按制造费用成本动因实际量制定的预算变动性制造费用时，变动性制造费用支出差异为有利差异。

分摊基础也称为成本动因，顾名思义，成本动因是成本（制造费用）产生的主要因素（primary factor）。过去，大部分制造商将直接人工工时或直接人工成本作为制造费用的成本动因（分摊基础）；而现今，更多的制造商使用机器设备制造产品，而非人工。机器运转将产生水电费用、维护费用和折旧费用，这些费用属于制造费用，因此机器运转时长（machine hour）也逐渐成为制造费用的成本动因（分摊基础）。

变动性制造费用效率差异（variable manufacturing overhead efficiency variance）测量是否有效地使用制造费用成本动因，而非测量是否有效地使用变动性制造费用。变动性制造费用效率差异等于制造费用成本动因实际量（actual quantity）与按产品实际数量制定的制造费用成本动因标准量（standard quantity）之间的差值乘以标准变动性制造费用分摊率（standard variable manufacturing overhead rate）（见说明8-11）。分摊变

动性制造费用（applied variable manufacturing overhead）等于按产品实际数量制定的
制造费用成本动因标准量乘以标准变动性制造费用分摊率。

说明 8 - 11：计算变动性制造费用效率差异

Variable manufacturing overhead（MOH）efficiency variance =
（Actual quantity of cost driver − Standard quantity of cost driver）× Standard variable MOH rate

　　请注意：当制造费用成本动因实际量低于按产品实际数量制定的制造费用成本
动因标准量时，有效地使用成本动因，因此变动性制造费用效率差异为有利差异；
而当制造费用成本动因实际量高于按产品实际数量制定的制造费用成本动因标准量
时，尚未有效地使用成本动因，因此变动性制造费用效率差异为不利差异。

案例 8 - 7

Travelling Corporation, which provides travel items, reported the following information
about manufacturing overhead（MOH）：

Budgeted fixed manufacturing overhead	$ 16,000
Budgeted variable manufacturing overhead	$ 30,000
Actual fixed manufacturing overhead	$ 16,120
Actual variable manufacturing overhead	$ 28,060
Budgeted direct labour（DL）hours	40,000 hours
Actual direct labour hours	37,200 hours
Standard direct labour hours allowed for actual production	37,000 hours

Required：

1. Calculate the variable manufacturing overhead spending variance. Be sure to label the
   variance as favourable or unfavourable.

2. Calculate the variable manufacturing overhead efficiency variance. Be sure to label the
   variance as favourable or unfavourable.

讲解： 标准变动性制造费用分摊率等于预估变动性制造费用总额除以预估分摊基础
总额。根据"案例8-7"信息，制造费用成本动因（分摊基础）为直接人工工时，
预估变动性制造费用总额为 $ 30 000，预估分摊基础总额为40 000小时，因此标准
变动性制造费用分摊率为 $ 0.75 per DL hour。

带你到北美学习
管理会计
Take You to
North America
to Learn
Managerial Accounting

变动性制造费用支出差异等于实际变动性制造费用减去标准变动性制造费用分摊率乘以制造费用成本动因实际量。实际变动性制造费用为 $28 060。制造费用成本动因为直接人工工时,直接人工实际工时为 37 200 小时,标准变动性制造费用分摊率为 $0. 75 per DL hour,因此按制造费用成本动因实际量制定的预算变动性制造费用为 $27 900（$0. 75 × 37 200 = $27 900）。实际变动性制造费用大于按制造费用成本动因实际量制定的预算变动性制造费用,所以变动性制造费用支出差异为不利差异 $160。

变动性制造费用效率差异等于制造费用成本动因实际量与按产品实际数量制定的制造费用成本动因标准量之间的差值乘以标准变动性制造费用分摊率。

根据"案例 8-7"信息,制造费用成本动因为直接人工工时,直接人工实际工时为 37 200 小时,按产品实际数量制定的直接人工标准工时为 37 000 小时,标准变动性制造费用分摊率为 $0. 75 per DL hour。直接人工实际工时超出按产品实际数量制定的直接人工标准工时 200 小时,即 Travelling Corporation 尚未有效地使用成本动因,因此变动性制造费用效率差异为不利差异 $150（$0. 75 × 200 = $150）。

变动性制造费用支出差异为不利差异 $160,变动性制造费用效率差异为不利差异 $150,因此变动性制造费用差异为不利差异 $310。

Variable MOH spending variance	$160(U)
Variable MOH efficiency variance	150(U)
Variable MOH variances	$310(U)

8.6.2 分析固定性制造费用差异
Analyzing Fixed Manufacturing Overhead Variances

固定性制造费用（fixed manufacturing overhead）指在相关范围内,成本总额不随活动作业量变化而变动的制造费用。换言之,在相关范围内,固定性制造费用是恒定不变的。理论上,分析固定性制造费用差异与分析直接材料差异、直接人工差异和变动性制造费用差异不同。

为分析固定性制造费用差异,可以将固定性制造费用差异（fixed manufacturing overhead variance）分为固定性制造费用预算差异（fixed manufacturing overhead budget variance）和固定性制造费用产量差异（fixed manufacturing overhead production volume variance）（见图 8-6）。

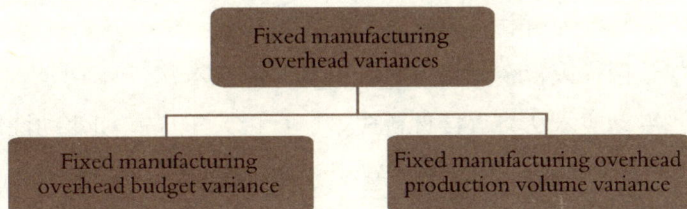

图 8 – 6　固定性制造费用差异分类

固定性制造费用预算差异也称为固定性制造费用支出差异（fixed manufacturing overhead spending variance）。固定性制造费用预算差异指实际固定性制造费用（actual fixed manufacturing overhead）与预算固定性制造费用（budgeted fixed manufacturing overhead）之间的差值（见说明 8-12）。因为固定性制造费用在相关范围内是恒定不变的，所以在相关范围内，弹性预算固定性制造费用和静态预算固定费用相同。预算固定性制造费用等于标准固定性制造费用分摊率乘以按产品预算数量（budgeted quantity）制定的制造费用成本动因标准量（制造费用成本动因预算数量）。标准固定性制造费用分摊率（standard fixed manufacturing overhead rate）就是预定固定性制造费用分摊率（predetermined fixed manufacturing overhead rate）（见说明 8-4）。

说明 8 - 12：计算固定性制造费用预算差异

Fixed manufacturing overhead budget variance =
　Actual fixed manufacturing overhead – Budgeted fixed manufacturing overhead

请注意：当实际固定性制造费用大于预算固定性制造费用时，固定性制造费用预算差异为不利差异；而当实际固定性制造费用小于预算固定性制造费用时，固定性制造费用预算差异为有利差异。

固定性制造费用产量差异指预算固定性制造费用（budgeted fixed manufacturing overhead）与分摊固定性制造费用（applied fixed manufacturing overhead）之间的差值（见说明 8-13）。分摊固定性制造费用等于标准固定性制造费用分摊率乘以按产品实际数量制定的制造费用成本动因标准量。

说明 8 - 13：计算固定性制造费用产量差异

Fixed manufacturing overhead production volume variance =
　Budgeted fixed manufacturing overhead – Applied fixed manufacturing overhead

带你到北美学习
管理会计
Take You to
North America
to Learn
Managerial Accounting

请注意：固定性制造费用产量差异不能解释为过度使用或未充分使用生产设施，因此这种差异不能解释为有利差异或不利差异。

为制定内部管理决策，企业管理者应使用变动成本法（variable costing）编写边际贡献收益表。变动成本法将直接材料成本、直接人工成本和变动性制造费用计入产品成本（product cost），固定性制造费用计入期间成本（period cost）。然而，为向投资人和债权人等外部使用者提供有价值的信息，财务会计报告准则要求，企业必须使用归纳成本法（absorption costing）编写传统收益表。归纳成本法将直接材料成本、直接人工成本、变动性制造费用和固定性制造费用计入产品成本。

对于使用变动成本法的企业，它们需要将固定性制造费用计入期间成本，因此无需将固定性制造费用分摊至产品。因为无需分摊固定性制造费用，所以对于这类企业，不用分析固定性制造费用产量差异。

对于使用归纳成本法的企业，它们需要将固定性制造费用计入产品成本，因此对于这类企业，需要分析固定性制造费用产量差异。

案例 8 - 8

Travelling Corporation, which provides travel items, reported the following information about manufacturing overhead:

Budgeted fixed manufacturing overhead	$ 16,000
Budgeted variable manufacturing overhead	$ 30,000
Actual fixed manufacturing overhead	$ 16,120
Actual variable manufacturing overhead	$ 28,060
Budgeted direct labour (DL) hours	40,000 hours
Actual direct labour hours	37,200 hours
Standard direct labour hours allowed for actual production	37,000 hours

Required:

1. Calculate the fixed manufacturing overhead budget variance. Be sure to label the variance as favourable or unfavourable.

2. Calculate the fixed manufacturing overhead production volume variance.

讲解： 固定性制造费用预算差异指实际固定性制造费用与预算固定性制造费用之间的差值。根据"案例8-8"信息，实际固定性制造费用为 $16 120，预算固定性制

造费用为 $ 16 000，实际固定性制造费用大于预算固定性制造费用 $ 120，固定性制造费用预算差异为不利差异 $ 120。

固定性制造费用产量差异指预算固定性制造费用与分摊固定性制造费用之间的差值。分摊固定性制造费用等于标准固定性制造费用分摊率乘以按产品实际数量制定的制造费用成本动因标准量。标准固定性制造费用分摊率等于预估固定性制造费用总额除以预估分摊基础总额。

根据"案例 8-8"信息，制造费用成本动因（分摊基础）为直接人工工时，预估固定性制造费用总额为 $ 16 000，预估分摊基础总额为 40 000 小时，因此标准固定性制造费用分摊率为 $ 0.40 per DL hour。

按产品实际数量制定的直接人工标准工时为 37 000 小时，标准固定性制造费用分摊率为 $ 0.40 per DL hour，因此分摊固定性制造费用为 $ 14 800。预算固定性制造费用为 $ 16 000，分摊固定性制造费用为 $ 14 800，固定性制造费用产量差异为 $ 1 200。

带你到北美学习
管理会计
Take You to
North America
to Learn
Managerial Accounting

例题综述
Summary of Examples

例题 8 - 1

A static budget _____.

A. can evaluate performance after the fiscal period ended but can not plan

B. reflects only variable costs but does not contains fixed costs

C. is a budget for a range of activity levels so that the budget can reflect changes in activity levels

D. is a budget for one level of activity and can not reflect changes in activity levels

讲解： 按某一产品数量制定的预算被称为静态预算（static budget），而按不同产品数量制定的预算则被称为弹性预算（flexible budget）。

答案： D

例题 8 - 2

A flexible budget _____.

A. can evaluate performance after the fiscal period ended but can not plan

B. reflects only variable costs but does not contains fixed costs

C. is a budget for a range of activity levels so that the budget can reflect changes in activity levels

D. is a budget for one level of activity and can not reflect changes in activity levels

讲解： 同 "例题 8-1"。

答案： C

例题 8 - 3

A sales volume variance occurs when _____.

A. the actual price of one unit is lower than the standard price originally planned for in the static budget

B. the actual number of units sold differs from the number of units originally planned for in the static budget

C. the actual price of one unit is higher than the standard price originally planned for in the static budget

D. the actual costs of inputs differ from the costs originally planned for in the static budget

讲解： 销量差异指静态预算与按产品实际数量制定的弹性预算之间的差值。销量差异产生的原因在于产品实际数量不同于制定静态预算的产品数量。

答案： B

例题 8 – 4

The formula for calculating a direct materials efficiency variance is _____.

A. （Actual direct materials price – Standard direct materials price） × Actual quantity of direct materials purchased

B. （Actual quantity of direct materials used – Standard quantity of direct materials） × Standard price per direct materials

C. （Actual rate per direct labour hour – Standard rate per direct labour hour） × Actual direct labour hours

D. （Actual direct labour hours – Standard direct labour hours） × Standard rate per direct labour hour

讲解： 见 "说明 8-7"。

答案： B

例题 8 – 5

The formula for calculating a direct materials price variance is _____.

A. （Actual direct materials price – Standard direct materials price） × Actual quantity of direct materials purchased

B. （Actual quantity of direct materials used – Standard quantity of direct materials） × Standard price per direct materials

C. （Actual rate per direct labour hour – Standard rate per direct labour hour） × Actual direct labour hours.

D. （Actual direct labour hours – Standard direct labour hours） × Standard rate per direct labour hour

带你到北美学习
管理会计
Take You to
North America
to Learn
Managerial Accounting

讲解: 见"说明8-6"。

答案: A

例题 8 - 6

The formula for calculating a direct labour rate variance is _____.

A. (Actual direct materials price − Standard direct materials price) × Actual quantity of direct materials purchased

B. (Actual quantity of direct materials used − Standard quantity of direct materials) × Standard price per direct materials

C. (Actual rate per direct labour hour − Standard rate per direct labour hour) × Actual direct labour hours

D. (Actual direct labour hours − Standard direct labour hours) × Standard rate per direct labour hour

讲解: 见"说明8-8"。

答案: C

例题 8 - 7

The formula for calculating a direct labour efficiency variance is _____.

A. (Actual direct materials price − Standard direct materials price) × Actual quantity of direct materials purchased

B. (Actual quantity of direct materials used − Standard quantity of direct materials) × Standard price per direct materials

C. (Actual rate per direct labour hour − Standard rate per direct labour hour) × Actual direct labour hours

D. (Actual direct labour hours − Standard direct labour hours) × Standard rate per direct labour hour

讲解: 见"说明8-9"。

答案: D

例题 8 - 8

A favourable direct materials efficiency variance indicates that _____.

A. the actual direct materials price is higher than the standard direct materials price

B. the actual direct materials price is less than the standard direct materials price

C. the actual quantity of direct materials used is less than the standard quantity of direct materials allowed for the actual quantity of output

D. the actual quantity of direct materials used is higher than the standard quantity of direct materials allowed for the actual quantity of output

讲解： 当直接材料实际使用量大于标准量时，直接材料效率差异为不利差异；而当直接材料实际使用量小于标准量时，直接材料效率差异为有利差异。

答案： C

例题 8 - 9

An unfavourable direct materials price variance indicates that _____.

A. the actual direct materials price is higher than the standard direct materials price

B. the actual direct materials price is less than the standard direct materials price

C. the actual quantity of direct materials used is less than the standard quantity of direct materials allowed for the actual quantity of output

D. the actual quantity of direct materials used is higher than the standard quantity of direct materials allowed for the actual quantity of output

讲解： 当直接材料实际价格大于标准价格时，直接材料价格差异为不利差异；而当直接材料实际价格小于标准价格时，直接材料价格差异为有利差异。

答案： A

例题 8 - 10

A unfavourable direct labour efficiency variance indicates that _____.

A. the actual rate of direct labour is higher than the standard rate of direct labour

B. the actual rate of direct labour is less than the standard rate of direct labour

C. the actual hours of direct labour worked is less than the standard hours of direct labour allowed for the actual quantity of output

带你到北美学习
管理会计
Take You to
North America
to Learn
Managerial Accounting

D. the actual hours of direct labour worked is higher than the standard hours of direct labour allowed for the actual quantity of output

讲解： 当直接人工实际工时高于标准工时，直接人工效率差异为不利差异；而当直接人工实际工时低于标准工时，直接人工效率差异为有利差异。

答案： D

例题 8 - 11

A favourable direct labour rate variance indicates that _____ .

A. the actual rate of direct labour is higher than the standard rate of direct labour

B. the actual rate of direct labour is less than the standard rate of direct labour

C. the actual hours of direct labour worked is less than the standard hours of direct labour allowed for the actual quantity of output

D. the actual hours of direct labour worked is higher than the standard hours of direct labour allowed for the actual quantity of output

讲解： 当直接人工实际工资率高于标准工资率，直接人工价格差异为不利差异；而当直接人工实际工资率低于标准工资率，直接人工价格差异为有利差异。

答案： B

例题 8 - 12

The mamufacturing overhead variances are composed of _____ .

A. variable manufacturing overhead spending variance and fixed manufacturing overhead production volume variance

B. fixed manufacturing overhead budget variance and variable manufacturing overhead efficiency variance

C. variable manufacturing overhead variance and fixed manufacturing overhead variance

D. price variance and efficiency variance

讲解： 制造费用差异（manufacturing overhead variance）分为变动性制造费用差异（variable manufacturing overhead variance）和固定性制造费用差异（fixed manufacturing overhead variance）。

答案： C

例题 8 - 13

The variable manufacturing overhead variances are composed of _____ .

A. variable manufacturing overhead spending variance and variable manufacturing overhead efficiency variance

B. variable manufacturing overhead budget variance and variable manufacturing overhead efficiency variance

C. variable manufacturing overhead variance and fixed manufacturing overhead variance

D. price variance and efficiency variance

讲解： 变动性制造费用差异（variable manufacturing overhead variance）分为变动性制造费用支出差异（variable manufacturing overhead spending variance）和变动性制造费用效率差异（variable manufacturing overhead efficiency variance）。

答案： A

例题 8 - 14

The fixed manufacturing overhead variances are composed of _____ .

A. variable manufacturing overhead variance and fixed manufacturing overhead variance

B. fixed manufacturing overhead spending variance and fixed manufacturing overhead efficiency variance

C. price variance and efficiency variance

D. fixed manufacturing overhead budget variance and fixed manufacturing overhead production volume variance

讲解： 固定性制造费用差异（fixed manufacturing overhead variance）分为固定性制造费用预算差异（fixed manufacturing overhead budget variance）和固定性制造费用产量差异（fixed manufacturing overhead production volume variance）。

答案： D

例题 8 - 15

The report provides the information about the corporation's budget and actual performance for May.

带你到北美学习
管理会计
Take You to
North America
to Learn
Managerial Accounting

	Actual Results	(I)	Flexible Budget	(II)	Static Budget
		Tom Corporation Income Statement Performance Report For the month ended by May 31			
Output units	40,000		(III)		48,000
Sales revenue	$320,000	$8,000(F)	(IV)		
Variable expenses			(V)		$300,000
Fixed expenses	24,000	(VI)			32,000

Required：

Fill in the missing data for letters I - VI. Be sure to label any variances as favourable or unfavourable.

讲解： 弹性预算差异（flexible budget variance）指按产品实际数量制定的弹性预算与实际结果之间的差值，所以 I 为 flexible budget variance。销量差异（sales volume variance）指静态预算与按产品实际数量制定的弹性预算之间的差值，因此 II 为 sales volume variance。

产品实际销量为 40 000 件，所以 III 为 40 000。

实际销售额为 $320 000，实际销售额与按产品实际销量制定的弹性预算销售额之间的差异为有利差异 $8 000，因此实际销售额超过弹性预算销售额 $8 000，按产品实际销量制定的弹性预算销售额为 $312 000，即 IV 为 $312 000。

对于静态预算和按产品实际销量制定的弹性预算，单件产品预算售价、单件产品预算变动成本、预算固定成本均相同，因此弹性预算的单件产品变动成本等于静态预算的单件产品变动成本，即 $6.25（$300 000 ÷ $48 000 = $6.25）。按产品实际销量制定的弹性预算变动费用为 $250 000（$6.25 × 40 000 = $250 000），因此 V 为 $250 000。

对于静态预算和按产品实际销量制定的弹性预算，单件产品预算售价、单件产品预算变动成本、预算固定成本均相同，因此静态预算固定费用等于弹性预算固定费用，即 $32 000。实际固定费用为 $24 000，而预算固定费用为 $32 000。实际固定费用低于预算固定费用 $8 000，这使经营收益增长 $8 000，产生有利差异 $8 000，VI 为 $8 000（F）。

答案：

<table>
<tr><td colspan="6" align="center">Tom Corporation
Income Statement Performance Report
For the month ended by May 31</td></tr>
<tr><td></td><td>Actual
Results</td><td>Flexible
Budget
Variance</td><td>Flexible
Budget</td><td>Sales
Volume
Variance</td><td>Static
Budget</td></tr>
<tr><td>Output units</td><td>40,000</td><td></td><td>40,000</td><td></td><td>48,000</td></tr>
<tr><td>Sales revenue</td><td>$ 320,000</td><td>$ 8,000(F)</td><td>$ 312,000</td><td></td><td></td></tr>
<tr><td>Variable expenses</td><td></td><td></td><td>250,000</td><td></td><td>$ 300,000</td></tr>
<tr><td>Fixed expenses</td><td>24,000</td><td>$ 8,000(F)</td><td></td><td></td><td>32,000</td></tr>
</table>

例题 8 - 16

A company's manager received the following incomplete performance report：

<table>
<tr><td colspan="6" align="center">Tom Corporation
Income Statement Performance Report
For the month ended by May 31</td></tr>
<tr><td></td><td>Actual
Results</td><td>Flexible
Budget
Variance</td><td>Flexible
Budget</td><td>Sales
Volume
Variance</td><td>Static
Budget</td></tr>
<tr><td>Output units</td><td>38,000</td><td></td><td>38,000</td><td>2,000(F)</td><td></td></tr>
<tr><td>Sales revenue</td><td>$ 219,000</td><td></td><td>$ 219,000</td><td>$ 24,000(F)</td><td></td></tr>
<tr><td>Variable expenses</td><td>81,000</td><td></td><td>80,000</td><td>10,000(U)</td><td></td></tr>
<tr><td>Fixed expenses</td><td>107,000</td><td></td><td>100,000</td><td>0(-)</td><td></td></tr>
<tr><td>Total expenses</td><td>(188,000)</td><td></td><td>(180,000)</td><td>10,000(U)</td><td></td></tr>
<tr><td>Operating income</td><td>$ 31,000</td><td></td><td>$ 39,000</td><td>$ 14,000(F)</td><td></td></tr>
</table>

Required：

Complete the performance report.

讲解： 销量差异指静态预算与按产品实际数量制定的弹性预算之间的差值，销量差异产生的原因在于产品实际数量不同于制定静态预算的产品数量，这也是两种预算之间的唯一差异。对于静态预算和按产品实际销量制定的弹性预算，单件产品预算售价、单件产品预算变动成本和预算固定成本均相同。

弹性预算差异（flexible budget variance）指按产品实际数量制定的弹性预算与实际结果之间的差值。弹性预算差异产生的原因：产品实际售价不同于预算售价，产品实际变动成本不同于预算变动成本，实际固定成本不同于预算固定成本。

使经营收益增长的差异被视为有利差异（favourable variance），如实际收入高于预算收入，实际成本低于预算成本；使经营收益降低的差异被视为不利差异（unfavourable variance），如实际收入低于预算收入，实际成本高于预算成本。

请注意：有利差异和不利差异仅代表对企业经营收益的影响，而非企业经营得"好"与"坏"。

答案：

Tom Corporation Income Statement Performance Report For the month ended by May 31					
	Actual Results	Flexible Budget Variance	Flexible Budget	Sales Volume Variance	Static Budget
Output units	38,000	0(-)	38,000	2,000(F)	36,000
Sales revenue	$219,000	$0(-)	$219,000	$24,000(F)	$195,000
Variable expenses	81,000	1,000(U)	80,000	10,000(U)	70,000
Fixed expenses	107,000	7,000(U)	100,000	0(-)	100,000
Total expenses	(188,000)	8,000(U)	(180,000)	10,000(U)	(170,000)
Operating income	$31,000	$8,000(U)	$39,000	$14,000(F)	$25,000

例题 8 - 17

The following is a partially completed performance report：

Tom Corporation Income Statement Performance Report For the month ended by May 31					
	Actual Results	Flexible Budget Variance	Flexible Budget	Sales Volume Variance	Static Budget
	10		10		8
Sales revenue	$121,000		$120,000		$96,000
Variable expenses	83,000		80,000		64,000
Fixed expenses	22,000		20,000		20,000
Total expenses	(105,000)		(100,000)		(84,000)
Operating income	$16,000		$20,000		$12,000

Required：

Complete the performance report.

讲解： 同 "例题 8-16"。

答案：

Tom Corporation Income Statement Performance Report For the month ended by May 31	Actual Results	Flexible Budget Variance	Flexible Budget	Sales Volume Variance	Static Budget
Output units	10	0(-)	10	2(F)	8
Sales revenue	$ 121,000	$ 1,000(F)	$ 120,000	$ 24,000(F)	$ 96,000
Variable expenses	83,000	3,000(U)	80,000	16,000(U)	64,000
Fixed expenses	22,000	2,000(U)	20,000	0(-)	20,000
Total expenses	(105,000)	5,000(U)	(100,000)	16,000(U)	(84,000)
Operating income	$ 16,000	$ 4,000(U)	$ 20,000	$ 8,000(F)	$ 12,000

例题 8 – 18

Chocolate Company produces milk chocolates in large batches. One batch of milk chocolates has the following standard costs and amounts：

Standard quantity of sugar	100 kilograms
Standard cost per kilogram of sugar	$ 1.90
Standard direct labour hours per batch of milk chocolates	2 hours
Standard direct labour rate	$ 18

Chocolate Company produced 400 batches of milk chocolates in the most recent month. Actual costs and usage levels were as follows：

Actual amount of sugar purchased and used per batch of milk chocolates	102 kilograms
Actual cost per kilogram of sugar	$ 2.10
Actual direct labour hours per batch of milk chocolates	1.80 hours
Actual direct labour rate	$ 17.50

Required：

1. Calculate the direct materials price variance and the direct materials efficiency variance.

带你到北美学习

管理会计

Take You to
North America
to Learn
Managerial Accounting

Be sure to label each variance as favourable or unfavourable.

2. Calculate the direct labour rate variance and the direct labour efficiency variance. Be sure to label each variance as favourable or unfavourable.

1. Calculate the direct materials price variance and the direct materials efficiency variance. Be sure to label each variance as favourable or unfavourable.

讲解： Chocolate Company 生产 400 块巧克力。为生产 1 块巧克力，糖的标准量为 100 千克，实际采购和使用糖 102 千克，因此糖的实际采购量和使用量均为 40 800 千克（400 × 102 = 40 800），按产品实际数量制定的、糖的标准量为 40 000 千克（400 × 100 = 40 000）。每千克糖的实际价格为 $2.10，而标准价格为 $1.90。

每千克糖的实际价格为 $2.10，每千克糖的标准价格为 $1.90，糖的实际采购量为 40 800 千克，因此直接材料价格差异为 $8 160（（$2.10 – $1.90）× 40 800 = $8 160）。每千克糖的实际价格超出标准价格 $0.20，即采购 1 千克糖，Chocolate Company 多支付 $0.20，所以直接材料价格差异为不利差异 $8 160。

糖的实际使用量为 40 800 千克，按产品实际数量制定的、糖的标准量为 40 000 千克，每千克糖的标准价格为 $1.90，所以直接材料效率差异为 $1 520（（40 800 – 40 000）× $1.90 = $1 520）。糖的实际使用量超出标准量 800 千克，即为生产 400 块巧克力，Chocolate Company 多使用 800 千克糖，因此直接材料效率差异为不利差异 $1 520。

答案： The unfavourable direct materials price variance is $8,160, the unfavourable direct materials efficiency variance is $1,520.

2. Calculate the direct labour rate variance and the direct labour efficiency variance. Be sure to label each variance as favourable or unfavourable.

讲解： Chocolate Company 生产 400 块巧克力。为生产 1 块巧克力，直接人工标准工时为 2 小时，直接人工实际工时为 1.80 小时，因此直接人工实际工时为 720 小时（400 × 1.80 = 720），按产品实际数量制定的直接人工标准工时为 800 小时（400 × 2 = 800）。每小时实际工资率为 $17.50，而标准工资率为 $18。

每小时实际工资率为 $17.50，标准工资率为 $18，直接人工实际工时为 720 小时，因此直接人工工资率差异为 $360（（$17.50 – $18）× 720 = $360）。每小时实际工资率低于标准工资率 $0.50,即工人工作 1 小时,Chocolate Company 少支付 $0.50,所以直接人工工资率差异为有利差异 $360。

直接人工实际工时为 720 小时,按产品实际数量制定的直接人工标准工时为 800 小时,每小时标准工资率为 $18,所以直接人工效率差异为 $1 440((720 - 800) × $18 = $1 440)。直接人工实际工时低于标准工时 80 小时,即为生产 400 块巧克力,工人比标准工时少工作 80 小时,因此直接人工效率差异为有利差异 $1 440。

答案: The favourable direct labour rate variance is $360, the favourable direct labour efficiency variance is $1,440.

例题 8 - 19

In order to manufacture 30,000 bags of frozen French fries, Potato Corporation purchased 99,000 kilograms of potatoes at a cost of $0.70 per kilogram and used 96,000 kilograms of potatoes last week. During the week, 2,300 direct labour hours were incurred at a rate of $12.30 per hour. Standards indicate that for the 30,000 bags of frozen French fries produced, the factory should have used 97,000 kilograms of potatoes and 2,200 direct labour hours. The standard cost per kilogram of potatoes is $0.90 and the standard direct labour rate is $12.05 per hour.

Required:

1. Determine the direct materials price and efficiency variances. Be sure to label each variance as favourable or unfavourable.

2. Determine the direct labour rate and efficiency variances. Be sure to label each variance as favourable or unfavourable.

1. Determine the direct materials price and efficiency variances. Be sure to label each variance as favourable or unfavourable.

讲解: 为生产 30 000 袋薯条,Potato Corporation 采购土豆 99 000 千克,使用土豆 96 000 千克,因此土豆实际采购量和使用量分别为 99 000 千克和 96 000 千克。按产品实际数量制定的直接材料标准量为 97 000 千克土豆。每千克土豆的实际价格为 $0.70,而标准价格为 $0.90。

带你到北美学习

管理会计

Take You to
North America
to Learn
Managerial Accounting

每千克土豆的实际价格为 $0.70、标准价格为 $0.90，土豆实际采购量为 99 000 千克，因此直接材料价格差异为 $19 800（（$0.70 – $0.90）× 99 000 = $19 800）。每千克土豆的实际价格低于标准价格 $0.20，即采购 1 千克土豆，Potato Corporation 少支付 $0.20，所以直接材料价格差异为有利差异 $19 800。

土豆的实际使用量为 96 000 千克，按产品实际数量制定的直接材料标准量为 97 000 千克土豆，每千克土豆的标准价格为 $0.90，所以直接材料效率差异为 $900（（96 000 – 97 000）× $0.90 = $900）。土豆的实际使用量低于标准量 1 000 千克，即为生产 30 000 袋薯条，Potato Corporation 少使用土豆 1 000 千克，所以直接材料效率差异为有利差异 $900。

答案： The favourable direct materials efficiency variance is $900, the favourable direct materials price variance is $19,800.

2. Determine the direct labour rate and efficiency variances. Be sure to label each variance as favourable or unfavourable.

讲解： 为生产 30 000 袋薯条，直接人工实际工作 2 300 小时。按产品实际数量制定的直接人工标准工时为 2 200 小时。每小时实际工资率为 $12.30，而标准工资率为 $12.05。

每小时实际工资率为 $12.30，每小时标准工资率为 $12.05，直接人工实际工时为 2 300 小时，因此直接人工工资率差异为 $575（（$12.30 – $12.05）× 2 300 = $575）。每小时实际工资率高于标准工资率 $0.25，即工人工作 1 小时，Potato Corporation 多支付 $0.25，所以直接人工工资率差异为不利差异 $575。

直接人工实际工时为 2 300 小时，按产品实际数量制定的直接人工标准工时为 2 200 小时，每小时标准工资率为 $12.05，所以直接人工效率差异为 $1 205（（2 300 – 2 200）× $12.05 = $1 205）。直接人工实际工时超出标准工时 100 小时，即为生产 30 000 袋薯条，工人比标准工时多工作 100 小时，所以直接人工效率差异为不利差异 $1 205。

答案： The unfavourable direct labour rate variance is $575, the unfavourable direct labour efficiency variance is $1,205.

例题 8 - 20

Potato Corporation, using standard costing, reported the following manufacturing overhead information for the last quarter of the year:

Actual fixed manufacturing overhead	$ 10,500
Actual variable manufacturing overhead	$ 66,810
Budgeted fixed manufacturing overhead	$ 11,000
Variable manufacturing overhead rate per direct labour (DL) hour	$ 5
Standard direct labour hours allowed for actual production	13,100 hours
Actual direct labour hours used	13,000 hours

Required:

1. Calculate the variable manufacturing overhead spending variance. Be sure to label the variance as favourable or unfavourable.

2. Calculate the variable manufacturing overhead efficiency variance. Be sure to label the variance as favourable or unfavourable.

1. Calculate the variable manufacturing overhead spending variance. Be sure to label the variance as favourable or unfavourable.

讲解： 变动性制造费用支出差异等于实际变动性制造费用减去标准变动性制造费用分摊率乘以制造费用成本动因实际量。

根据题目信息，制造费用成本动因为直接人工工时，直接人工实际工时为 13 000 小时，标准变动性制造费用分摊率为 $ 5 per DL hour，因此按制造费用成本动因实际量制定的预算变动性制造费用为 $ 65 000 （ $ 5 × 13 000 = $ 65 000）。实际变动性制造费用为 $ 66 810。实际变动性制造费用超出按制造费用成本动因实际量制定的预算变动性制造费用 $ 1 810，所以变动性制造费用支出差异为不利差异 $ 1 810。

答案： The unfavourable variable manufacturing overhead spending variance is $ 1,810.

2. Calculate the variable manufacturing overhead efficiency variance. Be sure to label the variance as favourable or unfavourable.

讲解： 变动性制造费用效率差异等于制造费用成本动因实际量与按产品实际数量制

带你到北美学习
管理会计
Take You to
North America
to Learn
Managerial Accounting

定的制造费用成本动因标准量之间的差值乘以标准变动性制造费用分摊率。

根据题目信息，制造费用成本动因为直接人工工时，直接人工实际工时为13 000小时，按产品实际数量制定的直接人工标准工时为13 100 小时，标准变动性制造费用分摊率为 $5 per DL hour。直接人工实际工时低于按产品实际数量制定的直接人工标准工时 100 小时，即 Potato Corporation 有效地使用成本动因，因此变动性制造费用效率差异为有利差异 $500（$5 × 100 = $500）。

答案： The favourable variable manufacturing overhead efficiency variance is $500.

例题 8 - 21

Tom Company budgets two direct labour (DL) hours for each unit of the 5,900 units that are planned for production. Last year, the company incurred actual direct labour hours of 11,800 hours, actual variable manufacturing overhead totaling $18,750, and actual fixed manufacturing overhead totaling $21,500 for the production of 6,000 units. The company applies variable manufacturing overhead at a rate of $1.50 per direct labour hour and fixed manufacturing overhead at a rate of $1.75 per direct labour hour.

Required：

1. Calculate the variable manufacturing overhead spending variance. Be sure to label the variance as favourable or unfavourable.

2. Calculate the variable manufacturing overhead efficiency variance. Be sure to label the variance as favourable or unfavourable.

3. Calculate the fixed manufacturing overhead budget variance. Be sure to label the variance as favourable or unfavourable.

4. Calculate the fixed manufacturing overhead production volume variance.

1. Calculate the variable manufacturing overhead spending variance. Be sure to label the variance as favourable or unfavourable.

讲解： 变动性制造费用支出差异等于实际变动性制造费用减去标准变动性制造费用分摊率乘以制造费用成本动因实际量。

根据题目信息，制造费用成本动因为直接人工工时，直接人工实际工时为 11 800 小时，标准变动性制造费用分摊率为 $1.50 per DL hour，因此按制造费用成本动因实际量制定的预算变动性制造费用为 $17 700（$1. 50 × 11 800 = $17 700）。实际变动性制造费用为 $18 750。实际变动性制造费用超出按制造费用成本动因实际量制定的预算变动性制造费用 $1 050，所以变动性制造费用支出差异为不利差异 $1 050。

答案： The unfavourable variable manufacturing overhead spending variance is $1,050.

2. Calculate the variable manufacturing overhead efficiency variance. Be sure to label the variance as favourable or unfavourable.

讲解： 变动性制造费用效率差异等于制造费用成本动因实际量与按产品实际数量制定的制造费用成本动因标准量之间的差值乘以标准变动性制造费用分摊率。

根据题目信息，制造费用成本动因为直接人工工时（direct labour hour），标准变动性制造费用分摊率为 $1. 50 per DL hour。产品实际数量为 6 000 件，生产 1 件产品的直接人工标准工时为 2 小时，因此按产品实际数量制定的直接人工标准工时为 12 000 小时（2 × 6 000 = 12 000）。直接人工实际工时为 11 800 小时。直接人工实际工时低于按产品实际数量制定的直接人工标准工时 200 小时，即 Tom Company 有效地使用成本动因，因此变动性制造费用效率差异为有利差异 $300（$1. 50 × 200 = $300）。

答案： The favourable variable manufacturing overhead efficiency variance is $300.

3. Calculate the fixed manufacturing overhead budget variance. Be sure to label the variance as favourable or unfavourable.

讲解： 固定性制造费用预算差异指实际固定性制造费用与预算固定性制造费用之间的差值。预算固定性制造费用等于标准固定性制造费用分摊率乘以按产品预算数量制定的制造费用成本动因标准量（制造费用成本动因预算数量）。

根据题目信息，产品预算数量为 5 900 件，生产 1 件产品的直接人工标准工时为 2 小时，因此按产品预算数量制定的制造费用成本动因标准量为 11 800 小时（2 × 5 900 = 11 800）。标准固定性制造费用分摊率为 $1. 75 per DL hour，按产品预算数量制定的制造费用成本动因标准量为 11 800 小时，所以预算固定性制造费用为 $20 650（$1. 75 × 11 800 = $20 650）。实际固定性制造费用为 $21 500。实际固定性制造费用大于预算固定性制造费用 $850，所以固定性制造费用预算差异为不利差异 $850。

带你到北美学习
管理会计
Take You to
North America
to Learn
Managerial Accounting

答案： The unfavourable fixed manufacturing overhead budget variance is ＄850.

4. Calculate the fixed manufacturing overhead production volume variance.

讲解： 固定性制造费用产量差异指预算固定性制造费用与分摊固定性制造费用之间的差值。分摊固定性制造费用等于标准固定性制造费用分摊率乘以按产品实际数量制定的制造费用成本动因标准量。

根据题目信息，产品实际数量为 6 000 件，生产 1 件产品的直接人工标准工时为 2 小时，因此按产品实际数量制定的直接人工标准工时为 12 000 小时（2 × 6 000 = 12 000）。标准固定性制造费用分摊率为 ＄1. 75 per DL hour，按产品实际数量制定的直接人工标准工时为 12 000 小时，所以分摊固定性制造费用为 ＄21 000（＄1. 75 × 12 000 = ＄21 000）。预算固定性制造费用为 ＄20 650，分摊固定性制造费用为 ＄21 000，所以固定性制造费用产量差异为 ＄350。

答案： The fixed manufacturing overhead production volume variance is ＄350.

专业名词汇编
Glossary of Accounting Terms

变动成本法	variable costing	标准成本	standard cost
标准量	standard quantity	不利差异	unfavourable variance
差异	variance	产品成本	product cost
弹性预算	flexible budget	弹性预算差异	flexible budget variance
归纳成本法	absorption costing	价格标准	price standard
价格差异	price variance	静态预算	static budget
静态预算差异	static budget variance	期间成本	period cost
实际量	actual quantity	数量标准	quantity standard
销量差异	sales volume variance	有利差异	favourable variance
主要因素	primary factor	总预算	master budget

变动性制造费用	variable manufacturing overhead
变动性制造费用差异	variable manufacturing overhead variance
变动性制造费用效率差异	variable manufacturing overhead efficiency variance
变动性制造费用支出差异	variable manufacturing overhead spending variance
标准变动性制造费用分摊率	standard variable manufacturing overhead rate
标准固定性制造费用分摊率	standard fixed manufacturing overhead rate
标准制造成本	standard manufacturing cost
标准制造费用	standard manufacturing overhead
标准制造费用分摊率	standard manufacturing overhead rate
分摊变动性制造费用	applied variable manufacturing overhead
分摊固定性制造费用	applied fixed manufacturing overhead
固定性制造费用	fixed manufacturing overhead
固定性制造费用差异	fixed manufacturing overhead variance
固定性制造费用产量差异	fixed manufacturing overhead production volume variance
固定性制造费用预算差异	fixed manufacturing overhead budget variance
固定性制造费用支出差异	fixed manufacturing overhead spending variance
间接制造成本	indirect manufacturing cost
实际变动性制造费用	actual variable manufacturing overhead
实际固定性制造费用	actual fixed manufacturing overhead
实际制造费用	actual manufacturing overhead

带你到北美学习
管理会计
Take You to
North America
to Learn
Managerial Accounting

预定变动性制造费用分摊率	predetermined variable manufacturing overhead rate
预定固定性制造费用分摊率	predetermined fixed manufacturing overhead rate
预估变动性制造费用总额	estimated total variable manufacturing overhead
预估分摊基础总额	estimated total amount of allocation base
预估固定性制造费用总额	estimated total fixed manufacturing overhead
预估制造费用总额	estimated total manufacturing overhead
直接材料差异	direct materials variance
直接材料价格差异	direct materials price variance
直接材料数量差异	direct materials quantity variance
直接材料效率差异	direct materials efficiency variance
直接材料用量差异	direct materials usage variance
直接人工差异	direct labour variance
直接人工工资率差异	direct labour rate variance
直接人工数量差异	direct labour quantity variance
直接人工效率差异	direct labour efficiency variance
直接人工用量差异	direct labour usage variance
制造费用差异	manufacturing overhead variance

企业管理者评估绩效

Managers Evaluate Performance

带你到北美学习
管理会计
Take You to
North America
to Learn
Managerial Accounting

9.1 绩效评估系统
Performance Evaluation System

由于经营规模较小，小微企业一般采用集中式决策（centralized decision making），企业所有者或高层管理者制定企业所有规划和经营决策，而当小微企业发展壮大之后，企业所有者或少数高层管理者没有足够精力和时间管理企业日常运营，不得不下放企业的经营权和决策权，设立下属部门负责企业日常运营，并给予部门经理相关决策权。此时，企业所有者或高层管理者将不再参与下属部门的日常运营，他们需要一个与下属部门交流企业长期战略目标、评估下属部门制定的决策是否符合企业长期战略的系统——绩效评估系统（performance evaluation system）。

绩效评估系统有如下五个主要目的：

（1）协助企业与下属部门交流未来愿景，以求达成共同目标；

（2）方便企业与下属部门的工作协调；

（3）激励下属部门管理者完成绩效目标，制定符合企业长期目标的决策；

（4）向企业所有者和高层管理者提供企业和下属部门的日常运营反馈；

（5）对比企业部门绩效与同行业中最佳部门绩效，比较企业及下属部门过去与当前绩效。

9.2 平衡计分卡
Balanced Scorecard

平衡计分卡是企业绩效评估的一次重大变革，即财务指标不再是评估企业绩效的唯一标准。根据平衡计分卡，在评定企业及下属部门绩效时，企业管理者应考虑财务绩效（financial performance）和经营绩效（operational performance）；换言之，企业管理者不能只考虑财务指标，也要考虑客户满意度、企业运营效率、市场份额和员工成长等。

平衡计分卡从如下四个不同角度评估企业：①财务角度；②客户角度；③内部业务角度；④学习与成长角度。

（1）财务角度帮助企业管理者回答这类问题——企业如何面对股东？我们知道，企业的最终目标是为股东创造利润。财务角度主要关注企业财务指标，如销售额增长（sales revenue growth）、毛利润增长（gross margin growth）、投资收益率（return on investment）、剩余价值（residual income）和经济附加值（economic value added）等。

（2）客户角度帮助企业管理者思考这类问题——客户如何看待企业？客户对企业产品与服务的满意度是企业实现财务目标、企业长期良性成长的决定性因素。客户一般关心以下四个问题：①产品价格；②产品质量；③服务质量；④产品交货时间。客户视角主要关注企业的客户满意度、产品市场份额、新增客户数量、产品准时交货率等。

（3）内部业务角度为企业解决这类问题——企业如何使客户长期满意，进而实现财务目标？为维持客户满意度，实现企业财务目标，必须从如下三个方面入手：①创新；②运营；③客户服务。企业必须持续更新现有产品、研发新产品，以维持老客户、吸引新客户。企业高效的内部运营可以缩短产品生产周期、提高产品质量，进而更好地满足客户需求。细致周到的客户服务是保持销售额的基础。内部业务角度主要关注企业研发新产品的数量与时间、受理保修产品的数量与平均维修时间、客服电话的平均等待时间等。

（4）学习与成长角度为企业处理这类问题——企业如何持续创造价值？企业的学习与成长是提高企业内部运营、维持客户满意度、实现财务目标的基石。为什么？因为缺乏有技能的员工、不断更新的技术、正面且积极的企业文化，企业很难持续创造价值。为了持续创造价值，企业必须从如下三个方面入手：①员工；②信息系统；③企业文化。企业应注重培养员工、提升员工能力、加强员工知识储备，以实现企业长期战略目标。为让员工及时获知准确的客户信息、企业内部运营与财务信息，企业需要维护和更新信息系统。为让员工积极参与企业经营和决策制定，企业应建立一种提倡创新、发展、沟通与协作的企业文化。学习与成长角度主要关注企业的员工培训成果、员工满意度、离职员工人数、采纳员工建议数、信息系统提供的有价值信息等。

9.3 责任会计

Responsibility Accounting

责任会计是评估每个责任中心绩效和中心管理者工作的系统。责任会计绩效报

带你到北美学习
管理会计
Take You to
North America
to Learn
Managerial Accounting

告对每个责任中心的实际运营结果与最初预算进行对比，因此责任会计可以协助企业管理者查明产生预算差异的原因，进而确定哪些差异是可控的、哪些差异是不可控的。责任中心（responsibility center）是企业的重要组成部分，中心管理者负责中心的具体事务。责任中心分为如下四类：①成本中心（cost center）；②收入中心（revenue center）；③利润中心（profit center）；④投资中心（investment center）。

(1) 成本中心管理者主要负责控制成本。通过比较实际成本（actual cost）和预算成本（budgeted cost），对中心管理者控制成本的能力进行评估。在其他条件相同的前提下，当实际成本低于预算成本时，中心管理者可以获得更好的评价。

(2) 收入中心管理者主要负责提升收入。收入中心绩效报告对实际收入（actual revenue）和预算收入（budgeted revenue）进行对比，进而评估中心管理者创造收入的能力。在其他条件相同的前提下，当实际收入超过预算收入时，中心管理者可以获得更好的评价。

(3) 利润中心管理者主要负责提高收入，降低成本，实现企业利润最大化。利润中心绩效报告不仅包括利润数据，也包含收入、成本数据。通过对比实际数据与预算数据，评估中心管理者提高收入、降低成本和最大化利润的能力。在其他条件相同的前提下，当实际利润超过预算利润时，中心管理者可以获得一个更好的评价。

(4) 投资中心管理者主要负责创造利润，有效地管理和使用投资中心资产。中心管理者有权决定如何使用投资中心资产。企业一般使用投资收益率（return on investment）、剩余价值（redsidual income）和经济附加值（economic value added），对中心管理者的工作进行评估。在其他条件相同的前提下，如果实际投资收益率、剩余价值和经济附加值高于相对应的预算数值，中心管理者可以获得更好的评价。

每个责任中心有各自的工作重心，因此不同责任中心运用不同的绩效指标。但无论是成本中心、收入中心，还是利润中心，每个中心的绩效报告均集中于财务信息，而不是以惩罚中心管理者为目的。

接下来，学习评估不同责任中心的财务绩效。

9.4 评估成本中心财务绩效
Evaluating the Financial Performance of Cost Centers

成本中心主要负责控制成本，因此成本中心绩效报告体现了实际成本与预算成本的对比。成本中心绩效报告（cost center performance report）主要关注实际成本与弹性预算成本之间的差异。我们知道，弹性预算差异（flexible budget variance）指按产品实际数量制定的弹性预算与实际结果之间的差值。造成弹性预算差异的原因包括产品实际售价不同于预算售价、产品实际变动成本不同于预算变动成本以及实际固定成本不同于预算固定成本。

通过例外管理法（management by exception），中心管理者确定成本中心绩效报告体现的哪些差异值得调查，比如管理者需要调查超过 $1 000 的弹性预算差异或超过 10% 的弹性预算差异百分比。更小的弹性预算差异说明，企业经营产生的成本更接近于最初预算，暂时无需企业管理层注意。弹性预算差异百分比等于弹性预算差异除以弹性预算。

如果调查超过 $2 000 的弹性预算差异或超过 20% 的弹性预算差异百分比，根据成本中心绩效报告（见说明 9-1）体现的弹性预算差异和弹性预算差异百分比，成本中心管理者需要调查 indirect labour。

说明 9-1：成本中心绩效报告				
	Actual Results	Flexible Budget	Flexible Budget Variance (U or F)	Percentage Variance (U or F)
Direct materials	$21,500	$20,000	$1,500(U)	7.50%(U)
Direct labour	14,250	15,000	750(F)	5%(F)
Indirect labour	29,250	25,000	4,250(U)	17%(U)
Utilities	10,950	10,000	950(U)	9.50%(U)
Depreciation	25,000	25,000	0(-)	0%(-)
Repairs and maintenance	4,200	5,000	800(F)	16%(F)
Total expenses	$105,150	$100,000	$5,150(U)	5.15%(U)

带你到北美学习
管理会计
Take You to
North America
to Learn
Managerial Accounting

9.5 评估收入中心财务绩效

Evaluating the Financial Performance of Revenue Centers

收入中心主要负责提升收入，因此收入中心绩效报告体现了实际收入与预算收入的对比。收入中心绩效报告（revenue center performance report）既关注弹性预算差异，又关注销量差异。我们知道，销量差异指静态预算与按产品实际数量制定的弹性预算之间的差值，销量差异产生的原因在于产品实际数量不同于制定静态预算的产品数量。弹性预算差异（flexible budget variance）指按产品实际数量制定的弹性预算与实际结果之间的差值，造成弹性预算差异的原因在于产品实际售价不同于预算售价、产品实际变动成本不同于预算变动成本以及实际固定成本不同于预算固定成本。通过分析销量差异和弹性预算差异，收入中心管理者可以了解实际收入不同于预算收入的原因（见说明9-2）。

说明9-2：收入中心绩效报告					
	Actual Results	Flexible Budget Variance (U or F)	Flexible Budget	Sales Volume Variance (U or F)	Static Budget
Model RI	$ 326,000	$ 6,000（F）	$ 320,000	$ 20,000（F）	$ 300,000
Model RII	155,000	10,000（U）	165,000	15,000（F）	150,000
Total revenues	$ 481,000	$ 4,000（U）	$ 485,000	$ 35,000（F）	$ 450,000

9.6 评估利润中心财务绩效

Evaluating the Financial Performance of Profit Centers

利润中心主要负责提升收入、降低成本和最大化企业利润，因此利润中心绩效报告（profit center performance report）既体现收入数据，又体现成本数据。根据利润中心绩效报告（见说明9-3），我们发现，Service department charges 在 Operating income before service department charges 下面单独出现。为什么单独列出 Service department charges，而不是归入 Operating expenses？因为企业为下属部门设立集中服务部门，以避免下属部门因重复设立服务部门造成资源浪费。下属部门不能免费使用企业提供的集中服务，所以企业需要将这些集中服务产生的费用分摊至下属部门。

下属部门承担的集中服务费用是由企业分摊所致，而非下属部门自身产生，所以 Service department charges 需要单独列出，而非归入 Operating expenses。

　　企业设立的集中服务部门一般包括薪资部门（payroll department）、人力资源部门（human resource department）、法务部门（legal department）、信息系统部门（information system department）等。

说明 9-3：利润中心绩效报告				
	Actual Results	Flexible Budget	Flexible Budget Variance (U or F)	Percentage Variance (U or F)
Sales	$486,000	$450,000	$36,000(F)	8%(F)
Cost of goods sold	(260,000)	(250,000)	10,000(U)	4%(U)
Gross profit	226,000	200,000	26,000(F)	13%(F)
Operating expenses	(52,000)	(50,000)	2,000(U)	4%(U)
Operating income before service department charges	174,000	150,000	24,000(F)	16%(F)
Service department charges (allocated)	(35,000)	(25,000)	10,000(U)	40%(U)
Operating income	$139,000	$125,000	$14,000(F)	11.20%(F)

9.7　评估投资中心财务绩效

Evaluating the Financial Performance of Investment Centers

　　投资中心管理者主要负责创造利润，有效管理和使用投资中心资产。投资中心管理者有权决定，是否开设新店、关闭老店、采购新设备，他们也有权制定持有库存商品数量的最低限、收取应收账款的政策。换言之，投资中心管理者对投资中心资产承担制定管理与使用决策的责任。

　　与评估利润中心财务绩效的方法不同，评估投资中心财务绩效必须考量两个要素：①创造的收益；②使用资产的效率。为准确评估投资中心财务绩效，企业普遍使用三个绩效指标：①投资收益率（return on investment）；②剩余收益（residual income）；③经济附加值（economic value added）。三个绩效指标均涉及经营收益（operating income）和资产（asset）。

带你到北美学习
管理会计
Take You to
North America
to Learn
Managerial Accounting

9.7.1 投资收益率

Return on Investment

投资收益率是评估投资中心财务绩效广泛使用的指标之一。投资收益率等于经营收益（operating income）除以平均运营资产（average operating asset）（见说明9-4）。因为经营收益覆盖整个财务周期，所以它与同一周期的平均运营资产共同使用。平均运营资产等于运营资产期初余额与期末余额之和除以2。

说明9-4：计算投资收益率
$$\text{Return on investment} = \frac{\text{Operating income}}{\text{Average operating assets}}$$

投资收益率也等于经营利润率（operating profit margin）乘以资产周转率（asset turnover）。经营利润率等于经营收益（operating income）除以净销售额（net sales）。净销售额（net sales）等于销售额（sales revenue）减去销售退货与折价（sales return and allowance）和销售折扣（sales discount）。经营利润率说明企业销售额带来的经营收益（见说明9-5）。

说明9-5：投资收益率展开公式
$$\text{Return on investment} = \text{Operating profit margin} \times \text{Asset turnover}$$ $$\text{Return on investment} = \frac{\text{Operating income}}{\text{Net sales}} \times \frac{\text{Net sales}}{\text{Average operating assets}}$$

资产周转率评估企业利用资产创造销售额的能力。资产周转率等于净销售额（net sales）除以平均运营资产（average operating asset）。因为净销售额涵盖整个财务周期，所以它与同一周期的平均运营资产共同使用。运营资产（operating asset）一般包括现金，应收账款，库存，经营企业所需的物业、厂房与设备（property, plant, and equipment）。为再次出售而持有的土地及其他资产、闲置资产均属于非运营资产（non-operating asset）。

企业管理层如何运用投资收益率对额外资金进行投资？管理层需要考量每个部门的投资收益率，拥有更高投资收益率的部门更有可能获得额外资金。

案例 9 - 1

The actual results from Tom Company's most recent year of operations are presented in the following table.

Operating income	$ 9,000
Average operating assets	$ 15,000
Total assets	$ 18,000
Current liabilities	$ 4,000
Net sales	$ 36,000
Minimum required rate of return	15%
Weighted average cost of capital	12%
Tax rate	30%

Required：

Calculate the operating profit margin, asset turnover, and return on investment.

讲解： 经营收益为 $ 9 000，平均运营资产为 $ 15 000，净销售额为 $ 36 000，因此经营利润率（operating profit margin）为 25%（ $ 9 000 ÷ $ 36 000 = 25%），资产周转率（asset trunover）为 2. 40（ $ 36 000 ÷ $ 15 000 = 2. 40），投资收益率（return on investment）为 60%（25% × 2. 40 = 60%）。

经营利润率为 25% 说明，当净销售额为 $ 1 时，产生经营收益 $ 0. 25。如何提升经营收益率？管理层可以通过削减产品成本与经营费用，进而提升企业经营收益，达到提高经营收益率的目的。削减成本虽然可以短期提升经营收益率，却严重影响长期投资收益率，这是因为以牺牲产品质量而达到降低产品成本、削减研发成本的目的，将严重损害企业未来的产品销售。

资产周转率为 2. 40 意味着，当资产为 $ 1 时，创造销售额 $ 2. 40。如何提升资产周转率？企业可以通过削减闲置资产、库存商品，加快收取应收账款，进而提升资产周转率。

案例 9 - 2

Ceramics Division, a division of Piper Corporation, has an operating income of $ 64,000 and an average operating assets of $ 400,000. The target rate of return for the company is

带你到北美学习
管理会计
Take You to
North America
to Learn
Managerial Accounting

12%. The manager of Ceramics Division has the opportunity to undertake a new project that will require an investment of ＄100,000. This investment would earn ＄14,000 for the division.

Required：

1. What is the original return on investment（ROI）for Ceramics Division（before making any additional investments）?

2. What is the ROI of this investment opportunity? Would the manager of Ceramics Division want to make this investment if he or she was evaluated based on the ROI? Why or Why not?

3. Would this investment be desirable from the standpoint of Piper Corporation? Why or why not?

讲解： 在投资新项目之前，Ceramics Division 的经营收益为 ＄64 000，平均运营资产为 ＄400 000，因此部门投资收益率为16% （＄64 000 ÷ ＄400 000 = 16%）。

新项目要求投资 ＄100 000，赚取利润 ＄14 000，因此新项目投资收益率为14% （＄14 000 ÷ ＄100 000 = 14%），低于 Ceramics Division 的投资收益率（16%）。如果投资新项目，将降低 Ceramics Division 的投资收益率，所以管理者不应考虑这项新投资。

新项目投资收益率为14%，高于企业目标收益率（12%），所以从企业角度出发，应考虑投资新项目。

通过"案例9-2"，我们发现一个问题：从部门角度，不建议投资新项目，因为投资新项目将降低 Ceramics Division 的投资收益率（16%），而从企业角度，投资新项目满足企业目标收益率（12%），所以建议投资新项目，这揭示了投资收益率的一个劣势，即不能实现企业与部门的目标一致（goal congruence）。

9.7.2 剩余收益

Residual Income

剩余收益是另一个普遍用于评估投资中心财务绩效的指标。剩余收益表明，企业部门是否拥有超过企业管理层期望的多余收益。剩余收益等于经营收益（operating income）减去平均运营资产（average operating asset）与最低所需收益率（minimum required rate of return）的乘积（见说明9-6）。与投资收益率相似，计算剩余收益也需要经营收益和平均运营资产的数据，因此剩余收益同样关注两个问题：①创造的利润；②使用资产的效率。与投资收益率不同，剩余收益需要考虑最低所需收益率。最低所需收益率说明，企业管理者期望每个部门使用资产赚取的最低收益率。

剩余收益体现，在给定资产的情况下，管理层期望的经营收益与实际经营收益的差异。当剩余收益为正值时，使用资产创造的实际经营收益超过了管理层期望的最低收益率；当剩余收益为负值时，使用资产创造的实际经营收益未满足管理层期望的最低收益率。

说明 9-6：计算剩余收益

Residual income = Operating income − Average operating assets × Minimum required rate of return

案例 9 – 3

The actual results from Tom Company's most recent year of operations are presented in the following table.

Operating income	$9,000
Average operating assets	$15,000
Total assets	$18,000
Current liabilities	$4,000
Net sales	$36,000
Minimum required rate of return	15%
Weighted average cost of capital	12%
Tax rate	30%

Required：

Calculate the residual income.

讲解： 经营收益为 $9 000，平均运营资产为 $15 000，最低所需收益率为 15%，因此剩余价值为 $6 750（$9 000 – $15 000 × 15% = $6 750）。

案例 9 – 4

Ceramics Division, a division of Piper Corporation, has an operating income of $64,000

带你到北美学习
管理会计
Take You to
North America
to Learn
Managerial Accounting

and an average operating assets of $400,000. The target rate of return for the company is 12%. The manager of Ceramics Division has the opportunity to undertake a new project that will require an investment of $100,000. This investment would earn $14,000 for the division.

Required:

1. What is the residual income (RI) of this investment opportunity? Would this investment be desirable from the standpoint of Piper Corporation? Why or why not?

2. What is the original RI for Ceramics Division (before making any additional investments)?

3. What would the RI be for Ceramics Division if this investment opportunity was undertaken? Would the manager of the division want to make this investment if he or she was evaluated based on RI? Why or why not?

讲解: 新项目要求投资 $100 000，赚取利润 $14 000，目标收益率为 12%，因此新项目剩余收益为 $2 000（$14 000 − $100 000 × 12% = $2 000），大于 $0，说明新项目创造的利润超过了企业目标收益率（12%）。从企业角度，应考虑这项投资。

在投资新项目之前，Ceramics Division 的经营收益为 $64 000，平均运营资产为 $400 000，目标收益率为 12%，因此剩余收益为 $16 000（$64 000 − $400 000 × 12% = $16 000）。

在投资新项目之后，Ceramics Division 的经营收益为 $78 000（$64 000 + $14 000 = $78 000），平均运营资产为 $500 000（$400 000 + $100 000 = $500 000），目标收益率为 12%，因此剩余收益为 $18 000（$78 000 − $500 000 × 12% = $18 000），说明这项投资增加了 Ceramics Division 的剩余收益 $2 000。从部门角度，也应考虑这项新投资。

通过"案例9-4"发现，从部门角度，建议投资新项目，因为这项投资增加了 Ceramics Division 的剩余收益 $2 000；从企业角度，也应投资新项目，因为这项投资也增加了企业剩余收益 $2 000。从上述分析发现，剩余收益可以弥补投资收益率的劣势，实现企业与部门的目标一致。

9.7.3 经济附加值

Economic Value Added

经济附加值是剩余收益的特别形式。我们知道，剩余收益考量了企业部门是否拥有超过企业管理层期望的多余收益。与剩余收益不同，经济附加值考量了企业部门是否拥有超过企业利益相关者（stakeholder）期望的多余收益；换言之，经济附加值是从企业利益相关者（投资者和长期债权人）的角度考量企业部门剩余收益的。

在计算经济附加值时，需要考虑三个因素：①对企业利益相关者的可用收益——税后经营收益（after-tax operating income）；②为创造收益，企业利益相关者使用的资产——资产总额（total asset）减去短期负债（current liability）；③企业利益相关者所需的最低收益率——加权平均资本成本（weighted average cost of capital）（见说明9-7）。

说明9-7：计算经济附加值
Economic value added =   After-tax operating income − (Total assets − Current liabilities) × Weighted average cost of capital

经济附加值体现，在给定资产和短期负债的情况下，企业利益相关者期望的经营收益与实际经营收益的差异。当经济附加值为正值时，使用资产创造的实际经营收益超过了企业利益相关者期望的最低收益率；当经济附加值为负值时，使用资产创造的实际经营收益未满足企业利益相关者期望的最低收益率。

经济附加值是从企业利益相关者（投资者和长期债权人）的角度，考量企业部门剩余收益的，因此与剩余收益相同，经济附加值也可以弥补投资收益率的劣势，实现企业与部门的目标一致。

案例 9 - 5

The actual results from Tom Company's most recent year of operations are presented in the following table.

Operating income	$9,000
Average operating assets	$15,000

带你到北美学习
管理会计
Take You to
North America
to Learn
Managerial Accounting

Total assets	$18,000
Current liabilities	$4,000
Net sales	$36,000
Minimum required rate of return	15%
Weighted average cost of capital	12%
Tax rate	30%

Required:

Calculate the economic value added.

讲解： 经营收益为 $9 000，税率为30%，因此税后经营收益为 $6 300（$9 000 ×（1 – 30%） = $6 300）。资产总额为 $18 000，短期负债为 $4 000，税后经营收益为 $6 300，加权平均资本成本为12%，所以经济附加值为 $4 620（$6 300 –（$18 000 – $4 000） × 12% = $4 620）。

例题综述
Summary of Examples

例题 9 - 1

Which performance measurement tool is most likely to cause goal incongruence between division managers and corporate headquarters?

A. Return on investment

B. Economic value added

C. Residual income

D. Balanced scorecard

讲解： 投资收益率有时不能实现企业与部门的目标一致（goal congruence），而剩余收益和经济附加值可以弥补投资收益率的劣势，实现企业与部门的目标一致。

答案： A

例题 9 - 2

For which type of responsibility center would it be appropriate to measure performance using return on investment?

A. Revenue center

B. Profit center

C. Cost center

D. Investment center

讲解： 与评估利润中心财务绩效的方法不同，评估投资中心财务绩效必须考量两个要素：①创造的收益；②使用资产的效率。为准确评估投资中心财务绩效，企业普遍使用三个绩效指标：①投资收益率（return on investment）；②剩余收益（residual income）；③经济附加值（economic value added）。三个绩效指标均涉及经营收益（operating income）和资产（asset）。

答案： D

例题 9 - 3

The performance evaluation of cost centers is typically based on its _____.

带你到北美学习
管理会计
Take You to
North America
to Learn
Managerial Accounting

A. residual income

B. return on investment

C. flexible budget variance

D. sales volume variance

讲解： 成本中心绩效报告（cost center performance report）主要关注实际成本与弹性预算成本之间的差异。我们知道，弹性预算差异（flexible budget variance）指按产品实际数量制定的弹性预算与实际结果之间的差值。弹性预算差异产生的原因在于产品实际售价不同于预算售价，产品实际变动成本不同于预算变动成本以及实际固定成本不同于预算固定成本。

答案： C

例题 9 - 4

Last year, Hotel Corporation had the following actual results:

Sales revenue	$ 15,000,000
Operating income	6,000,000
Operating assets	9,000,000
Total assets	10,000,000
Current liabilities	3,000,000

The management's target rate of return is 14% , the weighted average cost of capital is 10% , and the effective tax rate is 35% .

Required：

1. Calculate the return on investment.

2. Calculate the residual income.

3. Calculate the economic value added.

1. Calculate the return on investment.

讲解： 经营收益为 $6 000 000，平均运营资产为 $9 000 000，因此投资收益率为 66.67% 。

答案： The return on investment is 66.67% .

2. Calculate the residual income.

讲解： 经营收益为 $\$6\,000\,000$，平均运营资产为 $\$9\,000\,000$，目标收益率为 14% ，因此剩余价值为 $\$4\,740\,000$（ $\$6\,000\,000 - \$9\,000\,000 \times 14\% = \$4\,740\,000$ ）。

答案： The residual income is $\$4\,740\,000$.

3. Calculate the economic value added.

讲解： 经营收益为 $\$6\,000\,000$，税率为 35% ，因此税后经营收益为 $\$3\,900\,000$（ $\$6\,000\,000 \times (1-35\%) = \$3\,900\,000$ ）。资产总额为 $\$10\,000\,000$，短期负债为 $\$3\,000\,000$，税后经营收益为 $\$3\,900\,000$，加权平均资本成本为 10% ，所以经济附加值为 $\$3\,200\,000$（ $\$3\,900\,000 - (\$10\,000\,000 - \$3\,000\,000) \times 10\% = \$3\,200\,000$ ）。

答案： The economic value added is $\$3\,200\,000$.

例题 9 – 5

Home Company has two divisions: Professional and Residential. The following divisional information was available for the last month:

	Sales Revenue	Operating Income	Total Assets	Operating Assets	Current Liabilities
Residential	$\$635,000$	$\$63,500$	$\$205,000$	$\$160,000$	$\$70,000$
Professional	1,031,250	165,000	375,000	300,000	150,000

Assume that the management has a 25% target rate of return for each division. Also, assume that Home's weighted average cost of capital is 15% and its effective tax rate is 30% .

Required:

1. Calculate each division's return on investment. Interpret your results.

2. Calculate each division's residual income. Interpret your results.

3. Calculate each division's economic value added. Interpret your results.

1. Calculate each division's return on investment. Interpret your results.

讲解： Residential Division 的经营收益为 $\$63\,500$，运营资产为 $\$160\,000$，投资收益率为 39. 69% 。Professional Division 的经营收益为 $\$165\,000$，运营资产为 $\$300\,000$，投资收益率为 55% 。通过计算两个部门的投资收益率，Residential Divi-

带你到北美学习
管理会计
Take You to
North America
to Learn
Managerial Accounting

sion 和 Professional Division 均有很高的投资收益率。相比于 Residential Division 的投资收益率（39.69%），Professional Division 的投资收益率（55%）更高。

答案： The returns on investment（ROI）of Residential and Professional divisions are 39.69% and 55% respectively. Each division's ROI is very high, however, Professional Division has an higher ROI（55%）than Residential Division（39.69%）.

2. Calculate each division's residual income. Interpret your results.

讲解： Residential Division 的经营收益为 \$63 500，运营资产为 \$160 000，目标收益率为 25%，因此部门剩余收益为 \$23 500（\$63 500 - \$160 000 × 25% = \$23 500），而 Professional Division 的经营收益为 \$165 000，运营资产为 \$300 000，目标收益率为 25%，因此部门剩余收益为 \$90 000（\$165 000 - \$300 000 × 25% = \$90 000）。Residential Division 和 Professional Division 的剩余收益均为正值，说明两个部门的剩余收益超过了企业期望的目标收益率（25%）。

答案： The residual incomes of Residential and Professional divisions are \$23,500 and \$90,000 respectively. Both divisions have positive residual incomes. Therefore, both divisions' residual incomes exceed the management's target rate of return.

3. Calculate each division's economic value added. Interpret your results.

讲解： Residential Division 的经营收益为 \$63 500，税率为 30%，所以税后经营收益为 \$44 450（\$63 500 × （1 - 30%）= \$44 450）；Residential Division 的资产总额为 \$205 000，短期负债为 \$70 000，税后经营收益为 \$44 450，加权平均资本成本为 15%，因此部门经济附加值为 \$24 200（\$44 450 - （\$205 000 - \$70 000）× 15% = \$24 200）。然而，Professional Division 的经营收益为 \$165 000，税率为 30%，所以税后经营收益为 \$115 500（\$165 000 × （1 - 30%）= \$115 500）；Professional Division 的资产总额为 \$375 000，短期负债为 \$150 000，税后经营收益为 \$115 500，加权平均资本成本为 15%，因此部门经济附加值为 \$81 750（\$115 500 - （\$375 000 - \$150 000）× 15% = \$81 750）。Residential Division 和 Professional Division 的经济附加值均为正值，两个部门的经济附加值均超过了企业利益相关者的预期。

答案： The economic values added of Residential and Professional divisions are \$24,200 and $81,750 separately. Both divisions have positive economic values added. Therefore, both divisions have created incomes for their investors and long-term creditors at a rate that exceeds these stakeholders' expectations.

例题 9 - 6

Heavy Machine Corporation is preparing a capital budget for the coming year. The managers of the six divisions of the corporation have each submitted a capital investment proposal to the corporate headquater, which will decide which project (s) to be included in the capital budget. The proposals are listed below. All are considered equally risky.

Project	Investment Required	Expected Return
1	$4,800,000	$1,200,000
2	1,900,000	627,000
3	1,400,000	182,000
4	950,000	152,000
5	650,000	162,500
6	300,000	60,000

Heavy Machine Corporation has a cost of capital of 15%. The corporation has allocated $7. 50 million for capital investment purposes.

Required:

1. Calculate the return on investment (ROI) and residual income (RI) for each project.

2. The corporation has a rule that all projects with an expected return of 20% or more if the funds are available. Which project (s) should be included in the capital budget?

1. Calculate the return on investment (ROI) and residual income (RI) for each project.

答案:

Project	Investment Required	Expected Return	ROI	RI
1	$4,800,000	$1,200,000	25%	$480,000
2	1,900,000	627,000	33%	342,000
3	1,400,000	182,000	13%	(28,000)
4	950,000	152,000	16%	9,500

带你到北美学习
管理会计
Take You to
North America
to Learn
Managerial Accounting

Project	Investment Required	Expected Return	ROI	RI
5	650,000	162,500	25%	65,000
6	300,000	60,000	20%	15,000

2. The company has a rule that all projects with an expected return of 20% or more if the funds are available. Which project (s) should be included in the capital budget?

讲解： 企业规定，未来一年的新项目最低收益率为20%，因此3号、4号项目不在考虑范围内。2号项目的投资收益率为33%，需要资金 $ 1 900 000；1号、5号项目的投资收益率均为25%，共需资金 $ 5 450 000（$ 4 800 000 + $ 650 000 = $ 5 450 000）；6号项目的投资收益率为20%，需要资金 $ 300 000。

我们知道，当企业管理层考量每个新项目时，具有更高投资收益率的项目将更有可能获得额外资金。为投资新项目，企业准备了 $ 7 500 000，所以仅对2号、1号和5号项目进行投资，共需资金 $ 7 350 000（$ 1 900 000 + $ 4 800 000 + $ 650 000 = $ 7 350 000）。

答案：

Project	Investment Required	Expected Return	ROI	Accept or Not Accept
1	$ 4,800,000	$ 1,200,000	25%	Accept
2	1,900,000	627,000	33%	Accept
3	1,400,000	182,000	13%	Not Accept
4	950,000	152,000	16%	Not Accept
5	650,000	162,500	25%	Accept
6	300,000	60,000	20%	Not Accept

例题 9 - 7

Last year, one division of Sports Company had the following financial results：

	Actual Results	Flexible Budget	Flexible Budget Variance (U or F)	Percentage Variance (U or F)
Direct materials	$ 12,930	$ 12,000		
Direct labour	13,265	14,000		
Indirect labour	23,380	20,000		

	Actual Results	Flexible Budget	Flexible Budget Variance (U or F)	Percentage Variance (U or F)
Utilities	16,455	15,000		
Depreciation	30,250	30,250		
Repairs and maintenance	4,205	5,000		
Total expenses	$100,485	$96,250		

Required：

1. Complete the performance evaluation report.

2. Based on the performance evaluation report, what type of responsibility center is this division?

3. If part of management's decision criteria is to investigate all varianecs exceeding $2,500 or 10%, which items should be investigated?

1. Complete the performance evaluation report.

答案：

	Actual Results	Flexible Budget	Flexible Budget Variance (U or F)	Percentage Variance (U or F)
Direct materials	$12,930	$12,000	$930(U)	$7.75%(U)
Direct labour	13,265	14,000	735(F)	5.25%(F)
Indirect labour	23,380	20,000	3,380(U)	16.90%(U)
Utilities	16,455	15,000	1,455(U)	9.70%(U)
Depreciation	30,250	30,250	0(-)	0%(-)
Repairs and maintenance	4,205	5,000	795(F)	15.90%(F)
Total expenses	$100,485	$96,250	$4,235(U)	4.40%(U)

2. Based on the performance evaluation report, what type of responsibility center is this division?

讲解： 绩效评估报告体现实际成本与预算成本的差异。我们知道，成本中心绩效报告（cost center performance report）主要关注实际成本与弹性预算成本之间的差异，所以这个部门属于成本中心。

带你到北美学习
管理会计
Take You to
North America
to Learn
Managerial Accounting

答案: Based on the performance evaluation report, this division is a cost center.

3. If part of management's decision criteria is to investigate all varianecs exceeding $2,500 or 10%, which items should be investigated?

讲解: 调查超过 $2 500 的弹性预算差异或超过 10% 的弹性预算差异百分比。根据绩效评估报告中的弹性预算差异和弹性预算差异百分比，部门管理者需要调查 Indirect labour 和 Repairs and maintenance。

答案: Indirect labour, repairs and maintenance should be investigated.

例题 9 - 8

Last year, one division of Sports Company had the following financial results:

	Actual Results	Flexible Budget Variance (U or F)	Flexible Budget	Sales Volume Variance (U or F)	Static Budget
Model I	$326,000	$?	$?	$20,000(F)	$300,000
Model II	155,000	?	165,000	?	150,000
Model III	283,000	2,000(U)	285,000	?	300,000
Model IV	252,000	?	245,000	17,500(U)	262,500
Model V	425,000	5,000(F)	?	?	400,000
Total revenues	$1,441,000	$?	$?	$?	$1,412,500

Required:

1. Complete the performance evaluation report.

2. Based on the performance evaluation report, what type of responsibility center is this division?

3. Which items should be investigated if part of management's decision criteria is to investigate all variances exceeding $15,000?

1. Complete the performance evaluation report.

答案：

	Actual Results	Flexible Budget Variance (U or F)	Flexible Budget	Sales Volume Variance (U or F)	Static Budget
Model Ⅰ	$ 326,000	$ 6,000 (F)	$ 320,000	$ 20,000 (F)	$ 300,000
Model Ⅱ	155,000	10,000 (U)	165,000	15,000 (F)	150,000
Model Ⅲ	283,000	2,000 (U)	285,000	15,000 (U)	300,000
Model Ⅳ	252,000	7,000 (F)	245,000	17,500 (U)	262,500
Model Ⅴ	425,000	5,000 (F)	420,000	20,000 (F)	400,000
Total revenues	$ 1,441,000	$ 6,000 (F)	$ 1,435,000	$ 22,500 (F)	$ 1,412,500

2. Based on the performance evaluation report, what type of responsibility center is this division?

讲解： 该绩效评估报告体现实际收入与预算收入的差异，还体现弹性预算差异（flexible budget variance）和销量差异（sales volume variance）。我们知道，收入中心绩效报告体现实际收入与预算收入的差异；另外，收入中心绩效报告既关注弹性预算差异，又关注销量差异，所以这个部门属于收入中心。

答案： Based on the performance evaluation report, this division is a revenue center.

3. Which items should be investigated if part of management's decision criteria is to investigate all variances exceeding $ 15,000?

讲解： 调查超过 $ 15 000 的差异。根据绩效评估报告中的弹性预算差异（flexible budget variance）和销量差异（sales volume variance），部门管理者需要调查 Model Ⅰ，Model Ⅳ和 Model Ⅴ。

答案： Model Ⅰ, Model Ⅳ and Model Ⅴ should be investigated if part of management's decision criteria is to investigate all variances exceeding $ 15,000.

带你到北美学习
管理会计
Take You to
North America
to Learn
Managerial Accounting

专业名词汇编
Glossary of Accounting Terms

财务绩效	financial performance	成本中心	cost center
弹性预算差异	flexible budget variance	短期负债	current liability
法务部门	legal department	非运营资产	non-operating asset
经济附加值	economic value added	经营利润率	operating profit margin
经营收益	operating income	利润中心	profit center
毛利润增长	gross margin growth	平衡记分卡	balanced scorecard
平均运营资产	average operating asset	利益相关者	stakeholder
剩余收益	residual income	实际成本	actual cost
实际收入	actual revenue	收入中心	revenue center
投资收益率	return on investment	投资中心	investment center
销量差异	sales volume variance	销售额	sales revenue
销售额增长	sales revenue growth	净销售额	net sales
销售折扣	sales discount	薪资部门	payroll department
例外管理法	management by exception	预算成本	budgeted cost
预算收入	budgeted revenue	经营绩效	operational performance
运营资产	operating asset	责任会计	responsibility accounting
责任中心	responsibility center	资产	asset
资产周转率	asset turnover	资产总额	total asset
成本中心绩效报告	cost center performance report		
集中式决策	centralized decision making		
加权平均资本成本	weighted average cost of capital		
利润中心绩效报告	profit center performance report		
人力资源部门	human resource department		
收入中心绩效报告	revenue center performance report		
税后经营收益	after-tax operating income		
物业、厂房与设备	property, plant, and equipment		
销售退货与折价	sales return and allowance		
信息系统部门	information system department		
绩效评估系统	performance evaluation system		
最低所需收益率	minimum required rate of return		

企业管理者制定短期商业决策

Managers Make Short-Term Business Decisions

带你到北美学习
管理会计
Take You to
North America
to Learn
Managerial Accounting

在制定决策时，企业管理者需要评估与决策有关的成本、收入和利润，这些与决策有关的财务信息被视为相关财务信息（relevant financial information）。相关财务信息具有如下两个特点：①相关财务信息对未来产生影响；②在不同方案之间，相关财务信息是不同的。例如，一位客户希望按揭购买一辆汽车。在购买汽车之前，这位客户需要评估每个品牌和每款汽车的价格、贷款首付比例、汽车产生的油耗与保险、贷款带来的利息等。每个品牌和每款汽车的价格和贷款首付比例不同，油耗、保险费用和利息费用产生于贷款购车之后，均为未来数据，因此上述因素是贷款购车的相关财务信息，并影响这位客户的最终购车决定和贷款方案。

相关财务信息影响企业管理者的决策制定，而一些财务信息与决策制定无关，也不影响所制定的决策，这些信息被视为非相关财务信息（irrelevant financial information）。沉没成本（sunk cost）是非相关财务信息最典型的例子，沉没成本是过去产生的、未来商业决策和措施不能改变的成本。由于未来决策和措施不能改变过去产生的成本，所以沉没成本属于非相关财务信息。例如，这位客户购买了一辆价值为 $ 50 000 的汽车；在购车之后，这位客户无论继续使用该车、折价换车，还是出售这辆车，均无法改变汽车当初的购买价钱（ $ 50 000），因此当初的购买价钱就是沉没成本，属于非相关财务信息。

在制定决策时，企业管理者也要考虑相关非财务信息（relevant non-financial information）。相关非财务信息也称为相关特性信息（relevant qualitative information）。与相关财务信息相同，相关非财务信息也具备如下两个特点：①相关非财务信息对未来产生影响；②在不同方案之间，相关非财务信息是不同的，如在购车之前，这位客户需要考虑每个品牌和每款汽车的放脚空间、发动机性能、座椅舒适度、后备箱空间、仪表盘设计等诸多非财务因素。

用于制定短期决策（short-term decision）的方法被称为增量分析法（incremental analysis approach）。在使用增量分析法制定短期决策时，企业管理者应摒弃与决策方案无关的成本、收入和利润。

请注意：与决策无关的成本、收入和利润不影响企业的最终决策，所以应摒弃这类非相关财务信息。

10.1　特殊订单

Special Orders

客户要求的一次性减价的订单被称为特殊订单。在决定是否接受特殊订单之前，企业应考虑三个问题（见说明 10-1）。

> **说明 10 - 1：特殊订单考虑的核心问题**
>
> （1）企业是否拥有足够生产力完成特殊订单？
> （2）特殊订单创造的销售额是否可以承担订单产生的变动成本和额外固定成本？
> （3）特殊订单是否影响企业产品的常规销售？

案例 10 - 1

Jeweller Corporation is considering to accept a special order for 20 handcrafted golden rings for a wedding. The product costs of a golden ring are ＄149.

Direct materials	＄84
Direct labour	45
Manufacturing overhead	20

The manufacturing overhead of ＄4 is variable with respect to the number of golden rings produced. The customer who is interested in ordering would also like to have a new engraving for the 20 handcrafted golden rings, which would cost an additional ＄2 in direct labour cost per ring and require a new engraving machine of ＄300. The new engraving machine would be not useful for other purposes after the special order is fulfilled. Jeweller Corporation has enough capacity to take it on. The normal selling price of a golden ring is ＄189.95.

Required：

1. Should this order be accepted at a special price of ＄169.95?

2. What effects would accepting this order have on the company's operating income?

讲解：　一般情况下，制作 1 枚金戒指需要直接材料成本 ＄84、直接人工成本 ＄45、制造费用 ＄20。在制造费用中，变动性制造费用为 ＄4，固定性制造费用为 ＄16。

1 枚金戒指的正常零售价为 ＄189.95，而特殊订单的金戒指零售价仅为 ＄169.95。企业拥有足够生产力。Jeweller Corporation 正在考虑是否接受这张特殊订

带你到北美学习
管理会计
Take You to
North America
to Learn
Managerial Accounting

单——20 枚手工制作的金戒指。

1 枚戒指的零售价为 $169. 95，因此 20 枚手工制作的金戒指的销售额为 $3 399（ $169. 95 × 20 = $3 399）。

为完成这张特殊订单，Jeweller Corporation 同样需要承担直接材料、直接人工和变动性制造费用。此外，特殊订单要求对每枚戒指进行特殊雕刻；为对每枚戒指进行特殊雕刻，Jeweller Corporation 需要承担额外直接人工成本 $2，购买 1 台价值为 $300 的雕刻机。20 枚金戒指的直接材料成本为 $1 680，直接人工成本为 $940，变动性制造费用为 $80，因此变动成本为 $2 700；为完成这张特殊订单，企业还需新增固定成本 $300。

通过这张特殊订单，Jeweller Corporation 可以赚取销售额 $3 399，产生变动成本 $2 700、固定成本 $300，使企业经营收益增长 $399（ $3 399 – $2 700 – $300 = $399）。因此，企业应接受这张特殊订单。

Expected increase in sales revenue	$3,399
Expected increase in variable costs	(2,700)
Expected increase in fixed costs	(300)
Expected increase in operating income	$399

案例 10 - 2

Safety Company manufactures flotation vests. Safety Company's contribution margin income statement for the most recent month provides the following data:

Sales revenue (31,000 units)		$434,000
Variable expenses		
Manufacturing expenses	$93,000	
Marketing and selling expenses	124,000	(217,000)
Contribution margin		217,000
Fixed expenses		
Manufacturing expenses	120,000	
Marketing and selling expenses	90,000	(210,000)
Operating income		$7,000

Suppose Asian Tire is considering to purchase 5,000 vests from Safety Company. Acceptance of the special order will not increase any of Safety Company's variable marketing and selling expenses and fixed expenses. The Safety Company's plant has the full capacity to produce 35,000 vests. The current production volume of flotation vests is 31,000 vests. Asian Tire has offered $10 per vest, which is below the normal price of $14 per vest.

Required：

1. Should Safety Company accept the special order?

2. What is the minimum selling price for this special order?

讲解： 31 000 件浮力背心的销售额为 $434 000，产生变动性制造费用 $93 000、变动性市场与销售费用 $124 000，因此浮力背心的单件售价为 $14，单件变动性制造费用为 $3，单件变动性市场与销售费用为 $4。

1 件浮力背心的正常零售价为 $14，而这张特殊订单的浮力背心零售价仅为 $10。此外，Safety Company 的最大生产力为 35 000 件浮力背心，当前生产 31 000 件浮力背心，说明企业还能生产 4 000 件浮力背心。Safety Company 正在考虑是否接受这张来自于 Asian Tire 的特殊订单，即 5 000 件浮力背心。如果 Safety Company 接受这张特殊订单，生产 5 000 件浮力背心，将不得不暂时放弃 1 000 件浮力背心的常规生产。

为完成这张特殊订单，Safety Company 同样需要承担变动性制造费用，但无需承担变动性市场与销售费用和固定成本，因此 5 000 件浮力背心产生变动性制造费用 $15 000（$3 × 5 000 = $15 000）。此外，Safety Company 需要放弃 1 000 件浮力背心的常规生产，因此损失销售额 $14 000（$14 × 1 000 = $14 000），节省变动性制造费用 $3 000（$3 × 1 000 = $3 000）、变动性市场与销售费用 $4 000（$4 × 1 000 = $4 000），降低企业贡献毛利 $7 000（$14 000 − $3 000 − $4 000 = $7 000）。特殊订单（5 000 件浮力背心）导致企业贡献毛利降低 $7 000，这也是特殊订单的机会成本（opportunity cost）。机会成本指为获得一些东西，而放弃其他东西及其产生的最大价值。在"案例 10-2"中，机会成本指为完成这张特殊订单，不得不放弃 1 000 件浮力背心的常规生产及产生的贡献毛利 $7 000。

通过这张特殊订单，Safety Company 赚取销售额 $50 000（$10 × 5 000 = $50 000），产生变动性制造费用 $15 000、机会成本 $7 000，所以企业经营收益增长 $28 000（$50 000 − $15 000 − $7 000 = $28 000）。Safety Company 应接受这张特殊订单。

带你到北美学习
管理会计
Take You to
North America
to Learn
Managerial Accounting

Expected increase in sales revenue	$ 50,000
Expected increase in variable manufacturing costs	(15,000)
Expected increase in opportunity costs	(7,000)
Expected increase in operating income	$ 28,000

请注意：如果特殊订单带来的销售额超过产生的成本，企业应接受这张特殊订单；如果特殊订单带来的销售额低于产生的成本，企业不应接受这张特殊订单。除此之外，企业还应考虑特殊订单是否影响企业的常规销售？特殊订单的超低价格是否影响企业未来的常规销售？特殊订单的超低价格是否会引发企业与同行业竞争者之间的价格战？

如何计算特殊订单中产品的最低售价？特殊订单的产品最低售价等于特殊订单的单件产品变动成本加上损失的常规销售贡献毛利除以特殊订单的产品数量。损失的常规销售贡献毛利等于常规销售的单件产品贡献毛利乘以损失的常规销售产品数量（见说明 10-2）。

说明 10-2：计算特殊订单中产品的最低售价

$$\text{Minimum selling price} = \text{Variable cost per unit (special order)} + \frac{\text{Contribution margin lost (regular sales)}}{\text{Number of units (special order)}}$$

Contribution margin lost (regular sales) =
   Contribution margin per unit (regular sales) × Regular sales in units lost

根据"案例 10-2"信息，31 000 件浮力背心的销售额为 $ 434 000，产生变动性制造费用 $ 93 000、变动性市场与销售费用 $ 124 000，因此浮力背心的单件售价为 $ 14，单件变动性制造费用为 $ 3，单件变动性市场与销售费用为 $ 4，贡献毛利为 $ 7（$ 14 – $ 3 – $ 4 = $ 7）。

Safety Company 的最大生产力为 35 000 件浮力背心，当前生产 31 000 件浮力背心，说明企业还能生产 4 000 件浮力背心。如果 Safety Company 接受这张特殊订单，生产 5 000 件浮力背心，不得不暂时放弃 1 000 件浮力背心的常规生产。

为完成这张特殊订单，Safety Company 同样需要承担变动性制造费用，但无需承担变动性市场与销售费用和固定成本，因此特殊订单的单件浮力背心变动成本为 $ 3；此外，Safety Company 需要放弃 1 000 件浮力背心的常规生产和损失贡献毛利 $ 7 000（$ 7 × 1 000 = $ 7 000）。

计算得出，这张特殊订单的浮力背心最低售价为 $ 4.40。

$$\text{Minimum selling price} = \$ 3 + \frac{\$ 7\,000}{5\,000} = \$ 3 + \$ 1.40 = \$ 4.40$$

请注意：如果特殊订单的产品售价超过最低售价，企业应接受特殊订单；如果特殊订单的产品售价低于最低售价，企业不应接受特殊订单。

10.2 外包

Outsourcing

企业外包决策（outsourcing decision）也称为自制或外购决策（make or buy decision）。因为企业管理者需要选择自制产品还是外购产品，所以外包决策的核心问题是如何最好地利用可用资源。在抉择是自制产品还是外购产品时，企业应考虑三个问题（见说明 10-3）。

说明 10-3：外包考虑的核心问题
（1）自制产品产生的变动成本是否超过外包成本（oursourcing cost）？
（2）如果外购产品，是否可以节省固定成本？
（3）如果外购产品，如何利用闲置资源？

案例 10-3

Tech Corporation produces an TV switch that it uses in its final products. Last year, when Tech Corporation produced 68,000 switches, it incurred the following manufacturing costs:

Direct materials	$680,000
Direct labour	136,000
Variable manufacturing overhead	68,000
Fixed manufacturing overhead	374,000
Manufacturing costs	$1,258,000

A technology outside supplier has offered the switches for $14 per unit. If Tech Corporation buys the switches from the outside supplier, the manufacturing facilities can not be used for any other purposes, all of fixed costs can not be avoidable. This year, Tech Corporation will demand 70,000 switches.

带你到北美学习
管理会计
Take You to
North America
to Learn
Managerial Accounting

Required:

1. Should Tech Corporation make or buy the 70,000 switches?

2. Assume that Tech Corporation can avoid $200,000 of fixed manufacturing overhead a year by purchasing the switches from the outside supplier. Should Tech Corporation make or buy the 70,000 switches?

讲解：去年，Tech Corporation 生产电视开关 68 000 个，承担直接材料成本 $680 000、直接人工成本 $136 000、变动性制造费用 $68 000、固定性制造费用 $374 000，因此单个开关的直接材料成本为 $10，直接人工成本为 $2，变动性制造费用为 $1。

今年，Tech Corporation 需要电视开关 70 000 个。为生产 70 000 个电视开关，Tech Corporation 将承担直接材料成本 $700 000、直接人工成本 $140 000、变动性制造费用 $70 000、固定性制造费用 $374 000，产生总成本 $1 284 000。

供应商可以向 Tech Corporation 提供电视开关 70 000 个，单个开关价格为 $14。如果外购 70 000 个电视开关，Tech Corporation 不能节省固定成本，仍需承担固定性制造费用 $374 000，并向供应商支付 $980 000（$14 × 70 000 = $980 000），产生总成本 $1 354 000。

外购 70 000 个电视开关的成本（$1 354 000）超过自制 70 000 个电视开关的成本（$1 284 000），因此企业选择自制电视开关。

	Make Switches	Buy Switches
Variable costs		
Direct materials	$700,000	
Direct labour	140,000	
Variable manufacturing overhead	70,000	
Outsourcing cost（$14 × 70,000 = $980,000）		$980,000
Fixed manufacturing overhead	374,000	374,000
Total costs	$1,284,000	$1,354,000

根据"第2问"信息，如果外购 70 000 个电视开关，Tech Corporation 可以节省固定性制造费用 $200 000，则固定性制造费用降至 $174 000（$374 000 – $200 000 = $174 000），总成本降至 $1 154 000；而自制 70 000 个电视开关，Tech Corporation 仍需承担固定性制造费用 $374 000，总成本仍为 $1 284 000。

自制 70 000 个电视开关的成本（$1 284 000）超过外购 70 000 个电视开关的

成本（$1 154 000），因此企业选择外购电视开关。

	Make Switches	Buy Switches
Variable costs		
Direct materials	$700,000	
Direct labour	140,000	
Variable manufacturing overhead	70,000	
Outsourcing cost（$14 × 70,000 = $980,000）		$980,000
Fixed manufacturing overhead	374,000	174,000
Total costs	$1,284,000	$1,154,000

请注意：如果外购产品可以节省企业固定成本，固定成本与企业外包决策有关；如果外购产品不能节省企业固定成本，固定成本与企业外包决策无关。

案例 10 – 4

Sports Corporation manufactures snowboards. The costs of making 23,600 bindings are as follows：

Direct materials	$23,600
Direct labour	70,800
Variable manufacturing overhead	47,200
Fixed manufacturing overhead	94,400
Total manufacturing costs	$236,000

Suppose Binding Corporation is willing to offer bindings to Sports Corporation for $8 each. Sports Corporation predicts that outsourcing the bindings will enable the company to avoid $20,000 of fixed manufacturing overhead. The facilities freed by outsourcing the bindings can be used to manufacture another product that will contribute $30,000 to the company's net income.

Required：

Should Sports Corporation make bindings, buy bindings and leave facilities idle, or buy bindings and make another product?

讲解： 如果 Sports Corporation 自制 23 600 个滑雪板扣栓，将承担直接材料成本 $23 600、直接人工成本 $70 800、变动性制造费用 $47 200、固定性制造费用

带你到北美学习
管理会计
Take You to
North America
to Learn
Managerial Accounting

$94 400，产生总成本 $236 000。

如果 Sports Corporation 从供应商按单价 $8 外购 23 600 个滑雪板扣栓，并闲置生产资源，那么，企业将向供应商支付 $188 800（$8 × 23 600 = $188 800），节省固定性制造费用 $20 000，即承担固定性制造费用 $74 400（$94 400 – $20 000 = $74 400），产生总成本 $263 200（$188 800 + $74 400 = $263 200）。

如果 Sports Corporation 从供应商按单价 $8 外购 23 600 个滑雪板扣栓，并利用闲置资源生产另一种产品，进而获利 $30 000。那么，企业将向供应商支付 $188 800（$8 × 23 600 = $188 800），节省固定性制造费用 $20 000，即承担固定性制造费用 $74 400（$94 400 – $20 000 = $74 400），并利用闲置资源生产另一种产品，进而获利 $30 000，产生总成本 $233 200（$188 800 + $74 400 – $30 000 = $233 200）。

	Make	Buy & Leave Facilities Idle	Buy & Make Another Product
Variable costs			
Direct materials	$23,600		
Direct labour	70,800		
Variable manufacturing overhead	47,200		
Outsourcing cost		$188,800	$188,800
Fixed manufacturing overhead	94,400	74,400	74,400
Expected profit from another product			(30,000)
Total costs	$236,000	$263,200	$233,200

通过上述计算与分析，自制滑雪板扣栓产生总成本 $236 000；外购滑雪板扣栓且闲置生产资源，产生总成本 $263 200；外购滑雪板扣栓并利用闲置资源生产另一种产品，产生总成本 $233 200。在三种抉择中，外购滑雪板扣栓并利用闲置资源生产另一种产品的总成本最低，因此 Sports Corporation 选择外购 23 600 个滑雪板扣栓并利用闲置资源生产另一种产品。

请注意：如果企业外购产品并利用闲置资源生产另一种产品，生产另一种产品所产生的利润（亏损）与企业外包决策有关。

10.3 淘汰非盈利产品或部门
Dropping Unprofitable Products or Departments

企业抉择是否淘汰非盈利产品或部门涉及一个核心问题，即非盈利产品或部门的贡献毛利是否为正值。如果非盈利产品或部门的贡献毛利为负值，说明该产品或部门的销售额不能承担变动成本，企业应淘汰这样的产品或部门；如果非盈利产品或部门的贡献毛利为正值，说明该产品或部门的销售额可以承担变动成本和一部分固定成本，因此在抉择是否淘汰非盈利产品或部门时，企业管理者应考虑固定成本（见说明 10-4）。

说明 10-4：淘汰非盈利产品或部门考虑的核心问题
（1）非盈利产品或部门的贡献毛利是否为正值？
（2）即使淘汰非盈利产品或部门，固定成本是否仍将存在？
（3）如果淘汰非盈利产品或部门，是否可以节省直接固定成本？

案例 10-5

Bonds Corporation manufactures a fast-bonding adhesive, T-Bond. The normal sales volume of T-Bond is 40,000 litres per month. The selling price of T-Bond is $34 per litre and its variable costs are $21 per litre. Fixed costs per month include $280,000 in manufacturing costs and $300,000 in advertsing costs.

Currently, only 12,000 litres are being sold per month, which are projected to be below the normal sales volume. Bonds Corporation believes that this drop in sales volume will only last for two months and considers to close the plant that produces T-Bond for the two months after which the corporation expects the sales volume of T-Bond to return to the normal level of 40,000 litres per month.

If Bonds Corporation closes the plant, none of fixed costs can be avoided.

Required:

1. Would you recommend that Bonds Corporation closes the plant for those two months? Why or why not?

2. If Bonds Corporation closes the plant, the corporation anticipates that its fixed manufacturing costs can be reduced to $160,000 per month and fixed advertsing costs can be

带你到北美学习
管理会计
Take You to
North America
to Learn
Managerial Accounting

reduced by 15%. Would you recommend that Bonds Corporation closes the plant for those two months? Why or why not?

讲解： 每升黏合剂的售价为 $34，变动成本为 $21，因此贡献毛利为 $13。当前，Bonds Corporation 的黏合剂销量为 12 000 升。12 000 升黏合剂为企业带来销售额 $408 000、变动成本 $252 000、贡献毛利 $156 000。

当前，Bonds Corporation 的黏合剂销量为 12 000 升，远低于正常销量（40 000 升）。如果停止生产黏合剂 2 个月，Bonds Corporation 将损失销售额 $408 000，节省变动成本 $252 000，降低企业经营收益 $156 000，因此企业不应停产黏合剂 2 个月。

Expected decrease in sales revenue	($408,000)
Expected decrease in variable costs	252,000
Expected decrease in operating income	($156,000)

根据"案例 10-5"信息，即使在停产黏合剂之后，Bonds Corporation 的固定成本仍将存在，因此固定成本与企业淘汰非盈利产品或部门的决策无关，这种在淘汰非盈利产品或部门之后仍存在的固定成本被称为不可避免固定成本（unavoidable fixed cost）。

根据"第 2 问"信息，如果停止生产黏合剂 2 个月，企业固定性制造成本将从 $280 000 降至 $160 000，节省 $120 000；固定性广告成本下降 15%，节省 $45 000（$300 000 × 15% = $45 000），说明在黏合剂停产之后，Bonds Corporation 可以节省固定成本 $165 000。在停产黏合剂 2 个月之后，Bonds Corporation 将损失销售额 $408 000，节省变动成本 $252 000、固定成本 $165 000，增加企业经营收益 $9 000，因此企业应停产黏合剂 2 个月。

Expected decrease in sales revenue	($408,000)
Expected decrease in variable costs	252,000
Expected decrease in fixed costs	165,000
Expected increase in operating income	$9,000

在停产黏合剂之后，Bonds Corporation 节省固定成本 $165 000，因此这笔固定成本与企业淘汰非盈利产品或部门的决策有关，这种在淘汰非盈利产品或部门之后不存在的固定成本被称为可避免固定成本（avoidable fixed cost）。非盈利产品或部门的直接固定成本（direct fixed cost）均为可避免固定成本。

请注意：如果淘汰非盈利产品或部门损失的销售额大于节省的成本，企业应选择保留非盈利产品或部门，以免造成企业经营收益的进一步损失；如果淘汰非盈利产品或部门损失的销售额小于节省的成本，企业应选择淘汰非盈利产品或部门。在抉择是否淘汰非盈利产品或部门时，企业还应考虑，淘汰非盈利产品或部门是否影响企业的其他产品或部门、如何利用所淘汰非盈利产品或部门遗留的生产资源等问题。

10.4　分配有限生产资源
Allocating Limited Productive Resources

任何企业都不得不面对有限资源，有限资源限制了产品的生产与销售。对于制造商，生产受限因素（production constraint）一般指直接材料（direct materials）、直接人工工时（direct labour hour）和机器运转时长（machine hour）。对于商业类企业（merchandise company），主要限制因素是布展空间（display space）。面对有限资源，为使利润最大化，企业应强调某类产品的生产或销售。在抉择哪类产品应优先生产或销售时，企业应考虑三个问题（见说明 10-5）。

> **说明 10-5：分配有限生产资源考虑的核心问题**
> （1）什么资源阻碍了企业的产品生产或展示？
> （2）哪类产品的单位有限资源贡献毛利最高？
> （3）强调生产或销售一种产品是否会影响企业的固定成本？

案例 10 - 6

Clocks Corporation manufactures two styles of clocks: silver clock and goldlen clock. Clocks can sell a maximum of 25,000 clocks for each style clock annually. The machine hour capacity is 40,000 hours per year. Total fixed costs are $600,000. The following unit clock data are available:

	Silver Clock	Goldlen Clock
Selling price	$90	$108
Variable costs	60	75
Machine hours	1 hour	2 hours

带你到北美学习
管理会计
Take You to
North America
to Learn
Managerial Accounting

Required：

1. Calculate the unit contribution margin for each style clock.

2. Calculate the contribution margin per machine hour for each style clock.

3. Calculate the number of units of each style clock that Clocks Corporation should produce to maximize operating income. What is the dollar amount of the maximum operating income?

讲解： Clocks Corporation 生产 2 款钟表：Silver Clock 和 Goldlen Clock。1 台 Silver Clock 的售价为 $90，可变动成本为 $60，贡献毛利为 $30；1 台 Goldlen Clock 的售价为 $108，可变动成本为 $75，贡献毛利为 $33。生产 1 台 Silver Clock 需要运转机器 1 小时，而生产 1 台 Goldlen Clock 需要运转机器 2 小时，即运转机器 1 小时可以生产 1 台 Silver Clock、产生贡献毛利 $30 或 0.50 台 Goldlen Clock、带来贡献毛利 $16.50。

	Silver Clock	Goldlen Clock
Clocks produced per machine hour	1.00	0.50
Contribution margin per clock	× $30.00	× $33.00
Contribution margin per machine hour	$30.00	$16.50

加工 1 台 Goldlen Clock，需要机器运转 2 小时，产生贡献毛利 $33，即运转机器 1 小时生产 Goldlen Clock，带来贡献毛利 $16.50；加工 1 台 Silver Clock，需要运转机器 1 小时，创造贡献毛利 $30，即运转机器 1 小时生产 Silver Clock，带来贡献毛利 $30。通过上述分析，Goldlen Clock 的单位有限资源贡献毛利（$16.50）低于 Silver Clock 的单位有限资源贡献毛利（$30），所以企业应优先生产 Silver Clock。

每款钟表的年度最大销量为 25 000 台，Clocks Corporation 的机器运转能力为每年 40 000 小时。加工 1 台 Silver Clock，需要机器运转 1 小时，因此为生产 25 000 台 Silver Clock，企业运转机器 25 000 小时。Clocks Corporation 还可以运用剩余机器运转能力（15 000 小时）生产 Golden Clock；加工 1 台 Goldlen Clock，需要机器运转 2 小时，因此可以生产 7 500 台 Golden Clock。25 000 台 Silver Clock 的贡献毛利为 $750 000（$30 × 25 000 = $750 000），7 500 台 Golden Clock 的贡献毛利为 $247 500（$33 × 7 500 = $247 500），因此贡献毛利总额为 $997 500（$750 000 + $247 500 = $997 500）。

	Silver Clock	Goldlen Clock	Total
Contribution margin per machine hour	$30.00	$16.50	
Machine hours devoded to clocks	× 25,000	× 15,000	
Total contribution margin	$750,000	$247,500	$997,500

在 2 款钟表之间，Clocks Corporation 分配有限生产资源——机器运转能力，不影响企业固定成本，因此固定成本与企业分配有限生产资源（机器运转能力）的决策无关。生产 25 000 台 Silver Clock 和 7 500 台 Golden Clock，带来贡献毛利 $997 500，固定成本总额为 $600 000，因此企业经营收益为 $397 500。

	Silver Clock	Goldlen Clock	Total
Total contribution margin	$750,000	$247,500	$997,500
Total fixed costs			(600,000)
Operating income			$397,500

请注意：在产品搭配组合不变的前提下，在不同产品之间分配有限生产资源将不影响企业固定成本，因此固定成本与企业分配有限生产资源的决策无关。

10.5　出售或进一步加工产品
Selling or Processing Further Products

许多企业，特别是食品加工企业和自然资源开采企业，会面临这样的决策，即企业在加工过程中的哪个阶段出售产品？例如，一家肉制品加工企业是将生肉（raw meat）按原状出售，还是加工为午餐肉（lunch meat）出售？面对这样的决策，企业应考虑三个问题（见说明 10-6）。

> **说明 10 - 6：出售或进一步加工产品考虑的核心问题**
> （1）按原状出售产品，企业赚取多少销售额？
> （2）出售进一步加工的产品，企业赚取多少销售额？
> （3）进一步加工产品，将产生多少额外成本？

案例 10 - 7

Chemical Corporation has spent $243,000 to refine 73,000 litres of acetone, which can be sold for $2 per litre. Alternatively, Chemical Corporation can process the acetone fur-

带你到北美学习
管理会计
Take You to
North America
to Learn
Managerial Accounting

ther to create a total of 58,000 litres of lacquer thinner, which can be sold for $3.30 per litre. The further processing will cost $0.40 per litre of lacquer thinner. To sell the lacquer thinner, Chemical Corporation must pay advertising and shipping expenses of $0.38 per litre on the lacquer thinner.

Required:

Should Chemical Corporation sell the acetone as is or process it into the lacquer thinner?

讲解： Chemical Corporation 按原状出售 73 000 升丙酮，每升丙酮的售价为 $2，赚取收入 $146 000。

Chemical Corporation 还可以将 73 000 升丙酮提炼为 58 000 升挥发性漆稀释剂，每升挥发性漆稀释剂的售价为 $3.30，赚取收入 $191 400（$3.30 × 58 000 = $191 400）。提炼 1 升挥发性漆稀释剂产生额外成本 $0.40，1 升挥发性漆稀释剂的广告成本为 $0.38，因此 58 000 升挥发性漆稀释剂的提炼成本为 $23 200，广告成本为 $22 040，额外成本总额为 $45 240（$23 200 + $22 040 = $45 240）。通过计算，出售 58 000 升挥发性漆稀释剂，赚取净收入 $146 160（$191 400 − $45 240 = $146 160）。

出售 58 000 升挥发性漆稀释剂赚取的净收入（$146 160）超过出售 73 000 升丙酮赚取的收入（$146 000），因此 Chemical Corporation 应选择将 73 000 升丙酮提炼为 58 000 升挥发性漆稀释剂。

	Sell As Is	Process Further
Expected revenue from selling 73,000 litres of acetone	$146,000	
Expected revenue from selling 58,000 litres of lacquer thinner		$191,400
Additional costs to process acetone into lacquer thinner		(45,240)
Total net revenue	$146,000	$146,160

为什么不考虑金额为 $243 000 的提炼成本？因为无论出售丙酮，还是将丙酮加工为挥发性漆稀释剂，Chemical Corporation 均产生这笔提炼成本，所以这笔提炼成本（$243 000）属于沉没成本（sunk cost），与企业出售还是进一步加工产品的决策无关。

例题综述
Summary of Examples

例题 10 - 1

Sunglasses Corporation is considering to accept a special order from Lenses Corporation for 20,000 pairs of sunglasses at $76 per pair. Sunglasses Corporation incurs the following average costs for each glass:

Direct materials	$40
Direct labour	12
Variable manufacturing overhead	8
Variable marketing expenses	4
Fixed manufacturing overhead	20
Total costs	$84

Sunglasses Corporation has enough capacity to accept the special order from Lenses Corporation. Sunglasses Corporation will not incur any variable marketing expenses and fixed expenses.

Required:

1. Should this order be accepted at a special price of $76?

2. What other factors should Sunglasses Corporation consider in deciding whether to accept the special order?

1. Should this order be accepted at a special price of $76?

讲解: 根据题目信息,一般情况下,制作 1 副太阳镜需要直接材料成本 $40、直接人工成本 $12、变动性制造费用 $8、固定性制造费用 $20,每副太阳镜的变动性市场费用为 $4。

  Sunglasses Corporation 拥有足够生产力完成这张特殊订单,即 20 000 副太阳镜,但这张特殊订单的太阳镜零售价仅为 $76。Sunglasses Corporation 正在考虑是否接受这张特殊订单。

  1 副太阳镜的零售价为 $76,因此 20 000 副太阳镜的销售额为 $1 520 000 ($76 × 20 000 = $1 520 000)。

  为完成这张特殊订单,Sunglasses Corporation 同样需要承担直接材料、直接人工

带你到北美学习
管理会计
Take You to
North America
to Learn
Managerial Accounting

和变动性制造费用，但无需承担变动性市场费用和固定性制造费用。20 000 副太阳镜的直接材料成本为 $800 000，直接人工成本为 $240 000，变动性制造费用成本为 $160 000，所以产生变动成本 $1 200 000。

通过这张特殊订单，Sunglasses Corporation 赚取销售额 $1 520 000，产生变动成本 $1 200 000，因此企业经营收益增长 $320 000（$1 520 0000 – $1 200 000 = $320 000）。企业应接受这张特殊订单。

Expected increase in sales revenue	$1,520,000
Expected increase in variable costs	(1,200,000)
Expected increase in operating income	$320,000

答案：The special order should be accepted at a special price of $76.

2. What other factors should Sunglasses Corporation consider in deciding whether to accept the special order?

答案：In addition to the effect of this special order on the operating income, Sunglasses Corporation should consider whether regular customers will learn of the special price extended to Lenses Corporation. If regular customers learn of this special order, will it affect Sunglasses Corporation's ability to sell at its normal price? Also, what will be the effect on its industry competitors? Will the industry competitors view this special order as the start of a price war?

例题 10 – 2

Blue Company manufactures boats. Blue Company's contribution margin income statement for the most recent month provides the following data:

Sales revenue (31,000 units)		$434,000
Variable expenses		
Manufacturing expense	$124,000	
Marketing and selling expenses	124,000	(248,000)
Contribution margin		186,000
Fixed expenses		
Manufacturing expense	120,000	

Marketing and selling expenses	50,000	(170,000)
Operating income		$ 16,000

Suppose Black Inc. is considering to purchase 10,000 boats from Blue Company. Acceptance of the special order will not increase any of Blue Company's variable marketing and selling expenses and fixed expenses. The Blue Company's plant has the full capacity to produce 40,000 boats. The current production volume of boats is 31,000 units. Black Inc. has offered $ 8 per boat, which is below the normal price of $ 14 per boat.

Required：

1. Should Blue Company accept the special order?

2. What is the minimum selling price for this special order?

1. Should Blue Company accept the special order?

讲解： 根据题目信息，31 000 艘小船的销售额为 $ 434 000，产生变动性制造费用 $ 124 000、变动性市场与销售费用 $ 124 000，因此每艘小船的售价为 $ 14，变动性制造费用为 $ 4，变动性市场与销售费用为 $ 4。

1 艘小船的正常零售价为 $ 14，而这张特殊订单的小船零售价仅为 $ 8。此外，Blue Company 的最大生产力为 40 000 艘小船，当前生产 31 000 艘小船，说明企业还能生产 9 000 艘小船。Blue Company 正在考虑是否接受这张来自于 Black Inc. 的特殊订单，即 10 000 艘小船。如果 Blue Company 接受这张特殊订单，生产 10 000 艘小船，将不得不暂时放弃 1 000 艘小船的常规生产。

为完成这张特殊订单，Blue Company 同样需要承担变动性制造费用，但无需承担变动性市场与销售费用和固定成本，因此制造 10 000 艘小船将产生变动性制造费用 $ 40 000（ $ 4 × 10 000 = $ 40 000）。此外，Blue Company 需要放弃 1 000 艘小船的常规生产，因此损失销售额 $ 14 000（ $ 14 × 1 000 = $ 14 000），节省变动性制造费用 $ 4 000（ $ 4 × 1 000 = $ 4 000）、变动性市场与销售费用 $ 4 000（ $ 4 × 1 000 = $ 4 000），降低企业贡献毛利 $ 6 000（ $ 14 000 − $ 4 000 − $ 4 000 = $ 6 000）。这张特殊订单（10 000 艘小船）导致企业贡献毛利降低 $ 6 000，即特殊订单的机会成本。

通过这张特殊订单，Blue Company 可以赚取销售额 $ 80 000，产生变动性制造费用 $ 40 000、机会成本 $ 6 000，企业经营收益增长 $ 34 000（ $ 80 000 − $ 40 000 − $ 6 000 = $ 34 000）。因此，企业应接受这张特殊订单。

带你到北美学习
管理会计
Take You to
North America
to Learn
Managerial Accounting

Expected increase in sales revenue	$ 80 ,000
Expected increase in variable manufacturing costs	(40,000)
Expected increase in opportunity costs	(6,000)
Expected increase in operating income	$ 34 ,000

答案： Blue Company should accept the special order.

2. What is the minimum selling price for this special order?

讲解： 31 000 艘小船的销售额为 $ 434 000，产生变动性制造费用 $ 124 000、变动性市场与销售费用 $ 124 000，因此每艘小船的售价为 $ 14，变动性制造费用为 $ 4，变动性市场与销售费用为 $ 4，贡献毛利为 $ 6。

Blue Company 的最大生产力为 40 000 艘小船，当前生产 31 000 艘小船，说明企业还能生产 9 000 艘小船。如果 Blue Company 接受这张特殊订单，生产 10 000 艘小船，将不得不暂时放弃 1 000 艘小船的常规生产。

为完成这张特殊订单，Blue Company 同样需要承担变动性制造费用，但无需承担变动性市场与销售费用和固定成本，因此对于这张特殊订单，1 艘小船的变动成本为 $ 4。此外，Blue Company 需要放弃 1 000 艘小船的常规生产和损失贡献毛利 $ 6 000（$ 6 × 1 000 = $ 6 000）。

计算得出，对于这张特殊订单的小船的最低售价为 $ 4.60。

$$\text{Minimum selling price} = \$ 4 + \frac{\$ 6\ 000}{10\ 000} = \$ 4 + \$ 0.60 = \$ 4.60$$

答案： The minimum selling price for this special order is $ 4.60.

例题 10 - 3

Fin Corporation is a manufacturing company to produce e-communication systems. Fin is considering outsourcing its email applications. Fin's in-house email applications have 2,300 mailboxes. The information about making the 2,300 mailboxes is as follows:

Variable costs	
Email licence	$ 7
Virus protection licence	1
Other variable costs	8

Fixed costs	
Computer hardware	94,300
$8,050 monthly salaries for two information technology staff members who work only on email	16,100

As a provider of e-message outsourcing services, Mail Corporation wants to host Fin's email applications for $9 per mailbox per month. If Fin outsources its email applications to Mail, Fin will still need the virus protection software, the computer hardware, and one information technology staff member.

Required:

Should Fin Corporation accept Mail Corporation's offer? Why or why not?

讲解: 1 个邮箱的邮件许可费用为 $7，病毒防护许可费用为 $1，其他变动成本为 $8。如果 Fin Corporation 生产 2 300 个邮箱，将承担邮件许可费用 $16 100、病毒防护许可费用 $2 300、其他变动成本 $18 400；此外，Fin Corporation 还将承担计算机硬件费用 $94 300、2 名员工的薪资费用 $16 100，这些费用属于固定成本。通过上述分析与计算，自制 2 300 个邮箱将产生总成本 $147 200。

如果 Fin Corporation 从 Mail Corporation 按单价 $9 外购 2 300 个邮箱，需向供应商（Mail Corporation）支付 $20 700；此外，Fin Corporation 仍需支付病毒防护许可费用 $2 300、计算机硬件费用 $94 300、1 名员工的薪资费用 $8 050。通过上述分析与计算，外购 2 300 个邮箱将产生总成本 $125 350。

自制 2 300 个邮箱的成本（$147 200）超过外购 2 300 个邮箱的成本（$125 350），因此企业选择外购邮箱。

	Make Mailboxes	Buy Mailboxes
Variable costs		
Email licence	$16,100	
Virus protection licence	2,300	$2,300
Other variable costs	18,400	
Outsourcing cost ($9 × 2,300 = $20,700)		20,700
Fixed costs		
Computer hardware	94,300	94,300
Salaries	16,100	8,050
Total costs	$147,200	$125,350

带你到北美学习

管理会计

Take You to
North America
to Learn
Managerial Accounting

答案： Fin Corporation should accept Mail Corporation's offer and outsource 2,300 mail-boxes to Mail Corporation.

例题 10 - 4

Switch Corporation produces an transfer switch that it uses in its final products. Last year, when Tech Corporation produced 80,000 switches, it incurred the following actual manufacturing costs：

Direct materials per switch	$9.00
Direct labour per switch	1.50
Variable manufacturing overhead per switch	2.00
Fixed manufacturing overhead each year	455,000

A technology outside supplier has offered to the switch for $14 per unit. If Switch Corporation buys the switches from the outside supplier, $100,000 of fixed costs can be avoided. This year, Tech Corporation will demand 70,000 switches.

Required：

1. Should Switch Corporation make or buy the 70,000 switches?

2. Given the last scenario, what is the most Switch Corporation would be willing to pay to outsource the 70,000 switches?

1. Should Switch Corporation make or buy the 70,000 switches?

讲解： 单个转换开关的直接材料成本为 $9，直接人工成本为 $1.50，变动性制造费用为 $2。今年，Switch Corporation 需要转换开关 70 000 个。如果自制 70 000 个转换开关，将产生直接材料成本 $630 000、直接人工成本 $105 000、变动性制造费用 $140 000，固定性制造费用仍为 $455 000。通过计算，自制 70 000 个转换开关将产生总成本 $1 330 000。

供应商可以向 Switch Corporation 提供转换开关 70 000 个，单个开关的价格为 $14。如果外购 70 000 个转换开关，Switch Corporation 可以节省固定成本 $100 000，即仍需承担固定性制造费用 $355 000，并向供应商支付 $980 000（$14 × 70 000 = $980 000），产生总成本 $1 335 000。

外购 70 000 个转换开关的成本（$1 335 000）超过自制 70 000 个转换开关的

成本（＄1 330 000），因此企业选择自制转换开关。

	Make Mailboxes	Buy Mailboxes
Variable costs		
Direct materials	＄630,000	
Direct labour	105,000	
Variable manufacturing overhead	140,000	
Outsourcing cost		＄980,000
Fixed manufacturing overhead	455,000	355,000
Total costs	＄1,330,000	＄1,335,000

答案：Switch Corporation should make the 70,000 switches.

2. Given the last scenario, what is the most Switch Corporation would be willing to pay to outsource the 70,000 switches?

讲解：当外购 70 000 个转换开关的成本等于或低于自制 70 000 个转换开关的成本时，Switch Corporation 才会考虑外购转换开关，因此转换开关的最高采购价应使外购成本等于自制成本。我们知道，自制 70 000 个转换开关的成本为 ＄1 330 000，所以转换开关的最高采购价应使外购开关成本等于 ＄1 330 000。

	Make Mailboxes	Buy Mailboxes
Variable costs		
Direct materials	＄630,000	
Direct labour	105,000	
Variable manufacturing overhead	140,000	
Outsourcing cost		＄?
Fixed manufacturing overhead	455,000	355,000
Total costs	＄1,330,000	＄1,330,000

$$70\,000x + \$355\,000 = \$1\,330\,000$$

$$x = \$13.928\,517\,4 \approx \$13.93$$

答案：Switch Corporation will be willing to outsource if the outsourcing cost of one switch is less than ＄13.93.

带你到北美学习
管理会计
Take You to
North America
to Learn
Managerial Accounting

例题 10 - 5

Mc Corporation is considering discontinuing its French fries product line. Last year, the product line income statement showed the following information:

Sales revenue	$7,600,000
Cost of goods sold	(6,400,000)
Gross profit	1,200,000
Operating expenses	(1,400,000)
Operating income	($200,000)

Fixed manuafacturing costs account for 40% of the cost of goods sold, while only 30% of the operating expenses are fixed. Only $750,000 of direct fixed costs will be avoided if the French fries product line is dropped, the remainder of the fixed costs will continue to exist.

Required:

Should Mc Corporation drop the French fries product line?

讲解: 根据题目信息,售出商品成本为 $6 400 000,其中 40% 为固定成本,剩余 60% 为变动成本,即固定性售出商品成本为 $2 560 000,变动性售出商品成本为 $3 840 000;经营费用为 $1 400 000,其中 30% 为固定成本,剩余 70% 为变动成本,即固定性经营费用为 $420 000,变动性经营费用为 $980 000。变动性售出商品成本为 $3 840 000,变动性经营费用为 $980 000,因此变动成本为 $4 820 000。

如果关闭薯条生产线,Mc Corporation 将损失销售额 $7 600 000,节省变动成本 $4 820 000、固定成本 $750 000,企业经营收益下降 $2 030 000。企业不应关闭薯条生产线。

Expected decrease in sales revenue	($7,600,000)
Expected decrease in variable costs	4,820,000
Expected decrease in fixed costs	750,000
Expected decrease in operating income	($2,030,000)

答案: Mc Corporation should not drop the French fries product line.

例题 10 - 6

Video Corporation manufactures two products: CVD and DVD. The corporation is considering dropping the DVD product line because of its operating loss. During the last year, the income statements of two product lines showed the following information:

	CVD	DVD
Sales revenue	$300,000	$120,000
Variable expenses	(150,000)	(80,000)
Contribution margin	150,000	40,000
Fixed expenses	(125,000)	(70,000)
Operating income	$25,000	($30,000)

All of fixed costs attached with DVD are direct fixed costs and can be avoided if the corporation drops DVD. Unfortunately, CVD will be adversely affected by discontinuing the DVD product line. The production and sales of CVD will decline 10%.

Required:

What should the company do?

讲解: 如果关闭 DVD 产品线，Video Corporation 将损失销售额 $120 000，节省变动成本 $80 000、固定成本 $70 000；此外，关闭 DVD 产品线将使 CVD 的销售额下降 10%，即 CVD 的销售额下降 $30 000（$300 000 × 10% = $30 000），因此 CVD 产生的变动成本也随之降低 $15 000（$150 000 × 10% = $15 000）。通过上述分析，如果关闭 DVD 产品线，Video Corporation 将损失销售额 $150 000，节省变动成本 $95 000、固定成本 $70 000，因此企业经营收益增长 $15 000。企业应关闭 DVD 产品线。

Expected decrease in sales revenue	($150,000)
Expected decrease in variable costs	95,000
Expected decrease in fixed costs	70,000
Expected increase in operating income	$15,000

答案: Video Corporation should consider stopping the product line of DVD to increase its operating income by $15,000.

例题 10 - 7

Sports Corporation produces two types of exercise equipment: Regular and Deluxe. The Regular and Deluxe models are processed through the same production department, Sports Corporation could use all of its available machine hours to produce either model. (Hint:

带你到北美学习

管理会计

Take You to
North America
to Learn
Managerial Accounting

Allocating fixed manufacturing overhead based on machine hour. Using the allocation of fixed manufacturing overhead to determine the proportion of machine hours used by each model.)

	Per Unit	
	Deluxe	Regular
Selling price	$ 990	$ 560
Costs		
Direct materials	290	100
Direct labour	86	188
Variable manufacturing overhead	172	86
Fixed manufacturing overhead	80	40
Variable operating expenses	115	61
Total costs	(743)	(475)
Operating income	$ 247	$ 85

Required:

What the product mix will maximize operating income?

讲解: 根据题目信息, Sports Corporation 生产 2 种健身设备: Deluxe 和 Regular。1 台 Deluxe 的售价为 $ 990, 直接材料成本为 $ 290, 直接人工成本为 $ 86, 变动性制造费用为 $ 172, 变动性经营费用为 $ 115, 贡献毛利为 $ 327; 1 台 Regular 的售价为 $ 560, 直接材料成本为 $ 100, 直接人工成本为 $ 188, 变动性制造费用为 $ 86, 变动性经营费用为 $ 61, 贡献毛利为 $ 125。

	Per Unit	
	Deluxe	Regular
Selling price	$ 990	$ 560
Direct materials	(290)	(100)
Direct labour	(86)	(188)
Variable manufacturing overhead	(172)	(86)
Variable operating expenses	(115)	(61)
Contriburion margin	$ 327	$ 125

固定性制造费用的分摊基础为机器运转时长 (machine hour), 1 台 Deluxe 的固定性制造费用为 $ 80, 1 台 Regular 的固定性制造费用为 $ 40, 即生产 1 台 Deluxe 的

机器运转时长是生产 1 台 Regular 的 2 倍。换言之，如果生产 1 台 Deluxe 的机器运转时长为 1 小时，而生产 1 台 Regular 的机器运转时长为 0.50 小时，说明机器运转 1 小时可以生产 1 台 Deluxe、产生贡献毛利 $327 或 2 台 Regular、创造贡献毛利 $250。

通过上述分析，Deluxe 的单位有限资源贡献毛利（$327）超过 Regular 的单位有限资源贡献毛利（$250），因此企业应使用机器优先生产 Deluxe。

	Per Unit	
	Deluxe	Regular
Units produced per machine hour	1	2
Contribution margin per unit	× $327	× $125
Contribution margin per machine hour	$327	$250

在 2 种健身设备之间，Sports Corporation 分配有限生产资源——机器运转能力，不影响企业固定成本，因此固定成本与企业分配机器运转能力的决策无关。在产品搭配组合不变的前提下，在不同产品之间分配有限生产资源将不影响企业的固定成本，因此固定成本与企业分配有限生产资源的决策无关。

答案：Sports Corporation should produce only the Deluxe model.

例题 10 – 8

StoreAll makes two sizes of boxes (Large and Regular) and uses the same machine to produce them. The machine can be run for only 3,000 hours per year and can produce 10 Large Boxes or 15 Regular Boxes per hour. Fixed manufacturing overhead totals $100,000 per year. The following data are available：

	Per Unit	
	Regular	Large
Selling price	$7.00	$12.00
Direct materials	1.25	1.25
Direct labour	0.75	1.25
Variable manufacturing overhead	1.00	1.25

Required：

1. Assume that the annual demand for Regular Box is limited to be 30,000 units and the

带你到北美学习
管理会计
Take You to
North America
to Learn
Managerial Accounting

annual demand for Large Box is limited to be 25,000 units. How many of each size box should StoreAll produce?

2. Determine the annual operating profit using the optimal product mix.

1. Assume that the annual demand for Regular Box is limited to be 30,000 units and the annual demand for Large Box is limited to be 25,000 units. How many of each size box should StoreAll produce?

讲解： 根据题目信息，StoreAll 生产 2 种箱子：Regular Box 和 LargeBox。1 个 Regular Box 的售价为 $7，直接材料成本为 $1.25，直接人工成本为 $0.75，变动性制造费用为 $1，贡献毛利为 $4；1 个 Large Box 的售价为 $12，直接材料成本为 $1.25，直接人工成本为 $1.25，变动性制造费用为 $1.25，贡献毛利为 $8.25。

	Per Unit	
	Regular	Large
Selling price	$7.00	$12.00
Direct materials	(1.25)	(1.25)
Direct labour	(0.75)	(1.25)
Variable manufacturing overhead	(1.00)	(1.25)
Contribution margin	$4.00	$8.25

机器运转 1 小时可以生产 15 个 Regular Box 或 10 个 Large Box，即机器运转 1 小时可以生产 15 个 Regular Box、产生贡献毛利 $60 或 10 个 Large Box、带来贡献毛利 $82.50。通过上述分析，Regular Box 的单位有限资源贡献毛利（$60）低于 Large Box 的单位有限资源贡献毛利（$82.50），因此 StoreAll 应优先生产 Large Box。

	Per Unit	
	Regular	Large
Units produced per machine hour	15.00	10.00
Contribution margin per unit	× $4.00	× $8.25
Contribution margin per machine hour	$60.00	$82.50

Large Box 的最大需求量为 25 000 个，Regular Box 的最大需求量为 30 000 个。StoreAll 的机器运转能力为每年 3 000 小时。机器运转 1 小时可以生产 10 个 Large Box，因此生产 25 000 个 Large Box，机器需要运转 2 500 小时。机器运转 1 小时可以生产 15 个 Regular Box，利用剩余机器运转能力（500 小时）可以生产 7 500 个

Regular Box。

答案： StoreAll should produce 25,000 Large Boxes and 7,500 Regular Boxes.

2. Determine the annual operating profit using the optimal product mix.

讲解： 产品销售组合为 25 000 个 Large Box 和 7 500 个 Regular Box。1 个 Large Box 的贡献毛利为 $8.25，1 个 Regular Box 的贡献毛利为 $4，因此 25 000 个 Large Box 的贡献毛利为 $206 250，7 500 个 Regular Box 的贡献毛利为 $30 000，贡献毛利总额为 $236 250。固定性制造费用为 $100 000。贡献毛利总额（$236 250）减去固定性制造费用（$100 000）等于运营收益（$136 250）。

	Regular	Large	Total
Contribution margin	$30,000	$206,250	$236,250
Fixed manufacturing overhead			(100,000)
Operating income			$136,250

答案： Using the optimal product mix, the annual operating profit is $136,250.

例题 10 - 9

Chemical Corporation manufactures five compounds used in pharmaceutical. The following data are available：

	Products				
	C100	D100	D200	D300	E400
Units in demand for next year	26,000	42,000	40,000	46,000	450,000
Selling price per unit	$14.50	$13.50	$18.00	$12.50	$10.00
Direct materials per unit	3.50	2.30	4.50	3.10	1.50
Direct labour (DL) per unit	4.80	3.00	8.40	6.00	2.40

Additional information：

a. Present capacity is 130,000 direct labour hours per year.

b. Direct labour rate is $12 per hour.

c. Fixed costs total $356,000 per year.

d. Variable manufacturing overhead (MOH) rate is $4 per direct labour hour.

e. All of non-manufacturing costs are fixed.

带你到北美学习
管理会计
Take You to
North America
to Learn
Managerial Accounting

f．Inventories are ingored.

Required：

How would the corporation allocate the 130,000 direct labour hours to production? Indicate which product and how much would be 1st, 2nd, etc.

讲解：

第1步：计算每种产品的单位直接人工工时。

	C100	D100	D200	D300	E400
Direct labour per unit	$4.80	$3.00	$8.40	$6.00	$2.40
Direct labour rate	÷ $12	÷ $12	÷ $12	÷ $12	÷ $12
Direct labour hour per unit	0.40	0.25	0.70	0.50	0.20

第2步：计算每种产品的单位变动性制造费用。

	C100	D100	D200	D300	E400
Direct labour hour per unit	0.40	0.25	0.70	0.50	0.20
Variable MOH rate	× $4	× $4	× $4	× $4	× $4
Variable MOH per unit	$1.60	$1.00	$2.80	$2.00	$0.80

第3步：计算每种产品的单位贡献毛利。

	C100	D100	D200	D300	E400
Selling price per unit	$14.50	$13.50	$18.00	$12.50	$10.00
Direct materials per unit	(3.50)	(2.30)	(4.50)	(3.10)	(1.50)
Direct labour per unit	(4.80)	(3.00)	(8.40)	(6.00)	(2.40)
Variable MOH per unit	(1.60)	(1.00)	(2.80)	(2.00)	(0.80)
Contribution margin per unit	$4.60	$7.20	$2.30	$1.40	$5.30

第4步：计算直接人工工作1小时生产的每种产品数量。

	C100	D100	D200	D300	E400
Direct labour hour per unit	0.40	0.25	0.70	0.50	0.20
Units per DL hour	2.50	4.00	1.43	2.00	5.00

第5步：计算直接人工工作1小时创造的贡献毛利。

	C100	D100	D200	D300	E400
Contribution margin per unit	$4.60	$7.20	$2.30	$1.40	$5.30
Units per DL hour	× 2.50	× 4.00	× 1.43	× 2.00	× 5.00

Contribution margin per DL hour	$ 11. 50	$ 28. 80	$ 3. 29	$ 2. 80	$ 26. 50
Ranking	3	1	4	5	2

第 6 步：计算完成每种产品需求量所需的直接人工工时。

	C100	D100	D200	D300	E400
Ranking	3	1	4	5	2
Units in demand for next year	26,000	42,000	40,000	46,000	450,000
Units per DL hour	÷ 2.50	÷ 4.00	÷ 1.43	÷ 2.00	÷ 5.00
Direct labour hours required	10,400	10,500	27,972	23,000	90,000

通过上述计算与分析，D100 的单位有限资源贡献毛利为 $ 28. 80，E400 的单位有限资源贡献毛利为 $ 26. 50，C100 的单位有限资源贡献毛利为 $ 11. 50，D200 的单位有限资源贡献毛利为 $ 3. 29，D300 的单位有限资源贡献毛利为 $ 2. 80。根据每种产品的单位有限资源贡献毛利，StoreAll 应优先生产 D100，其次分别为 E400，C100，D200 和 D300。

当前，直接人工可用工时为 130 000 小时，在完成 D100（42 000 件）、E400（450 000 件）、C100（26 000 件）之后，直接人工工时还剩 19 100 小时（130 000 − 10 500 − 90 000 − 10 400 = 19 100）。利用直接人工剩余工时（19 100 小时）可以生产 27 313 件 D200（19 100 × 1.43 = 27 313）。

答案：

Ranking	Products	Contribution Margin per DL Hour	Units to be Produced
1	D100	$ 28. 80	42,000
2	E400	26. 50	450,000
3	C100	11. 50	26,000
4	D200	3. 29	27,313
5	D300	2. 80	0

例题 10 − 10

Soda Water Corporation has spent $ 100,000 to produce 70,000 litres of soda water, which can be sold for $ 2 per litre. Alternatively, Soda Water Corporation can process the soda water further to create a total of 65,000 litres of coke, which can be sold for $ 2. 50 per litre. The further processing will cost $ 0. 30 per litre of coke.

Required:

Should Soda Water Corporation sell the soda water as is or process it into the coke?

讲解： 每升苏打水的售价为＄2，Soda Water Corporation 按原状出售 70 000 升苏打水，赚取收入＄140 000。

Soda Water Corporation 还能将 70 000 升苏打水加工为 65 000 升可乐，每升可乐的售价为＄2.50，赚取收入＄162 500（＄2.50 × 65 000 ＝ ＄162 500）。加工 1 升可乐产生额外成本＄0.30，因此 65 000 升可乐的加工成本为＄19 500（＄0.30 × 65 000 ＝ ＄19 500）。通过计算，出售 65 000 升可乐赚取净收入＄143 000（＄162 500 – ＄19 500 ＝ ＄143 000）。

出售 65 000 升可乐赚取的净收入（＄143 000）超过出售 70 000 升苏打水赚取的收入（＄140 000），因此 Soda Water Corporation 选择将 70 000 升苏打水加工为 65 000升可乐。

因为无论出售苏打水，还是将苏打水加工为可乐，Soda Water Corporation 均产生生产成本＄100 000，因此这笔生产成本属于沉没成本，与企业出售还是进一步加工产品的决策无关。

	Sell As Is	Process Further
Expected revenue from selling 70,000 litres of soda water	$ 140,000	
Expected revenue from selling 65,000 litres of coke		$ 162,500
Additional costs to convert soda water into coke		(19,500)
Total net revenue	$ 140,000	$ 143,000

答案： Soda Water Corporation should process 70,000 litres of soda water further into 65,000 litres of coke.

例题 10 - 11

Chocolate Corporation always processes cocoa beans into cocoa powder. The entire batch of processed cocoa powder can be sold for ＄15,500. Chocolate Corporation is considering further processing the cocoa powder into chocolate syrup or boxed chocolates. It would cost additional ＄75,800 to process the cocoa powder into 138,000 litres of chocolate syrup, which would be sold for ＄103,500. Also, it would cost additional ＄187,000 to process the cocoa powder into 75,000 boxes of chocolates, which would be sold for

420

$206,250.

Required:

Regardless of the choice made, Chocolate Corporation will be able to sell all it can produce. What should Chocolate Corporation do?

讲解：Chocolate Corporation 按原状出售一批可可粉，赚取收入 $15 500。

Chocolate Corporation 还可以将这批可可粉加工为 138 000 升巧克力糖浆或 75 000 盒巧克力。138 000 升巧克力糖浆的销售额为 $103 500，加工成本为 $75 800；75 000 盒巧克力的销售额为 $206 250，加工成本为 $187 000。通过计算，出售 138 000 升巧克力糖浆赚取净收入 $27 700（$103 500 - $75 800 = $27 700），出售 75 000 盒巧克力赚取净收入 $19 250（$206 250 - $187 000 = $19 250）。

出售 138 000 升巧克力糖浆赚取的净收入（$27 700）超过出售 75 000 盒巧克力赚取的净收入（$19 250）或按原状出售可可粉赚取的收入（$15 500），因此 Chocolate Corporation 选择将这批可可粉加工为 138 000 升巧克力糖浆。

	Cocoa Powder	Chocolate Syrup	Boxed Chocolates
Revenue	$15,500	$103,500	$206,250
Additional processing costs	(0)	(75 800)	(187,000)
Total net revenue	$15,500	$27,700	$19,250

答案：Chocolate Corporation should process the cocoa powder into 138,000 litres of chocolate syrup.

带你到北美学习
管理会计
Take You to
North America
to Learn
Managerial Accounting

专业名词汇编
Glossary of Accounting Terms

沉没成本	sunk cost	短期决策	short-term decision
固定成本	fixed cost	机会成本	opportunity cost
特殊订单	special order	外包决策	outsourcing decision
直接固定成本	direct fixed cost	不可避免固定成本	unavoidable fixed cost
非相关财务信息	irrelevant financial information		
可避免固定成本	avoidable fixed cost		
生产受限因素	production constraint		
相关财务信息	relevant financial information		
相关非财务信息	relevant non-financial information		
相关特性信息	relevant qualitative information		
增量分析法	incremental analysis approach		
自制或外购决策	make or buy decision		

企业管理者制定资本投资决策

Managers Make Capital Investment Decisions

带你到北美学习
管理会计
Take You to
North America
to Learn
Managerial Accounting

评估企业资本投资项目和制定企业资本投资决策的过程被称为资本预算（capital budgeting）。资本投资（capital investment）也称为长期投资（long-term investment）。资本投资包括采购新设备，建立新厂房、自动化生产流程，研发商业网站等。无论制造商，还是服务类企业或商业类企业，企业管理者均需要评估资本投资项目和制定资本投资决策。

分析资本投资项目，企业管理者一般使用以下四种指标：①现金回收期（cash payback period）；②年度收益率（annual rate of return）；③净现值（net present value）；④内部收益率（internal rate of return）。

分析短期资本投资，企业管理者应使用现金回收期和年度收益率，短期资本投资包括购买使用寿命仅为 2~3 年的电脑设备或软件；分析长期资本投资，企业管理者应使用净现值和内部收益率，而不是现金回收期和年度收益率。这是因为现金回收期和年度收益率不考虑货币时间价值（time value of money），属于非贴现法（non-discounted method），而净现值和内部收益率考虑货币时间价值，属于贴现法（discounted method）。

虽然四种资本投资分析指标均具有精准的计算过程，但这些投资分析指标仅预测不确定的未来，考量不确定的未知因素（消费者偏好的变化、市场竞争和政府新规等），因此资本预算仅属于一种预测。

资本预算主要考虑现金流（cash flow），评估资本投资项目创造出的净现金流入（net cash inflow）。净现金流入指现金流入（cash inflow）超出现金流出（cash outflow）的部分。资本投资项目的现金流入包括资本投资项目创造的未来现金收入（cash revenue）、资本投资项目节省的未来现金运营费用、资本投资项目的剩余价值（residual value），而资本投资项目的现金流出包括资本投资项目的初始投资（initial investment）和未来现金运营费用（cash operating expense）。

在第 7 章讲解预算收益表时，我们知道，销售额（sales revenue）减去售出商品成本（cost of goods sold）等于毛利润（gross profit），毛利润减去经营费用（operating expense）等于经营收益（operating income），经营收益减去利息费用（interest expense）等于税前收益（income before tax），税前收益乘以所得税税率（income tax rate）等于所得税费用（income tax expense），税前收益减去所得税费用等于净收益（net income）。经营费用包括折旧费用（depreciation expense）和坏账费用（bad debt expense）等非现金费用（non-cash expense）。

计算资本投资项目的净收益与编写收益表的流程相同。资本投资项目产生的所得税费用和非现金费用将使资本投资项目的净收益与净现金流入出现不同。如何将资本投资项目的净收益转化为资本投资项目的净现金流入？同学们将在大学金融课程中学习，本书对此问题不赘言。

我们知道，分析资本投资项目，企业管理者一般使用四种指标：现金回收期、年度收益率、净现值和内部收益率。现金回收期、净现值和内部收益率从净现金流入方面分析资本投资项目，而年度收益率从运营收益方面分析资本投资项目。

如何使用上述四种分析指标进行资本预算？

首先，企业管理者鉴别资本投资项目；这些项目包括提高企业生产和市场竞争能力的扩建型项目（expansion project），替换对企业已无经济价值、生产力的老旧设备的重置型项目（replacement project），为持续运营企业的强制型项目（mandatory project）。在鉴别资本投资项目的同时，企业管理者应评估各个资本投资项目创造的净现金流入。

其次，企业管理者使用现金回收期和年度收益率筛选不良投资项目。为什么使用现金回收期和年度收益率进行初步筛选？现金回收期和年度收益率不考虑货币时间价值且容易计算。在摒弃不良投资项目之后，管理者利用净现值和内部收益率选出最具投资潜力的项目。为什么使用净现值和内部收益率进行进一步筛选？因为净现值和内部收益率考虑货币时间价值，提供关于资本投资项目未来利润的准确信息。由于每种分析指标是从不同角度评估投资项目的，所以企业管理者一般使用四种分析指标，以获得关于各项投资项目的全面、准确的信息。

最后，根据四种指标提供的分析结果，企业管理者制定资本投资决策并执行。对于拥有充足资金和资源的企业，管理者可以投资所有满足或超过决策标准（decision criteria）的项目；然而，由于受限于有限的资金和资源，一些企业管理者不得不使用资本配额（capital rationing），先对满足或超过决策标准的项目进行选择，然后再投资。在对项目投入资金之后，企业管理者对项目产生的实际净现金流入（actual net cash inflow）与当初预计净现金流入（predicted net cash inflow）进行评估与比较；这种评估可以帮助企业管理者决定，是进一步追加投资该项目，还是终止该项目并出售相关资产。

接下来，将学习现金回收期、年度收益率、净现值和内部收益率的计算。

带你到北美学习
管理会计
Take You to
North America
to Learn
Managerial Accounting

11.1 现金回收期
Cash Payback Period

现金回收期指收回初始投资的时间长度。现金回收期可以告诉企业管理者，收回初始投资需要多长时间。现金回收期越短，投资项目越具吸引力。一个投资项目越快收回初始投资，这个项目面临亏损的固有风险（inherent risk）就越低。通过"案例 11-1"，学习现金回收期的计算及利用现金回收期选择投资项目。

案例 11 – 1

A company is considering investing $350,000 in Project A and Project B. The Project A will generate $50,000 in Year 1, $140,000 in Year 2, $70,000 in Year 3, and $500,000 in Year 4. The Project B will generate $170,000 in Year 1, $110,000 in Year 2, $170,000 in Year 3, and $110,000 in Year 4. Assume the company has a preset payback limit of three years.

Year	Net Cash Inflows of Project A	Net Cash Inflows of Project B
0	($350,000)	($350,000)
1	50,000	170,000
2	140,000	110,000
3	70,000	170,000
4	500,000	110,000

Required：

If the company apply the cash payback criterion, which project will the company choose? Why?

讲解： 项目 A 的初始投资为 $350 000。在第 1 年收回 $50 000 之后，项目 A 亏损 $300 000；在第 2 年收回 $140 000 之后，项目 A 仍亏损 $160 000；在第 3 年收回 $70 000之后，项目 A 还亏损 $90 000；在第 4 年收回 $500 000 之后，项目 A 扭亏为盈，盈利 $410 000，所以项目 A 的现金回收期为 3.18 年（3 + $90 000 ／ $500 000 = 3.18）。

Year	Investment	Net Cash Inflows of Project A	Cumulative Net Cash Inflows of Project A
0	($350,000)		
1		$50,000	$50,000
2		140,000	190,000
3		70,000	260,000
4		500,000	760,000

项目 B 的初始投资同样为 $350 000。在第 1 年收回 $170 000 之后，项目 B 亏损 $180 000；在第 2 年收回 $110 000 之后，项目 B 仍亏损 $70 000；在第 3 年收回 $170 000 之后，项目 B 扭亏为盈，盈利 $100 000，所以项目 B 的现金回收期为 2.41 年（2 + $70 000 / $170 000 ≈ 2.41）。

Year	Investment	Net Cash Inflows of Project B	Cumulative Net Cash Inflows of Project B
0	($350,000)		
1		$170,000	$170,000
2		110,000	280,000
3		170,000	450,000
4		110,000	560,000

根据"案例 11-1"信息，企业预先设定的现金回收期为 3 年。项目 A 的现金回收期为 3.18 年，超过预先设定的现金回收期；项目 B 的现金回收期为 2.41 年，未超过预先设定的现金回收期，因此选择项目 B。

如果投资项目的现金回收期未超过预先设定的现金回收期，企业管理者应考虑这项投资项目；如果投资项目的现金回收期超过预先设定的现金回收期，企业管理者应摒弃这项投资项目。如果没有预先设定现金回收期，企业管理者应尽量考虑具有更短现金回收期的投资项目（见图 11-1）。

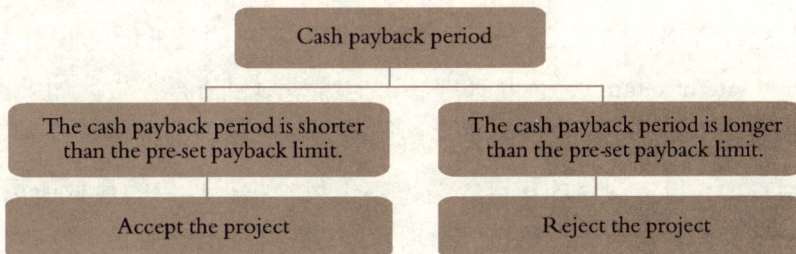

Cash payback period

The cash payback period is shorter than the pre-set payback limit.

The cash payback period is longer than the pre-set payback limit.

Accept the project

Reject the project

图 11 - 1　现金回收期决策定则

带你到北美学习
管理会计
Take You to
North America
to Learn
Managerial Accounting

现金回收期具有方便计算和益于理解的优势，但也饱受争议。第一，现金回收期仅关注收回投资项目初始投资的时间长短，而非投资项目利润；第二，现金回收期仅涉及投资项目在现金回收期的现金流（cash flow），忽略了包括投资项目剩余价值（residual value）在内的现金回收期之后的现金流和货币时间价值（time value of money）。在"案例 11-1"中，项目 A 在现金回收期（3.18 年）之后，产生净现金 $410 000；项目 B 在现金回收期（2.41 年）之后，产生净现金 $210 000。如果从现金回收期角度，项目 B 的现金回收期短于项目 A 的现金回收期，企业应选择项目B；而从利润角度，项目 A 与项目 B 的初始投资额均为 $350 000，但相比于项目 B，项目 A 可以提供更高的利润。现金回收期只能说明收回项目初始投资需要多长时间，却不能给企业管理者提供投资项目利润的相关信息，因此企业管理者很少将现金回收期作为选择投资项目的标准。对于企业管理者，现金回收期仅是一种筛选工具，它协助企业管理者摒弃现金回收期太长、甚至不能收回初始投资的项目。

11.2 年度收益率

Annual Rate of Return

与现金回收期仅说明投资项目收回初始投资的时间长度不同，年度收益率关注投资项目利润。投资项目年度收益率等于投资项目平均年度净收益（average annual net income）除以投资项目平均投资（average investment）（见图 11-2）。

图 11-2　年度收益率计算公式

通过年度收益率计算公式发现，年度收益率关注投资项目产生的净收益，而非净现金流入。投资项目平均投资等于投资项目初始投资与剩余价值之和除以 2。

通过对比投资项目的年度收益率与风险相近项目的最低所需收益率（minimum required rate of return），企业管理者决定哪些项目值得投资。如果投资项目的年度收益率大于风险相近项目的最低所需收益率，企业管理者可以考虑接受这项投资项目；如果投资项目的年度收益率小于风险相近项目的最低所需收益率，企业管理者可以放弃这项投资项目。根据年度收益率，企业管理者如何在可投资项目中选择更具投资潜力的项目？在特定风险下，年度收益率越大的投资项目更具投资潜力（见图 11-3）。

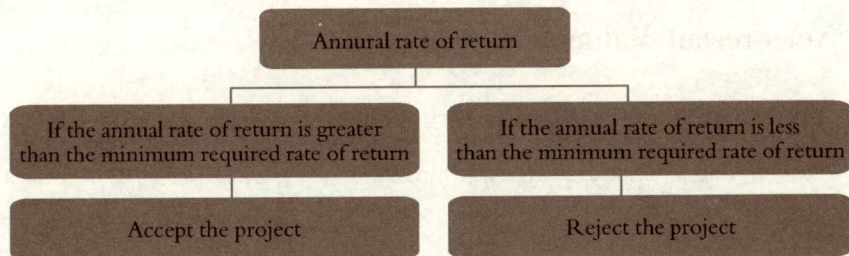

图 11 – 3　年度收益率决策定则

案例 11 – 2

A company is considering to add an item of new equipment that will require an investment of ＄1,000,000. Its manager predicts that this investment will have a 10-year life and generate net income of ＄200,000 the first year, ＄150,000 the second year, and ＄100,000 each year thereafter for eight years. The investment has a residual value of ＄200,000. The company has a required rate of return of 20%.

Required：

1. Compute the annual rate of return for the new equipment.

2. Should the company invest the new equipment?

讲解： 新设备的初始投资为 ＄1 000 000，10 年后的剩余价值为 ＄200 000，所以新设备的平均投资为 ＄600 000。新设备创造的第 1 年净收益为 ＄200 000，第 2 年净收益为 ＄150 000，剩余 8 年的年度净收益均为 ＄100 000，因此新设备的平均年度净收益为 ＄115 000。平均年度净收益（＄115 000）除以平均投资（＄600 000）等于年度收益率（19.17%）。新设备的年度收益率（19.17%）小于所需收益率（20%），所以企业不考虑投资这项新设备。

　　与现金回收期相同，年度收益率也具有方便计算和益于理解的优势，忽略货币时间价值的劣势。与现金回收期不同，年度收益率关注投资项目利润（净收益），而非净现金流入，说明投资项目如何影响企业净收益。

带你到北美学习
管理会计
Take You to
North America
to Learn
Managerial Accounting

11.3　净现值

Net Present Value

现金回收期和年度收益率拥有一个共同劣势——忽略了货币时间价值（time value of money），而净现值正弥补了这一劣势。什么是货币时间价值？我们知道，今天获得的 1 元钱比未来获得的 1 元钱具有更高价值。为什么？因为今天获得的 1 元钱可以用于投资，赚取额外收益。这种投资随时间获取收益的事实被称为货币时间价值。货币时间价值解释了为什么资本投资项目需要尽早收回现金，为什么企业管理者需要考虑资本投资项目产生净现金流入的时机。

货币时间价值一般受三个因素影响：①本金金额（principal amount）；②利率（interest rate）；③周期数（number of periods）。

（1）本金金额指投资或借款金额。本金既可以一次性支付（single lump sum），也可按年金（annuity）支付。例如，1 名大一学生想在 4 年后购买 1 辆新车，这名大学生可以在今天一次性存入 $20 000，也可以在未来 4 年，每年年底存入 $5 000。年金指每隔一段相等时长收取或支付相等金额的钱款。年金分为期初年金（annuity due）和期末年金（ordinary annuity），在周期初收取或支付的年金被称为期初年金，而在周期末收取或支付的年金则被称为期末年金。

（2）利率一般指一年期利息与本金金额的百分比。因为利率的计量期限不同，所以利率可以表述为年利率、半年利率、月利率和日利率等。我们在本章假定，利率为年利率。利息分为单利（simple interest）和复利（compound interest）。单利指在计算到期利息时，仅考虑借贷本金金额。复利指在计算到期利息时，需要考虑借贷本金金额和先前产生的所有利息。

（3）周期数指从投资开始至投资结束的时长。周期期限可以是日、周、月、季度、半年或年。我们在本章假设，周期期限为 1 年，即周期数为年数。在其他条件相同的前提下，投资时长越短，投资赚取的收益越低。

案例 11 - 3

John invests $1,000 today at 5% annual simple interest. How much will he have after three years?

讲解： 今天，John 投资 $1 000，年度单利利率为 5%。第 1 年利息收入为 $50

（＄1 000 × 5% ＝ ＄50），第 2 年利息收入为 ＄50，第 3 年利息收入为 ＄50，因此 John 在 3 年后收到 ＄1 150。

案例 11 - 4

Nancy invests ＄1,000 today at 5% annual compound interest. How much will she have after three years?

讲解： 今天，Nancy 投资 ＄1 000，年度复利利率为 5%。第 1 年利息收入为 ＄50（＄1 000 × 5% ＝ ＄50），第 2 年利息收入为 ＄52.50（（＄1 000 ＋ ＄50）× 5% ＝ ＄52.50），第 3 年利息收入约为 ＄55.13（（＄1 000 ＋ ＄50 ＋ ＄52.50）× 5% ＝ ＄55.125 ≈ ＄55.13），因此 Nancy 在 3 年后收到 ＄1 157.63（＄1 000 ＋ ＄50 ＋ ＄52.50 ＋ ＄55.13 ＝ ＄1 157.63）。

资本投资现值（present value）和终值（future value）指资本投资在不同时间点的价值。无论计算资本投资现值，还是计算资本投资终值，均需要使用上述三个影响货币时间价值的因素。

首先，讲解计算一次性支付现值（见说明 11-1）、期末年金现值（见说明11-2）和期初年金现值（见说明11-3）。

说明 11 - 1：计算一次性支付现值
$$PV = \frac{FV}{(1+r)^n}$$
PV : present value
FV : future value
n : number of periods
r : interest rate

说明 11 - 2：计算期末年金现值
$$PV = C\left[\frac{1 - \dfrac{1}{(1+r)^n}}{r}\right]$$
PV : present value
C : net cash inflow for each period
n : number of periods
r : interest rate

带你到北美学习
管理会计
Take You to
North America
to Learn
Managerial Accounting

说明 11-3：计算期初年金现值
$$PV = C \left[\dfrac{1 - \dfrac{1}{(1+r)^n}}{r} \right](1+r)$$
PV：present value
C：net cash inflow for each period
n：number of periods
r：interest rate

其次，讲解计算一次性支付终值（见说明 11-4）、期末年金终值（见说明11-5）和期初年金终值（见说明11-6）。

说明 11-4：计算一次性支付终值
$$FV = PV(1+r)^n$$
PV：present value
FV：future value
n：number of periods
r：interest rate

说明 11-5：计算期末年金终值
$$FV = C \left[\dfrac{(1+r)^n - 1}{r} \right]$$
FV：future value
C：net cash inflow for each period
n：number of periods
r：interest rate

说明 11-6：计算期初年金终值
$$FV = C \left[\dfrac{(1+r)^n - 1}{r} \right](1+r)$$
FV：future value
C：net cash inflow for each period
n：number of periods
r：interest rate

净现值由复利和现值决定。为什么使用现值计算（present value computation），而非终值计算（future value computation）？因为企业今天投资，而投资却在未来才能为企业带来净现金流入（net cash inflow），初始投资和未来产生的净现金流入不在同一时间点，所以为对比初始投资和未来产生的净现金流入，需要将它们统一在同一时间点。投资项目初始投资就是投资项目现值，所以需要计算投资项目未来净现金流入现值，以求在同一时间点对比投资项目初始投资和未来产生的净现金流入。

投资项目净现值指投资项目净现金流入现值与投资项目初始投资的差值（见图 11-4）。计算投资项目净现金流入现值时，需要使用贴现率（discounted rate）。贴现率是现值计算中的所用利率，它也称为所需收益率（required rate of return）。投资项目风险决定贴现率数值。换言之，投资项目风险越高，贴现率越大，投资项目风险越低，贴现率越小。对于风险适中的投资项目，资本机会成本（opportunity cost of capital）、加权平均资本成本（weighted average cost of capital）和所需收益率相同，均可作为贴现率用于计算投资项目净现金流入现值。

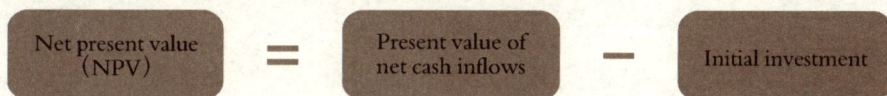

Net present value （NPV）	=	Present value of net cash inflows	−	Initial investment

图 11 - 4　净现值计算公式

对比投资项目净现金流入现值和投资项目初始投资，以确定投资项目是否满足或超过企业管理层设定的所需收益率。当投资项目净现值为正值时，投资项目收益率超过所需收益率，企业可以考虑这项投资；当投资项目净现值为负值时，投资项目收益率低于所需收益率，企业可以放弃这项投资（见图 11-5）。

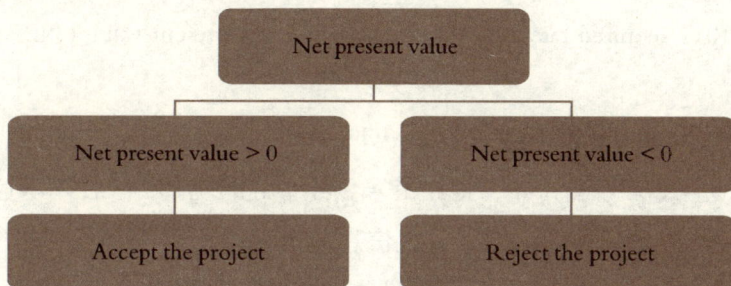

Net present value

Net present value > 0

Net present value < 0

Accept the project

Reject the project

图 11 - 5　净现值决策定则

案例 11 - 5

A new project invested by ABC corporation costs ＄350,000 and offers ＄70,000 at the

带你到北美学习
管理会计
Take You to
North America
to Learn
Managerial Accounting

end of each year for nine years. The corporation's projects demand an annual rate of 12% on investments of this nature.

Required:

Using the net present value (NPV) method to determine whether the corporation should invest in the new project.

讲解： 未来 9 年，新项目在每年年末为企业带来现金 $70 000，因此使用"说明 11-2"公式计算新项目的现金流现值。年度现金流（C）为 $70 000，贴现率（$r$）为 12%，周期数（$n$）为 9，带入"说明 11-2"公式，新项目现金流现值约为 $372 977.49。新项目初始投资为 $350 000，因此新项目净现值约为 $22 977.49。新项目净现值大于 0，企业应投资此项目。

$$\text{NPV} = -\$350\,000 + \$70\,000\left[\frac{1 - \dfrac{1}{(1+0.12)^9}}{0.12}\right] \approx \$22\,977.49$$

案例 11 - 6

An item of new equipment manufactured by ABC corporation costs $800,000 and will last five years and have an expected residual value of $100,000. The new equipment will generate the following net cash inflows：$150,000 the first year, $200,000 the second year, $300,000 the third year, $250,000 the fourth year, and $200,000 the fifth year.

Required:

1. Assume a 10% required rate of return, what is the net present value (NPV) of the new equipment?

2. Is this an attractive investment? Why or why not?

讲解： 未来 5 年，新设备每年为企业带来金额不等的现金；在使用寿命结束之际，新设备剩余价值为 $200 000。根据上述信息，使用"说明 11-1"公式计算新设备的净现金流入现值和剩余价值现值。新设备初始投资为 $800 000，净现金流入现值约为 $821 984.96，剩余价值现值约为 $62 092.13，因此新设备净现值约为 $84 077.09。新设备净现值大于 0，所以这是一项有潜力的投资。

$$\text{NPV} = -\$800\,000 + \frac{\$150\,000}{(1+0.10)^1} + \frac{\$200\,000}{(1+0.10)^2} + \frac{\$300\,000}{(1+0.10)^3} + \frac{\$250\,000}{(1+0.10)^4} +$$

$$\frac{\$\,200\,000}{(1+0.10)^5}+\frac{\$\,100\,000}{(1+0.10)^5}$$

NPV $\approx$ \$ 84 077. 09

根据"案例 11-5"和"案例 11-6",新项目和新设备的净现值分别为 \$ 22 977. 49 和 \$ 84 077. 09,均为正值,说明无论是新项目,还是新设备,对于企业均有投资价值。虽然新设备净现值大于新项目净现值 \$ 61 099. 60（\$ 84 077. 09 - \$ 22 977. 49 = \$ 61 099.60），但新设备初始投资需要 \$ 800 000,而新项目初始投资仅需 \$ 350 000。如果企业资金充足,可以既投资新项目,又投资新设备;而如果企业资金有限,怎么办? 这里,我们引入一个新概念——盈利指数（profitability index）。

投资项目盈利指数等于投资项目净现值除以投资项目初始投资加 1（见图 11-6）。盈利指数反映了投资 1 元钱所获取的回报。投资项目盈利指数大于 1,说明投资项目收益率高于所需收益率,企业可以考虑这项投资;投资项目盈利指数小于 1,说明投资项目收益率低于所需收益率,企业可以放弃这项投资。投资项目盈利指数越大,投资项目越具投资潜力（见图 11-7）。

| Profitability index | **=** | NPV | **÷** | Initial investment | **+** | 1 |

图 11 - 6 盈利指数计算公式

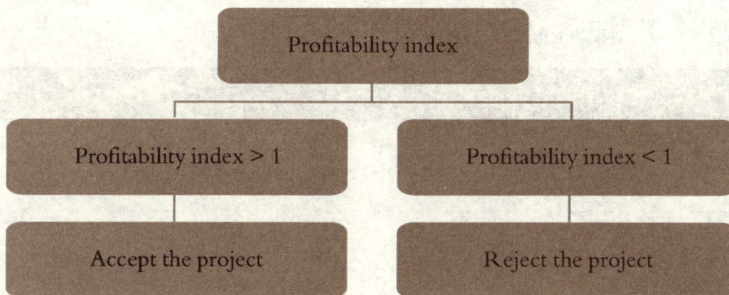

Profitability index
Profitability index > 1 / Profitability index < 1
Accept the project / Reject the project

图 11 - 7 盈利指数决策定则

根据"案例 11-5"和"案例 11-6"的结果,计算新项目和新设备的盈利指数。新项目净现值为 \$ 22 977. 49,初始投资为 \$ 350 000,因此新项目盈利指数约为 1. 07（\$ 22 977. 49 ÷ \$ 350 000 + 1 ≈ 1. 07）。新设备净现值为 \$ 84 077. 09,初始投资为 \$ 800 000,因此新设备盈利指数约为 1. 11（\$ 84 077. 09 ÷ \$ 800 000 + 1 ≈ 1. 11）。由于资金有限,ABC 公司只能选择投资新设备。

带你到北美学习
管理会计
Take You to
North America
to Learn
Managerial Accounting

11.4 内部收益率

Internal Rate of Return

内部收益率指净现值等于 0 时的贴现率。与净现值相同，内部收益率同样由复利和现值决定。当投资项目内部收益率大于所需收益率时，企业可以考虑这项投资；当投资项目内部收益率小于所需收益率时，企业可以放弃这项投资。投资项目内部收益率越大，投资项目越具投资潜力（见图 11-8）。

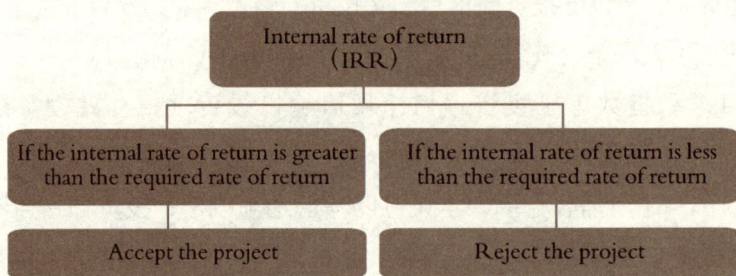

图 11 - 8　内部收益率决策定则

如何计算内部收益率？运用金融计算器（financial calculator）计算内部收益率，既容易又方便；如果没有金融计算器，如何计算内部收益率？通过"案例 11-7"，学习使用试错法（trial and error method）和线性插值法（linear interpolation method）（见说明 11-7）计算内部收益率。

> **说明 11 - 7：计算内部收益率的线性插值法公式**
>
> $$\frac{\text{IRR} - \text{lower}}{\text{higher} - \text{lower}} = \frac{\text{NPV}_{\text{IRR}} - \text{NPV}_{\text{lower}}}{\text{NPV}_{\text{higher}} - \text{NPV}_{\text{lower}}}$$

案例 11 - 7

ABC corporation is considering purchasing new equipment. The new equipment will cost \$450,000 and have no residual value. The management predicts the new equipment will generate the following net cash inflows: \$150,000 the first year, \$200,000 the second year, and \$300,000 the third year.

Required:

1. What is the internal rate of return（IRR）of the new equipment?

2．Assume a 15% required rate of return，is this a favourable investment? Why or why not?

讲解： 内部收益率指净现值等于 0 时的贴现率。根据"案例 11-7"信息，新设备的初始成本为 $450 000，第 1 年净现金流入为 $150 000，第 2 年净现金流入为 $200 000，第 3 年净现金流入为 $300 000。

$$NPV = -\$450\,000 + \frac{\$150\,000}{(1+r)^1} + \frac{\$200\,000}{(1+r)^2} + \frac{\$300\,000}{(1+r)^3} = \$0$$

我们不能直接解出内部收益率（r），所以不得不使用试错法，分别设定不同数值的贴现率并计算出相应净现值。内部收益率指净现值等于 0 时的贴现率，所以需要找到一个"净现值小于 0"时的贴现率和一个"净现值大于 0"时的贴现率，以确定内部收益率的数值区间。

首先，计算贴现率为 10% 的新设备净现值。新设备净现值约为 $77 047.33。

$$NPV_{10\%} = -\$450\,000 + \frac{\$150\,000}{(1+0.10)^1} + \frac{\$200\,000}{(1+0.10)^2} + \frac{\$300\,000}{(1+0.10)^3} \approx \$77\,047.33$$

贴现率（r）上升，分母数值随之增加，分数数值降低，因此净现值下降。我们知道，当贴现率为 10% 时，新设备净现值约为 $77 047.33，所以下一步设定贴现率为 15%。

计算贴现率为 15% 的新设备净现值。新设备净现值约为 $28 918.39。

$$NPV_{15\%} = -\$450\,000 + \frac{\$150\,000}{(1+0.15)^1} + \frac{\$200\,000}{(1+0.15)^2} + \frac{\$300\,000}{(1+0.15)^3} \approx \$28\,918.39$$

相比于贴现率为 10% 的净现值（$77 047.33），贴现率为 15% 时，新设备净现值约为 $28 918.39，所以继续提升贴现率，以求进一步降低净现值。

计算贴现率为 20% 的新设备净现值。新设备净现值为 -$12 500。

$$NPV_{20\%} = -\$450\,000 + \frac{\$150\,000}{(1+0.20)^1} + \frac{\$200\,000}{(1+0.20)^2} + \frac{\$300\,000}{(1+0.20)^3} = -\$12\,500$$

当贴现率为 15% 时，新设备净现值约为 $28 918.39；当贴现率为 20% 时，新设备净现值为 -$12 500，因此新设备的内部收益率应大于 15%、小于 20%。

在知道内部收益率的数值区间之后，使用线性插值法解出新设备的内部收益率。

$$\frac{IRR - lower}{higher - lower} = \frac{NPV_{IRR} - NPV_{lower}}{NPV_{higher} - NPV_{lower}}$$

$$\frac{IRR - 15\%}{20\% - 15\%} = \frac{NPV_{IRR} - NPV_{15\%}}{NPV_{20\%} - NPV_{15\%}}$$

$$\frac{IRR - 15\%}{20\% - 15\%} = \frac{\$0 - \$28\,918.39}{-\$12\,500 - \$28\,918.39}$$

带你到北美学习
管理会计
Take You to
North America
to Learn
Managerial Accounting

$$\frac{IRR - 15\%}{5\%} = \frac{-\$28\ 918.\ 39}{-\$41\ 418.\ 39}$$

$$\frac{IRR - 15\%}{5\%} = 0.\ 698\ 201\ 7$$

$$IRR - 15\% = 0.\ 698\ 201\ 7 \times 5\%$$

$$IRR \approx 18.\ 49\%$$

根据线性插值法，新设备的内部收益率约为 18.49% 。

请注意：线性插值法仅提供内部收益率的近似值（18.49%），而金融计算器可以计算出内部收益率的精确值（18.412 675%）。

我们知道，当投资项目内部收益率大于所需收益率时，企业可以考虑这项投资；当投资项目内部收益率小于所需收益率时，企业可以放弃这项投资。根据"第2问"信息，所需收益率为 15%。新设备内部收益率（18.49%）大于所需收益率（15%），因此购买新设备是一项具有潜力的投资。

例题综述
Summary of Examples

例题 11 - 1

The internal rate of return is _____ .

A. the discounted rate at which the net present value of the investment is zero

B. the same as the annual rate of return

C. the same as the required rate of return

D. All of the above

讲解： 内部收益率（internal rate of return）指净现值等于 0 时的贴现率（discounted rate）。

答案： A

例题 11 - 2

Which of the following methods uses net income rather than net cash inflows as a basis for calculations?

A. Internal rate of return

B. Annual rate of return

C. Cash payback period

D. Net present value

讲解： 投资项目年度收益率等于投资项目平均年度净收益（average annual net income）除以投资项目平均投资（average investment）。

答案： B

例题 11 - 3

Which of the following methods does not consider the capital investment's profit?

A. Cash payback period

B. Internal rate of return

C. Annual rate of return

D. Net present value

带你到北美学习
管理会计
Take You to
North America
to Learn
Managerial Accounting

讲解： 现金回收期具有方便计算和益于理解的优势，但也饱受争议。第一，现金回收期仅关注收回投资项目初始投资的时间长短，而非投资项目利润；第二，现金回收期仅反映投资项目在现金回收期的现金流（cash flow），忽略了包括投资项目剩余价值（residual value）在内的现金回收期之后的现金流和货币时间价值（time value of money）。

答案： A

例题 11 - 4

Which of the following methods is the most reliable for making capital investment decisions?

A. Cash payback period

B. Annual rate of return

C. Net present value

D. All of the above

讲解： 现金回收期和年度收益率拥有一个共同劣势——忽略了货币时间价值，而净现值正弥补了这一劣势。投资项目净现值指投资项目净现金流入现值与投资项目初始投资的差值，因此净现值直接考量投资项目利润，而不是投资项目收益率和收回投资项目初始投资的时长。

答案： C

例题 11 - 5

Which of the following affects the time value of money?

A. The principal amount

B. The interest rate

C. The number of periods

D. All of the above

讲解： 货币时间价值一般受三个因素影响：①本金金额；②利率；③周期数。

答案： D

例题 11 - 6

Which of the following is not true regarding capital rationing decisions?

A. The management should choose the investment with the highest internal rate of return.

B. The management should choose the investment with the highest net present value.

C. The management should choose the investment with the highest annual rate of return.

D. All of the above

讲解： 根据四个指标提供的分析结果，企业管理者制定资本投资决策并执行。对于拥有充足资金和资源的企业，管理者可以投资所有满足或超过决策标准（decision criteria）的项目；然而，由于受限于有限的资金和资源，一些企业管理者不得不使用资本配额（capital rationing），先对满足或超过决策标准的项目进行选择再投资。

答案： D

例题 11 - 7

If the size of an initial investment required may differ among alternative investments, the net present value can be used in conjunction with which of the following methods to help managers make capital investment decisions?

A. Profitability index

B. Cash payback period

C. Annual rate of return

D. Internal rate of return

讲解： 投资项目盈利指数等于投资项目净现值除以投资项目初始投资加 1。盈利指数反映投资 1 元钱所获取的回报。投资项目盈利指数大于 1，说明投资项目收益率高于所需收益率，企业可以考虑这项投资；投资项目盈利指数小于 1，说明投资项目收益率低于所需收益率，企业可以放弃这项投资。投资项目盈利指数越大，投资项目越具投资潜力。

答案： A

例题 11 - 8

Lucy wants to receive $1,070.58 five years from now. If she can earn 6% compounded annually, how much does she need to invest today?

讲解： Lucy 在 5 年后想获得 $1 070.58，年度复利利率为 6%，因此使用"说明 11-1"公式计算 Lucy 今天需要投资多少钱。

带你到北美学习
管理会计
Take You to
North America
to Learn
Managerial Accounting

$$PV = \frac{FV}{(1+r)^n} = \frac{\$1\,070.58}{(1+0.06)^5} = \$800$$

答案： Lucy needs to invest $800 today.

例题 11 – 9

XYZ company is considering adding an item of new equipment that will require an initial investment of $1,500,000. The management estimates that the new equipment will have a 10-year life and no residual value. The new equipment will generate net income of $260,000 the first year, $300,000 the second year, and $240,000 the third year, and $200,000 each year thereafter for seven years.

Required：

Compute the annual rate of return for the new equipment.

讲解： 新设备初始投资为 $1 500 000，10 年后的剩余价值为 $0，所以新设备的平均投资为 $750 000。新设备第 1 年净收益为 $260 000，第 2 年净收益为 $300 000，第 3 年净收益为 $240 000，剩余 7 年的年度净收益为 $200 000，因此平均年度净收益为 $220 000。平均年度净收益（$220 000）除以平均投资（$750 000）等于年度收益率（29.33%）。

答案： The annual rate of return for the new equipment is 29.33%.

例题 11 – 10

Use the profitability index method to determine whether ABC company should make the following investments：

Investment A costs $270,000 and offers eight annual net cash inflows of $60,000. ABC company requires an annual rate of return of 12% on this investment.

Investment B costs $350,000 and generates ten annual net cash inflows of $70,000. ABC company needs an annual rate of return of 10% on this investment.

Required：

What is the profitability index of each investment? Which investment will ABC company choose? Why?

讲解： 未来 8 年，项目 A 每年年末产生净现金流入 $60 000，因此年度净现金流入

（ C ）为 $\$ 60\,000$ ；所需收益率（ r ）为 12% ，周期数（ n ）为 8 。将上述数据带入"说明 11-2"公式，计算出项目 A 的净现金流入现值（PV）约为 $\$ 298\,058.39$ 。项目 A 的初始投资为 $\$ 270\,000$ ，因此项目 A 的净现值（NPV）约为 $\$ 28\,058.39$ ，盈利指数约为 1.10 （ $\$ 28\,058.39 \div \$ 270\,000 + 1 \approx 1.10$ ）。

$$\text{NPV}_A = -\$ 270{,}000 + \$ 60\,000 \left[\frac{1 - \frac{1}{(1+0.12)^8}}{0.12} \right] \approx \$ 28\,058.39$$

未来 10 年，项目 B 每年年末产生净现金流入 $\$ 70\,000$ ，因此年度净现金流入（ C ）为 $\$ 70\,000$ ；所需收益率（ r ）为 10% ，周期数（ n ）为 10 。将上述数据带入"说明 11-2"公式，计算出项目 B 的净现金流入现值（PV）约为 $\$ 430\,119.70$ 。项目 B 的初始投资为 $\$ 350\,000$ ，因此项目 B 的净现值（NPV）约为 $\$ 80\,119.70$ ，盈利指数约为 1.23 （ $\$ 80\,119.70 \div \$ 350\,000 + 1 \approx 1.23$ ）。

$$\text{NPV}_B = -\$ 350{,}000 + \$ 70\,000 \left[\frac{1 - \frac{1}{(1+0.10)^{10}}}{0.10} \right] \approx \$ 80\,119.70$$

项目 A 的盈利指数约为 1.10 ，项目 B 的盈利指数约为 1.23 。投资项目盈利指数越大，投资项目越具投资潜力，因此 ABC 公司应投资项目 B 。

答案： The profitability index of Investment A is about 1.10, the profitability index of Investment B is approximately 1.23. The higher the profitability index, the more desirable the investment, so ABC company should choose Investment B.

例题 11 - 11

Auto Industries is deciding whether to automate its production process. The new manufacturing machine costs $\$ 930{,}000$ and will have a six-year useful life and a residual value of $\$ 200{,}000$. The new machine will generate the following net cash inflows: $\$ 264{,}000$ the first year, $\$ 254{,}000$ the second year, $\$ 222{,}000$ the third year, $\$ 210{,}000$ the fourth year, $\$ 204{,}000$ the fifth year, and $\$ 178{,}000$ the sixth year.

Required：

Assume a 16% required rate of return, what is the net present value (NPV) of the new machine? Should Auto Industries invest in the new machine? Why or why not?

讲解： 未来 6 年，新机器每年为企业带来金额不等的现金。在使用寿命结束之际，

新机器剩余价值为 $200 000。根据题目信息，使用"说明 11-1"公式计算新机器的净现金流入现值和剩余价值现值。新机器初始投资为 $930 000，净现金流入现值约为 $844 742.49，剩余价值现值约为 $82 088.45，因此新机器净现值约为 – $3 169.05。新设备净现值小于 0，所以这不是一项具有潜力的投资。

$$\text{NPV} = -\$930\,000 + \frac{\$264\,000}{(1+0.16)^1} + \frac{\$254\,000}{(1+0.16)^2} + \frac{\$222\,000}{(1+0.16)^3} + \frac{\$210\,000}{(1+0.16)^4} +$$

$$\frac{\$204\,000}{(1+0.16)^5} + \frac{\$178\,000}{(1+0.16)^6} + \frac{\$200\,000}{(1+0.16)^6} \approx -\$3\,169.05$$

答案： The net present value of the new machine is about – $3,169.05, less than 0, so Auto Industries should not invest in the new machine.

例题 11 – 12

A company is considering investing $10,000 in Investment A and $10,000 in Investment B. The Investment A will generate $2,000 in Year 1, $4,500 in Year 2, $3,500 in Year 3, and $4,000 in Year 4. The Investment B will generate $3,000 in Year 1, $2,000 in Year 2, $3,000 in Year 3, and $8,000 in Year 4. Assume the company has a pre-set payback limit of three years.

Year	Net Cash Inflows of Investment A	Net Cash Inflows of Investment B
0	($10,000)	($10,000)
1	2,000	3,000
2	4,500	2,000
3	3,500	3,000
4	4,000	8,000

Required：

1. If the company apply the cash payback criterion, which investment will the company choose? Why?

2. Assume a 10% required rate of return, what is the net present value (NPV) of each investment?

3. What is the internal rate of return (IRR) of each investment? Which investment will the company choose? Why?

1. If the company apply the cash payback criterion, which investment will the company choose? Why?

讲解： 项目 A 的初始投资为 $10 000。在第 1 年收回 $2 000 之后，项目 A 亏损 $8 000；在第 2 年收回 $4 500 之后，项目 A 仍亏损 $3 500；第 3 年收回 $3 500，使项目 A 收回初始投资，因此项目 A 的现金回收期为 3 年。

Year	Investment	Net Cash Inflows of Invenstment A	Cumulative Net Cash of Inflows Invenstment A
0	($10,000)		
1		$2,000	$2,000
2		4,500	6,500
3		3,500	10,000
4		4,000	14,000

项目 B 的初始投资同样为 $10 000。在第 1 年收回 $3 000 之后，项目 B 亏损 $7 000；在第 2 年收回 $2 000 之后，项目 B 仍亏损 $5 000；在第 3 年收回 $3 000 之后，项目 B 还亏损 $2 000；第 4 年收回 $8 000，使项目 B 扭亏为盈，盈利 $6 000，所以项目 B 的现金回收期为 3.25 年（3 + $2 000 / $8 000 = 3.25）。

Year	Investment	Net Cash Inflows of Invenstment B	Cumulative Net Cash Inflows of Invenstment B
0	($10,000)		
1		$3,000	$3,000
2		2,000	5,000
3		3,000	8,000
4		8,000	16,000

根据题目信息，企业预先设定的现金回收期为 3 年。项目 A 的现金回收期为 3 年，与预先设定的现金回收期相同；项目 B 的现金回收期为 3.25 年，超过预先设定的现金回收期，因此选择项目 A。

答案： The cash payback period of Investment A of three years is matched with the pre-set payback limit, but the cash payback period of Investment B exceeds the pre-set payback limit, so the company will choose Investment A.

2. Assume a 10% required rate of return, what is the net present value (NPV) of each in-

带你到北美学习
管理会计
Take You to
North America
to Learn
Managerial Accounting

vestment?

讲解： 项目 A 的初始成本为 $10 000，第 1 年净现金流入为 $2 000，第 2 年净现金流入为 $4 500，第 3 年净现金流入为 $3 500，第 4 年净现金流入为 $4 000。我们使用 "说明 11-1" 公式计算项目 A 的净现金流入现值。根据计算，项目 A 的净现金流入现值约为 $10 898.84。项目 A 的初始投资为 $10 000，因此项目 A 的净现值约为 $898.84。

$$\text{NPV}_A = -\$10\,000 + \frac{\$2\,000}{(1+0.10)^1} + \frac{\$4\,500}{(1+0.10)^2} + \frac{\$3\,500}{(1+0.10)^3} + \frac{\$4\,000}{(1+0.10)^4} \approx \$898.84$$

项目 B 的初始成本为 $10 000，第 1 年净现金流入为 $3 000，第 2 年净现金流入为 $2 000，第 3 年净现金流入为 $3 000，第 4 年净现金流入为 $8 000。我们使用 "说明 11-1" 的公式计算项目 B 的净现金流入现值。根据计算，项目 B 的净现金流入现值约为 $12 098.22。项目 B 的初始投资为 $10 000，因此项目 B 的净现值约为 $2 098.22。

$$\text{NPV}_B = -\$10\,000 + \frac{\$3\,000}{(1+0.10)^1} + \frac{\$2\,000}{(1+0.10)^2} + \frac{\$3\,000}{(1+0.10)^3} + \frac{\$8\,000}{(1+0.10)^4}$$
$$= \$2\,098.217\,33 \approx \$2\,098.22$$

答案： The net present value of Investment A is about $898.84, and the net present value of Investment B is approximately $2,098.22.

3. What is the internal rate of return (IRR) of each investment? Which investment will the company choose? Why?

讲解： 内部收益率指净现值等于 0 时的贴现率。

根据题目信息，项目 A 的初始成本为 $10 000，第 1 年净现金流入为 $2 000，第 2 年净现金流入为 $4 500，第 3 年净现金流入为 $3 500，第 4 年净现金流入为 $4 000。

$$\text{NPV}_A = -\$10\,000 + \frac{\$2\,000}{(1+r)^1} + \frac{\$4\,500}{(1+r)^2} + \frac{\$3\,500}{(1+r)^3} + \frac{\$4\,000}{(1+r)^4} = \$0$$

我们不能直接解出内部收益率（r），所以不得不使用试错法，分别设定不同数值的贴现率并计算出相应净现值。内部收益率指净现值等于 0 时的贴现率，所以需要找到一个 "净现值小于 0" 时的贴现率和一个 "净现值大于 0" 时的贴现率，以确定内部收益率的数值区间。

首先，计算贴现率为 10% 的项目 A 的净现值。项目 A 的净现值约为 $898.84。

$$\text{NPV}_{10\%}^{A} = -\$10\,000 + \frac{\$2\,000}{(1+0.10)^1} + \frac{\$4\,500}{(1+0.10)^2} + \frac{\$3\,500}{(1+0.10)^3} + \frac{\$4\,000}{(1+0.10)^4}$$

$$\approx \$898.84$$

贴现率（r）上升，等式分母数值随之增加，分数数值降低，因此净现值下降。我们知道，当贴现率为 10% 时，项目 A 的净现值约为 $898.84，所以我们下一步设定贴现率为 15%。

计算贴现率为 15% 的项目 A 的净现值。项目 A 的净现值约为 -$269.90。

$$\text{NPV}_{15\%}^{A} = -\$10\,000 + \frac{\$2\,000}{(1+0.15)^1} + \frac{\$4\,500}{(1+0.15)^2} + \frac{\$3\,500}{(1+0.15)^3} + \frac{\$4\,000}{(1+0.15)^4}$$

$$\approx -\$269.90$$

当贴现率为 15% 时，项目 A 的净现值约 -$269.90；当贴现率为 10% 时，项目 A 的净现值约为 $898.84，因此项目 A 的内部收益率应大于 10%、小于 15%。

在知道内部收益率的数值区间之后，我们使用线性插值法，得出项目 A 的内部收益率约为 13.85%。

$$\frac{\text{IRR}_A - \text{lower}}{\text{higher} - \text{lower}} = \frac{\text{NPV}_{\text{IRR}}^{A} - \text{NPV}_{\text{lower}}^{A}}{\text{NPV}_{\text{higher}}^{A} - \text{NPV}_{\text{lower}}^{A}}$$

$$\frac{\text{IRR}_A - 10\%}{15\% - 10\%} = \frac{\text{NPV}_{\text{IRR}}^{A} - \text{NPV}_{10\%}^{A}}{\text{NPV}_{15\%}^{A} - \text{NPV}_{10\%}^{A}}$$

$$\frac{\text{IRR}_A - 10\%}{15\% - 10\%} = \frac{\$0 - \$898.84}{-\$269.90 - \$898.84}$$

$$\frac{\text{IRR}_A - 10\%}{5\%} = \frac{-\$898.84}{-\$1\,168.74}$$

$$\frac{\text{IRR}_A - 10\%}{5\%} = 0.769\,067\,5$$

$$\text{IRR}_A - 10\% = 0.769\,067\,5 \times 5\%$$

$$\text{IRR}_A \approx 13.85\%$$

根据题目信息，项目 B 的初始成本为 $10\,000，第 1 年净现金流入为 $3\,000，第 2 年净现金流入为 $2\,000，第 3 年净现金流入为 $3\,000，第 4 年净现金流入为 $8\,000。

$$\text{NPV}_B = -\$10\,000 + \frac{\$3\,000}{(1+r)^1} + \frac{\$2\,000}{(1+r)^2} + \frac{\$3\,000}{(1+r)^3} + \frac{\$8\,000}{(1+r)^4} = \$0$$

带你到北美学习
管理会计
Take You to
North America
to Learn
Managerial Accounting

首先, 计算贴现率为 10% 的项目 B 的净现值。项目 B 的净现值约为 $2 098.22。

$$NPV_{10\%}^B = - \$10\ 000 + \frac{\$3\ 000}{(1+0.10)^1} + \frac{\$2\ 000}{(1+0.10)^2} + \frac{\$3\ 000}{(1+0.10)^3} + \frac{\$8\ 000}{(1+0.10)^4}$$

$$\approx \$2\ 098.22$$

贴现率 (r) 上升, 等式分母数值随之增加, 分数数值降低, 因此净现值下降。我们知道, 当贴现率为 10% 时, 项目 B 的净现值约为 $2 098.22, 所以下一步设定贴现率为 15%。

计算贴现率为 15% 的项目 B 的净现值。项目 B 的净现值约为 $667.56。

$$NPV_{15\%}^B = - \$10\ 000 + \frac{\$3\ 000}{(1+0.15)^1} + \frac{\$2\ 000}{(1+0.15)^2} + \frac{\$3\ 000}{(1+0.15)^3} + \frac{\$8\ 000}{(1+0.15)^4}$$

$$\approx \$667.56$$

相比于贴现率为 10% 的净现值 ($2 098.22), 贴现率为 15% 时, 项目 B 的净现值约为 $667.56, 所以继续提升贴现率, 以求进一步降低净现值。

计算贴现率为 20% 的项目 B 的净现值。项目 B 的净现值约为 -$516.98。

$$NPV_{20\%}^B = - \$10\ 000 + \frac{\$3\ 000}{(1+0.20)^1} + \frac{\$2\ 000}{(1+0.20)^2} + \frac{\$3\ 000}{(1+0.20)^3} + \frac{\$8\ 000}{(1+0.20)^4}$$

$$\approx -\$516.98$$

当贴现率为 15% 时, 项目 B 的净现值约为 $667.56; 当贴现率为 20% 时, 项目 B 的净现值约为 -$516.98, 因此项目 B 的内部收益率应大于 15%、小于 20%。

在知道内部收益率的数值区间之后, 我们使用线性插值法, 得出项目 B 的内部收益率约为 17.82%。

$$\frac{IRR_B - lower}{higher - lower} = \frac{NPV_{IRR}^B - NPV_{lower}^B}{NPV_{higher}^B - NPV_{lower}^B}$$

$$\frac{IRR_B - 15\%}{20\% - 15\%} = \frac{NPV_{IRR}^B - NPV_{15\%}^B}{NPV_{20\%}^B - NPV_{15\%}^B}$$

$$\frac{IRR_B - 15\%}{20\% - 15\%} = \frac{\$0 - \$667.56}{-\$516.98 - \$667.56}$$

$$\frac{IRR_B - 15\%}{5\%} = \frac{-\$667.56}{-\$1\ 184.54}$$

$$\frac{IRR_B - 15\%}{5\%} = 0.563\ 560\ 5$$

$$\text{IRR}_B - 15\% = 0.563\ 560\ 5 \times 5\%$$

$$\text{IRR}_B \approx 17.82\%$$

项目 A 的内部收益率约为 13.85% ，项目 B 的内部收益率约为 17.82% 。投资项目内部收益率越大，投资项目越具投资潜力，因此选择投资项目 B。

答案： The internal rate of return for Investment A is approximately 13.85% , and the internal rate of return for Investment B is about 17.82% . The higher the internal rate of return , the more attractive the investment , so the company choose Investment B.

带你到北美学习
管理会计
Take You to
North America
to Learn
Managerial Accounting

专业名词汇编
Glossary of Accounting Terms

本金金额	principal amount	单利	simple interest
非贴现法	non-discounted method	非现金费用	non-cash expense
复利	compound interest	固有风险	inherent risk
坏账费用	bad debt expense	货币时间价值	time value of money
金融计算器	financial calculator	经营费用	operating expense
经营收益	operating income	净收益	net income
净现金流入	net cash inflow	净现值	net present value
决策标准	decision criteria	扩建型项目	expansion project
利率	interest rate	利息费用	interest expense
毛利润	gross profit	内部收益率	internal rate of return
年度收益率	annual rate of return	年金	annuity
平均投资	average investment	期初年金	annuity due
初始投资	initial investment	期末年金	ordinary annuity
强制型项目	mandatory project	剩余价值	residual value
实际净现金流入	actual net cash inflow	试错法	trial and error method
售出商品成本	cost of goods sold	税前收益	income before tax
所得税费用	income tax expense	所得税税率	income tax rate
所需收益率	required rate of return	贴现法	discounted method
贴现率	discounted rate	现金回收期	cash payback period
现金流	cash flow	现金流出	cash outflow
现金流入	cash inflow	现金收入	cash revenue
现金运营费用	cash operating expense	现值	present value
销售额	sales revenue	一次性支付	single lump sum
盈利指数	profitability index	长期投资	long-term investment
折旧费用	depreciation expense	终值	future value
终值计算	future value computation	重置型项目	replacement project
资本机会成本	opportunity cost of capital	资本配额	capital rationing
资本投资	capital investment	资本预算	capital budgeting
加权平均资本成本	weighted average cost of capital		
现值计算	present value computation		

线性插值法	linear interpolation method
预计净现金流入	predicted net cash inflow
平均年度净收益	average annual net income
预算收益表	budgeted income statement
最低所需收益率	minimum required rate of return

重要公式与定则

Important Formulas and Rules

带你到北美学习
管理会计
Take You to
North America
to Learn
Managerial Accounting

第1章 管理会计概述
An Introduction to Managerial Accounting

◎ **对比管理会计与财务会计**

Issue	Managerial Accounting	Financial Accounting
1. Who are the primary users of the accounting information?	内部使用者一般包括首席执行官、市场营销主管、人力资源经理、生产主管和财务总监等	外部使用者一般包括投资人、债权人、税务机关、监管机构和工会等
2. What is the purpose of the accounting information?	帮助管理者筹划、监督和控制企业运营，制定企业相关决策	帮助外部使用者制定投资与借贷决策
3. What are the primary accounting products?	提供对企业管理者有价值和有益的内部会计报告	收益表、股东权益变化表、资产负债表和现金流量表
4. What must be included in the accounting reports, and how must they be formatted?	企业管理层决定管理会计报告的内容与形式。当管理会计报告带来的益处超过编写报告产生的成本时，企业管理层编写管理会计报告	财务会计报告标准包括《国际财务报告准则》(International Financial Reporting Standards, IFRS)、《美国通用会计准则》(Generally Accepted Accounting Principles, US GAAP)和《非上市企业会计准则》(Accounting Standards for Private Enterprises, ASPE)
5. How often are the accounting reports prepared	根据企业管理层的不同需求，有些管理会计报告需要每日编写一次，而有些管理会计报告则在需要时方才编写	每年和每季度
6. What are the underlying basises of the accounting information?	虽然有些管理会计信息与企业历史交易有关，但管理会计更注重企业未来，提供更多关于企业决策方面的信息。管理会计既呈现企业内部交易信息，又揭示企业外部交易信息	财务会计信息与企业外部历史交易有关
7. What accounting information characteristics are emphasized?	管理会计信息必须是相关的（relevant）	财务会计信息必须是可靠的（reliable）和客观的（objective）
8. Does anyone verify the accounting information?	企业无需对管理会计进行独立审计（independent audit），但企业内部审计工作可以对管理会计报告的编写流程进行审查	独立注册会计师（certified public accountant）对上市公司的年度财务报表进行审计，并针对所公布财务信息的公正性提出自己的意见
9. What business unit is the accounting report about?	关于企业的具体业务部门、地区分支机构，如产品部门、市场部门和人力资源部门等	关于整个企业

Issue	Managerial Accounting	Financial Accounting
10. Is the accounting information required by a government agency	政府部门不要求企业公布管理会计报告	政府部门要求上市企业公布经审计的年度财务报表（annual audited financial statement）

● 企业组织架构

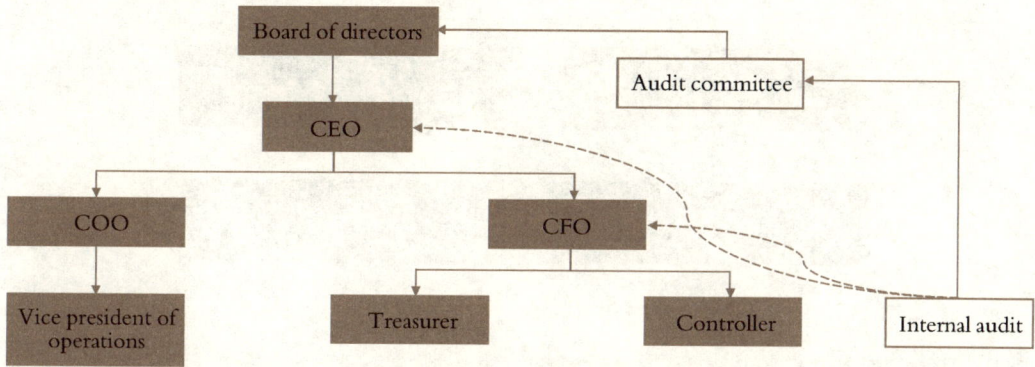

```
                    Board of directors ◄──────────────┐
                           │                           │
                           ▼                   Audit committee ◄─────┐
                          CEO ┄┄┄┄┄┄┄┄┄┄┄┄┄┄┄┄┄┄┄┄┄┄┄┄┄┄┄┄┄┄┐   │
                ┌──────────┴──────────┐                          ┊   │
               COO                   CFO ◄┄┄┄┄┄┄┄┄┄┄┄┄┄┄┄┄┄┄┄┄┄┘   │
                │              ┌───────┴───────┐                       │
                ▼             ▼               ▼                        │
        Vice president    Treasurer       Controller         Internal audit
         of operations
```

● 制造类企业价值链

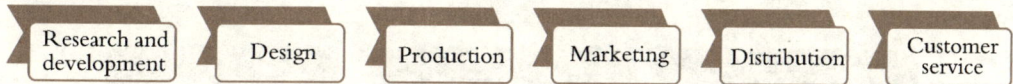

| Research and development | Design | Production | Marketing | Distribution | Customer service |

● 商业类企业价值链

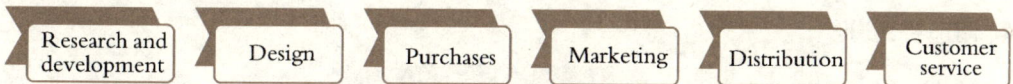

| Research and development | Design | Purchases | Marketing | Distribution | Customer service |

带你到北美学习
管理会计
Take You to
North America
to Learn
Managerial Accounting

第 2 章　管理会计的主要内容
The Main Contents of Managerial Accounting

◉ **直接成本与间接成本之间的区别**

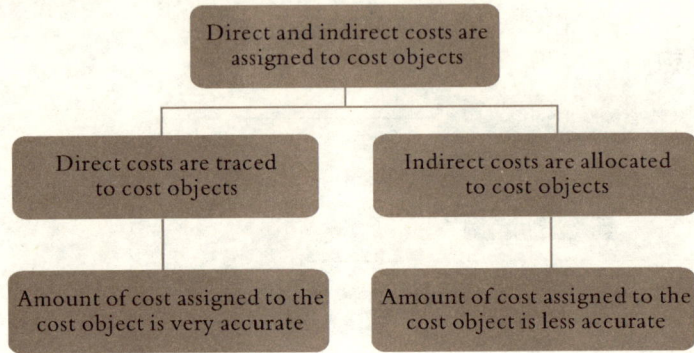

```
           Direct and indirect costs are
              assigned to cost objects
                       |
         ┌─────────────┴─────────────┐
   Direct costs are traced      Indirect costs are allocated
      to cost objects                to cost objects
         │                             │
   Amount of cost assigned to the   Amount of cost assigned to the
   cost object is very accurate     cost object is less accurate
```

◉ **制造成本分类**

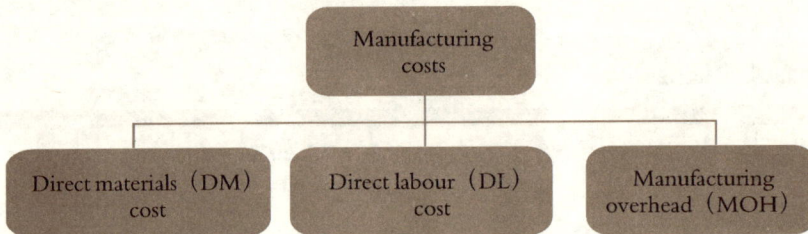

```
                   Manufacturing
                      costs
                        |
      ┌─────────────────┼─────────────────┐
Direct materials (DM)   Direct labour (DL)   Manufacturing
      cost                  cost              overhead (MOH)
```

◉ **制造费用分类**

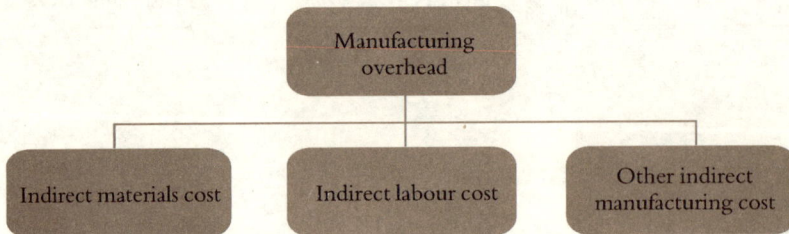

```
                   Manufacturing
                     overhead
                        |
      ┌─────────────────┼─────────────────┐
Indirect materials cost   Indirect labour cost   Other indirect
                                                  manufacturing cost
```

◉ **主要成本计算公式**

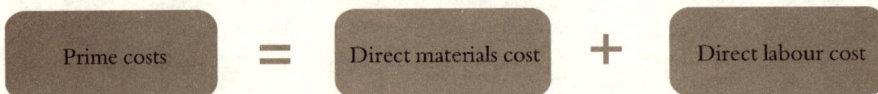

$$\text{Prime costs} = \text{Direct materials cost} + \text{Direct labour cost}$$

◉ 加工成本计算公式

| Conversion costs | = | Direct labour cost | + | Manufacaturing overhead |

◉ 商业类企业售出商品成本计算公式

| Beginning merchandise inventory | + | Cost of goods purchased | = | Cost of goods available for sale |

| Cost of goods available for sale | − | Ending merchandise inventory | = | Cost of goods sold |

◉ 制造类企业售出商品成本计算公式

| Beginning finished goods inventory | + | Cost of goods manufactured | = | Cost of goods available for sale |

| Cost of goods available for sale | − | Ending finished goods inventory | = | Cost of goods sold |

◉ 制造工厂内的成本流转

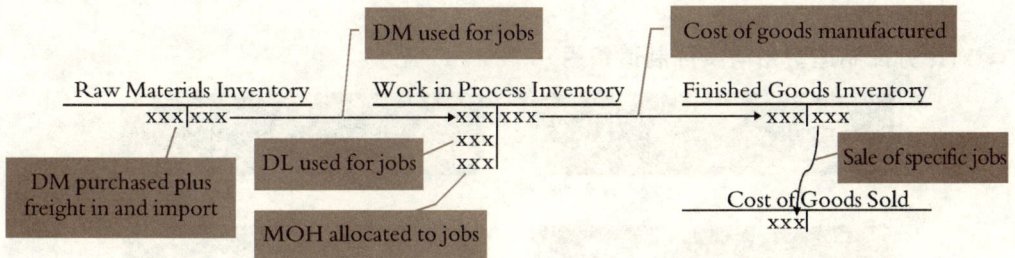

DM used for jobs   Cost of goods manufactured

Raw Materials Inventory   Work in Process Inventory   Finished Goods Inventory
xxx|xxx   →xxx|xxx   →xxx|xxx
                xxx
DM purchased plus   DL used for jobs   xxx   Sale of specific jobs
freight in and import   Cost of Goods Sold
        MOH allocated to jobs   xxx

带你到北美学习
管理会计
Take You to
North America
to Learn
Managerial Accounting

第 3 章　分批成本计算法
Job Costing

◉ **对比分批成本计算法与分步成本计算法**

	Job Costing	Process Costing
Cost Object	Job	Process
Outputs	Unique, custom-ordered products or small batches of different products	Large number of identical units
How to Average?	Costs are averaged over the small number of units in a job (often one unit in a job).	Costs are averaged over the large number of identical products that pass through a series of uniform production steps or processes.

◉ **计算预定制造费用分摊率**

$$\text{Predetermined manufacturing overhead rate} = \frac{\text{Estimated total manufacturing overhead}}{\text{Estimated total amount of allocation base}}$$

◉ **计算一张订单的分摊制造费用**

Manufacutring overhead allocated to a job =

　　Predetermined manufacutring overhead rate × Actual amount of allocation base used by the job

◉ **对比分摊制造费用与实际制造费用**

MOH allocated > actual MOH	MOH allocated < actual MOH
⇩	⇩
MOH has been overallocated	MOH has been underallocated
⇩	⇩
Jobs have been overcosted	Jobs have been undercosted

◉ **调整售出商品成本账目**

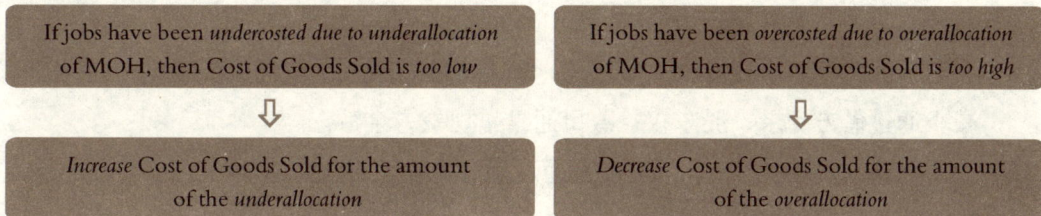

If jobs have been *undercosted due to underallocation* of MOH, then Cost of Goods Sold is *too low*	If jobs have been *overcosted due to overallocation* of MOH, then Cost of Goods Sold is *too high*
⇩	⇩
Increase Cost of Goods Sold for the amount of the *underallocation*	*Decrease* Cost of Goods Sold for the amount of the *overallocation*

◉ **对比三种成本分摊系统**

	全厂成本分摊系统	部门成本分摊系统	作业成本法分摊系统
第1步	预估未来一年的制造费用总额	预估每个部门未来一年的制造费用总额	鉴别主要加工作业活动，预估每种作业活动未来一年的制造费用总额
第2步	选择分摊基础，预估未来一年的分摊基础总额	为每个部门选择分摊基础，预估每个部门未来一年的分摊基础总额	为每种作业活动选择分摊基础，预估每种作业活动未来一年的分摊基础总额
第3步	计算全厂制造费用分摊率	计算部门制造费用分摊率	计算作业活动成本分摊率
第4步	一张订单的分摊制造费用＝全厂制造费用分摊率×该订单所用分摊基础的实际数额	一张订单的分摊制造费用＝部门制造费用分摊率×该订单所用部门分摊基础的实际数额	一张订单的分摊制造费用＝作业活动成本分摊率×该订单所用作业活动分摊基础的实际数额

◉ **成本层级**

Facility-level

Product-level

Batch-level

Unit-level

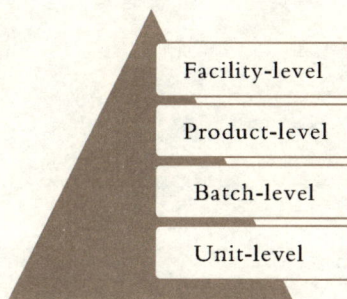

◉ **日记账分录的借贷记账定则**

（1）资产账目（asset account）增长通过借方（debit）记录，资产账目减小通过贷方（credit）记录；资产账目通常呈现借方余额（debit balance）。

带你到北美学习
管理会计
Take You to
North America
to Learn
Managerial Accounting

（2）负债账目（liability account）增长通过贷方记录，负债账目减小通过借方记录；负债账目通常呈现贷方余额（credit balance）。

（3）股东权益账目（shareholders' equity account）增长通过贷方记录，股东权益账目减小通过借方记录；股东权益账目通常呈现贷方余额。

（4）收入账目（revenue account）增长通过贷方记录，收入账目减小通过借方记录；收入账目通常呈现贷方余额。

（5）费用账目（expense account）增长通过借方记录，费用账目减小通过贷方记录；费用账目通常呈现借方余额。

（6）股息账目（dividend account）增长通过借方记录，股息账目减小通过贷方记录；股息账目通常呈现借方余额。

◉ **成本加成定价法计算公式**

$$\text{Cost - plus price} = \text{Cost} + \text{Markup on cost}$$

第4章 分步成本计算法
Process Costing

● 分批成本计算法的成本流转

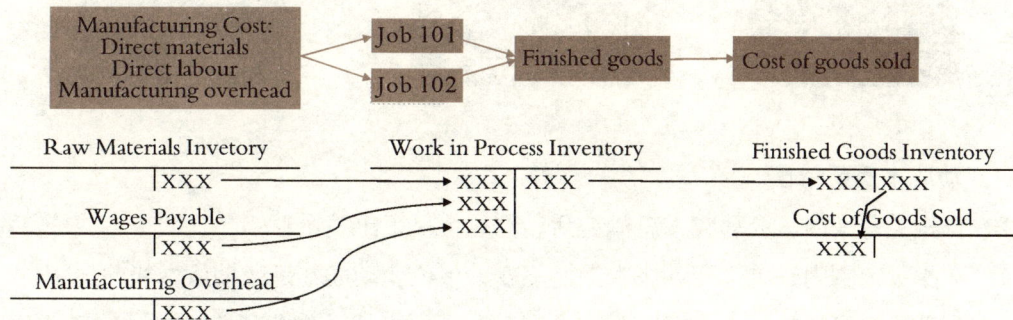

```
Manufacturing Cost:        Job 101
   Direct materials                    Finished goods  →  Cost of goods sold
   Direct labour           Job 102
Manufacturing overhead
```

Raw Materials Inventory	Work in Process Inventory	Finished Goods Inventory
XXX	XXX │ XXX	XXX │ XXX
Wages Payable	XXX	Cost of Goods Sold
XXX	XXX	XXX │
Manufacturing Overhead		
XXX		

● 分步成本计算法的成本流转

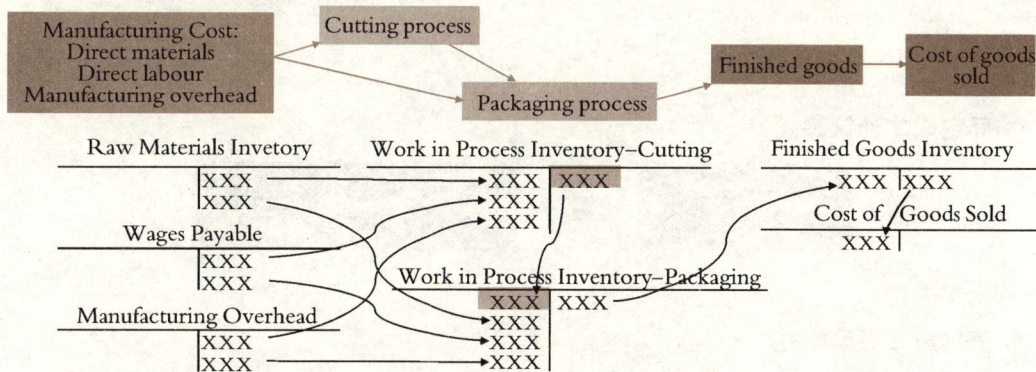

```
Manufacturing Cost:      Cutting process
   Direct materials
   Direct labour                        Finished goods → Cost of goods
Manufacturing overhead   Packaging process                    sold
```

Raw Materials Inventory	Work in Process Inventory–Cutting	Finished Goods Inventory
XXX	XXX │ XXX	XXX │ XXX
XXX	XXX	Cost of Goods Sold
Wages Payable	XXX	XXX │
XXX		
XXX	Work in Process Inventory–Packaging	
Manufacturing Overhead	XXX │ XXX	
XXX	XXX	
XXX	XXX	

● 约当产量计算公式

$$\text{Number of equivalent units} = \text{Number of partially completed goods} \times \text{Percentage of process completed}$$

461

带你到北美学习
管理会计
Take You to
North America
to Learn
Managerial Accounting

第 5 章　成本习性与边际贡献收益表
Cost Behaviour and Contribution Margin Income Statement

◉ **变动成本计算公式**

Total variable cost (y)	$=$	Variable cost per unit (v)	$\times$	Volume of activity (x)

◉ **变动成本重要特性**

（1）在相关范围内，变动成本总额与活动作业量呈正比关系；

（2）在相关范围内，单位变动成本保持不变，单位变动成本是变动成本线的斜率；

（3）变动成本线通常始于坐标原点、没有截距，即当活动作业量为 0 时，变动成本总额也为 \$ 0；

（4）变动成本等式为 $y = vx$，y 代表变动成本总额，v 代表单位变动成本，x 代表活动作业量。

◉ **固定成本计算等式**

Total fixed cost (y)	$=$	Fixed cost over a period of time (f)

◉ **固定成本重要特性**

（1）在相关范围内，固定成本总额不随活动作业量的变动而变化；

（2）在相关范围内，单位固定成本的变化与活动作业量的变动呈反比关系；

（3）固定成本线不始于坐标原点，没有斜率；

（4）固定成本线与 y 轴相交，与 y 轴的交点是 y 轴截距，即固定成本总额；

（5）固定成本等式为 $y = f$，y 代表固定成本总额，f 代表给定财务周期的固定成本金额。

◉ **混合成本计算公式**

$$\boxed{\text{Total mixed cost} \atop (y)} \quad = \quad \boxed{\text{Total variable cost} \atop (vx)} \quad + \quad \boxed{\text{Total fixed cost} \atop (f)}$$

◉ **混合成本重要特性**

（1）混合成本中的变动成本部分使混合成本总额随着活动作业量的变动而变化，但混合成本中的固定成本部分使混合成本总额的变化与活动作业量的变动不呈正比关系；

（2）混合成本中的固定成本部分使单位混合成本的变化与活动作业量的变动呈反比关系；

（3）混合成本线不始于坐标系原点；混合成本线与 y 轴相交，与 y 轴的交点是 y 轴截距，即固定成本总额；混合成本线的斜率为单位变动成本；

（4）混合成本等式为 $y = vx + f$，y 代表混合成本总额，v 代表单位变动成本，x 代表活动作业量，f 代表固定成本总额。

◉ **对比归纳成本法与变动成本法**

	Absorption Costing	Variable Costing
Product Costs	Direct materials Direct labour Variable manufacturing overhead *Fixed manufacturing overhead*	Direct materials Direct labour Variable manufacturing overhead
Period Costs	Variable non-manufacturing costs Fixed non-manufacturing costs	*Fixed manufacturing overhead* Variable non-manufacturing costs Fixed non-manufacturing costs
Focus	*External reporting*	*Internal reporting*
Income Statement Format	*Traditional income statement*	*Contribution margin income statement*

带你到北美学习
管理会计
Take You to
North America
to Learn
Managerial Accounting

第6章 本量利分析
Cost – Volume – Profit Analysis

◉ 边际贡献率计算公式

$$\text{Contribution margin ratio} = \frac{\text{Unit contribution margin}}{\text{Selling price}}$$

$$\text{Contribution margin ratio} = \frac{\text{Contribution margin}}{\text{Sales revenue}}$$

◉ 收益表法

Operating income = Sales revenue – Variable costs – Fixed costs

Operating income =
(Sales price per unit × Units sold) – (Variable costs per unit × Units sold) – Fixed costs

◉ 单位贡献毛利法

$$\text{Sales in units} = \frac{\text{Fixed costs} + \text{Operating income}}{\text{Unit contribution margin}}$$

◉ 边际贡献率法

$$\text{Sales in dollars} = \frac{\text{Fixed costs} + \text{Operating income}}{\text{Contribution margin ratio}}$$

◉ 售价改变引起的变化

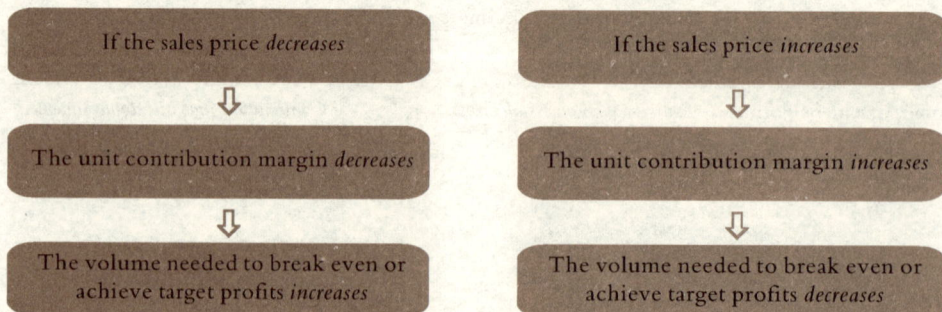

If the sales price *decreases*	If the sales price *increases*
⇩	⇩
The unit contribution margin *decreases*	The unit contribution margin *increases*
⇩	⇩
The volume needed to break even or achieve target profits *increases*	The volume needed to break even or achieve target profits *decreases*

● **变动成本改变引起的变化**

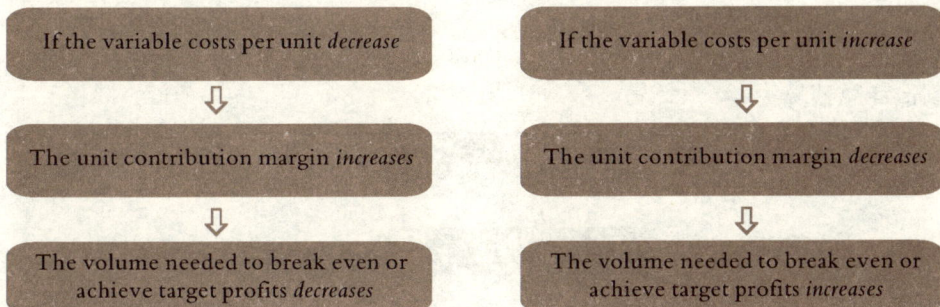

If the variable costs per unit *decrease*	If the variable costs per unit *increase*
⇩	⇩
The unit contribution margin *increases*	The unit contribution margin *decreases*
⇩	⇩
The volume needed to break even or achieve target profits *decreases*	The volume needed to break even or achieve target profits *increases*

● **固定成本改变引起的变化**

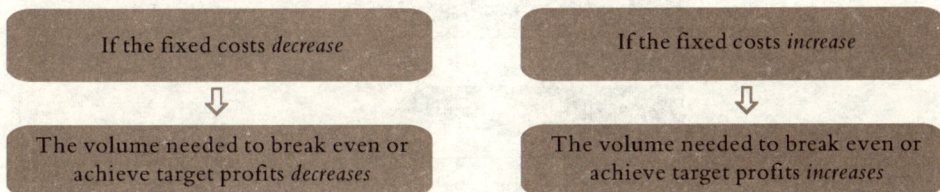

If the fixed costs *decrease*	If the fixed costs *increase*
⇩	⇩
The volume needed to break even or achieve target profits *decreases*	The volume needed to break even or achieve target profits *increases*

● **安全边际计算公式**

Margin of safety in units = Expected or Actual sales in units − Breakeven sales in units

Margin of safety in dollars = Expected or Actual sales in dollars − Breakeven sales in dollars

$$\text{Margin of safety as a percentage} = \frac{\text{Margin of safety in units}}{\text{Expected or Actual sales in units}}$$

$$\text{Margin of safety as a percentage} = \frac{\text{Margin of safety in dollars}}{\text{Expected or Actual sales in dollars}}$$

● **经营杠杆计算公式**

$$\text{Operating leverage} = \frac{\text{Contribution margin}}{\text{Operating income}} = \frac{(\text{Sales revenue} - \text{Variable costs})}{\text{Operating income}}$$

$$= \frac{(\text{Fixed costs} + \text{Operating income})}{\text{Operating income}}$$

$$\text{Operating leverage} = \frac{\text{Percentage in operating income}}{\text{Percentage in sales revenue}}$$

带你到北美学习
管理会计
Take You to
North America
to Learn
Managerial Accounting

第 7 章　总预算
Master Budget

◉ **制造商总预算**

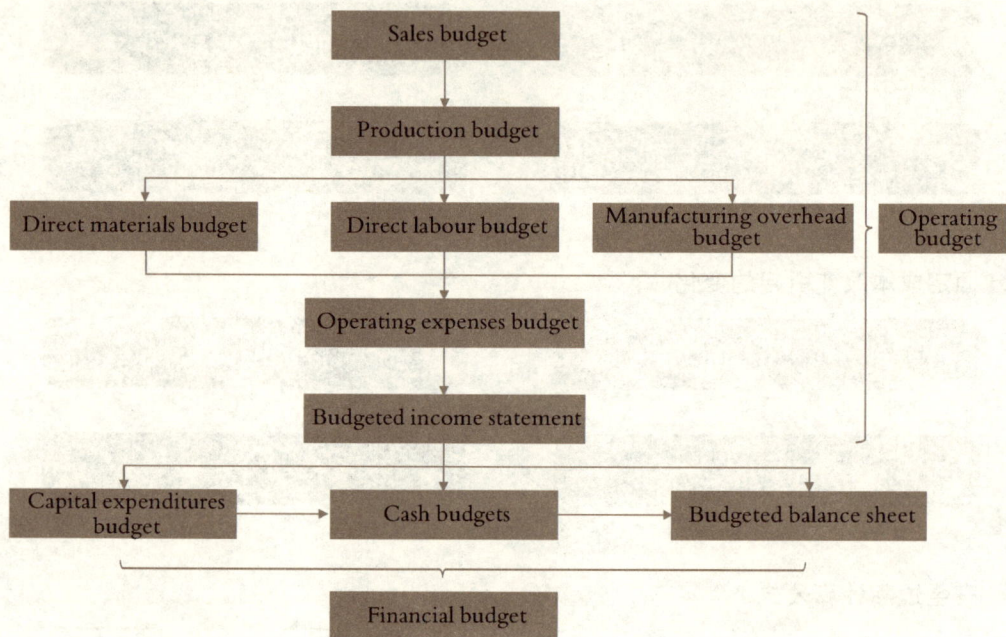

```
                    Sales budget
                         │
                  Production budget
                         │
   ┌─────────────────────┼─────────────────────┐
Direct materials    Direct labour    Manufacturing overhead    Operating
   budget              budget              budget                budget
   └─────────────────────┼─────────────────────┘
                Operating expenses budget
                         │
              Budgeted income statement
                         │
Capital expenditures ──► Cash budgets ──► Budgeted balance sheet
   budget
                  Financial budget
```

◉ **销售预算计算公式**

$$\text{Expected sales revenue} = \text{Expected sales in units} \times \text{Expected sales price}$$

◉ **生产预算计算公式**

$$\text{Expected sales in units} + \text{Desired units in ending inventory} = \text{Total units needed}$$

$$\text{Total units needed} - \text{Units in beginning inventory} = \text{Units to produce}$$

● **直接材料预算计算公式**

| Direct materials needed for production | + | Desired ending direct materials inventory | = | Total direct materials needed |

| Total direct materials needed | − | Beginning direct materials inventory | = | Direct materials to purchase |

● **直接人工预算计算公式**

| Units to be produced | × | Direct labour hours needed per unit | = | Direct labour hours needed for production |

| Direct labour hours needed for production | × | Direct labour rate | = | Total direct labour cost |

● **现金预算计算公式**

| Beginning cash balance | + | Cash collections for the fiscal period | = | Total cash available |

| Total cash available | − | Cash payments for the fiscal period | = | Ending cash balance before financing |

带你到北美学习
管理会计
Take You to
North America
to Learn
Managerial Accounting

第 8 章 标准成本与差异分析
Standard Costs and Variance Analysis

◉ **标准成本计算公式**

$$\boxed{\text{Standard cost}} \quad \textbf{=} \quad \boxed{\text{Quantity standard}} \quad \times \quad \boxed{\text{Price standard}}$$

◉ **标准变动性制造费用分摊率计算公式**

$$\text{Standard variable manufacturing overhead rate} = \frac{\text{Estimated total variable manufacturing ovehead}}{\text{Estimated total amount of allocation base}}$$

◉ **标准固定性制造费用分摊率计算公式**

$$\text{Standard fixed manufacturing overhead rate} = \frac{\text{Estimated total fixed manufacturing ovehead}}{\text{Estimated total amount of allocation base}}$$

◉ **标准制造费用分摊率计算公式**

$$\text{Standard manufacturing overhead rate} = \frac{\text{Estimated total manufacturing ovehead}}{\text{Estimated total amount of allocation base}}$$

◉ **直接材料差异分类**

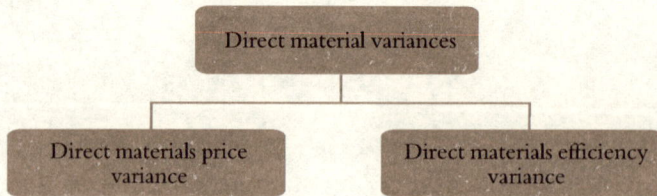

$$\boxed{\text{Direct material variances}}$$

$$\boxed{\text{Direct materials price variance}} \qquad \boxed{\text{Direct materials efficiency variance}}$$

◉ **直接材料价格差异计算公式**

Direct materials (DM) price variance =
(Actual DM price − Standard DM price) × Actual quantity of DM purchased

● **直接材料效率差异计算公式**

> Direct materials (DM) efficiency variance =
> (Actual quantity of DM used − Standard quantity of DM) × Standard price per DM

● **直接人工差异分类**

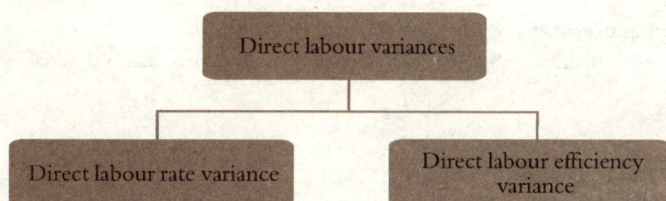

```
            Direct labour variances
            /                    \
Direct labour rate variance    Direct labour efficiency
                               variance
```

● **直接人工工资率差异计算公式**

> Direct labour (DL) rate variance =
> (Actual rate per DL hour − Standard rate per DL hour) × Actual DL hours

● **直接人工效率差异计算公式**

> Direct labour (DL) efficiency variance =
> (Actual DL hours − Standard DL hours) × Standard rate per DL hour

● **制造费用差异分类**

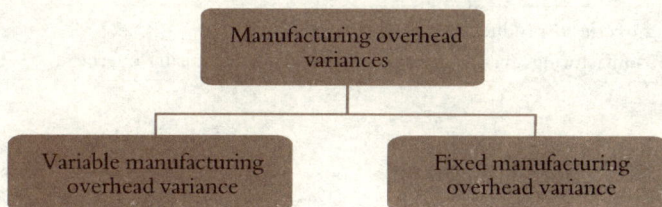

```
            Manufacturing overhead
                  variances
            /                    \
Variable manufacturing         Fixed manufacturing
overhead variance              overhead variance
```

● **变动性制造费用差异分类**

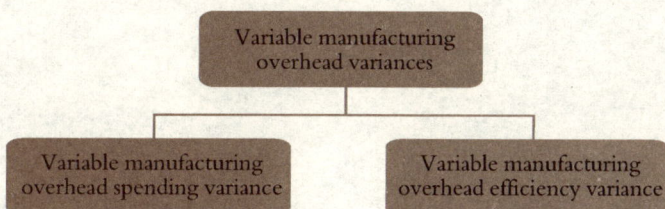

```
            Variable manufacturing
              overhead variances
            /                        \
Variable manufacturing          Variable manufacturing
overhead spending variance      overhead efficiency variance
```

带你到北美学习
管理会计
Take You to
North America
to Learn
Managerial Accounting

◉ **变动性制造费用支出差异计算公式**

Variable manufacturing overhead（MOH）spending variance =
   Actual variable MOH − Standard variable MOH rate × Actual quantity of cost driver

◉ **变动性制造费用效率差异计算公式**

Variable manufacturing overhead（MOH）efficiency variance =
   （Actual quantity of cost driver − Standard quantity of cost driver）× Standard variable MOH rate

◉ **固定性制造费用差异分类**

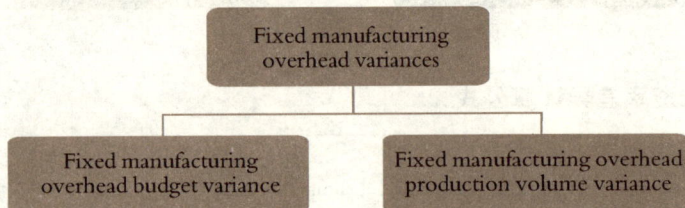

Fixed manufacturing
overhead variances

Fixed manufacturing
overhead budget variance

Fixed manufacturing overhead
production volume variance

◉ **固定性制造费用预算差异计算公式**

Fixed manufacturing overhead budget variance =
   Actual fixed manufacturing overhead − Budgeted fixed manufacturing overhead

◉ **固定性制造费用产量差异计算公式**

Fixed manufacturing overhead production volume variance =
   Budgeted fixed manufacturing overhead − Applied fixed manufacturing overhead

第 9 章　企业管理者评估绩效
Managers Evaluate Performance

◉ 投资收益率计算公式

$$\text{Return on investment} = \frac{\text{Operating income}}{\text{Average operating assets}}$$

◉ 投资收益率展开公式

Return on investment = Operating profit margin × Asset turnover

$$\text{Return on investment} = \frac{\text{Operating income}}{\text{Net sales}} \times \frac{\text{Net sales}}{\text{Average operating assets}}$$

◉ 剩余收益计算公式

Residual income = Operating income − Average operating assets × Minimum required rate of return

◉ 经济附加值计算公式

Economic value added =
　　After-tax operating income − (Total assets − Current liabilities) × Weighted average cost of capital

带你到北美学习
管理会计
Take You to
North America
to Learn
Managerial Accounting

第 10 章　企业管理者制定短期商业决策
Managers Make Short-Term Business Decisions

● 特殊订单考虑的核心问题

（1）企业是否拥有足够生产力完成特殊订单？

（2）特殊订单创造的销售额是否可以承担订单产生的变动成本和额外固定成本？

（3）特殊订单是否影响企业产品的常规销售？

● 特殊订单中产品的最低售价计算公式

$$\text{Minimum selling price} = \text{Variable cost per unit (special order)} + \frac{\text{Contribution margin lost (regular sales)}}{\text{Number of units (special order)}}$$

$$\text{Contribution margin lost (regular sales)} =$$
$$\text{Contribution margin per unit (regular sales)} \times \text{Regular sales in units lost}$$

● 外包考虑的核心问题

（1）自制产品产生的变动成本是否超过外包成本（oursourcing cost）？

（2）如果外购产品，是否可以节省固定成本？

（3）如果外购产品，如何利用闲置资源？

● 淘汰非盈利产品或部门考虑的核心问题

（1）非盈利产品或部门的贡献毛利是否为正值？

（2）即使淘汰非盈利产品或部门，固定成本是否仍将存在？

（3）如果淘汰非盈利产品或部门，是否可以节省直接固定成本？

● 分配有限生产资源考虑的核心问题

（1）什么资源阻碍了企业的产品生产或展示？

（2）哪类产品的单位有限资源贡献毛利最高？

（3）强调生产或销售一种产品是否会影响企业的固定成本？

● 出售或进一步加工产品考虑的核心问题

（1）按原状出售产品，企业赚取多少销售额？

（2）出售进一步加工的产品，企业赚取多少销售额？

（3）进一步加工产品，将产生多少额外成本？

带你到北美学习
管理会计
Take You to
North America
to Learn
Managerial Accounting

第 11 章　企业管理者制定资本投资决策
Managers Make Capital Investment Decisions

◉ **现金回收期决策定则**

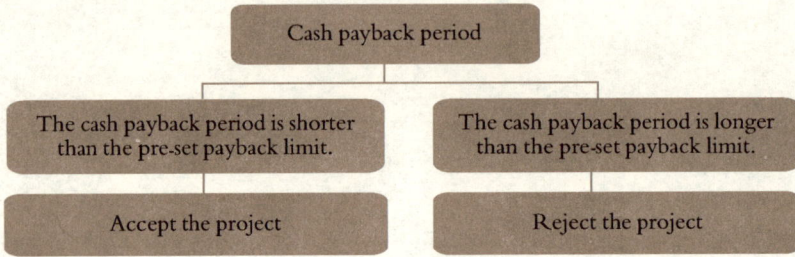

```
                    Cash payback period

   The cash payback period is shorter        The cash payback period is longer
   than the pre-set payback limit.           than the pre-set payback limit.

        Accept the project                        Reject the project
```

◉ **年度收益率计算公式**

$$\text{Annual rate of return} = \text{Average annual net income} \div \text{Average investment}$$

◉ **年度收益率决策定则**

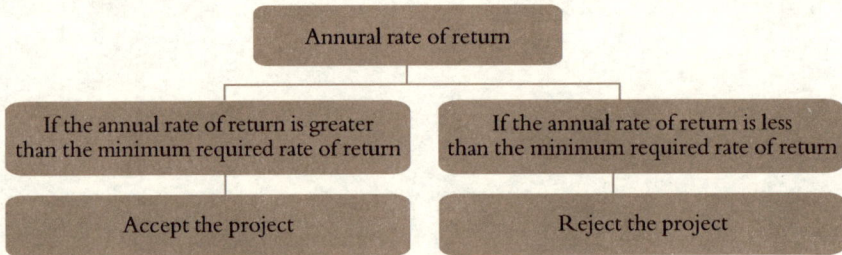

```
                    Annural rate of return

   If the annual rate of return is greater    If the annual rate of return is less
   than the minimum required rate of return   than the minimum required rate of return

        Accept the project                        Reject the project
```

◉ **一次性支付现值计算公式**

$$PV = \frac{FV}{(1+r)^n}$$

PV : present value
FV : future value
n : number of periods
r : interest rate

◉ 期末年金现值计算公式

$$PV = C \left[\frac{1 - \frac{1}{(1+r)^n}}{r} \right]$$

PV : present value	
C : net cash inflow for each period	
n : number of periods	
r : interest rate	

◉ 期初年金现值计算公式

$$PV = C \left[\frac{1 - \frac{1}{(1+r)^n}}{r} \right] (1+r)$$

PV : present value	
C : net cash inflow for each period	
n : number of periods	
r : interest rate	

◉ 一次性支付终值计算公式

$$FV = PV(1+r)^n$$

PV : present value	
FV : future value	
n : number of periods	
r : interest rate	

◉ 期末年金终值计算公式

$$FV = C \left[\frac{(1+r)^n - 1}{r} \right]$$

FV : future value	
C : net cash inflow for each period	
n : number of periods	
r : interest rate	

带你到北美学习
管理会计
Take You to
North America
to Learn
Managerial Accounting

◉ **期初年金终值计算公式**

$$FV = C\left[\frac{(1+r)^n - 1}{r}\right](1+r)$$

| FV : future value |
| C : net cash inflow for each period |
| n : number of periods |
| r : interest rate |

◉ **净现值计算公式**

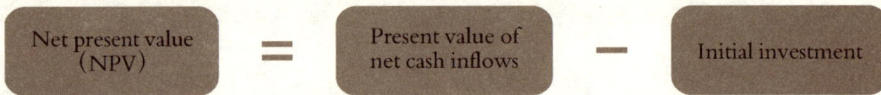

Net present value（NPV）　＝　Present value of net cash inflows　－　Initial investment

◉ **净现值决策定则**

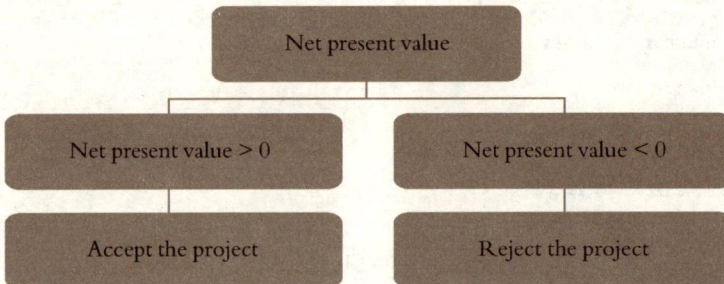

Net present value

Net present value > 0 → Accept the project

Net present value < 0 → Reject the project

◉ **盈利指数计算公式**

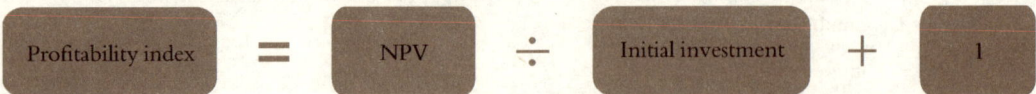

Profitability index　＝　NPV　÷　Initial investment　＋　1

◉ **盈利指数决策定则**

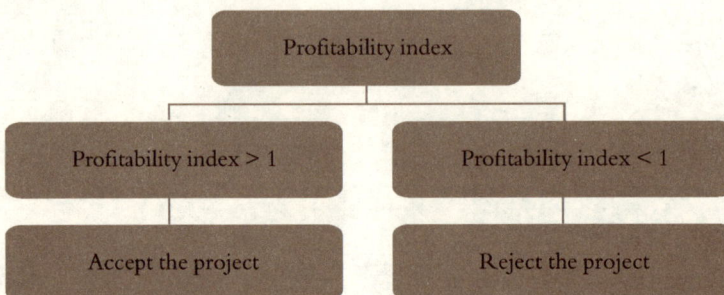

Profitability index

Profitability index > 1 → Accept the project

Profitability index < 1 → Reject the project

◉ **内部收益率决策定则**

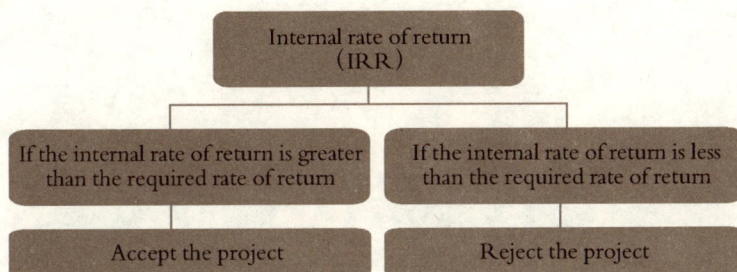

Internal rate of return
（IRR）

If the internal rate of return is greater than the required rate of return

If the internal rate of return is less than the required rate of return

Accept the project

Reject the project

◉ **计算内部收益率的线性插值法公式**

$$\frac{\text{IRR} - \text{lower}}{\text{higher} - \text{lower}} = \frac{\text{NPV}_{\text{IRR}} - \text{NPV}_{\text{lower}}}{\text{NPV}_{\text{higher}} - \text{NPV}_{\text{lower}}}$$